THE **Bicycling**® GUIDE TO COMPLETE

Bicycle Maintenance & Repair

RODALE
LIVE YOUR WHOLE LIFE™

Every day our brands connect with and inspire millions of
people to live a life of the mind, body, spirit — a whole life.

THE **Bicycling**® GUIDE TO COMPLETE

Bicycle Maintenance & Repair

FOR ROAD & MOUNTAIN BIKES

Todd Downs

RODALE®

Interior book design by Rita Baker

Cover and interior photos by Mitch Mandel/Rodale Images
"Anatomy of a Recumbent" photo on pages xiv to xv copyright © 1997 by Barry Gregg
Photo on page 12 courtesy of Dave Hawkins/United Bicycle Institute
Interior illustrations © Beau Daniels/Artistic License Inc.

Library of Congress Cataloging-in-Publication Data

Downs, Todd.
    The bicycling guide to complete bicycle maintenance & repair : for road & mountain bikes /
Todd Downs.
        p.   cm.
    Includes index.
    ISBN-13 978–1–57954–883–4 paperback
    ISBN-10 1–57954–883–0 paperback
    ISBN-13 978–1–59486–342–4 hardcover
    ISBN-10 1–59486–342–3 hardcover
    1. Bicycles—Maintenance and repair—Handbooks, manuals, etc.   I. Title.
TL430.D68 2005
629.28'772—dc22   2004024331

Distributed to the trade by Holtzbrinck Publishers

2 4 6 8 10 9 7 5 3 1   paperback
2 4 6 8 10 9 7 5 3 1   hardcover

We inspire and enable people to improve their lives and the world around them
For more of our products visit **rodalestore.com** or call 800-848-4735

*To the memories of
Carl Emery, my friend and mentor,
and Albert Leslie Howsen, my grandfather.
Diolch yn fawr.*

Anatomy of a Road Bike

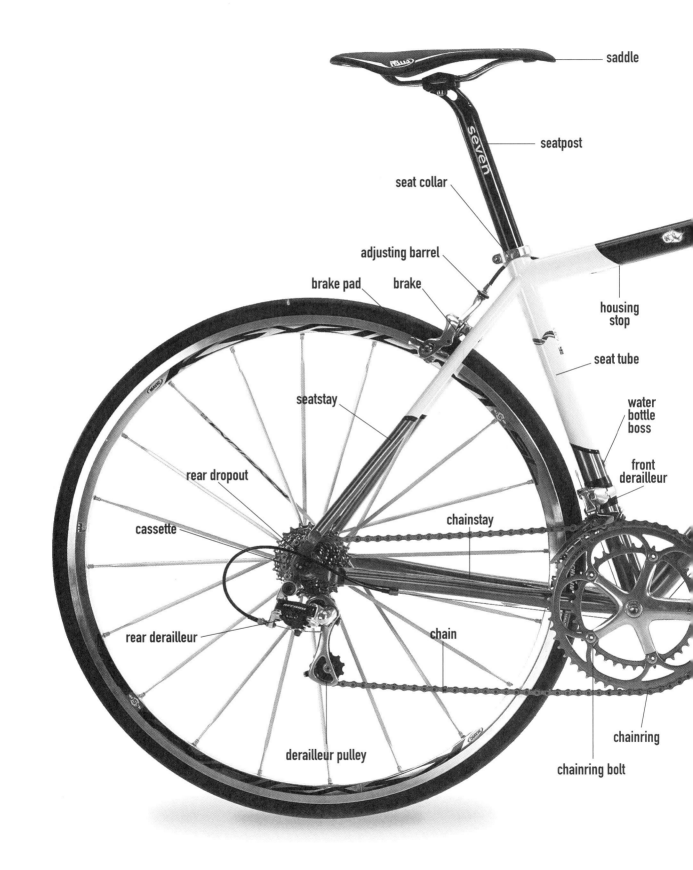

saddle

seatpost

seat collar

adjusting barrel

brake pad

brake

housing stop

seat tube

seatstay

water bottle boss

rear dropout

front derailleur

cassette

chainstay

rear derailleur

chain

derailleur pulley

chainring

chainring bolt

stem

head tube

handlebar wrap

integrated brake/shift lever

top tube

cable housing

head badge

drop handlebar

down tube

fork

quick release

crankarm

fork dropout

pedal

tire

rim

Anatomy of a Mountain Bike

saddle

saddle rail

seatpost

saddle clamp

seat collar

monocoque

seat tube

rear shock

seatstay

cassette

rear dropout

rear derailleur

chainstay

crankarm

chainring

chain

grip

stem

brake lever

shift lever

head tube

fork crown

fork stanchion

fork arch

down tube

fork slider

brake disc

front derailleur

pedal

hub

brake caliper

fork dropout

tire

rim

Anatomy of a Tandem

saddle

bullhorn handlebar

stoker stem

seatpost

seat collar

seat tube

lateral tube

seatstay

front derailleur

cassette

chainstay

chainring

rear derailleur

bottom tube (boom tube)

chain

stem

integrated
brake/shift lever

top tube

drop handlebar

head tube

cantilever brake

down tube

fork

timing
chain

fork dropout

hub

pedal

crankarm

tire

rim

Anatomy of a Recumbent

seat

direct–pull
cantilever brake

rear stay

cassette

rear dropout

chain

rear derailleur

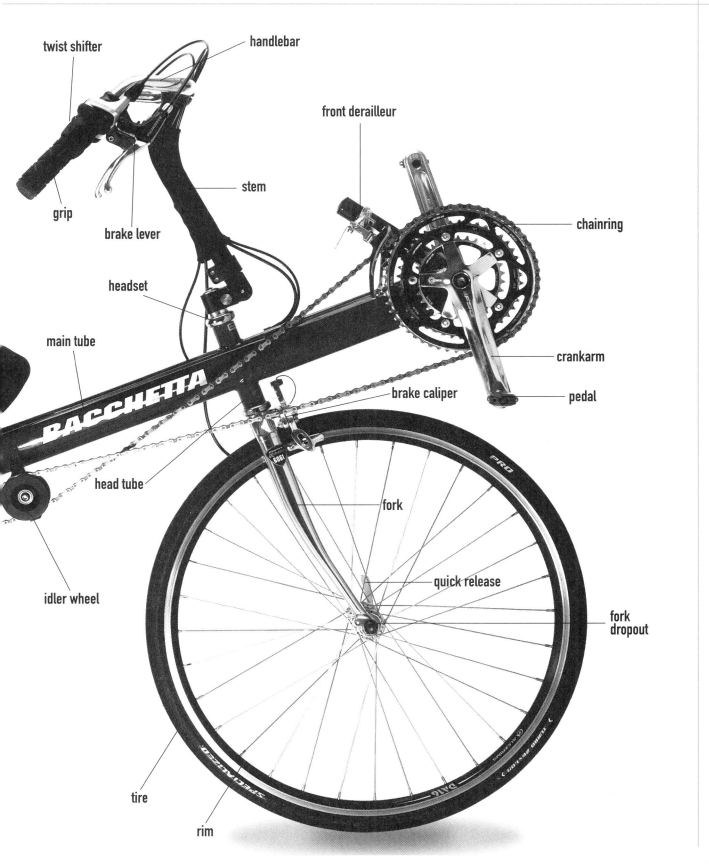

twist shifter

handlebar

front derailleur

grip

stem

brake lever

chainring

headset

crankarm

main tube

pedal

brake caliper

head tube

fork

idler wheel

quick release

fork
dropout

tire

rim

BACCHETTA

Contents

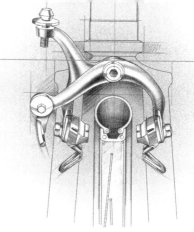

Acknowledgments

The 5th edition of *The Bicycling Guide to Complete Bicycle Maintenance & Repair* could never have been possible without the help of dozens of people and organizations. This book has been a collaborative effort between the author and many talented and knowledgeable mechanics and product designers, as well as photographers, artists, and editors.

There is hardly time or space to personally thank everyone who has been involved, but here are the key people who've gone to great lengths to ensure that this is the most comprehensive and up-to-date resource of bicycle maintenance available.

Heidi Rodale
Nancy N. Bailey
Rita Baker
Mark Bowman
Alan Daniels
Sarah S. Dunn
Drew Frantzen
Kathy LeSage
Mitch Mandel
Matt Reigner

Thank you to all the companies that loaned their time, knowledge, and products:

Ace and Belmont Wheelworks, Somerville and Belmont, Massachusetts
Answer-Manitou
Avid
Bacchetta
Bianchi USA
Bike Sport, Tracce, Pennsylvania
Bontrager
Burley Design Cooperative
Campagnolo USA
Cane Creek Components
Cannondale
Chris King Components
Crank Brothers
Euro-Asia Imports
Finish Line
FSA
Giant Bicycles
Hayes Disc Brake
Hope Technology
Hutchinson
Independent Fabrication
Iron Horse
LeMond Bicycles
Magura
Marzocchi
Maverick American
Michelin
Nault's Nashua Cyclery, Nashua, New Hampshire
Park Tool
Pedro's
Phil Wood
Quality Bicycle Products
RaceFace
RockShox
Seven Cycles
Shimano
South Mountain Cycles, Emmaus, Pennsylvania
Specialized Bicycles
SRAM
Trek Bicycle Corp.
Titec
Tri-Flow
Ultimate Support Systems
United Bicycle Institute
United Bicycle (Tool) Supply

Finally, thanks to some of the people who've been influential and supportive, both in making this book and throughout my years as a writer and professional bicycle mechanic.

John and Jill Downs
Marjorie Howsen
Danielle Ciraulo
John Allis
Butch Balzano
Michael Browne
Chipps Chippendale
Ralph Cronin
Matt Eames
Leif Erickson
Chris Fallon
Adrian Fletcher
Clint Paige
JuliRae Mitchell
Jack Mowatt
Ed Nasjleti
Rob Reed
Matt Roy
Merlyn Townley
Dave Weagle
Karl Wiedermann
Tripp Wyckoff

Introduction

Almost two decades ago, the first edition of this book was published. Much has changed in those years. But edition after edition, the goal of *The Bicycling Guide to Complete Bicycle Maintenance & Repair* has remained to keep up with and anticipate the pace of that change, and to be the definitive source of bicycle maintenance and repair techniques for cycling enthusiasts of every stripe.

The craft of bicycle mechanics, though well developed and documented for more than a century, is still largely passed on from master to apprentice through guidance and experience shared, much the same way any other traditional craft is taught. Through this text, you will benefit in the same spirit from the knowledge and experience of not one, but many bicycle mechanics that have helped to shape this guide through the years. With, no doubt, hundreds of years' experience among them, you could not hope to find yourself in better company.

Within the pages of this book, you will be introduced to all the parts of your bike. You will learn which components perform what functions, and you will learn how they all come together to make your bicycle work. Tools and supplies will be explained, lending you insight as to what ones you will need and what, though perhaps less necessary, can improve the speed, accuracy, and ease of each repair. Then, you will take all of this together and discover how all those bits and pieces are kept in top working order by cleaning, inspecting, lubricating, and adjusting.

A great deal of new information has been added to this, the 5th edition, but not at the expense of the old. Changes in technology occur every year, but perhaps there has never been a period where those changes have come so quickly and so frequently as they have in the last decade. The advent and evolutions of suspension and disc brakes are the most obvious advancements in the way bicycles function, but more subtle improvements in frame construction, bearing design, and component manufacture have made the past several years an exciting and challenging time for bicycle mechanics.

Still, there are a good many tried-and-true designs that have withstood the test of time and that remain as functional today as they did decades ago; these are highlighted and explained in the same detail as the most current technology. This is a complete guide, after all. So, in it, you will find topics of maintenance and repair covered for bicycles ranging from the trusty 1970s ten-speed through to the latest in dual-suspension mountain bikes.

Even if you don't want to perform your own repairs, knowing your bike, its component parts, and how they work together can dramatically improve your cycling experiences. By learning to recognize when something is out of adjustment before it leads to a more serious—and expensive—problem, you will save time, money, and possibly skin. This book may be all the reference you need.

Then, there are those of you who want to save even more by performing basic maintenance tasks at home. You will likely be pleasantly surprised at just how easy many of these procedures can be. You will quickly learn that most components of a bicycle are much more simple than they appear; and that, with every new technique you learn and apply, the savings will grow greater and greater.

Of course, there are those who want to go even deeper. If you want to begin performing all of your own routine maintenance, and to explore the possibilities of taking on more major repairs, this is the ideal first volume of an entire library of guides, manuals, and catalogs that you can build, covering every minute detail of bicycle maintenance.

Remember: The key to knowledge is not in knowing everything, but in knowing where to look and whom to ask.

1 HOME BICYCLE REPAIR

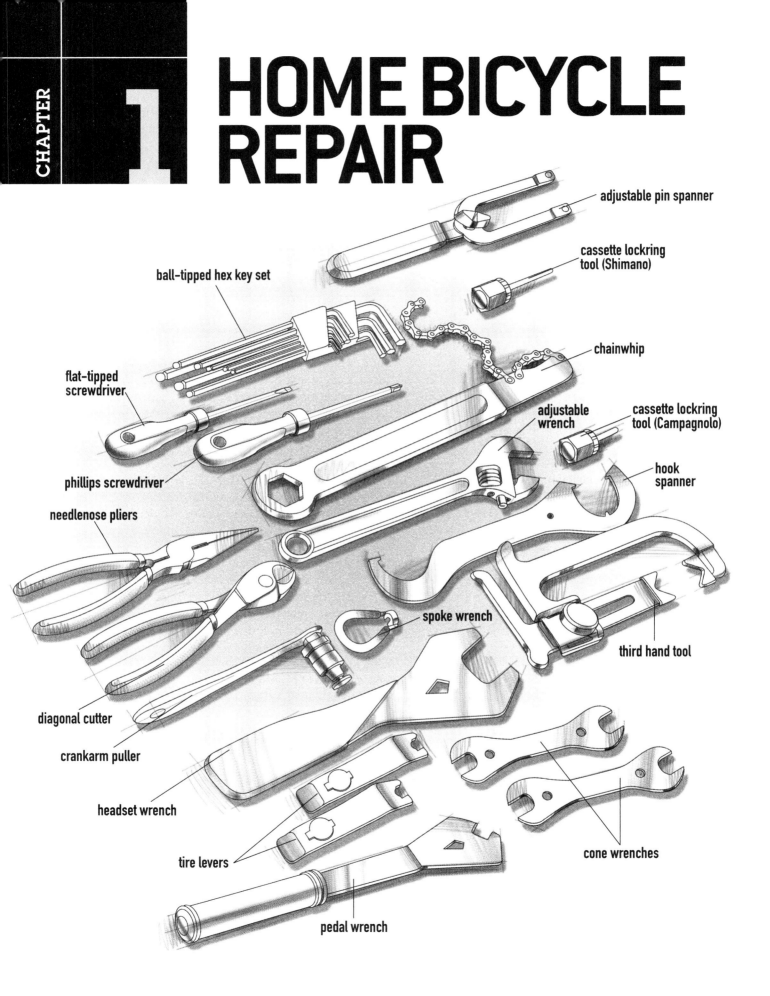

adjustable pin spanner

cassette lockring tool (Shimano)

ball-tipped hex key set

chainwhip

flat-tipped screwdriver

adjustable wrench

cassette lockring tool (Campagnolo)

phillips screwdriver

hook spanner

needlenose pliers

spoke wrench

third hand tool

diagonal cutter

crankarm puller

headset wrench

cone wrenches

tire levers

pedal wrench

Whether you ride a bicycle for fun, fitness, transportation, or an adrenalin fix—or maybe all of these—you need this book. Even if you think you never want to perform your own repairs, knowing your bike intimately, as you can after reading this text, is an invaluable tool for any cyclist. Just in taking this book from the shelf, you've shown yourself to be a cycling enthusiast: someone who has more than a passing interest in bicycles and cycling. You ride your bike (maybe several) far, frequently, or both. Perhaps you ride only in fair weather, or perhaps you're out even when the Postal Service wants to stay in. In either case, all that time spent in the saddle of any bike results in wear and tear, no matter what the quality of the bike.

Luckily for us, bicycles are nearly as fun and easy to service as they are to ride. The bicycle is one of the few things left in our lives that just about anyone—with a small amount of coaching—can understand and maintain at home. Your car, as a comparison, is intentionally shrouded in mystery, with anything not integral to its daily use hidden behind plastic and glossy paint. Lights on the dashboard hint that something is amiss, but only your dealer can coax the car to reveal its ailment with special diagnostic equipment that reads the millions of bits of information that the car's computer tracks. The bicycle, though, is open and obvious. A lightweight framework of tubes proudly presents all the bicycle's mechanisms for inspection and adjustment. Shapes, materials, and dimensional standards have changed slightly as technology has progressed over the bicycle's nearly 150-year history, but form still follows function on the bicycle, and the same simple mechanical principles make it go and stop.

If you're a numbers person, you'll be pleased to find that geometry and dimensional tolerances can dictate how and when your bike works and doesn't work. And if you're not a numbers person, you're equally in luck. How's this possible? Despite the fact that bicycle components are designed with very specific dimensions that allow them to work seamlessly together, it's important to remember that human interface is what makes a bicycle work. Without a person, a bicycle cannot stand on its own two wheels; it can't steer; it can't shift. It needs a rider to be a bicycle. And like your favorite pair of jeans, when something "feels" right, it's usually right.

"So what does it really take?" you ask. "And have I got it?" Every cyclist needs a pump, a patch kit, a folding tool or mini tool kit, and just a little bit of know-how to keep a favorite bike—or any bike, for that matter—rolling along smoothly. That's it. Really.

Hand tools are easy. There are many high-quality options available from several manufacturers, and the good folks at your local bike shop can help you decide which suits you and your bike best. *The Bicycling Guide to Complete Bicycle Maintenance & Repair* can take care of the rest; giving you the knowledge and the confidence to start you on your way to knowing your bike better than you ever have before—because knowing your bike will make every ride more enjoyable. And isn't that what it's really all about?

YOU ARE IN THE SADDLE

Maintaining your own bicycle can be relaxing, rewarding, and financially liberating. As parts wear, they need to be replaced—and you'll pay the same amount for these whether the bike shop installs them or you do it yourself. A good mechanic costs money, though, and a cheap mechanic may end up costing you more in the long run. So it stands to reason that the cost (in time) of performing your own labor may be repaid both in dollars—and in pride.

There are other good reasons to become your own bike mechanic, too. The more you work on your bike, the more you learn about it, and the better it runs. You soon discover that a tweak here and a tweak there is often all it takes to keep things

Servicing your bicycle is easiest when the bike is held off the ground by a quality workstand. Shown here are models from Ultimate, Pedro's, and Park.

running right. You learn that some problems are easy to correct and that some are difficult, and then you learn a few tricks to prevent the difficult ones. You see the value of preventive maintenance in minimizing the need for expensive repairs.

Think how much more enjoyable, too, your rides with friends will be if you can quickly diagnose and correct a roadside or trailside problem on a riding partner's bike. You can be a hero and preserve precious ride time that might otherwise be spent hobbling home.

Of course, unless you've made the greatest commitment of all—to open your own full-service bicycle repair shop—there will be repairs that are simply out of your grasp for lack of specialized tools. Things like frame-alignment tables and facing tools are just too expensive and infrequently needed to justify for any home workshop. When these kinds of situations arise, knowing the root cause can help a qualified professional help you much more quickly and efficiently— the way a physician is more able to treat your physical ailments when you've stated your symptoms clearly. These procedures will be discussed in this book so you can understand and identify them.

CREATING A SPECIAL WORK SPACE

Your home workshop should be in a comfortable, open space with sufficient ventilation. Garages and basements are the most popular locations for a home work space, but be certain that the lighting is good and the surrounding area is kept relatively clean. A floor clean enough to eat off isn't necessary, but you don't know frustration until you've chased a ⅛-inch ball bearing across a cluttered basement!

In a space of about 7 by 7 feet, you can create a pretty comfortable bicycle repair station. This allows for a workbench about 4 to 6 feet long by 2 feet deep for resting tools, small parts, and a supply of lubricants and cleaners. Opposite the workbench, you will want a workstand to hold your bike. An ideally placed workstand will hold your bike about 36 to 40 inches from the workbench, giving you enough room to move while still keeping both bike and bench within easy reach. On the back of your workbench, a pegboard with hooks to hold your most frequently used tools will keep things organized and efficient. Paint the pegboard a light color to make

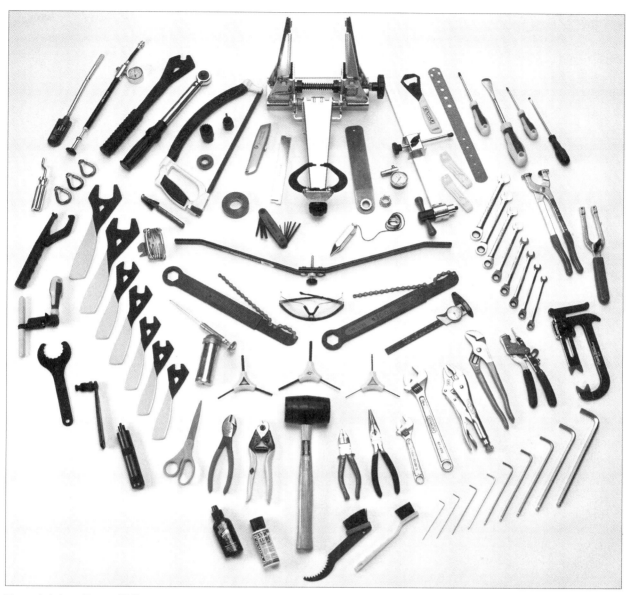

To maintain a fleet of bikes requires a fleet of tools. This assortment is more than the average home mechanic would likely need, but it would make a good start for an aspiring pro wrench.

your tools more visible, then outline the tools with a black marker on the board to help remind you where things go and what isn't put away. A short piece of 2×4 with holes drilled through makes a great storage solution for screwdrivers, loose hex keys, pens, picks, and other small tools. Lastly, a shelf under your workbench is handy for housing a small toolbox with less frequently used tools, a small trash bucket, a rag bin, and some small bins for hardware and spare parts.

Hardware stores sell kits for building workbenches just like the one described, but the sturdiest are easily constructed with just a few 2×4s and a sheet of ¾-inch plywood (Spend a little extra on exterior-grade plywood. It's more resistant to liquids that can cause your workbench top to warp and peel.) Build your workbench about 34 to 36 inches tall (or a little higher or lower if you're over 6 feet or under 5 feet tall). If you have a larger area to play with, go ahead and build your workbench 8

Good Tool Assortment

GENERAL TOOLS

- Phillips screwdrivers (#1 and #2)
- flat screwdrivers (⁷/₃₂", ¼", and ⁵/₁₆")
- standard pliers
- water pump pliers (Channel Lock, etc.)
- needle-nose pliers
- locking pliers (small, medium - Vise Grip, etc.)
- diagonal cutter
- hex keys (2, 2.5, 3, 4, 5, 6, 8, and 10mm)
- Torx keys (T-7, T-25, and T-40 for disc brake maintenance and some chainring bolts)
- metric combination wrench set (6 through 17mm)
- adjustable wrenches (8 and 12 inch)
- 8-ounce ballpeen hammer
- plastic, rubber, or leather mallet
- scissors
- tape measure (in centimeters and inches)
- hacksaw frame and blades (18 and 32 tpi)
- utility knife
- awl
- cold chisels (for cutting or carving metal)
- punches (for driving out or aligning things)
- outside calipers
- small magnet (useful for extracting ball bearings from components)
- rubber gloves
- safety glasses or goggles

BICYCLE TOOLS

- floor pump with gauge
- repair stand
- tire levers
- pedal wrench (long-handled wrench with strong jaws for removing and installing pedals)
- cone wrenches (13 through 19mm for adjusting wheel axle bearings)
- Schrader valve core remover (to fix slow leaks in car-type valves)
- cable cutter (cuts brake and shift cables without fraying)
- third hand tool (for brake cable adjustments)
- chain rivet extractor (for removing, installing, and repairing chains)
- cassette lockring remover or freewheel remover that fits the cogset(s) on your wheel(s)
- chain whips (for holding cassettes steady during lockring removal or to disassemble freewheels)
- spoke wrench(es) that fit your spoke nipples
- crank bolt wrench or 14mm socket and ratchet handle
- crankarm remover(s)
- chainring bolt spanner
- bottom bracket tool(s) to fit your bottom bracket(s)
- headset wrenches (if you have a threaded headset)
- suspension pump (if you have air-sprung shocks)

feet long, and revel in all that extra elbowroom.

It's easiest to work on your bike when it's suspended a couple of feet off the floor. This can be achieved in a number of ways. A system as simple as two cords hanging from a rafter with hooks to hold your bike at the correct level or a rack made from scrap 2×4s to hold your bike up by the frame (the same way a rack on the back of a car works) serves just fine for the purposes of most simple maintenance tasks. Just be sure that there is clearance for the crank and wheels to spin freely. For frequent

use or for more complex jobs, though, nothing beats a proper bicycle repair stand. Ready-made stands come in versions to suit anyone from the most casual home tinkerer to the seasoned pro. They work by clamping onto the seatpost or a frame tube (be careful and read the manual—some of these clamps are powerful enough to crush a frame if not applied properly) and allow you to rotate the bike up or down to bring the area you are working on closer to you.

All this talk of garages, basements, and extra

Ultimate Tool Assortment

Includes all of the tools from the Good Tool Assortment list, plus:

- *Sutherland's Handbook for Bicycle Mechanics* (the definitive source for component measurements)
- stainless steel ruler (6 inch/15cm)
- sturdy bench vise
- solvent tank (a safe place to clean parts and store solvent)
- truing stand
- Vernier caliper (a precise tool for checking component dimensions)
- dishing gauge (for centering the rim over the axle when building or truing wheels)
- taps (for repairing threads; 5mm x 0.8, 6mm x 1.0, 7mm x 1.0, 8mm x 1.0, and 10mm x 1.0)
- spoke tensiometer (for measuring spoke tension)
- tap handle
- dropout alignment tools (for repairing bent dropouts)
- thread pitch gauge (for measuring threads)
- headset installation tools (for installing headset cups and crown races)
- spoke ruler
- derailleur hanger alignment tool (for repairing bent hangers)

- tapered reamer (for enlarging holes by hand)
- rear triangle alignment indicator bar (for checking frame alignment)
- medium and coarse, round and flat files (for machining metal parts by hand)
- electric drill and drill bits
- Bondhus hex keys (hex keys with a ball-shaped end ideal for working in tight spaces; 2 through 6mm, and 8 and 10mm)
- inside caliper
- torque wrench
- grinder with wire wheel
- hex key bits (to fit torque wrench; 4, 5, 6, and 8mm)
- air compressor with blower attachment (simplifies tire inflation and grip installation)
- snap ring pliers
- lockwire pliers and lockwire (for securing disc brake hardware and for wiring mountain bike grips in place)
- tubing cutter
- hydraulic disc brake bleed kit(s)

space may be making the apartment dwellers among us feel left out in the cold, but there's no need to despair. Folding workbenches and repair stands can disappear into a closet quickly and easily, along with a small tool tote. Pick up a small linoleum remnant from a flooring store and you can even save your carpet (and security deposit!). Lay it down when working on your bike; when you're finished, wipe it down and roll it up to hide away with your portable bike shop.

It is likely that you already have many of the basic hand tools you will need to get started working on your own bike. If not, things like adjustable wrenches, pliers, screwdrivers, and combination wrenches can be most economically purchased from your local hardware store. Of course, if you like to "keep it in the neighborhood," bicycle-specific tool manufacturers like Pedro's and Park make shop-quality versions of these, as well as all the specialty tools you may eventually want or need. We have provided lists of what makes a "good" assortment of tools for the casual home mechanic and what could be an "ultimate" assortment for those who want to be entirely self-sufficient. You'll also need cutting oil (if you plan to tap or chase threads), electrical tape, grease, solvents, spray lube, thread adhesive, and wax. If you're not sure where you fall, start small and add tools to your collection as the need arises.

Now that your workspace is organized, you may want to create a list of periodic maintenance tasks to hang next to your favorite cycling calendar.

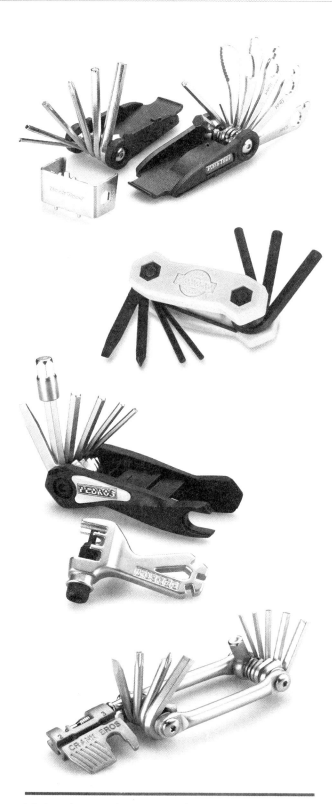

Mini-tools come in many configurations to suit different needs. Even the most basic can mean the difference between riding home and walking home.

AVOID PROBLEMS THROUGH PREVENTIVE MAINTENANCE

Everybody has heard the saying "An ounce of prevention is worth a pound of cure." Well, when it comes to bikes, an ounce of preventive maintenance is worth a pound of expensive repair.

The first part of preventive maintenance is also the simplest—keeping your tires properly inflated. You'll find the recommended pressure written on the tire's sidewall. At least every other ride for road bikes or once a week for mountain bikes, check the pressure with a floor pump that has a gauge. Maintaining the proper tire pressure makes the bike roll most efficiently. More important, it ensures that when you hit a rut or pothole or rock, your wheels will have the best chance of escaping damage (you can help, too, by getting off the saddle and absorbing the shock in your knees and elbows).

Next priority should be keeping your bike clean and lubricated. Freeing your bike of grime and grit by wiping it down regularly will help your machine perform better and prevent corrosion. It's also easier to inspect your frame for signs of corrosion and cracks at the tube junctions when the frame is clean. Discovering these issues early gives you the best chance of mitigating the problem and saving the frame (or your front teeth).

At least once a month (or after every muddy ride), wipe down your frame with a damp cloth. While you're at it, polish it with a car wax or an all-in-one bike cleaner (even Lemon Pledge furniture polish for a quick spray and spruce-up). Polish or wax will give your paint job a slick surface that dirt and grit will less easily adhere to and makes each subsequent cleaning easier.

Clean the rims of your wheels frequently because the grime that builds up on them is passed along to your brake pads and can reduce the brakes' effectiveness. At least once a month (more frequently if you do a lot of riding on dirty road surfaces), clean your rims and brake pads with alcohol.

Inspect the brake pad surfaces that strike the rims, and use an awl or pick to dig out any small stones, metal, and debris embedded in the pads. These will quickly cut into the rims, damaging them over time. Then, scuff off the glaze that may develop on your brake pads with a piece of emery cloth, sandpaper, or a fine file.

The grit and grime that makes its way into your

Bicycle Tool Kit

Here are tools to carry when you ride. Carry them in a bag under your seat or in a backpack.

- spare tube (even if you use tubeless tires)
- tube patch kit (contains patches, glue, and sandpaper; check the glue frequently since it tends to dry out once opened)
- tire boots (special patches to repair cuts in the tire; a dollar bill works in a pinch)
- tire levers
- all-in-one mini-tool such as the Crank Brothers Multi 17 (a small tool that includes 2, 2.5, 3, 4, 5, 6, and 8mm hex keys; chain tool; flat screwdriver; Phillips screwdriver; T-25 Torx key; spoke wrenches; and 8 and 10mm open wrenches)
- frame pump or mini pump (set to fit your type of valve)
- small length of wire (handy for making temporary, 'get-home' repairs on the road- or trail-side)
- emergency money
- identification (written inside your helmet, too)

hubs, headset, and bottom bracket is a little more difficult to remove. In this case, you must disassemble the parts, clean them, and repack them in fresh grease. There are also preventive measures that you can take. Wrapping pipe cleaners around the openings into your hubs or pulling sections of old tire tubes over the upper and lower stacks on your headset are cheap, effective ways of making a mechanical seal. These techniques are described further in the chapters devoted to these bike parts.

Besides inflating tires and cleaning and lubricating, the other primary maintenance tasks on a bike are to make sure that parts are properly fastened and adjusted.

Some loose or improperly adjusted parts are dangerous. Others simply lead to unnecessary wear and deterioration of components. Both types of problems can be avoided by frequent checking to make sure all parts of your bike are properly tightened and adjusted.

CHOOSING CLEANING MATERIALS

What do you use to clean a bike? Water, for starters. Some cyclists hose down their bikes after a dirty ride. This technique is fine when using the trickle from a garden hose or squirts from a spray bottle. When you do this, just bounce the bike on its tires a couple times to shake off some of the water, then let it air-dry in a warm place. Treat it the same way after riding in a drenching rain. In both cases, if you have a leather saddle, you don't want to get it too wet, so wrap it in a plastic bag to protect it. Avoid using pressurized water streams, like those at a car wash for example, though. Too much force can push water past the seals in your hubs, headset, and bottom bracket and force the grease out, increasing the frequency with which you will need to service these bearings.

Along with the water, use a sponge and a mild soap such as dish soap. Some parts get too greasy and grimy to be cleaned with soap and water. Parts such as chainrings, chains, the insides of hubs, headsets, and bottom brackets need to be cleaned with a degreaser or solvent. Which one you use depends on how difficult the part is to clean. In general, the most aggressive solvents are the most volatile, which means in part that their vapors will quickly permeate the air around you and may pose a hazard to your health.

Gasoline and lacquer thinner are examples of readily available solvents of this type. Both are very effective cleaners but also are highly volatile and highly flammable. Don't use them.

WD-40 is a well-known product that contains several different solvents mixed with a light oil. The most aggressive solvent in the mixture quickly evaporates into the air if you leave it sitting in an open container. For cyclists, WD-40 may be most useful in its spray form for loosening gummed-up parts in derailleurs and chains. Bicycle-specific degreasers are available in varying strengths from Pedro's, Finish Line, and Simple Green. The advantage to using a bicycle-specific cleaner or degreaser is that most are formulated to not harm plastic or composite components that make up many of today's high-performance parts. As a general rule, keep citrus-based cleaners on chains, cogs, and chainrings and away from shifters, and minimize their contact with your bike's paint. "Green" cleaners like Pedro's Bio Cleaner (formerly Bio Degreaser) and Simple Green Bike Cleaner are milder and will not harm

Maintenance Schedule

BEFORE EVERY RIDE

- Check tire pressure.
- Make sure that the chain is properly lubricated.
- Make sure that brakes grab firmly.
- Make sure the wheels are centered in the frame and that the quick releases are firmly closed.
- Check that brakes are properly aligned and that the pads are in good condition.
- Check and adjust pressure of air-sprung suspension components.
- Check hydraulic brake lines for kinks or splits.
- Bounce the bike to detect rattles that might indicate loose or mis-adjusted parts.
- Make sure bags and panniers are secure and that no loose straps can get caught in the wheels.
- Check that your pump and repair kit are present.

AFTER EVERY RIDE

- Brush foreign objects off the tread and check the overall condition of the tires.
- Wipe down or hose down the bike if it's very dirty; be careful not to direct water at bearings or other sensitive components; bounce the bike to shake off excess water and store it in a warm, dry place.
- Dry off the saddle if it's wet.
- If the chain got wet, wipe it down and apply some fresh chain lube.
- After a wet ride, remove the seatpost, turn the bike upside down, and let the seat tube drain; apply fresh grease or antiseize before reinstalling the post (except where carbon fiber is involved).
- Check hydraulic brake lines for kinks or splits.

EVERY MONTH (OR MORE OFTEN IF RIDING FIVE OR MORE DAYS PER WEEK)

- Wipe down the entire bike with a wet rag.
- Check for cracks or signs of stress on the frame, rims, crank, fork, handlebar, and stem.
- Hold the front wheel between your knees and try to turn the handlebar with one hand; if it moves easily, tighten the stem bolt(s), give the chain, cogs, and chainrings a quick degreasing on the bike, and relubricate the chain.
- Lubricate the bushings of the idler and jockey pulleys on the rear derailleur.
- Lubricate the pivot points on the front and rear derailleurs.
- Check crankbolts and chainring bolts for tightness.
- Clean the legs of suspension forks and the body of the rear shock; then apply lubricant

---

plastics or paint in any concentration. Use these to clean greasy residue anywhere on your bike.

Best of all, these cleaners are environmentally friendly and, in most cases, biodegradable. Despite the relatively benign nature of these biodegradable cleaning products, wear rubber gloves idea whenever using cleaning agents. In fact, wearing gloves like Park's Nitrile rubber gloves is a good way to protect your hands and keep clean while you're performing any bicycle repair.

Alcohol is less harsh to your skin than most solvents and works for lighter jobs, such as cleaning brake pads and the braking surfaces of your wheel rims.

Besides soap, water, and degreaser, all you need to get your bike parts clean are a bucket, plenty of rags, a few sponges, pads, and brushes. Scouring pads made of synthetic materials that are kind to shiny metal surfaces are useful aids in cleaning rims and removing road tar from bike frames. Old toothbrushes can be put to good use cleaning freewheel cogs, chainring teeth, and chains. Larger brushes work well for getting between spokes, around brakes, and into the tight spots on the frame. Experiment to find what works best for you, put together a kit, and store it in a bucket.

Disc brakes are extremely sensitive to oil, so special care must be taken when cleaning the brake disc, or rotor. Even the small amount of oil on the surface of your skin is enough to hinder disc brakes' performance or even ruin the brake pads perma-

to the dust wipers to keep them from drying out.

- Lubricate springs and pivot points on clipless pedals.
- Check that all brake hardware is secure.
- Check the spoke tension and truness of wheels and adjust as needed.
- Check cables for kinks and fraying.
- Measure the chain and check the cogs and chainrings for excessive wear; replace if necessary.
- Check the condition of the brake pads; replace if excessively or unevenly worn; for rubber rim-brake pads, pick out debris with an awl and remove glazing by scuffing with a half-round file.
- Clean rims with isopropyl rubbing alcohol.
- Check accessory hardware (racks, bottle cages, etc.) for tightness.
- Check the condition of glue on tubular (sew-up) tires.
- Add two to four drops of oil to three-speed hubs.
- Clean and treat leather saddles with saddle soap or leather dressing.
- Check headset for proper adjustment.
- Check rear suspension pivot bolts for proper torque.

EVERY SIX MONTHS

- Check the bearing adjustment on front and rear hubs.
- Check the adjustment on pedal bearings.
- Check the bottom bracket for proper adjustment.
- Check the seat tube for rust on steel frames.
- Clean cables and flush cable housings with a light aerosol solvent.
- Check all hardware on the bike.
- Overhaul suspension forks, rear shocks, and rear suspension pivots

EVERY YEAR

- Overhaul hubs.
- Overhaul headset.
- Replace cables and housings.
- Replace worn parts such as tires and brake pads.
- Replace grips or handlebar wrap.

nently. Use a cleaner specifically intended for disc brakes, such as White Lightning Clean Streak or Disc Doctor, and a perfectly clean rag to spray and wipe off the rotors. In the absence of these products, rubbing alcohol is an acceptable substitute for cleaning rotors. Disc brake pads generally should not be cleaned, but in a case of oil contamination, it is sometimes possible to revive the pads by soaking them in rubbing alcohol and then gently scuffing them on a piece of sandpaper or emery cloth laid flat on your workbench.

LUBRICANTS

Along with thorough cleaning, properly lubricating the moving parts of your bike is extremely impor-

tant. There are many lubricants on the market, and here are some general guidelines.

Grease. This book frequently calls for the use of medium-weight grease. This is the lubricant recommended for all bearing installations on a bike as well as for threaded parts on freewheels, bottom brackets, headsets, pedals, and wheel axles. The same grease can be used to lubricate as well as rust-protect brake and gear cables.

The bike greases marketed by Finish Line, Park, Pedro's, and Phil Wood, among other bike-product companies, are the type we have in mind. These greases are generally sold in tubes. If you expect to use a lot of grease, you may want to purchase a tub of white lithium grease at an auto parts store.

This is similar to bike grease and works just as well. Just make sure you buy white lithium grease and not automotive bearing grease, which contains molybdenum disulfide to help it handle high temperatures. This grease is too thick and sticky for use on a bike.

When servicing suspension forks, be sure to read the manual provided with the fork. Some models must be lubed with a certain grease type. Using a lithium-based grease, for instance, may damage the bushings inside the fork.

Oil. Oils are used to lubricate the pivot points of brakes and derailleurs, the cassette bearings (inside the cluster of gears on the rear wheel), and the chain links. The internally geared hubs on three-speed bikes also need a periodic healthy dose of oil, as do suspension forks. In fact, most suspension forks use oil as a way to control travel.

Many companies offer quality oils. Pedro's, Finish Line, ProGold (the only lubricant to ever win *Bicycling* Magazine's Editor's Choice Award), DT Swiss, and a host of others offer a wide variety of oils for different applications. Avoid the familiar three-in-one oil because it is vegetable-based and will gum up your bike's moving parts. For suspension forks, get the oil recommended by the manual.

As with grease, so with oil. The automotive industry provides an alternative to the oil sold in bike shops. Ordinary 30-weight motor oil is a workable substitute. Pour it into a squirt can and apply a few drops where needed. Fight the temptation, however, to be frugal and put used motor oil to use on your bicycle. Used motor oil contains microscopic metal filings and develops an acidic quality from the introduction of carbon and heat in the combustion chamber. Both of these will compromise metal surfaces and increase wear.

There is much debate over the question of the best lubricant for chains, the bike component that is particularly subject to the ravages of dirt and water. This is partly because riding conditions vary so much. What works in southern California isn't going to be much good in Maine, for instance. Here we offer general recommendations. Try various types to determine what is best for you.

As a general rule, wet lubricants (oils) work year-round but are messier and require more frequent cleaning of your drivetrain than dry lubricants, which are best suited to warm, dry conditions but don't tend to hold dirt and grime as much.

What you use on your chain is somewhat less important than how you use it. Contrary to what some may believe, it is not necessary to have a heavy coating of lubricant on the outside of the chain or on the teeth of your chainrings and cogs. Rather, it's the inner surfaces of the chain where wear takes place—the interfaces of the pins, plates, and rollers.

The correct way to lubricate your chain begins with a clean chain. Removing the chain and soaking it in a solvent or degreaser is a great way to do this, but not necessary. Chain cleaning devices that soak and scrub the chain while it is still in place on your bike do a great job, save you a step, and keep the whole process neat and tidy. In the absence of a chain-cleaning box, you can simply soak a rag in degreaser and grip it loosely on the chain while pedaling your drivetrain backward. You'll need to repeat this several times to achieve the results of soaking or of a mechanical chain-cleaning box. If there are thick clumps of dry, dirty lubricant between the chain links, scrub these out with an old toothbrush. If time allows, it's best to let the chain dry for several hours.

Once your chain is clean, drip lubricant over the chain while pedaling the drivetrain backward. After lightly coating the entire chain, continue the pedaling motion for 20 to 30 seconds to allow the lubricant to work its way into the deepest parts of the chain. Use a clean rag to wipe the excess lubricant from the outside of the chain. This last step leaves a thin film of lubricant on the outside of the chain to inhibit corrosion but minimizes the amount of grit that will stick to the chain. Your chainring and cog teeth will receive enough lubricant just from contact with the chain to fight corrosion.

Use these same steps before installing a new chain, as well. New chains are coated with a protective, oil-based wax to prevent rust while in shipping and storage, but it is not an ideal lubricant. This protectant is very sticky and will attract dirt and debris.

Keeping cables freely flowing through their housings follows two schools of thought. The first says that grease on the cables will prevent water and grit from entering the housing. However, some dirt will always be dragged into the housing by the motion of the cable, so greased cables should be removed, cleaned, and regreased regularly. The other says that a perfectly clean cable and housing allows the cable to move quickly and smoothly, especially in modern, Teflon-lined cable housings. Care, too, should be taken to ensure that the cables and housings remain clean by removing the cables periodically and spraying a solvent or very light oil like White Lightning Clean Streak or WD-40 through the housings to flush them.

DON'T BE A STATISTIC

There's nothing like a trip to the emergency room to put a dent in the Sunday that you were devoting to tuning up your road rocket. Worse, it's a terrible irony when you can't ride because you hurt yourself

Recommended Lubricants

PART	LUBRICANT
Ball bearings	Medium weight bike grease
Bottom bracket spindle	Medium weight bike grease (do not lubricate square-taper spindles unless directed to by the crankarm manufacturer
Brake cable	Flush housing with aerosol solvent; if desired, lubricate using a lightweight oil
Brake pivot	Medium weight bike grease or Teflon-based oil
Brake spring	Medium weight bike grease
Chain	Pick a chain lubricant; there are lots out there for different conditions
Derailleur pivots	Teflon-based oil
Internal gear hubs	Lightweight machine oil with no particulate additives
Seatposts (steel or aluminum frame and/or seatpost)	Medium weight bike grease
Seatposts (titanium frame with steel, aluminum, or titanium seatpost; titanium seatpost with steel, aluminum, or titanium frame)	Antiseize compound
Seatposts (carbon fiber frame with any material seatpost; carbon fiber seatpost with any material frame)	Nothing (any type of lubricant could cause slipping and possibly compromise the carbon fiber)
Stem (quill-type)	Medium weight bike grease; substitute antiseize compound if any titanium component is involved
Stem (threadless type)	Nothing
Suspension fork dust wipers	Teflon-based oil
Threads	White lithium grease, medium weight bike grease, antiseize compound, or thread-locking compound, depending on the application

A bike repair school, like this class being held at United Bicycle Institute in Ashland, Oregon, is the ideal starting point for a career in bicycle mechanics.

cranking on your sled. Fortunately for you, we've made every dumb mistake a mechanic can make and are here to tell you about them. Keep these in mind as you wrench and you'll escape the embarrassment and downtime of an injury. Also, take your time, use common sense, and be careful.

Bad jab. When you're pushing down with a screwdriver, knife, awl, electric drill—anything sharp—make sure your free hand and any other body part aren't directly behind the object you're operating on. If you slip, you'll likely cut, poke, or drill yourself.

Face job. Likewise, whenever you're pulling on things, keep your face out of the way. The classic goof is pulling up hard to remove something, say a frozen seatpost or seat. When it releases, you bash

yourself in the face. Ouch.

Slice of life. Watch out for sharp parts. When removing pedals, for instance, you're working around the chainrings with all those nasty teeth (not just sharp, but greasy, too). A good way to protect yourself is to always shift the chain onto the large chainring before trying to remove or install a pedal. That way, the teeth are covered. And watch out for frayed cables, which can stick you like splinters.

Can clumsiness. When using spray lubes or cleaners, be sure the nozzle is pointing away from your face. And don't drop the cans because that can knock the nozzles off, leading to broken cans that won't stop spraying. Also, read the labels before use so you know what to do if you get the stuff in your eyes. Be sure to work with spray lubes in ventilated areas only.

Splish-splash guard. When working with solvents, wear rubber gloves to protect your skin and goggles to protect your eyes from splashback.

Test-ride. After finishing a repair, test-ride the bike—but take it easy. Even the best mechanics forget things. It's better to pedal gently and test things at slow speeds than to vault into the saddle and sprint down the road.

TAKING IT TO THE NEXT LEVEL

If you get hooked on fixing bikes, you may want to pursue it as a career or learn as much as you can. While it's a tough field in which to earn a living, if you love bikes, wrenching from 9:00 to 5:00 (okay, more like 10:00 to 8:00, but love knows no time) can sure be satisfying. So how do you get the experience needed to land a job or to do advanced work? One approach is to attend a bike-repair school such as those offered by Barnett's Bicycle Institute in Colorado Springs, Colorado, and the United Bicycle Institute in Ashland, Oregon.

These extensive courses plunge you headfirst into the world of bicycle mechanics, similar to what it would be like working in a shop. You'll graduate having worked on many different bikes and problems, confident in your ability to troubleshoot whatever bicycle failure comes your way. The courses even provide manuals that you keep for use in the real world.

If you're not ready to attend a repair school or you don't want to spend the tuition for one, Park Tool has put together a program called Park Tool School that is run through local bike shops across the country. Here you can learn bicycle repair on your own bike in small classes with lots of one-on-one time with the instructor. You might also check community colleges or universities that may have a bike co-op. These often offer much more affordable bike-repair classes where you can get hands-on experience. If you can't find one, consider rounding up some friends who'd like to learn repair, and then approach local shops to see if they'd be willing to put together a course. They may not have thought of it before and might be happy to test the profit potential of such an idea.

BASIC PRINCIPLES OF BICYCLE MAINTENANCE AND REPAIR

Here are the guidelines that we live by when it comes to bicycle maintenance and repair.

Think safety first. Wear rubber gloves to protect your hands from solvents and grease. Don goggles to protect your eyes when using hammers or power tools. Wear a face mask and ventilate your shop when working with chemicals.

Don't wait until severe problems arise before doing anything. Preventive maintenance is the best way to take care of your bike.

When lubricating your bike, use plenty of oil or grease, then wipe away any excess that will attract grit. Don't wipe off dirty grease that appears on the outside of bearings until overhaul time; doing so will only shove grit inside the bearings.

Most parts are turned to the right to tighten and to the left to loosen. One way to remember this is to repeat, "Righty, tighty; lefty, loosey." The common exceptions to this rule are the left pedal and the right side of the bottom bracket.

Before installing any threaded part, check the threads to see that they match. Don't mismatch threaded parts. And never force things: Always grease threads first, then start threading them together carefully and gently.

Take it easy when tightening things. Bicycle components are often small and made of lightweight materials. Tighten, then check the tightness, then tighten some more if needed. That's better than stripping threads and breaking parts.

Some repair jobs are better left to experts. Learn to recognize your skills and limitations. Learn to make wise choices as to what you can handle and what's better left to a trained shop mechanic.

BOXING A BIKE

Though it's not really a repair topic, knowing how to properly box a bike for shipping can come in handy. Most airlines require that a bike be placed in a box before you can take it on a flight. Another good way to get your machine somewhere is to ship it via United Parcel Service (UPS) or Federal Express. Both require that the bike be boxed in a proper bike container.

More important, a careful packing job will protect the bike and improve the chances that baggage handlers won't trash your prize possession. The first step is getting a good box, and the place to do that is a bike shop. Tell them the type of bike it is and the frame size so they can select the correct box. It's a good idea to call first because shops may have spare boxes only when they're building new bikes, which isn't necessarily every day.

Some shops sell bike boxes for a nominal fee; others give them away. Besides the box, pick up some 2-inch-wide packing tape. Get good tape that's difficult to tear and that will stick fast, like the kind UPS sells. Other things you'll need include a permanent black marker (to address the box and cross out old addresses), pipe insulation (or newspaper or bubble wrap), string, elastics, a fork spacer (ask at the shop or make a 1-inch by 1-inch wood block that's 100 mm long), and a shoebox-size box for small-parts storage.

The fork-spacer block is an important piece because it will prevent the fork from being damaged should some gorilla-like handler abuse your box. If you get a plastic fork spacer from a shop, it will press into the dropouts and stay in place. If you make your own spacer out of wood, however, you'll need to fasten it in place. Pressing it between the blades usually isn't sufficient, and it will do no good if it falls out the first time that someone bumps or drops the box. One way to attach the spacer is to drill holes in each end and drive in sheetrock screws. Also, insert washers between the screws and the dropouts.

It's also a good idea to reinforce the box. Some careful packers get an oversize box and put the correct size box inside the first to create a double-wall box. This adds weight but pretty much guarantees that the box will protect your prize possession from damage.

If you don't want to double the box, you can simply put in pieces of cardboard on the sides of the box to reinforce it. Or, if you have some ¼-inch plywood or old paneling, use pieces of that to reinforce the cardboard.

Keep in mind that airlines charge an additional fee for bringing your bike on the plane—usually about $75 to $100 one way. It's often cheaper to ship the bike using UPS or FedEx. This is also easier than dragging the bike through the airport. In today's time of heightened security awareness, it's best not to try to fool the airlines by disguising boxes or lying about their contents. It could mean the difference between making your flight and spending 3 hours in a security shakedown.

The step-by-step instructions on boxing a bike that begin on page 15 refer to mechanical skills described later in the book. If you don't understand a step, jump to the chapter pertaining to the component being described to learn how to work on the part. Most of the skills required to box a bike are not advanced.

Boxing a Bike

1 To prevent cuts, remove any protruding staples from the box lids. Start bike preparation by removing the pedals with a pedal wrench. Turn the left pedal clockwise to loosen; turn the right pedal counterclockwise. Place the pedals in the small-parts box. Shift onto the largest rear cog and smallest chainring. To prevent damage, cover all the tubes and the left crankarm with pipe insulation (see photo), bubble wrap, or many sheets of newspaper wrapped and taped. Loosen and remove the seat and seatpost as a unit. If necessary, remove the handlebar and computer, carefully unwinding the cable from the brake wire. Wrap the seat and seatpost, aero bar, and computer. Place the computer in the small-parts box.

2 If you are taking your bike on a plane or shipping by air, the lower atmospheric pressure in the cargo compartment should be taken into consideration. Deflate tires to about 25 psi so they won't burst. Air-sprung shocks and suspension forks should also be aired down to prevent blown seals and oil weeping.

3 Open both sidepull brake quick-releases, unhook cantilever link wires, or release the noodle from direct-pull cantilevers. If you have slotted cable stops, lift the brake housings out of the stops. For the shift cables, click the right lever several times as if you're shifting to smaller cogs, then pull on the front derailleur to create slack and release the derailleur housing sections. Some bikes have stems that open so that the handlebars can be removed intact (that is, with the levers and grips attached). If you have this type, open the stem, remove the bar, and reattach the stem parts (see photo).

Boxing a Bike *continued*

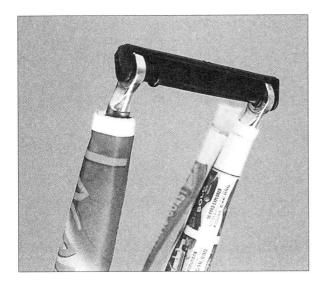

4 For a nonopening stem, loosen and remove the top cap bolt on threadless forks (most mountain bikes) and loosen the stem bolts. On threaded forks (most road bikes), loosen the stem bolt on top of the stem and tap it with a mallet to loosen the stem. Remove the front sidepull brake by unscrewing the 5 mm hex key bolt (don't disconnect the cable). For cantilevers, remove the side connected to the cable. Reattach the sidepull nut and any washers and tape the cantilever parts together. Wrap the brake so it can't scratch the frame. Lift off the stem and handlebar. For threadless forks, place a cardboard tube that's about the same width as your stem over the fork and reinstall the top cap and nut (see photo).

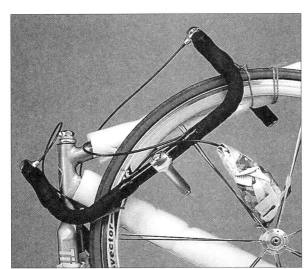

5 Remove the front wheel. Unscrew and extract the front quick-release, reassemble it, and place it in the small-parts box. Install a fork spacer or wood block (1 inch by 1 inch by 100 mm) between the dropouts (see photo) with screws or tape. This prevents the fork from getting bent and from poking through the box. Put the bike on the ground, level the crankarms, and wrap an elastic around the seatstays and valve stem, which will keep the rear wheel from rotating and changing the crankarm position.

6 Place the front wheel on the left side of the bike, fitting it snugly by working the left crankarm inside the spokes. When the wheel is in the correct position, the axle will be between the seat tube and down tube and won't be able to contact them. Just be certain that the hub is situated so it cannot damage the frame. Then tie the wheel to the frame at the seat, down, and top tubes.

Place the handlebar/stem assembly alongside the top tube to find the narrowest way to attach it. Loosen the stem if necessary to rotate the bar inside the stem. For drop handlebars, try placing the bar's hooks over the top tube with the levers pointing upward and the stem inside the wheel (see photo).

7 Experiment to find the safest position for the brake levers, and wrap them if they seem vulnerable. Rotate the fork 180 degrees.

Check the small-parts box to ensure that all pieces are inside, tape it shut, and place it in one end of the bike box. Lift and lower the bike into the box, keeping the small-parts box between the fork and downtube. Make sure that the crankarms are horizontal. Put the front brake wherever it fits. Wrap the seat, aero bar/ seatpost assembly and tie it next to the rear wheel. If the front hub rubs the side of the box, tape a piece of cardboard over the axle as a buffer.

2 FRAMES

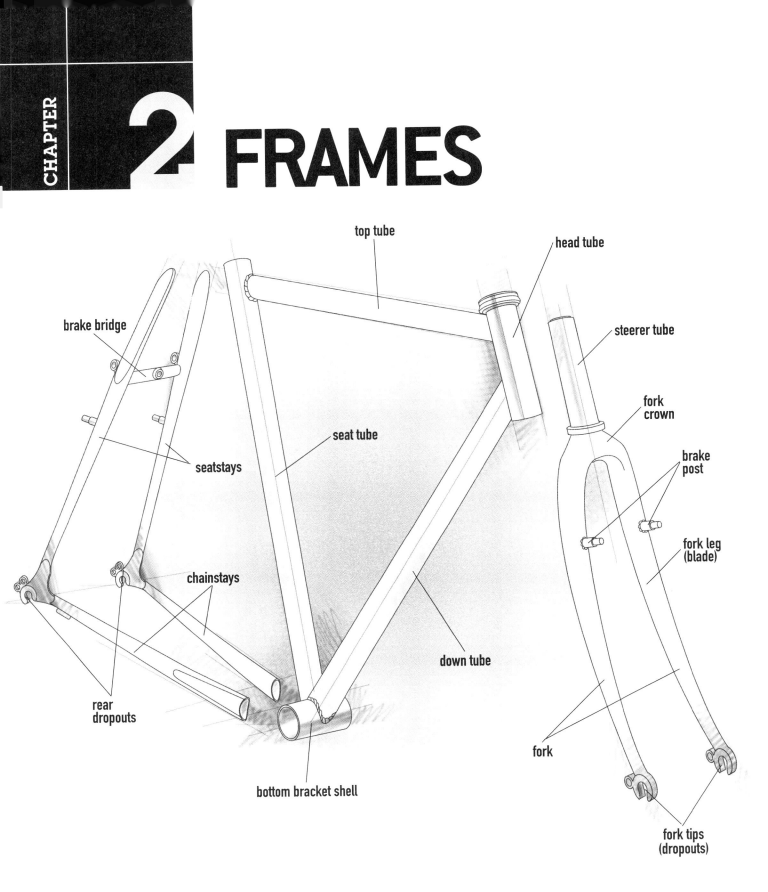

top tube

head tube

brake bridge

steerer tube

seatstays

seat tube

fork crown

brake post

chainstays

fork leg (blade)

rear dropouts

down tube

bottom bracket shell

fork

fork tips (dropouts)

When asked, "What kind of bike do you ride?" most of us will quickly utter the name that appears on the bike's frame. Indeed, though every bike is made up of a collection of parts from several manufacturers, the frame builder gets credit for making the bike what it is. This is not entirely incorrect, as the details of each frame's construction determine how the bike will behave more than any other single component.

Frames require little maintenance, and a damaged frame can be properly repaired only by a qualified frame builder or experienced professional mechanic. Still, your bicycle's frame should not be taken for granted, so the focus of this chapter will be to familiarize you with the aspects of frame construction, geometry, and inspection for signs of trouble.

The frame is the most important part of your bicycle for many reasons. The first aspect is geometry. Geometry is a blanket term that refers to all the angles and dimensions that make the bike fit and handle the way it does. It positions your body for efficient pedaling by determining the locations of the saddle, crankset, and handlebars. The same geometry also determines the handling, or behavior, of a bike. How stable it is when racing down trails, its willingness to cut corners, and its ability to carry loads are all determined by the specific relationships between each dimension of the frame's geometry.

It's simply not possible to build a frame that optimizes all of these factors, so trade-offs are made among them to make your bike a racer, sports tourer, loaded tourer, or mountain bike. Beyond your frame's geometry, its construction material, combined with the type of tires, determines how comfortably or sportily it will ride.

You can change your bike's personality to some extent by changing the parts that are hung on it. Lighter wheels, for example, will liven up your bike's ride and make it climb and accelerate more easily.

Your bike's frame, though, determines its general handling and comfort. Therefore, it's valuable to learn to identify the principal parts of a typical frame and to recognize different types of frames.

FRAME NOMENCLATURE

A bicycle's frame is often described by its halves: the front and the rear triangles. The front triangle, also known as the main triangle, is actually a quadrilateral. It consists of the following tubes.

Head tube. This is located at the front of the frame and holds the headset, or steering bearings.

Top tube. This connects the head tube and the seat tube, which is under the saddle.

Seat tube. This runs from the seat down to the bottom bracket and the bottom of the down tube.

Down tube. This runs from the head tube down to the bottom bracket. The bottom bracket holds the bearings and axle of the crankset.

The rear triangle consists of the chainstays and the seatstays. The chainstays are the twin tubes that connect the bottom bracket and two rear axle holders known as the dropouts. The seatstays are the twin tubes that connect the dropouts and the junction of tubes under the saddle called the seat cluster. Technically, the seat tube completes the triangle.

Completing the frame are the fork and the steerer tube. The fork consists of two fork blades that are attached to a horizontal piece known as the fork crown. On suspension forks, the blades are most often referred to as "legs," each of which is made up of two primary parts. The smaller-diameter part of the leg, generally stationary and press-fit or clamped into the crown, is the stanchion; and the larger diameter part that fits over it is the slider. Some mountain bike downhill forks have stanchions that extend up past the crown to a secondary crown at the top of the head tube. These are most commonly referred to as double crown forks. At the

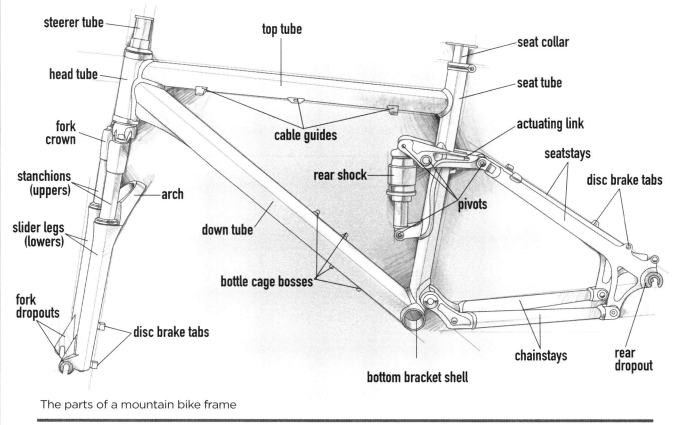

steerer tube

head tube

fork crown

stanchions (uppers)

arch

slider legs (lowers)

fork dropouts

disc brake tabs

top tube

cable guides

down tube

bottle cage bosses

rear shock

pivots

bottom bracket shell

seat collar

seat tube

actuating link

seatstays

disc brake tabs

chainstays

rear dropout

The parts of a mountain bike frame

lower end of the blades are the two front axle holders known as fork tips or fork dropouts. The steerer tube rises out of the crown at the top of the blades and is normally hidden in the head tube. It connects the fork crown to the headset.

The materials used in manufacturing the frame affect the way it feels. But as we said before, the length of the tubes and the way they relate to one another—that is, the frame geometry—play the major role in determining the way a bike behaves.

There are two critical parts of frame geometry. The first is the fork rake, which is the amount that the front axle is offset from the centerline of the fork. The second is the bottom bracket position, which is given either from the line drawn between the front and rear axles (called the drop), or from the ground (called the bottom bracket height). Other important aspects of the frame are the seat angle, which is the smaller of the two angles formed by the seat tube and any horizontal line, and the head angle, which is the smaller of the two angles formed by the centerline of the head tube or the fork and

any horizontal line. All of these factors combine to determine the bike's wheelbase, or the distance between the axles of the two wheels.

HISTORY OF THE BICYCLE FRAME

The typical bicycle frame—sometimes called the diamond frame because of its shape, but more commonly known as the men's frame—has been around for more than 100 years, even though it has seen competition from many other frame designs. Ladies' and mixte frames may provide easier mounting and dismounting because they don't have a top tube, but the diamond frame still provides the best combination of rigidity, strength, and light weight, and it is the predominant frame in use today.

Rigidity is important in a bicycle frame because a frame that's too flexible wastes pedaling energy. Frames that do not have a top tube are essentially incomplete from a structural standpoint. To regain some of the strength lost because of their poor struc-

The top tube on a ladies' frame is replaced by a second down tube, which makes mounting and dismounting the bike easier but eliminates much of its structural strength.

ture, ladies' frames have traditionally been constructed with heavy tubing. Not surprisingly, these bikes have also been quite heavy in weight. In an earlier time, this wasn't a major concern, since most men's frames were also made from the same heavy, cheap tubing. But in recent years, the bike market has changed considerably.

Technology developed over the past several years has provided less expensive ways to manufacture high-quality lightweight steel, aluminum, carbon, and even titanium tubing. At the same time, the demand for better-performing, lighter bikes has greatly increased. As a result, most beginners now expect to purchase a lightweight bike.

Because a ladies' frame can't be made with light-gauge tubing, a few manufacturers offer mixte

frames. These frames can be made of light tubing because they are structurally superior to the ladies' design. If you need a frame without a top tube for clearance reasons, a mixte frame bike provides much more rigidity and strength and is much lighter than a ladies' frame bike. Even so, the traditional diamond frame is still stronger and more rigid.

Today, smaller riders once forced to ride compromise frames like the mixte design benefit from the increased availability of slightly smaller-than-standard, 650c size wheels (as compared to the current standard, 700c size wheel) and sloping top tubes (like those on mountain bikes). With the 650c size wheel, it is possible to have a lower frame for stand-over clearance and a shorter top tube length without the danger of excessive toe-overlap (when your foot

The mixte frame is a compromise between the diamond frame and the ladies' frame. It replaces the top tube with twin lateral tubes that run from the head tube all the way back to the rear axle.

at the forward-most part of the pedal stroke extends past the rear-most part of the front wheel, making steering difficult or impossible).

The basic shape of the men's or diamond frame has remained largely recognizable from the turn of the last century to the turn of the present one. Geometries have evolved over this time, sometimes drastically and at other times more subtly; and all despite the fact that the human body has hardly changed in this time. The places we ride, however, have changed over and over; and this has been the impetus behind changes in geometries.

Dramatic advances in materials technology, construction techniques, and the understanding of the mechanics of the human body have also affected frame geometry. Cyclists can now enjoy riding a single bicycle that deftly combines drivetrain efficiency, precise handling, and a compliant ride.

FRAME MATERIALS

Even though you can't change the type of tubing used in your frame, it can be very helpful to be able to identify it from the tubing sticker displayed prominently on one of the frame's main tubes. This helps you determine the value of the frame. So, before you sink a lot of money into repairing or upgrading an old bike, check to see if the frame is made of tubing good enough to warrant the expense. And the next time you spot an awesome-looking but unfamiliar brand going for a great price at a garage sale, read the tubing sticker so you can see whether it is a lemon or a bargain.

LEGENDARY STEEL

Even today, purists tout that all the technology that has gone into new, exotic materials can't match the mystical ride quality of a well-built steel-frame bicycle. Whether you agree with this or not, there is one fact that is beyond dispute: There are still a lot of very good frames out there, some old and some new, that are made out of good old-fashioned steel. Here's how you can determine whether yours is a gem or just a rock.

Once there were only a handful of tubing suppliers making all the tubing used by bicycle manufacturers. At that time, it was easy to gauge your bike's quality by the tubing sticker. Today, many bike manufacturers have taken to designing their own proprietary tube sets. What's more, manufacturers of lower-priced bikes have gotten wise to the tubing sticker and have begun giving fancy names to what are essentially mild steel budget bikes. So beware. We can't possibly list here every tubing brand and type, but we can let you know what a few of the most common, high-quality tube sets are.

If there's no sticker at all on your frame and the tubes are approximately 1 inch in diameter, it's probably made of mild steel. That means the tubing walls are very thick and heavy. The frame will be adequate in the utilitarian sense, but will have no appreciable value of its own. Frames that read "high-tensile," "high-ten," "steel," or any similar term on their stickers won't be much lighter or worth much more.

The first level of quality in steel bike frames generally involves "high-carbon" tubing, which may also be called by a name particular to a certain

Tubing stickers help identify frame material and can hint at the quality of the bicycle.

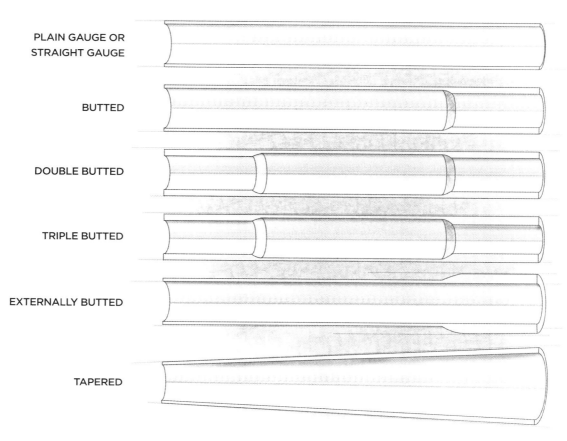

PLAIN GAUGE OR
STRAIGHT GAUGE

BUTTED

DOUBLE BUTTED

TRIPLE BUTTED

EXTERNALLY BUTTED

TAPERED

Manipulating tube diameter, wall thickness, and tube shape put strength and rigidity where they are needed and reduce weight where they are not.

brand. Examples of this are Columbus Aelle, Reynolds 500, and VALite.

Approaching the highest level of steel quality are steel alloy tubes such as Reynolds 853, True Temper OX Platinum, and Columbus Foco. Frames made of these materials are substantially lighter and better riding than all high-tensile and many high-carbon steel frames. A frame made of these materials might be worth rehabilitating, but not if you have to pay a lot to do so.

Tubes with stickers labeled "chrome-molybdenum," "chrome moly," or "manganese-molybdenum" steel are made of the finest steel alloys. Reynolds, Columbus, Dedacciai, and True Temper are the best-known and most highly regarded brands, although Ritchey, Tange, and Ishiwata all make tubing of similar quality.

But there's more to bike tubing than just its alloy. One way that manufacturers market the use of a name brand of tubing is to use the expensive tubing in just the three tubes of the frame's main triangle. The tubing sticker of such a frame might state the well-known alloy followed by the words "three main tubes" or "Main Frame." That makes a better frame than one made of high-tensile steel, but not as good as one constructed entirely of high-quality alloy.

Another important tubing factor displayed on many stickers is butting. This refers to the process of making one section of a tube with a thicker wall than another part of the same tube. Single-butted tubing is usually found only in seat tubes, with the thicker end placed in the bottom bracket shell to resist pedaling forces. Double-butted tubing has thicker walls at both ends. You can think of it as tubing that has two wall thicknesses: one thickness in the middle of the tube, and the other at the two ends. Triple-butted tubing is similar, except that it has three gauges: the end thicknesses are not the same. Quad-butted tubing not only has two different endwall thicknesses but the middle section also tapers from one gauge to another. Triple- and quad-butted tubes, not often used anymore, are designed to handle loads at the two ends of a tube that may be substantially different, requiring different strengths.

Butted tubing offers a couple of advantages. First, butting reduces weight by allowing lighter gauges to be used in the center sections of the tubes where there is less stress and where there is no welding and filing, such as takes place at the tube ends. (Both brazing and filing slightly weaken tubing.) Second, butted tubes are more resilient, or have more give, which means they provide a more comfortable ride. Don't totally discount straight-gauge tubing, however. There are places, such as tandem or mountain bike down tubes, where it may be superior to butted tubing. In any case, even on lightweight frames, butted tubing is found only in the three tubes of the main triangle and in the fork's steerer tube.

ALUMINUM, TITANIUM, AND COMPOSITES

Materials such as titanium, aluminum, and composites made from carbon, boron, and Kevlar fibers are quite popular and are becoming more affordable. In fact, aluminum has taken the place of steel as the bike manufacturers' material of choice for even inexpensive road, hybrid, and mountain bikes. Frames made from these advanced materials offer lighter weight—and often increased comfort. They're also amazingly corrosion resistant, which is great for mountain bikes that frequently get doused with plenty of water while crossing streams.

Today, aluminum is the most popular material for bike frames. Advantages include a slight weight savings, no rust problems, and excellent rigidity, which ensures that every pedal stroke goes directly into forward motion and isn't lost in frame flex.

As with steel, aluminum tubes can be butted to save weight while putting strength where it's needed. Beyond butting, though, aluminum tubes can also be formed into radical shapes that help it reach new levels of performance and at the same time make for a more comfortable frame than believed possible in years past. Aluminum's main drawback is its relatively short fatigue life. Unlike steel, carbon, or titanium,

aluminum fatigues a little bit every time the frame flexes even just a small amount. It takes years before the average rider can fatigue an aluminum frame enough for it to develop into a problem, though.

Carbon is one of the most interesting frame materials because there are so many ways it can be used. You'll see it in tube form, as on Trek OCLV frames, and in monocoque form, as on Kestrel or older Trek "Y" frames. The former resembles other bike frames. The latter has a striking one-piece, molded look, resembling the body of a race car.

What is unique about carbon as a material is how it's used. It starts as a fabric, and the frame designers custom-build each tube or frame section by precisely adding or removing fibers to get the strength and compliance exactly where it's needed. This level of "tube tuning" isn't possible with metal tubes, and it has produced some of the lightest bicycle frames in the world. The ride quality is also impressive because the builder can so accurately dial in the frame design.

Nevertheless, to most cyclists, titanium stands as the dream material for bike frames. From an engineering standpoint, carbon holds more promise, but titanium has a better reputation for durability and an amazing ride quality that most riders cannot forget. Titanium feels alive and springy, like there's energy inside the tubes. It also compares with carbon, weight-wise, and enjoys excellent corrosion resistance. The only negative is that it's costly.

THE BASICS OF FRAME GEOMETRY

Depending on the use for which a bike is designed, the seat angle, head angle, fork rake, chainstay length, and bottom bracket drop (you'll often hear it called B/B drop) are varied within a narrow range of values. Small differences in the dimensions of any of these factors can make a great difference in the performance of a bike and in your performance on it.

The seat angle's primary function is to determine your leg position in relation to the crankset, which can influence the way you pedal. In general, steeper angles are better for high-cadence spinning, while shallower angles are more conducive to muscling a bigger gear at slower cadence.

The head angle is instrumental, along with the

fork rake, in determining how your bike handles. This includes stability, whether at cruising speed or in high-speed descents, and cornering capability.

Generally, performance-orientated bikes like road racing bikes or cross-country mountain bikes will have a steeper head angle than will touring bikes, downhill and freeride bikes, or other bikes built for all-day comfort on longer rides.

To decide what's right for you, think about your favorite road or trail. Is it a fast, windy patch of mountain road or a twisty singletrack in the hills? You'll probably be happiest with a steeper head angle. On the other hand, do you love spending hours working your way deep into the backcountry or taking in the sights on a country lane? Is your idea of bliss finding the steepest, most treacherous descent around? In these cases, you'd likely be best served by a shallower or less steep head angle.

But head angle isn't the be-all and end-all of a bicycle's steering feel. The head angle, fork rake, and wheel diameter all combine to create a dimension called trail, which is a critical determining factor in a bike's steering characteristics. Trail is calculated by following an imaginary line drawn through the center of the head tube to the ground. The distance from where this line intersects the ground to the point directly below the axle, measured horizontally, is the trail measurement.

Put most simply, a longer trail measurement is more stable and a shorter one handles more quickly. Since trail is nearly impossible to measure except on paper, and because changing tire size can change the dimension, most frame builders report head angle and fork rake only on their geometry tables. When comparing bikes built for similar purposes, using similar size wheels and tires, this is enough information to allow you to make an informed decision about handling characteristics.

Chainstay length also affects in many ways the way a bike rides. Shorter chainstays, like those on road racing frames, can make a bike ride a bit more harshly but with less flexing in the rear triangle, which is especially important in hill climbing and sprinting. Shorter chainstays also decrease a bike's wheelbase, and the shorter that is, the more nimble and quick the bike feels. Loaded touring bikes, on the other hand, need longer chainstays for heel clearance with rear panniers, or rack bags. Those

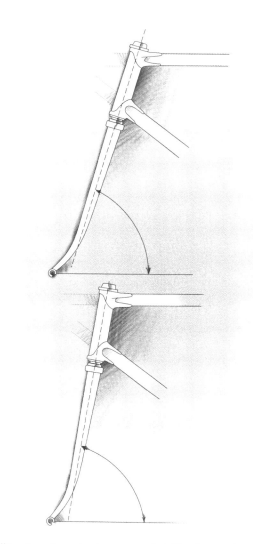

Shallow head angles increase stability for a relaxed ride, while steeper head angles sharpen handling for top performance.

long chainstays also provide the more stable ride that a tourist usually wants.

A larger drop, or a lower bottom bracket height, is also often found on loaded touring bikes. The lower the bottom bracket, the lower the saddle and the lower the center of gravity (CG) for the combination of the bike and its rider. A bike with a lower CG is more stable without losing any handling quickness. That's a desirable characteristic for most bikes. Unfortunately, most racing events involve cornering, and many racers like to pedal out of corners. For such riders, higher bottom brackets are necessary for the clearance needed between their pedals and the road. Tight-cornering criterium-racing bikes usually have high bottom brackets, while traditional road racing bikes fall somewhere in between. Mountain bikes have higher bottom brackets, which helps in clearing obstacles and in pedaling over cluttered terrain.

A similar trade-off between low-CG stability and ground clearance figures into the various frame designs for mountain bikes. Once you get off the beaten path, you can expect to encounter some large rocks and fallen trees, not to mention deep weeds.

With these general observations in mind, let's take a closer look at the main types of bicycle use and the frame geometry appropriate to each.

Road racing bike. The frame of a racing bicycle is designed for stability at high speeds, easy cornering, quick steering response, and a stiff, efficient ride that minimizes energy losses. As a direct result of these virtues, the racing bike usually has poor low-speed stability, handles worse if any load is carried on the frame, requires constant attention to maintain a straight line, and very efficiently transmits even the tiniest bump in the road straight to your body. You can identify a racing frame by the following measurements.

• **Seat angle:** 73 to 74 degrees. Add 1 degree to that range for frames with a seat tube smaller than 21 inches/54 centimeters (measured from the center of the bottom bracket to the top edge of the seat lug) and subtract 1 degree for frames larger than 24 inches.

• **Head angle:** 73 to 74 degrees. Subtract up to 2 degrees from that range for frames smaller than 21 inches/54 centimeters and add 1 degree for frames larger than 24 inches/61 centimeters.

• **Fork rake:** 1½ to 1¾ inches (38 to 45 mm) for a 73-degree head angle. Subtract or add ⅛ inch (3 mm) for every degree of head angle greater or smaller, respectively.

• **Chainstay length:** 16 to 16½ inches.

• **Drop:** 2⅜ to 2⅞ inches (60 to 75 mm). That equals bottom bracket heights of 11 to 10½ inches.

Road sport touring bike. Sport tourers are the midsize sports cars of the biking world. They're not all-out racers, but they're not loaded touring bikes either. They can carry a load with racks and small panniers, but not too much. Their major attribute is their stable handling, which is predictable, if a little slow by racing standards. Sport tourers just want to have fun, so to speak, and can do just about anything well enough for you to enjoy it. Look for the following dimensions.

• **Seat angle:** 72 to 73 degrees. Add 1 degree to that range for frames with a seat tube smaller than 21 inches/54 centimeters (measured from the center of the bottom bracket to the top edge of the seat lug) and subtract 1 degree for frames larger than 24 inches/61 centimeters.

• **Head angle:** 72 to 73 degrees. Subtract 1 degree from that range for frames smaller than 21 inches/54 centimeters and add 1 degree for frames larger than 25 inches/63 centimeters.

• **Fork rake:** 1⅝ to 2⅛ inches (43 to 55 mm) for a 73-degree head angle. Subtract or add ⅛ inch for every degree of head angle greater or smaller, respectively.

• **Chainstay length:** 16½ to 17½ inches.

• **Drop:** 2⅝ to 3 inches (68 to 78 mm). That equals bottom bracket heights of 10¾ to 10 inches.

Loaded touring bike. The pack mules of the two-wheel road, loaded touring bikes exhibit great stability and straight-line tracking, even with up to 40 or 50 pounds of cargo. You can watch the scenery from aboard one of these without the constant fear of either meandering off the road or straying into traffic lanes. In addition, they are comfortable over rough roads and also come with gearing low enough to allow you to climb over any mountain. This all adds up to a bike that's perfect, loaded or not, for those whose main interest is being there, rather than speeding on by.

• **Seat angle:** 71 to 72 degrees. Add 1 degree to that range for frames smaller than 21 inches/54 centimeters.

• **Head angle:** 71 to 72 degrees. Subtract 1 degree from that range for frames smaller than 21 inches/54 centimeters and add 1 degree for frames larger than 25 inches/63 centimeters.

- **Fork rake:** 2 to 2¼ inches for a 72-degree head angle. Subtract or add ⅛ inch for every degree of head angle greater or smaller, respectively.

- **Chainstay length:** 17 to 18 inches.

- **Drop:** 2⅝ to 3⅛ inches. That equals bottom bracket heights of 10¾ to 10¼ inches.

Mountain bike. Whether you want to explore deep into the backcountry or you seek the rush of a woodland rollercoaster ride, the mountain bike can take you there and back. Mountain bike design has become more and more specialized over its 20-some year evolution. Walking into your local bike shop, you may hear things said like "Cross Country" (or "XC"), "Freeride," "DH" (or "Downhill"), "Epic," "Enduro," "Hucking," "Two-Niner," "Trials," "Marathon," or any number of other descriptors for what we all used to just call mountain biking. But the root formula is still the same: wide, sturdy wheels and a straight (or slightly rising) handlebar suit these bikes to life on dirt (or rocks, or logs . . . you get the idea).

Mountain bikes are equally as comfortable around the town, too. In fact, it's been said that only about 10 percent of all mountain bikes sold are purchased with the intention of riding off-road. Wide, deeply treaded tires are far better suited to take the knocks of curbs, potholes, sewer grates, broken glass, and other roadside debris than the slender, lightweight wheels of a road racing bike. And the mountain bike's upright riding position allows a better view of traffic and pedestrians around you.

Most mountain bikes you see on the showroom floor will still be of the cross-country (XC) variety. The XC bike is the most direct descendent of the classic mountain bike we all recognize. It's an all-purpose machine that is as comfortable on the trail with a pair of knobbed off-road tires as it is cruising around town on a milder set of street rubber. Such is the mountain bike's greatest appeal: Its more upright riding position and balance of weight and strength make it the ideal "one bike" to own for most casual cyclists. XC bikes can be had fully rigid (no suspension in front or rear), front-suspended (also called "hardtails" for their lack of rear suspension), or dual-suspended. Typically, front-suspended models will have a suspension fork with 63 to 80 mm (2½ to 3 inches) of travel, and dual-suspended models will have between 80 and 100 mm (3 to 4 inches) of travel both front and rear.

When selecting a mountain bike, most shops will recommend you have 3 or more inches of standover clearance (the amount of clearance between you and the top tube when straddling the bike, flat-footed). Not having enough standover clearance can be downright painful should you need to put a foot or two down on rough terrain. If you're buying the bike to use only for commuting, running errands around town, and occasional riding along dirt roads or sandy beaches, something with a longer top tube may suit your needs better.

- **Seat angle:** 70 to 73 degrees. Add 1 degree to that range for frames smaller than 19 inches.

- **Head angle:** 69 to 72 degrees. Subtract 1 degree from that range for frames smaller than 19 inches and add 1 degree for frames larger than 23 inches.

- **Fork rake:** 1⅝ to 2 inches (43 to 50 mm).

- **Chainstay length:** 16 to 17 inches, or shorter (if you can find it) for really steep climbing.

Mountain bikes are sometimes likened to the SUVs of the bike world. Wide, durable tires and an upright riding position make them well suited to getting around downtown as well as negotiating off-road trails.

- **Drop:** 1⅛ to 2 inches (30 to 50 mm). That equals bottom bracket heights of 12 to 11¼ inches.

All rules go out the window when you stray from the pure XC bike. We'll break down a few "typical" specialty bikes for identification purposes.

Enduro bike. A dual-suspension mountain bike largely similar to the cross-country bike but with more suspension travel, usually in the range of 100 to 130 mm (4 to 5 inches), and a slightly shallower head angle for stability on long rides deep in the backcountry.

Two-niner. Based around a 29-inch-diameter tire, Two-niners are built for speed. The larger-diameter wheel rolls more smoothly over uneven terrain than the standard 26-inch wheel at the expense of some agility. These bikes rely on a longer-than-usual top tube coupled with a shorter-than-usual stem to minimize toe overlap, but they maintain the relationship between crankset, saddle, and handlebar similar to that of a smaller-wheeled bike.

Downhill bike. With as much as 10 inches of suspension travel, front and rear, downhill bikes can roll over almost anything short of a brick wall. Very shallow head angles and high bottom brackets make these bikes lumber along on smooth ground and their weight makes climbing seem futile, but that's probably why they're not called "uphill bikes."

Freeride bike. Freeride bikes have the toughest job of all mountain bikes in my opinion. They need to handle the abuse of high drops and steep descents, but they're also expected to climb and steer well at low speeds. The geometry of freeride bikes leans toward that of downhill bikes, but with suspension travel in the range of 6 to 8 inches, slightly lower ⅜ heights, and marginally steeper head angles to sharpen handling.

Hucking bike. Hucking bikes are generally very small-framed hardtails with front suspension ranging from 4 to 6 inches. The frames are built to handle the rigors of jumping and other stunts and have clearance for extra-wide tires to absorb impact.

Trials bike. Observed trials is a form of mountain bike competition that focuses on obstacle negotiation. Trials bikes have ultrashort chainstays (as short as 15 inches), high bottom brackets, and very low top tubes to help them up and over boulders and logs as well as man-made obstacles and through streams—often moving only inches at a time.

Cyclocross. Cyclocross is a form of competition where bicycles that appear to the untrained eye to be road racing bikes are raced off-road. In a cyclocross or 'cross race, riders negotiate a short, tight course over varying terrain with occasional barriers that are intended to make the racers dismount and run with their bikes for short distances. As a result, 'cross bikes are designed and built to be as sharp-handling and lightweight as their road racing counterparts, but with the added demands for durability to survive this intense sport.

Hybrid bike. Part mountain bike and part touring bike is the nearest way to describe the hybrid bike. The frame geometry is closely related to that of the touring bike, with relaxed angles and clearance for wide 700c tires. The mountain bike's donation to the equation is its flat or rising handlebar and sloping top tube to make for a comfortable, upright riding position and to make mounting and dismounting easy.

Recumbent. You can throw out all the rules for frame geometry when it comes to a recumbent. On these bikes the cyclist is in a reclining position and pedals feet-first. They're among the most comfortable and fastest of bicycles, but there are no fast rules on frame configurations. There are short, medium, and long wheelbase recumbents with padded seats or with seats that resemble lawn chairs. There are two- and three-wheel recumbents; bikes with above-the-seat and below-the-seat handlebars; dual-suspended and rigid-frame recumbents; even tricycles and bikes with complete bodies such as you find on automobiles.

FITTING TO THE FRAME

For starters, you should be able to comfortably straddle the top tube of a bike with both feet placed flat on the ground. For mountain bikes that will be ridden off road, 3 or more inches of clearance is a comfortable margin. Next, adjust the height of the saddle (first make sure that the saddle is level) so you can maintain a slight bend in your knee at the bottom of your pedal stroke with your feet held level and the balls of your feet placed over the pedal centers.

For this next step, you'll probably need some help. Get on the bike, then rotate your crankset backward until your right crankarm points straight ahead. With the crankarm horizontal, a vertical line passing through the pedal axle should intersect your knee about ½ inch behind its front surface. Loosen the saddle clamp and slide the saddle either forward or back to get closer to this ideal position, if it's possible.

With your saddle correctly adjusted, your arms locked straight, and your hands in position on top of the brake lever hoods, your back and the bike's top tube should form an angle that's equal to or slightly smaller than 45 degrees. Raise or lower the stem to get the correct position. If the length, or forward reach, of your bike's stem is correct, the angle formed by your arms and body, with your arms straight (but don't ride with straight arms, always keep them bent) and your hands on top of the brake lever hoods, shouldn't be greater than 100 degrees or less than 90 degrees. If you ride a lot, it's worth the money to change stems if yours is more than ½ inch too short or too long.

FRAME MAINTENANCE

Now that you're fitted correctly to your machine and you understand its design and function better than ever before, what maintenance can you perform to ensure the long life of your bike's frame? A lot more than you might think.

Kicking corrosion. Besides accidents, the greatest enemy your frame may face is corrosion. You needn't worry about this much if you ride an aluminum, carbon, or titanium frame. But if yours is steel (if you're not sure, check it with a magnet), take care. If you sweat a lot on your bike while you ride it, either indoors or out, thoroughly rinse it off as frequently as is practical. Salt deposits form in any kind of corner, especially underneath clamps, and continue the process of corrosion, even if the bike is dry. Braze-on parts contribute less to this severe problem than clamp-on parts, but they still trap unwanted salt. Salt can effect aluminum, carbon, and composite (made of two or more different materials, like carbon tubes mated to aluminum lugs, for example) frames and components, too.

Prompt attention to your bike after sweaty rides or workouts on rollers or indoor trainers means a thorough, gentle water rinse. Don't use high-pressure hoses or concentrated spray patterns because they'll force water, and maybe also dirt, into your bike's bearings.

Clear silicone-rubber bathroom caulk can help

The right position is crucial for efficiency and comfort.

Proper fit improves control and makes riding more enjoyable.

keep sweat and water out of the inside of your bike's frame. Unless the locknut on your headset has an O-ring seal, sweat can seep down the sides of your stem into the steerer tube. The resulting corrosion can sometimes require the use of a hacksaw to remove the stem from the steerer. A thin bead of clear caulk around the base of the stem (wipe away the excess) will prevent the problem.

If you ride in the rain even occasionally, the same caulk treatment applied to the junction of the seat tube and the seatpost will prevent water thrown up under your saddle from leaking into your seat tube and collecting in your bottom bracket. Even if you have a shield protecting the bearings, the threads of your bottom bracket shell can rust—a situation that could eventually make it difficult to keep your bottom bracket cups tight. It's a good idea to remove your seatpost periodically and tip the bike upside down to drain it.

While the best defense against corrosion is to prevent moisture from entering your frame tubes, it is also a good idea to help fight corrosion from the inside. Anytime you have your seatpost out of the frame or your headset or bottom bracket dismantled for an overhaul, use the opportunity to spray or swab a rust inhibitor such as WD-40 inside the exposed tubes.

Also consider treating the inside of your steel frame with a rust inhibitor such as J. P. Weigle's Frame Saver. Spray it inside the tubes and allow to dry, and it forms a barrier that will prevent rust from developing inside the frame. We can't recommend this treatment strongly enough if you ride a steel frame and cycle in wet conditions.

Painting over chips. Paint chips can allow rust to start even on a dry, salt-free frame. To prepare the surface for touch-up paint, don't sand the chipped area except to remove rust. Most manufacturers treat their frames' bare surfaces with a very thin phosphate coating that inhibits rust; sanding will remove it. Instead of sanding, use a solvent, such as lacquer thinner, to clean any oil from the chipped area. Then cover the chip with one or more coats of almost any type of paint that matches your bike's original color. If rust has already reared its ugly head through the hole in your frame's finish, use fine sandpaper to remove all of it before you touch up the frame. Don't expect miracles: The main purpose of your touch-up work is to minimize rust damage to your frame until you have it repainted.

There are some other steps worth taking to protect the paint on your frame. Because the chain is close to the right rear chainstay, it can slap against it when you hit bumps. This makes a metallic clank sound and can lead to chipping paint on the chainstay. A simple way to protect the stay and muffle the chain slap is to put a vinyl or foam chainstay protector over the stay. These are adhesive-backed and cost only a couple of dollars at your local bike shop. For more complete protection, you can wind electrical tape or an old inner tube over the entire stay.

Chainstay protectors made of neoprene, the same material used to make surfers' wetsuits, also do an excellent job of protecting your chainstay and quieting chain slap. When using one of these, though, you should make it part of your maintenance routine to remove periodically and after rainy rides, as they can absorb some moisture and hold it against the frame.

Another good way to protect paint is to stick tape beneath cables where they rub the frame, such as Shimano STI cables that strike the frame by the head tube. This will prevent them from wearing a hole in the paint. Just cut a small oval of tape (get clear tape or tape the same color as your frame so it's not noticeable) and stick it on under the housing.

To stop the rattling and resultant paint scratches you might get from bare cable sections (such as the rear brake cable under the top tube), install cable O-rings. Shops should have these. These tiny rubber doughnut-shaped O-rings slip over the cable and prevent it from vibrating when you're riding.

Fixing bends. Obviously, the best way to help your frame last is to avoid twisting it out of shape in an accident. A good bike frame has considerable resilience but cannot be expected to regain its original shape after being wrapped around a tree. If you're unlucky enough to crash and bend your frame or fork, take it to a mechanic for evaluation. A shop with alignment tools can sometimes straighten metal frames and rigid (non-suspension) forks enough that they still ride fine. Bent suspension forks can often be repaired by replacing the damaged parts.

Repairing dents. Sometimes a crash dents a frame tube. Though unsightly, these dents rarely weaken the frame much. If you can't stand looking at a dent and if you have a steel frame, you can have a framebuilder fill the dent with brazing material. After painting over it, for all practical purposes, your frame will be as good as new.

Unbending a derailleur hanger. Another type of frame damage that often occurs in a crash is a bent rear derailleur hanger. This can also happen if you shift into the spokes or drop your bike on its side. Both cause the derailleur to get pulled forcefully inward. Because the derailleur is attached to a tab built into the bottom of the right-hand dropout, the tab, too, gets bent, sometimes severely.

The proper way to repair a bent hanger is to use a derailleur hanger alignment tool that has a feeler and references the hanger against the rear wheel, keeping the hanger perfectly aligned. This is especially important for modern indexing systems that allow for little margin of error in the alignment of the derailleur and cogs. In a pinch, though, or on an older bike with friction shifting, you can often repair a bent hanger by removing the rear derailleur and pulling the hanger straight with an adjustable wrench (set the jaws to just fit over the hanger). On a ride, it's unlikely that you or your friends are carrying a hanger alignment tool or large adjustable wrench. In these cases, use the rear wheel to bend it by removing the quick-release, screwing the axle into the hanger, installing the quick-release, and using the wheel to bend the hanger back close enough to get you home.

Sometimes, the accident tears the threads in the hanger and if you try to remove the derailleur, you'll remove the threads with it. Fortunately, there's a clever fix even if you have a frame with a one-piece hanger that's part of the dropout. A Boulder, Colorado, company named Wheels Manufacturing makes a threaded piece that fits into the damaged hole to restore it. All you have to do is bend the hanger straight and install this part, and the frame will be as good as new. After such a home repair, it is always a good idea to have a shop with alignment tools check your work because the shifting can suffer if the derailleur alignment is off.

Bending the hanger and repairing damaged threads are easier to do and more likely to be done successfully on a steel frame than on an aluminum frame. Because of this, most aluminum frames now use a replaceable hanger that is simply removed and disposed of in the event of a bad bend or break. These replacements will run anywhere from about $15 to $30. Riders of aluminum bikes should pick one of these up and keep it in a take-along tool kit.

Dealing with loose water bottle mounts or stuck screws. One possible glitch on aluminum and composite frames is loosening of the water bottle mounting bosses, or getting a water bottle screw stuck in the boss. These fittings are pressed into the frame at the factory and should stay fixed. If they start rattling or spinning in the frame, making it impossible to remove the screw, take your frame to your dealer or a shop that carries your brand of bike. He should have the factory tools to remove a stuck screw, reseat the boss, and stop the rattling.

Steadying speed wobble or shimmy. A han- dling glitch that is often blamed on the frame is speed wobble, the tendency of a bike to shake violently at fast speeds on a downhill. Obviously, this is a dangerous problem, and every cyclist should know what to do if it happens. Though it may not always work, try clamping your knees together on the top tube, which should stop the wobbling.

Speed wobble is usually related to component adjustments (faulty or improperly installed tires, a loose headset, or untrue or under-tensioned wheels) and sizing mistakes (usually a too-high seat). Check these things first and test-ride the bike to see if the wobble goes away.

If the wobble doesn't stop, there's another possible culprit: a frame made of tubing that is too light for the person using it. This might happen if you purchase a used custom frame that was built for someone else, or if you're on the big side, say, over 6 feet tall and 200 pounds but riding an ultralight bike (always test-ride before buying). In this case, the best bet is to sell the bike.

Waxing the frame. An occasional waxing when your bike is clean and dry helps its appearance and improves your chances of staying ahead of rust. There are many bike-specific polishes on the market, such as Pedro's Bike Lust, that are formulated to be kind to the high-quality paint finishes found on many custom bikes. For titanium frames, a wipe-down with a furniture polish such as Pledge will keep your frame showroom new-looking (and lemony fresh).

BASIC FRAME-ALIGNMENT CHECKS

Alignment of the bicycle frame is important because it affects many things. For example, if the fork is slightly bent, taking your hands off the bar may result in the bike steering off the trail. Or if the rear triangle isn't aligned with the front triangle, the chain may fall off the chainrings every time you shift onto the small chainring.

Frame alignment is usually spot-on when a bike first comes from the bike shop. When a mechanic assembles a bike, he looks for signs of alignment problems and makes adjustments to the frame as needed. Or if the frame is really out of whack, he'll return it to the manufacturer.

Unfortunately, just because a frame is straight

when you buy it doesn't guarantee that it will remain so. Accidents, abuse, or even just dropping the bike on its side can lead to alignment problems if the impact is hard enough.

Some shops have impressive alignment tables and fixtures for precisely measuring and straightening frames to very exacting standards. If you bend a frame severely, it makes sense to use their services. Keep in mind that a bent frame cannot always be repaired if the damage is serious, and not all types of frames can be aligned. Signs of serious damage include wrinkles in frame tubes that indicate the tube has been buckled, and cracks that mean that the frame will likely break soon if you continue riding on it. Don't mess with that type of damage. It's best to replace the frame.

Frame material makes a difference, as well. Steel frames are much more easily repaired than most titanium, carbon, or welded-aluminum frames. If a titanium or welded-aluminum frame proves out of alignment when you check it, take it to a shop. It may be a warranty issue. Usually, it's impossible to make anything but minor corrections to these types of frames; let a professional mechanic handle the work.

Frame spacing. For the wheels to slide smoothly in and out of the frame, the widths of the front and rear forks should match the widths of the wheels (measured from the outer edges of the two axle locknuts). To check fork width, measure from the inside surface of one dropout to the inside surface of the other. Front forks should measure 100 mm wide. Rear forks should measure 120 mm for five-speed rear wheels, 127 for six- and seven-speed wheels, 130 for eight-, nine-, and ten-speed road wheels, and 135 for mountain bike wheels.

If the measurement is off by more than 2 mm, it's usually still relatively easy to install and remove the wheel. But if the measurement is off and it's a struggle to get the wheels in, not only are the dropouts probably too narrow but it could also be that they've been bent out of parallel to each other. If that's the case, take the frame to a shop and to have the dropouts aligned. Shops have special tools that make this job easy. Not only will fixing the dropouts ease wheel installation and removal, but also it will eliminate uneven pressure on the axle that often leads to broken axles.

Alignment of the rear triangle with the front triangle. Shifting problems are often related to im-

proper chainline, which occurs anytime the crankset and the cassette cogs are out of alignment. Ideally, an imaginary line would bisect the chainrings and the cassette. If the rear triangle isn't correctly aligned with the front triangle, this isn't the case, and it results in a misaligned chain and derailleurs, which causes shifting problems.

Here's an easy way to check the alignment of the rear end. First, do the frame spacing check, as this affects rear-triangle alignment. Next, get a piece of fine but strong thread or fishing line. Tie it to the right rear dropout in such a way that you can repeat the exact placement on the left dropout. Run the thread around the head tube of the bike, and pull it back to the left dropout. Pull the thread so it's taut, and tie it in exactly the same position in which you tied it on the other side.

You should now have a piece of thread running from the rear of the bike, around the head tube, and back to the rear of the bike. Now, hold one end of a ruler against the seat tube of the bike, extending it out so that the thread rests on the ruler's gauge and you can read the measurement. Jot the number down, then repeat the measurement on the other side, making sure that you hold the ruler the same way that you did on the first side. The two numbers should match if the rear triangle is aligned correctly with the front triangle. If they're off by more than 4 mm and you're experiencing problems with shifting or the chain falling off, have a shop align the rear end.

Wheel tracking. This alignment check determines whether the front and rear wheels are tracking in line with each other. To do this check, remove the tires and tubes and reinstall the wheels, taking care to center them in the fork and rear triangle. Hold one end of a 5-foot straightedge or a straight piece of wood or metal against the front wheel so that it touches two points on the rim. Then swing the straightedge up (or down, if you're working on the bike when it's upside down) toward the rear wheel. If the wheels are in line with each other, the straightedge should contact two points on the rear rim, too.

These alignment checks aren't necessary unless you suspect problems. Most modern bikes are built to fine standards. But if you have a problem or you crash hard and are concerned, a careful inspection could put your mind at ease or alert you to the need to have a professional repair the frame.

REPAINTING A FRAME

Steel frames occasionally require repainting. You may also want to get an aluminum, carbon, or titanium frame repainted if the finish gets chipped. Repainting your color not only looks good but also provides an opportunity to stop any ongoing corrosion. On steel frames, repainting gives you an excuse to acquire any braze-on fittings you've been wanting.

We don't recommend painting a bike yourself. It's a big job that is best left to professionals. If you can't locate either a framebuilder or a bike-finishing specialist in your area, check with the nearest bike shop. People there will probably be able to point you toward a reputable refinisher.

When arranging for refinish work, make sure that the firm has experience with the type of frame you're having redone. Thin-wall metal tubes need to be stripped carefully so as not to remove any of the tubing material. Carbon frames are usually not stripped, just lightly sanded before being refinished. The refinisher should know all about these things. If you can't find a trustworthy refinisher in your area, consider shipping your frame to the professionals at

CyclArt in Vista, California, who've been turning out show-stopping bicycle paint jobs for almost three decades now.

As for types of paint, baked enamels and catalyzed enamels provide the most durable topcoats, whereas lacquers should be avoided because they chip easily. Imron, a single-layer paint once favored for its durability and ease of application, is not often used anymore. Instead, multilayer paint jobs using a color coat followed by a protective clear coat are most often used now, giving color saturation and depth that can not be duplicated by single-layer paints.

A WORTHY INVESTMENT

Your bicycle's frame can accompany you for many years and tens of thousands of miles if given proper consideration and care. Deal with paint chips promptly; don't allow perspiration or road salts to accumulate; don't beat on your bike by riding recklessly and jumping a lot; store it inside, out of the weather; and once in a while treat your frame to a new paint job.

3 SUSPENSION

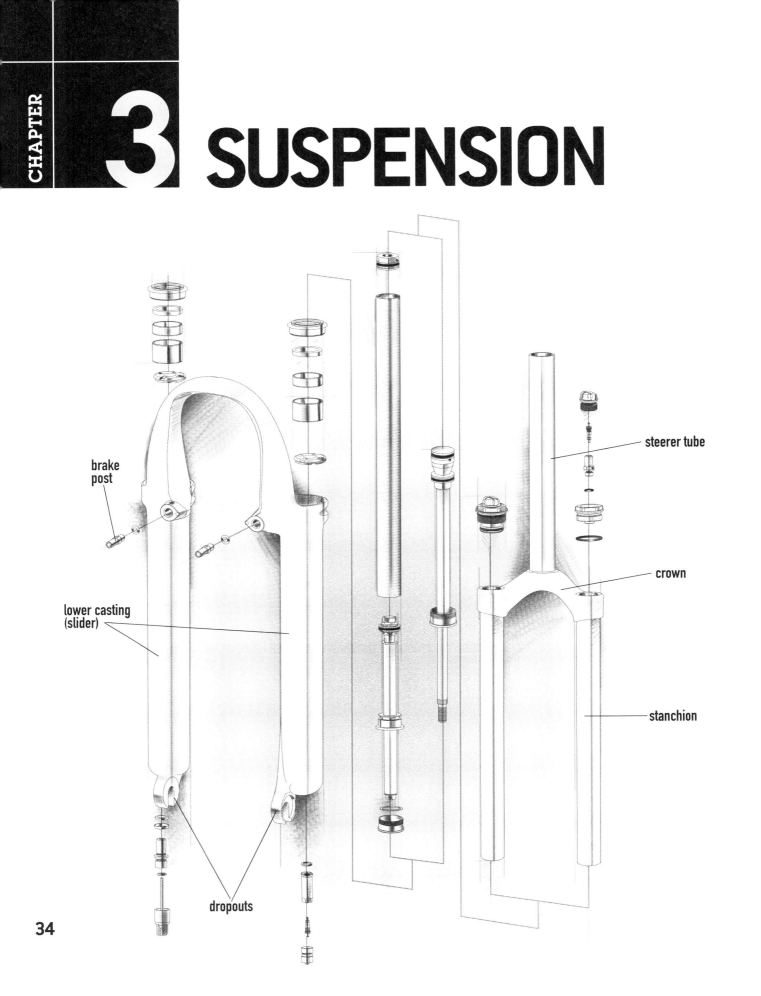

brake post

lower casting (slider)

dropouts

steerer tube

crown

stanchion

The subject of bicycle suspension could easily fill its own book. What once was only a tool of mountain bike racers and the most avid of enthusiasts is now commonplace on nearly all types of bicycles, not just mountain bikes. Hybrid bikes, recumbent bikes, tandems, and even some road bikes now benefit from a little extra cushion. Still, the mountain bike is where the modern era of bicycle suspension got its start and remains where manufacturers turn when time comes for refinement. This chapter will serve to introduce you to the concepts and basic design principles of many of the most current suspension systems.

We begin with the basics.

While most may recognize that air-filled tires will compress and rebound with changes in the terrain, what may not seem obvious is that every part of any bicycle—suspended or not—absorbs shock in some small amount. Handlebars, wheels, seatposts, saddles, even the most rigid aluminum racing frames have a measurable amount of flex or give that equates to a shock-absorbing property. While all these things working in concert may effectively smooth out a rough patch of pavement, as the going gets rougher you'll need a little more to stay on track.

Beyond making your ride more comfortable, suspension plays a vital role in your bike's handling on rough terrain. A nonsuspended or "rigid" bike will tend to bounce over obstacles like rocks, roots, and potholes, relying on the rider's skill to keep it pointed in a safe direction. By introducing a shock absorber into the equation, the wheel will read and react to changes in terrain on its own, leaving the rider a little less to think about on the road or trail. This peace of mind while riding comes with a price, however. Suspension frames and forks require periodic maintenance to keep them performing well.

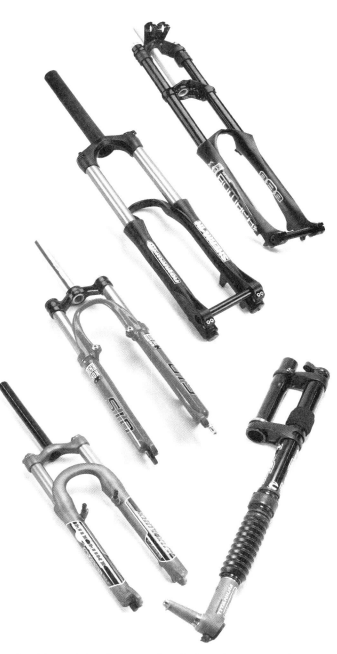

A wide variety of suspension forks exists to match every riding style.

SUSPENSION FORKS

With a few rare exceptions, suspension forks on bicycles today are of the telescopic variety. This means there are two main components to each leg of the fork, one that slides over the other. The stationary part of the leg is called the stanchion; the moving part is the slider. The stanchions are press-fit into a crown that also holds the steerer tube. These three tubes clamped into the crown give it its other common name, the triple clamp.

What appears to be simplistic on the exterior is a marvel of technology in its interior. The internals of suspension forks are closely guarded secrets through the development of new models. Springs, pistons, valves, and air and oil chambers are all carefully engineered to perform at the highest level while minimizing weight and maximizing durability. It's a delicate balancing act to say the least. Essentially, though, all telescoping suspension forks rely on two basic principles.

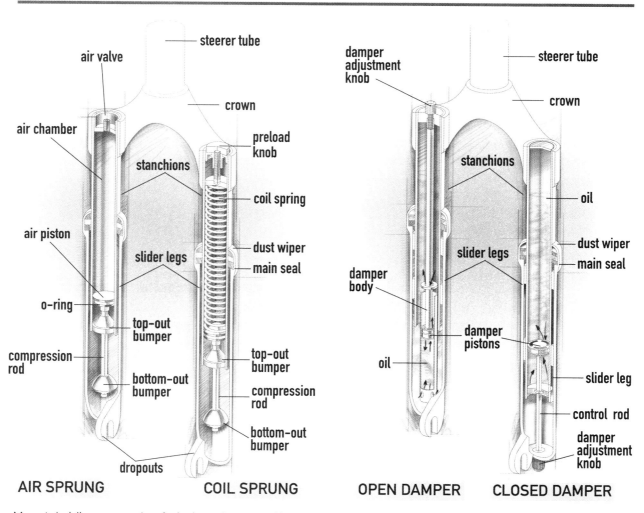

AIR SPRUNG   **COIL SPRUNG**   **OPEN DAMPER**   **CLOSED DAMPER**

Mountain bike suspension forks have borrowed heavily from the motorcycle industry. Most forks now use either a coil spring or a chamber of compressed air to give a fork its bounce, and a piston riding in a volume of oil, called a damper, to provide compression and rebound speed control.

A polyurethane material commonly referred to as elastomer saw widespread use several years ago but is much less common now. Elastomers become brittle over time and lose their bounce, and replacements are more and more difficult to find. In many cases, it's best to cut your losses and replace elastomer forks when this happens.

BOUNCE

First and most obvious is the spring. This is what gives the fork the ability to absorb an impact and return to absorb another. Springs used for bicycles come in three types: coil, air, and elastomer. The coil is readily recognizable as a spring. Usually made from steel wire of varying gauge or thickness, the wire is wound into a coil that compresses with a given amount of force.

Less obviously, air can also be used as a spring. The most recognizable use of air as a spring is in your bike's air-filled tires. In your suspension fork, air can be used as a spring by inflating a sealed chamber inside the fork. Air offers two benefits over steel coils. For one, air is light. Also, incrementally changing the pressure inside the fork allows a great range of adjustment for different riders that can be made without disassembling the fork (as must be done to change a coil spring).

The last type of spring is the elastomer. Elastomers were used frequently in the early days of mountain bike suspension, but are much less common now. Made of a urethane material, elastomers are light, simple, and relatively low-maintenance. However, as suspension travels have increased over the years, elastomers have become less and less viable because a stack of elastomers needs to be much longer than a coil spring or air chamber to achieve the same amount of travel.

CONTROL

The second basic principle of suspension is damping. Damping is the ability to control the speed of compression and rebound of the fork. An unchecked spring will compress and rebound too quickly, making your bike bounce like a pogo stick. To control this motion, most performance suspension forks use a volume of oil and a piston that flows through it. By changing the size of the hole in the piston and the weight (or viscosity) of the oil, it is possible to slow down the motion of the fork to a useable rate.

There are two common types of oil dampers being used today. An open damper uses one volume of oil to handle the duties of lubricating the fork's slider bushings and stanchions and to flow through the damper to control compression and rebound speed. A cartridge damper incorporates a sealed tube in which the oil and damper piston work, relying on a separate volume of oil or grease to lubricate the slider bushings and stanchions. Each has a benefit and a drawback. A cartridge damper remains sealed inside the fork, requiring service less frequently than an open damper, which can become contaminated as dirt makes its way past the dust wiper and main oil seal at the top of the slider leg. But when a seal does wear out or split on a cartridge damper, it won't be instantly obvious why damping has been lost. The seals on open systems can be viewed and inspected for "oil weeping" without disassembly, but the greater volume of oil used in these designs makes them slightly heavier in most cases.

KEEP IT CLEAN

Manufacturers' recommendations vary, but most will agree that you should visually inspect your fork

Cannondale equips some bikes with a suspension fork called HeadShok—a system that puts the suspension components inside an oversize fork steerer tube.

Suspension Maintenance

These maintenance recommendations are general guidelines. You should check your owner's manual for your suspension manufacturer's specific, recommended maintenance schedule.

DO WHAT	WHEN
Check air pressure for air-sprung shocks	Before every ride
Clean and inspect, visually	Before and after every ride
Check torque and tightness of rear suspension pivots	Every 10 hours of riding
Change oil and replace seals	Every 50 to 100 hours or if a leak develops
Complete fork rebuild including new bushings	Every 100 to 200 hours or if excessive play develops
Replace suspension pivots	Every 100 to 200 hours or if excessive play develops

for signs of oil weeping or stress before every ride. Your fork should be disassembled and cleaned after every 50 hours of riding in fair conditions, or as frequently as every 25 hours of riding in wet or muddy conditions. A complete overhaul of the fork, including replacement of seals, wipers, and slider bushings, is a good idea every 200 hours. Of course, when there are signs of oil leaking from the fork, the offending seals should be replaced immediately before performance begins to suffer.

Maintaining your suspension fork is relatively easy with the right tools. The most important one to have is a service manual specific to the model of your fork, provided by the manufacturer. If you don't have your manual, you may be able to track one down at your local bike shop or by visiting the Web site of your fork's manufacturer. Here are a few of the most common:

Cannondale, www.cannondale.com
Fox Racing Shox, www.foxracingshox.com
Manitou, www.answerproducts.com
Marzocchi, www.marzocchi.com
Risse, www.risseracing.com
Rockshox, www.rockshox.com
White Brothers,
   www.whitebrotherscycling.com

SUSPENSION STEMS

Though less common today, suspension stems offer a light, simple, and inexpensive option for adding comfort to the front of a bike. Since frame geometries had to be modified slightly with the advent of suspension forks, suspension stems could be used to upgrade older bikes without worry of adverse effects to the bike's head angle, causing slow or floppy steering.

REAR SUSPENSION

Sometimes it seems there are as many unique designs of rear suspension as there are trails to ride. From the simplest soft-tail design, yielding an inch or so of travel, to downhill strokers with sophisticated, computer-designed linkages allowing 8 to 10 inches or more of wheel movement, there's a dual suspension mountain bike to suit any riding style.

REAR-SUSPENSION BASICS

Swingarm rear-suspension design is complicated by the presence of the chain, which pulls on the rear wheel. If the rear axle doesn't move at a right angle to chain force, then these pulses will compress or extend the drivetrain. This means that pedaling will raise or lower the rider with every stroke ("bob"). Conversely, the rider will feel the crankarms slow or quicken every time the rear wheel hits a bump and compresses the suspension ("biopacing").

Another unintentional input that rear-suspension designs need to fight is the tendency for braking forces to try to freeze the swingarm in place ("brake jack"). Brake jack is of greater concern for racers looking to shave precious seconds. Still, for enthusiasts seeking top performance, certain rear-suspension designs are less susceptible to brake jack than others.

Here's how various rear-suspension designs address these problems.

Four-bar linkage (*right*). Also known as the Horst link (named for its innovator, Horst Leitner) or as the FSR linkage (named so by the patent's owner, Specialized bicycles), the four-bar linkage produces a roughly vertical axle path that minimizes bob and brake jack.

High-forward pivot (*right*). Many bicycle manufacturers use a simple swingarm, pivoted above and ahead of the front derailleur. A line drawn through the pivot and rear axle will be roughly in line with the top of the middle chainring. This pivot placement keeps the suspension active while pedaling in the large or middle chainring, and it works to lock the suspension out while using the small chainring.

Low pivot (*right*). A single pivot point, located directly behind the bottom bracket shell, allows the suspension to remain very active at all times. As a result, this design is most susceptible to bob and biopacing. Some low-pivot bikes bear a striking resemblance to the four-bar design described above. Here's how to tell the difference: The key to the four-bar or FSR linkage is the location of the rear pivots on the chainstay, just ahead of the rear dropout. If the rear pivots are on the seatstays, above the dropouts, it's a low pivot, not a four bar.

Highly coupled linkage (*right*). Two very short "coupling links" to connect the main triangle to the rear triangle and a lot of heavy math come together to make the highly coupled linkage work. By carefully manipulating the length of each link and the location of each pivot point, the travel path of the rear axle can be tuned to make the suspension firm at the beginning of the stroke (for efficiency while pedaling) and more active as the suspension compresses farther.

Floating drivetrain (*page 40*). A floating drivetrain design like Maverick American's ML7 makes strategic use of a chainstay length that grows slightly as the swingarm compresses. The rear wheel is driven downward while pedaling to aid in climbing on loose terrain. The floating drivetrain is unique in that it can be very active while coasting—as you might be on a technical descent—and will firm up while pedaling for efficient climbing or sprinting.

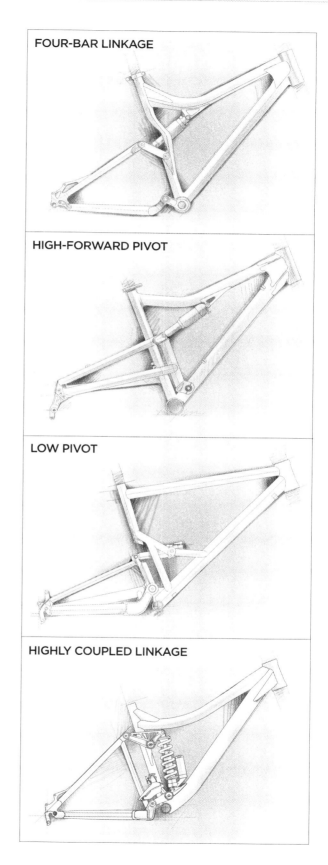

FOUR-BAR LINKAGE

HIGH-FORWARD PIVOT

LOW PIVOT

HIGHLY COUPLED LINKAGE

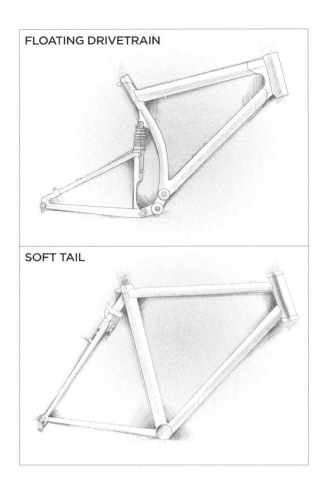

FLOATING DRIVETRAIN

SOFT TAIL

Soft tail (*above*). The soft tail is the simplest of rear suspension designs. A short section of the seatstays is removed near the seat cluster and replaced with a small shock. With only about an inch of travel at the rear wheel, lightweight soft tails work with no pivots anywhere on the rear end. Instead, the seatstays are allowed to bow in the middle. At first, the idea sounds questionable, but with such a small amount of deflection, the seatstays remain well within their safe limit to flex and return without fatiguing.

SADDLE SUSPENSION

Sprung seatposts—as well as the Softride beam—eliminate many of the maintenance issues that accompany swingarms, linkages, and oil-filled and pressurized shocks. By offering extra comfort while seated and maintaining the efficiency and simplicity of a rigid rear triangle, saddle suspensions are often the first choice of both casual cyclists in need of a little extra cushion while seated as well as many elite racers in search of a lightweight alternative to full suspension.

LONG TRAVEL BIKES

Downhill (DH) and freeride bikes represent the outer limits of bicycle suspension design. It's here on the wild fringe, where bicycles begin to look like motorcycles-sans-motor, that new suspension designs are imagined, developed, and tested.

DH bikes are custom-built race machines that evolve much more quickly than the publishing world can hope to keep up. Internal gearboxes, 12-plus inches of wheel travel, and disc brakes were all only experimental "what-ifs" just a few short years ago. Now these technologies are the norm on the World Cup level and all but commonplace at local amateur DH events all around the globe.

Freeride is a term that gets widely interpreted. In the early days of the freeride movement, freeride bikes were essentially long-travel cross-country bikes with short stems and riser handlebars. 100 mm (4 inches) of wheel travel was pushing the limits of what was reasonable for an all-around bike that was a capable descender and a passable climber. These early freeride rigs weighed in around 32 pounds or so. A result of this was the birth of "shuttling," where a group would take turns driving a vanload of bikes and riders to the top of a descent, eliminating all that pesky climbing on a pig of a bike that didn't like going up all that well, anyway. Around this same time, a small group of riders from the North Shore of Vancouver, British Columbia, began testing just how steep the fall line could get before freeriding became freefalling. Darlings of the magazines, these North Shore riders legitimized a style of riding that had previously been viewed as merely a failed suicide attempt. The terms North Shore and freeride rapidly became synonymous. Manufacturers keen on the trend began to push out bikes even more heavily built, with longer travel, which became the freeride bikes we know today. (It's interesting to note that those early North Shore riders rode hard tail cross-country bikes fitted with "long" (3-inch) travel forks and riser handlebars. Many North Shore and freeriders today still prefer the handling of a bike with a rigid rear end.)

What of up?

Early freeride purists have not been forgotten.

Today's all-mountain type bikes reflect the spirit of the first freeride bikes. Thanks to leaps in technology, all-mountain riders enjoy bikes with 4 to 6 inches of wheel travel that weigh less than 30 pounds and benefit from swingarm and shock designs that help the bikes descend and climb equally well.

SUSPENSION ADJUSTMENTS

As we said before, if you own a suspension bike or added a suspension component to your bike, you probably received a manual explaining basic adjustment and maintenance requirements. If not, contact the manufacturer and request one. This is important—there are so many different types of suspensions available that you must follow the manufacturer's recommendations on setup and adjustments. If you don't have a manual, you may be able to get advice from a shop mechanic, provided your suspension is not too unusual.

The first adjustment to make is preload. This sets the suspension to your weight. For instance, if your air/oil rear shock is low on air pressure, you may bottom it out on bumps. And if you're a light rider and the pressure is set too high, you won't get enough action from the suspension to do you any good.

For air shocks, this is a fairly simple adjustment. First, use the manual to determine what pressure is required for your weight. Most air-sprung forks have a Schrader valve for pressurizing, but some require specific adapters or a needle, like you might use for a basketball. Forks that require an adapter usually come supplied with one. If your fork requires an adapter and did not include one, or if the adapter has become lost or damaged, you'll need to pick up a new one from your local shop. A custom-built suspension pump with a built-in gauge works best for pressurizing air-filled forks. They can push a very small volume of air to extremely high pressures, making them both powerful and precise. Additionally, most suspension pumps incorporate a bleed valve that allows you to release pressure in small increments, which is tough to do with a floor pump.

Rear air shocks usually require a lot of pressure—sometimes more than 200 psi—so a proper suspension pump works best for these, as well. A floor pump may be substituted in a pinch, but it may have a difficult time achieving the necessary pressure.

Once you adjust the preload on air shocks, it's important to check them regularly. Because they contain small volumes of air, the loss of only a few pounds can make the shock operate poorly, so it's wise to check the pressure every week if you're riding regularly.

Coil-spring suspensions are adjusted for rider weight by turning knobs that compress the spring, an adjustment called preload. Preload on coil-sprung shocks is a fine-tuning adjustment only. Applying too much preload can make the shock bottom out. In time, it will also overstress the coil and cause it to crack, so it's important to begin with springs that are rated for the specific rider's weight and work from there. Your fork's or rear shock's owner's manual should provide guidelines detailing how much preload is acceptable and what spring is the correct one to start with for your weight.

Changing springs on rear shocks is relatively easy and requires only a few basic hand tools. Changing the spring or springs in your fork, however, is another matter. The tools required are still not very specialized, but the procedures vary from manufacturer to manufacturer and can be a little tricky. As always when dealing with the unknown, read the manual first, then start in after you understand the whole process.

Many elastomer suspensions can be adjusted for rider weight by preloading the elastomers inside, also. Some, however, are tuned by changing the urethane bumpers. Manufacturers once offered bumpers in various densities, but as elastomers have fallen out of favor with most manufacturers, it may be difficult to find new ones. If you have the necessary bumpers, it's usually fairly easy to disassemble the suspension, remove them, and replace them with softer or stiffer ones.

On some forks, changing the bumpers may require special tools, such as superlong hex keys. Check your manual for directions. Again, parts and tools were once readily available from suspension manufacturers. Now, it may take a little detective work to find what you need.

Besides these basic preload adjustments, most suspensions require regular maintenance to keep them functioning properly. Check your front wheel quick-release regularly to ensure that it's tight, because it's the key to keeping the two fork legs moving as one. A simple thing to do every couple of

SPRING RATE PROGRESSIONS OF AIR SPRINGS AND COIL SPRINGS

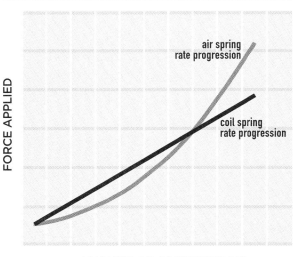

FORCE APPLIED

air spring rate progression

coil spring rate progression

AMOUNT OF COMPRESSION

rides is to wipe dirt from the legs (carefully lift up the boots if your fork has them), apply a light fork oil, and compress the fork a few times to work the oil past the seals. This will help keep dirt out of the fork and lubricate the legs, keeping the fork action smooth and friction-free. Once a month or so, put a wrench on the top caps, brake posts, and shaft bolts (on the bottom of the legs), and gently snug them if they've loosened. And always keep an eye on the brake arch and dropouts for signs of damage.

If you race or ride hard, you'll want to clean and relube the fork about every 2 months, or more often if you ride in wet or muddy conditions. On some forks, this is easy. On others, you'll want to take the bike to a shop. Also, many fork and shock makers have service centers ready to quickly take care of oil changes and rebuilds at a reasonable cost.

Elastomer shocks are usually simpler to maintain than models with air shocks and hydraulic damping. For forks, keep the slider surfaces clean and lightly lubricated with a spray or drip Teflon-based oil. On stems and rear shocks, about the only upkeep you might have to do is to tighten the pivot bolts if the parts develop play. And if you ride a lot, you'll probably want to replace the elastomers yearly because they lose resiliency with enough riding.

All suspensions that rely on mechanical linkages may loosen over time, so it's always wise to check the bolts occasionally and tighten them if necessary. Rear swingarms are particularly susceptible. You can push and pull laterally on the rear wheel to feel for play; it shouldn't move much. If there's any clunking or looseness, the bolts securing the swingarm probably need to be tightened.

GENERAL SUSPENSION TIPS

Here are some handy tips to keep your suspension in top shape.

• Forks come factory-set to provide suspension for the average rider. Which means, of course, that if you're not average, the fork may not work very well. How can you tell? Even though you try all available preload settings, when you hit bumps, either the fork barely reacts (small riders) or it overreacts by bottoming out (large riders). The solution? Have the fork tuned differently by an expert. Almost all models can be modified to work for a wide range of riders, though it may sometimes require purchasing different internals.

• Magnesium is used in many forks because it's a lightweight material, but it's also quite susceptible to corrosion when exposed to salty winter conditions where road crews use salt to melt snow. If you must ride in these conditions, wash, dry, and relube the fork after every ride or you may ruin it.

• When checking bolts on suspension forks, follow the torque specifications in the owner's manual. This will ensure that things are tight enough. But more important, it'll guarantee that you don't break or strip parts of the fork.

• Always check the fork after a crash. If it doesn't rebound like it did before, it probably was damaged in the crash. (Usually, replacing the damaged parts will repair it.)

• Oil-damped forks often weep oil. A trace is usually nothing to worry about. Pooling oil, however, usually indicates a blown seal or O-ring, which means disassembly and repair are needed.

• The bushings that separate the inner and outer fork legs will wear with abuse or lots of use. This creates play in the fork legs. Check for it by applying the front brake and rocking the bike forward and back. A knocking sensation indicates either a loose headset or worn bushings. Check the headset. If it's okay, the bushings need to be replaced, which is a job for a shop with the appropriate tools.

• When lubricating forks, use only those lubes recommended by the manufacturer; other types may break down internal plastic and rubber parts.

• Disc brakes are quickly becoming the number-one choice for serious off-road enthusiasts looking for powerful, consistent braking in all conditions. But don't make the mistake of installing one on a fork that was not made for it—the forces from this type of brake can overload the fork leg and even break it.

• Use care when putting a mountain bike with a shock fork (or any bike with any fork, for that matter) on a rooftop car rack that grabs the fork. It's possible to damage or break the dropout if the bike tips over when only one dropout is held by the rack (as could happen when you're putting the bike up there).

• To check sag, or fork travel, place a zip-tie at the top of the fork leg. Sitting on the bike will compress the fork and move the zip-tie. When you get off the bike, the fork will extend and you'll be able to measure how far the zip-tie moved, or the amount of sag, and adjust preload accordingly (recommended sag is listed in your manual and is typically in the range of 30 percent of full travel of your fork or shock). After a ride, you'll be able to see the maximum travel of the fork (assuming you rode hard and hit bumps that could bottom the fork).

• If your suspension fork was equipped by the manufacturer with rubber boots to protect the stanchions and seals, use them. There is some argument that boots trap dirt and moisture against the fork's seals, but a little careful cleaning under the boots after every ride will prevent this from becoming a genuine problem. Newer-model forks, on the other hand, benefit from more sophisticated dust-wiper designs and stanchion finish coatings that make boots often unnecessary.

• When cleaning the bike after a muddy ride, don't spray water at the fork seals because it can work its way inside the legs and cause corrosion.

• On double-crown forks, check the rubber bumpers on the upper legs occasionally. These have an important job: When the fork swings completely to the side, they ensure that the legs won't smack into the frame and damage it. The bumpers must be placed just right to provide this protection.

TROUBLESHOOTING

PROBLEM: The fork or rear suspension doesn't feel like it moves much over bumps.

SOLUTION: The spring preload may be set too high. Change the adjustment.

PROBLEM: The fork or rear suspension moves too much over bumps.

SOLUTION: Increase the spring preload until the suspension sags very slightly when you're sitting on the bike.

PROBLEM: The fork doesn't move over bumps like it used to.

SOLUTION: Clean and lubricate the inner legs and bushings.

PROBLEM: The fork doesn't move like it used to and you crashed.

SOLUTION: Have the alignment checked by a shop. You may have bent the fork legs.

PROBLEM: Oil is leaking out of one leg.

SOLUTION: You may have a bad or leaking seal in the damping cartridge. Replace the cartridge.

PROBLEM: The top caps on the fork legs repeatedly loosen.

SOLUTION: Replace the O-rings on the caps (if there are any) and check the threads on the caps. Replace caps if they're damaged.

PROBLEM: After hitting a bump, the fork kicks back too quickly.

SOLUTION: Stiffen the rebound damping.

PROBLEM: On steep climbs, when you're standing and pedaling, you hear a rubbing noise.

SOLUTION: The legs of the fork are moving independently, allowing the rim to brush the brake. Make sure the wheel is centered in the fork and securely fasten the quick-release skewer. Still rubbing? Upgrade the fork bridge or the front hub.

PROBLEM: You hear knocking, clicking, or creaking sounds from the rear suspension.

SOLUTION: Put a wrench on all the pivot bolts to tighten loose ones. Check the manual to determine which pivots require lubing and lubricate them.

PROBLEM: You strike your heel on the rear brake when pedaling.

SOLUTION: If the bike is equipped with cantilever brakes, try installing a direct-pull brake (these fit closer to the frame). If the bike has direct-pulls, try rerouting the cable to increase clearance. If it's a Shimano V-Brake, shorten the noodle. Or install a cable pulley.

Basic Suspension Adjustment

1 Suspension improves control and cushions the ride, but it's not maintenance-free. First, adjust it to accommodate your weight. On air shocks, do this by adding or releasing pressure according to the settings that the manual recommends for your weight.

Forks usually have two valves, one located on the top of each leg. To prevent valves from being contaminated by dirt, they're sealed with either a screw (for needle valves) or a regular plastic cap (for Schrader valves). Remove needle-type caps with a Phillips screwdriver or Schrader caps by hand to expose the valves.

Now attach the pump. In a pinch, you can use a standard bicycle pump, but it's best to use a special suspension pump. This usually resembles a syringe with a gauge attached. It allows more minute pressure adjustments, so it's easier to use, and the gauge is higher quality than on most bicycle pumps, so it's more accurate.

Place the pump on the valve and operate the plunger to inflate each leg to the recommended pressure (see photo). If you overdo it or if the fork already indicates too much pressure, let some air out by depressing the bleed button in the side of the pump. When you have the correct pressure in both legs, replace the screws or caps.

2 Rear air shocks require much more pressure than fronts, so exact pressure is less critical. For accuracy, it's still best to use the pump supplied by the manufacturer. But if you're willing to ballpark pressure, you can do okay with a regular bicycle pump. The procedure is identical to working on the fork, except there's only one valve and the pressure is much greater. Remove the valve cap, install the pump, and inflate the shock to recommended pressure (see photo).

Fine-tuning the ride of your coil-sprung fork or rear shock is as simple as a twist of the wrist. To firm things up, turn the preload knob clockwise. To soften, turn it counterclockwise. If the available preload adjustment isn't enough to achieve the ride quality you want, you'll need to change the spring to one recommended for your weight.

Because the coil on a rear shock rides on the outside of the shock body, changing it is pretty easy and usually doesn't require any special tools. Changing springs in a fork is a bit more involved. You will need to partially disassemble the fork to perform this job, so it's advisable that you consult your fork's owner's manual before turning so much as a single bolt.

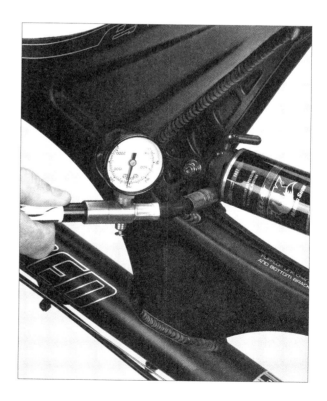

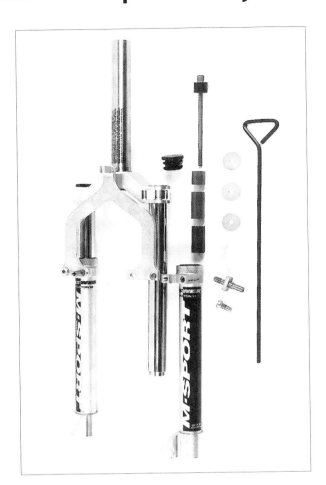

3 Replacement parts for elastomer suspensions are rapidly disappearing. If you're lucky enough to have what you need, it's pretty easy to adjust elastomer suspension to your weight by changing the urethane bumpers. On forks, it is more difficult than adding air pressure; however, it's not so tough that you shouldn't attempt it if your fork doesn't have enough travel or feels too stiff. It's usually necessary to disassemble the legs. This may be as simple as unscrewing the top caps, or it may require special tools such as long hex keys (see photo). These and the different-density urethane bumpers are available from some shops or the fork manufacturer. You should also have a manual that explains how to disassemble and reassemble the fork and bumpers because there are so many different types of forks.

For stems and rear shocks, which employ elastomers, it's usually fairly obvious how to disassemble the mechanism to change bumpers. And it generally requires only basic hand tools.

To keep shock forks as friction-free as possible, once a week or so, lift the boots (if your fork has them), clean any dirt from the legs, drip on a little lube containing Teflon, and compress the fork to work the lube past the seals. To ensure optimum steering precision, check the front wheel quick-release. It has to be tight to tie the fork legs together. To prevent problems due to loose parts, put a wrench on the top caps, brake bosses, and shaft bolts regularly.

4 The last type of shock maintenance that you can do yourself is checking linkages. Since many suspensions rely on moving parts, such as swingarms, that are bolted to the frame, it's important to occasionally check them for play. Do this by wiggling the parts laterally. If there's side-to-side play, the wheels won't track in line, which can lead to squirrelly handling. You can prevent this by regularly checking the linkages and tightening any bolts that have loosened (see photo).

Some shocks that rely on oil damping also require regular oil changes, but this service is best performed by an authorized service center. Some shop mechanics can handle this, or you may have to send the shock back to the manufacturer. If you must do the latter, the job usually isn't too expensive, and the manufacturer can generally turn it around quickly.

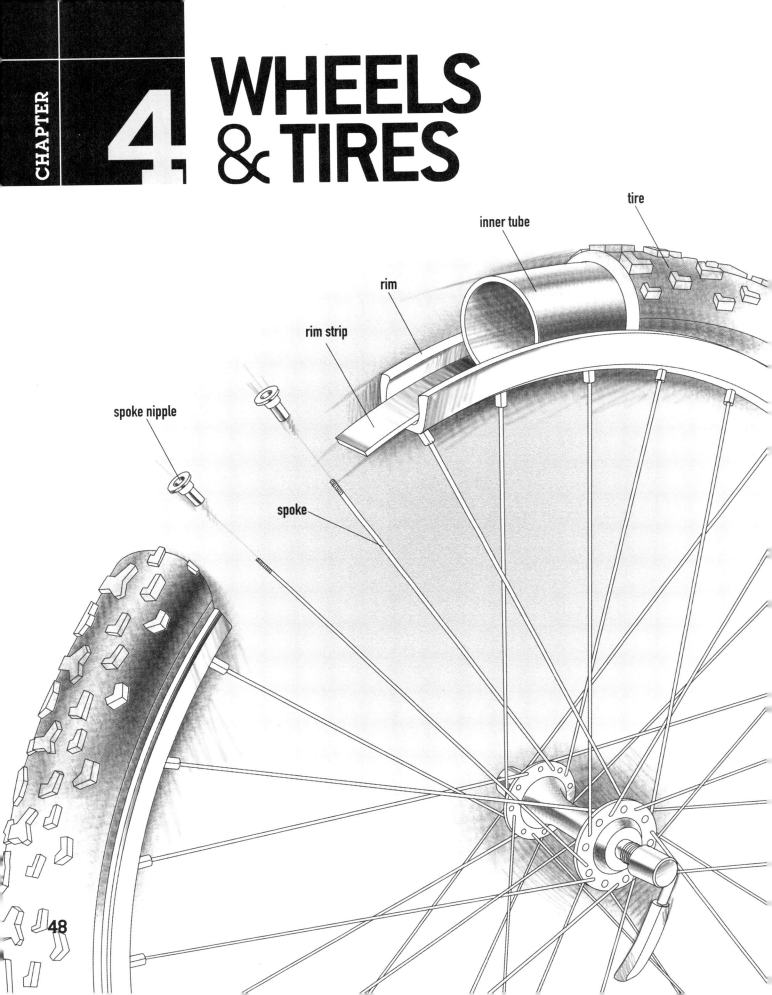

4. WHEELS & TIRES

tire

inner tube

rim

rim strip

spoke nipple

spoke

48

Most folks know that the term "bicycle" means "two wheels." While the bike's frame may determine how the bike handles, none of it would be possible without its wheels. A bike's ride quality and some aspects of handling are heavily influenced by the quality of wheels and tires. A well-built wheel—tight and true, with a properly inflated tire—makes for an enjoyable ride every time. On the other hand, a loose, bent wheel or a soft, underinflated tire can make just a few minutes in the saddle a miserable—or worse, dangerous—experience. A bad wheel makes steering difficult, especially at high speeds, and braking suffers similarly.

WHAT MAKES A GOOD WHEEL?

Quality rims and hubs are both important, but the keys to a wheel's strength are the spokes. Even a mediocre hub and rim can become a great wheel when properly strung with quality spokes by an expert wheelbuilder. By carefully balancing tension all the way around the wheel, a wheelbuilder creates a straight, round, and durable melding of art and science—the bicycle wheel. Correct spoke tension enables wheels to stay round and to withstand the pressures of weight and shocks transmitted from the road or trail.

When weight is applied to a wheel, the spokes beneath the hub lose some of their tension. If this tension is inadequate to begin with, the rim is in danger of becoming permanently deformed. A well-built and well-maintained wheel is thus a tight wheel, one in which all the spokes are at optimum tension. Such a wheel can better withstand pressures both from above and from the side than a loose wheel can. A tight wheel flexes less than a loose one, and so it experiences less metal fatigue. It's more durable and less likely to go out of true, or round.

Luckily, chances are good that almost any wheelset you get from your local bike shop, whether alone or as part of a new bike, have been well built. It's still a smart idea to check them before taking them home. Spin the wheels to check for true (the straightness of the rim) and round. Then (after they've stopped spinning, of course) pluck at the spokes or squeeze them in pairs to listen or feel for firm and equal tension. Bear in mind that it is normal for the left-side spokes of a multispeed rear wheel to have a lower tension than the right side. This is called "dish" (and will be explained in further detail later in this chapter). Any shop selling you a new bike or wheelset should be willing and eager to touch up the true and tension for you before leaving the store with your purchase. A pair of wheels properly tensioned from the start will require less attention in the future.

Exactly what you need. The ultimate option is to have a pair of wheels custom-built for you by an experienced wheelbuilder. Custom-built wheels are pricier than a factory-built set, but what you get is a wheelset built with your specific riding style in mind by a true craftsman who takes the greatest pride in his or her work.

Learning to build your own wheels is another possibility. Wheel building requires patience, attention to detail, and a high level of skill. In fact, it may be too much for most home mechanics to pick up, but the process should be well within reach of those with an above-average mechanical aptitude. It takes several wheels before you become truly proficient; in the end, though, the satisfaction and feeling of accomplishment gained from building and riding your own wheels is well worth all the effort.

The right rubber. Good tires are constructed with a fabric casing made of nylon fibers and may include the addition of some exotic materials like aramid fibers (such as Kevlar) to increase puncture resistance or reduce weight. Rubber compounds are selected to match the intended use of the tire.

Racing tires use thin, lightweight treads made of grippy rubber, touring tires use compounds developed to maximize tread life, and mountain bike rubber is formulated to be durable and maximize traction in a variety of conditions.

Avoid cheap tires like those you might find in a department store. These are most often made of low-grade cotton or polyester fabric and low-quality rubber that wears quickly. The biggest problem, though, with cheap tires like these is their low recommended inflation pressure that makes for a mushy, vague ride.

A cushion of air. With correct inflation pressure, a tire rolls quickly and smoothly while at the same time conforms to and grips the road or trail surface. A properly inflated tire also affords the rim protection from bumps, rocks, and potholes. So what is the correct inflation pressure? Every tire has a recommended range printed on the sidewall. Generally speaking, for road tires you want to be right at the top of the recommended range and for off-road tires, you will want to tailor the pressure to given conditions. On pavement or smooth, fast, hard-packed trails like converted railroad beds, traction is abundant, so you should pump your tires right up to

their recommended maximum, often around 60 to 65 psi to minimize rolling resistance. The usual range for off-road riding is between 35 and 45 psi, but finding the right pressure requires a bit of trial and error. For top performance, the correct pressure is as low as you can go without pinch-flatting or folding the tire over while cornering. Rocky trails require higher pressure to avoid flats; lower pressures allow the tire to conform to the terrain, maximizing traction.

Variety. Tires don't last; it's just the way things are. Take advantage of this by experimenting with widths, tread patterns, rubber compounds, etc. Work boots aren't right for running a marathon, and casual shoes wouldn't be the best choice for hiking deep into the backcountry. Similarly, bicycle tires are specialized—and only through trying lots of different tires will you discover what works best for your bike, your region, and your riding style. It's not at all unusual for an enthusiastic mountain biker to have a closet full of tires for different conditions or for roadies to have heavy, long-wearing tires for early-season training and slender, lightweight ones for racing season.

SELECTING WHEELS

Bicycle wheels come in an impressive array of sizes and types, ranging from 12- to 29-inch diameters and ¾- to 3-inch widths. The bicycle world contains several rim-and-tire numbering systems: the English-American and the European standards are the most common. Although many wheels are essentially interchangeable, the exact tire-to-rim fit is unique to each system.

The English-American standard uses two-digit numbers to indicate the approximate wheel diameter (measured tread to tread) in inches, followed by a tire-width number. For instance, 26 × 1.9 describes a wheel that, with its tire, is about 26 inches in diameter and 1.9 inches wide.

The European system is metric, and wheel diameter is designated by a three-digit number, the approximate diameter in millimeters. This number is some-

MOUNTAIN BIKE TIRES　　　　**ROAD BIKE TIRES**

Tires are available in many sizes and tread patterns. From narrow, high-pressure tires for maximum speed on smooth roads to wide, soft, heavily treaded tires for the roughest trails (with many options in between), there is a tire available to suit almost any terrain.

Rim and Tire Compatibilities and Uses

RIM CATEGORY OR NAME	RIM WIDTH (MM)	RIM WEIGHT (G)	TIRE SIZES	TYPICAL USES
Road clincher	19–21	395–500	700c x 19–32mm and 27" x ⁷⁄₈–1¹⁄₈"	Road racing and sport/light touring
Touring/hybrid/29" clincher	22–28	500–600	700c x 28–47mm, 29" x 2.0", and 27" x 1¹⁄₈–1³⁄₈"	All-purpose touring, tandem, casual riding, and 29" mountain bike racing
Mountain bike clincher	25–32	500–1100	26" x 1.25–3.0"	Mountain bike racing, general off-road riding, casual riding, off-road and third-world touring
Tubular	19–21	300–420	700c x 18-32mm	Road, track, and cyclocross racing

times accompanied by a two-digit number, which indicates the tire width. Usually a letter (A, B, or C) indicating rim width is placed after one of these numbers. So, for example, the European counterpart to the English 26 × 1.9 might be labeled 650 × 48B or simply 650B. The two tires are similar in size but not interchangeable.

Factors that must be considered when choosing wheels include diameter (you'll most likely be dealing with a 26, 27, or 700C), rim width (this dimension affects tire selection but isn't formally numbered), and tire size.

Wheel diameter. This is determined by the frame designer, who proportions the fork and stays for a specific size. Most road bicycles made for 27-inch wheels will not take 700Cs. Some will, but to be sure of the interchangeability, do a trial fit. Surprisingly, it's possible to fit 700C wheels in some mountain bike frames to make the bike better for road use. When trying these exchanges, always make certain that the brake pads reach the rims (don't buy until you're sure they'll fit).

Rim width. This affects road-tire choice. Although there are no hard-and-fast rules on rim-tire compatibility, most rims will fit several road-tire sizes. For instance, a narrow rim with an outside width of 20 mm (often called a 1-inch rim) will carry tires with widths of 19 to 32 mm. In making your rim selection, anticipate the full range of riding conditions you wish to encounter. The table above

shows which tires are suited for different types of riding. Find the road tires that you'll be using, then select a compatible rim.

Tire size. When selecting road and dirt tires, beware that although makers can be trusted to list diameters correctly, their way of indicating width is undependable. One company's 25 mm tire is the same size as another's 28. Some 26 × 1.75 labels would be labeled 26 × 1.5 by another maker. So the exact size of a tire can be determined only by measuring the width of an inflated tire. The International Standards Organization (ISO) tire size system, a five-digit sequence, is potential salvation from this measurement confusion. Although tire engineers understand and adhere to it, this form of labeling is just starting to find its way to consumers as a guide to tire choice.

Besides size, tires vary in many other ways, casing construction and tread pattern foremost among them. When choosing tires, keep in mind that the rougher the pavement, the coarser the casing (which means larger and fewer cords, around 20 to 36 per inch) and the larger the tread pattern should be. Dry, loose ground calls for numerous large knobs. Wet, muddy conditions, on the other hand, are best met with shorter, more widely spaced knobs that don't collect mud.

On smoother surfaces, such as well-maintained pavement, casings can be made of finer, more numerous threads (from 36 to more than 100 per inch),

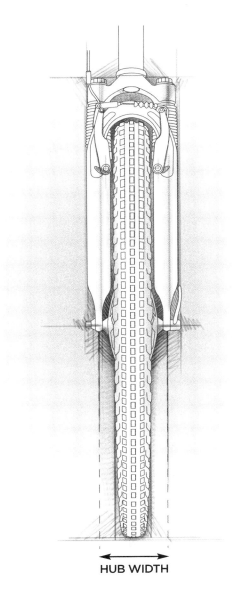

and the tread patterns can be less aggressive. On good roads, in the wet or dry, some of the best results are obtained with entirely smooth tires.

COMPATIBILITY OF WHEELS AND BIKE

When considering a change of wheels, you must not overlook wheel and bike compatibility. The factors affecting compatibility are wheel diameter, rim width, hub axle size and width, and cassette type compatibility or, if you have an older bike, freewheel threading.

Wheel diameter. The wheel diameter is important because it must be compatible with the brakes. Brake pads must make solid and secure contact with the sidewalls of the rim, which serve as the braking surface. Because brakes are made in many different lengths and are mounted to frames in different locations, don't assume your brakes will reach any size wheel. For instance, bicycles equipped with 27-inch wheels will occasionally not accommodate the slightly smaller 700C size because the brake pads can't be lowered even 1/16 inch. With such small distances to measure, a trial fitting of the wheel you hope to use becomes very helpful. Borrow a friend's or visit a bike shop to see if the wheel you want to use will fit.

Rim width. This is a measure of wheel strength and indicates the range of tire options. Refer to the table on page 51 for suggestions on tire and rim sizes. Select a rim that is suited to your type of riding.

Hub axle size and width. These must be appropriate for your bike frame. Hub width is measured from locknut to locknut and needs to conform to the space between the two blades of the fork (see the illustration below) and between the two rear dropouts on the frame. Otherwise, fitting your new wheel can be a real thumb buster.

Most front hubs come 100 mm wide. Exceptions to this rule include juvenile sidewalk bikes, which have even narrower hubs, and the rare tandem equipped with a front hub brake, which requires a dished wheel and a hub of 110 to 115 mm width. The same width consideration should be observed for the rear wheel, where the range of sizes is wider. Road bikes today run 130 mm wide and mountain bikes run 135 mm with a few very rare ex-

HUB WIDTH

Hub width is measured from the outer edges of the two axle locknuts. This distance should be equivalent to the space between the dropouts of the frame or fork.

ceptions, but older bikes may be 120, 125, 126, 127, and 130 mm (for older mountain bikes) wide. Try to achieve a close fit so the difference between wheel and frame is no more than 3 mm.

The goal of racing teams is to set up all their bikes with the same exact spacing for all rear wheels and frames. If all derailleurs are set up for the same cassette cog space, then lightning-fast wheel changes are possible. Whenever you expect to regularly use several different rear wheels on your bicycle, take the time to make each overall width and cassette spacing the same. Damaging chain overshifts from misadjusted derailleurs can occur after wheel swaps, but they're avoidable.

Axle diameter varies according to the axle type. Quick-release axles are thicker by ½ mm than most nutted axles. Many bicycle frames can handle either type, but some designed for nutted hubs have dropout slots that are too narrow to permit the thicker quick-release axle. Since the convenience and popularity of the quick-release system is so overwhelming, consider filing your dropouts to enlarge the slot openings. The amount of metal to remove is small; work very carefully and don't misshape the dropout and cause the wheel to sit crooked.

Downhill and freeride mountain bikes with long travel forks often come equipped with a very large-diameter axle called a through-axle that helps resist unequal compression of the fork legs. (We'll touch on this design further in Chapter 5.) Chances are that if you have one of these, you already know it.

Be aware that the quick-release axle must protrude past the locknut so the dropouts can rest on it—but the amount that protrudes past the locknut must not be longer than the dropout is wide. On inexpensive bicycles fitted with higher-class hubs, this is often the case. If so, the clamping skewer won't secure the hub when tightened and the wheel can pull out when you pedal. The solution is to file the end of the axle until it's the correct length to allow the quick-release to clamp the frame.

Cassette-type compatibility. A big issue any time you're swapping rear wheels is gearing compatibility. Two types of mechanisms are in common use for holding gears (cogs) on the rear wheel. The standard today is cassette cogs, which slide onto a splined body built into the hub called a freehub. The freehub contains bearings for coasting and a ratchet mechanism for driving the bike, hence the clicking sound when you're coasting.

The advantage of cassettes is that because the freehub is part of the hub, the main hub bearings are placed farther apart, which reinforces the all-important hub axle and prevents breakage (formerly a common problem). Also, the cogs are held in place by a lockring, which is relatively easy to

remove for simple cog replacement.

Naturally, the two big component manufacturers couldn't agree on a standard spline that the cassette cogs slide onto, so now we have two standards, the Shimano and Campagnolo spline patterns, which are not interchangeable. When purchasing wheels or planning upgrades, be sure to get a wheel that matches the cassette you're planning to use.

The other bugaboo is the number of gears on the cassette. It's best if this matches also (though for upgrades there are spacer kits that allow you to add a cog). Standards keep changing as competitors and engineers up the ante on what's best for serious riders. The important thing to know is what you're trying to match when you're doing repairs or replacements.

If you have an older bike or if you purchased a bike at a department store, it's also possible that you have a freewheel instead of a cassette on your rear wheel. Freewheels preceded cassettes and are different to work with. The basic difference is that a freewheel contains the cogs and the bearing and drive mechanism in one unit that is threaded onto the rear hub (remember that on cassette systems, the bearing and drive mechanism is built into the freehub, which is part of the hub, and the cogs are separate).

Because freewheels are threaded onto the hub, a special removal tool is required to unscrew the freewheel from the hub. And because the cogs and bearing/driving mechanism are combined, it can be more difficult to remove the cogs than on cassette systems. Special tools may be required (depending on the type of freewheel).

In any case, when upgrading wheels, it's the perfect time to upgrade to a cassette system. This is best because freewheels are getting hard to find. Even if you find one, you may be out of luck later on when you need parts for it. If you have a cassette system, on the other hand, it'll be easy to find the parts you need.

If you must go with a freewheel, make sure that the threading matches that on your hub. The standard is English, and that's what's found on all mountain bikes and most road bikes made after 1980 or so. The only bike that might give you trouble is an older (1960s or early 1970s) French road bike, such as a Peugeot or Gitane. On these, it's possible, even likely, that the freewheel is French-threaded. Don't try to screw on an English-threaded freewheel in this case. It's slightly larger and it'll seem to go on, but the first time you go for a ride, it'll strip the hub threads. Consequently, if you have this type of bike and want to upgrade, the best bet is to get a cassette wheel or at least a used wheel that's threaded to accept an English freewheel threading, because some English freewheels are still available.

SPECIAL-USE WHEELS

Specialty bicycles often use very different equipment than day-to-day machines. Track bicycles don't use brakes, and punctures are rare on the velodrome surface. This explains why lightweight glued-on sew-up tires (also known as tubulars) are so universal for track racing. For explosive events like matched sprinting, which features unpredictable maneuvering and sudden acceleration, 32- and 36-spoke wheels with sturdy rims in the 350-gram range abound. But for individual pursuit, in which speed is steady and riders have the track mostly to themselves, rims can weigh as little as 260 grams and have 24 or fewer spokes.

Mass-start road racing is a rough-and-tumble world governed by weather and pavement conditions. Potholes, crashes, and punctures are facts of life, so the most popularly used rims are "team weight," that is, from 395 to 420 grams supported by 32 or 36 spokes of full 14 (2.0 mm) gauge. In certain circumstances, such as lighter-weight riders and on better roads, as few as 28 spokes are used and rims can be as light as 340 grams. Composite aero wheels are also becoming common due to the wind-cheating effect they offer.

Triathlon racing has room for all equipment. Since it's a timed, largely individual race over usually good roads, many competitors employ the lightest possible wheels and tires. Because the emphasis is on steady speed and not acceleration, rim and tire weight are not terribly important. Many smaller triathlons are won with everyday clincher rims and tires, in good condition and inflated from 100 to 155 psi.

Some of the best bicycle touring these days is on infrequently traveled rural roads. These roads are safer due to low traffic, but they're poorly maintained. To ride a bike carrying loaded panniers, wheels must be sturdy and tires generous. Use 27-inch and 700C rims of 500-gram weights capable of handling larger tires, or 26-inch rims in the 450-gram range. The same formula applies to tandem bikes, which also benefit from an increased number of spokes in the wheels. Where most bikes have 32 spokes per wheel, tandems sometimes have as many as 48.

Freeride and downhill mountain bikers use special wheels that are designed to be almost indestructible, with heavy rims, tires, hubs, and spokes. When disc brakes are used on the bikes, the wheels often have special rims without braking surfaces. Unlike cross-country wheels, weight is a secondary consideration for downhill racing, where races are won and lost in tenths or even hundredths of a second, so reliability is paramount. This is even more so in freeriding, where anything less than ultimate durability could result in serious injury.

WHEEL SYSTEMS

A hot trend in the last several years has been the wheel system. Sometimes referred to as "aero wheels" or "low-spoke-count wheels," wheel systems are complete wheels from the manufacturer designed as a single unit that includes rim, spokes, and hub, to balance weight and strength. They look very unique and high-tech, too. By building wheel systems in large quantities with specially trained assemblers, manufacturers are able to produce high-performance wheels that compare favorably in price to the high-quality, hand-built wheels you might get from an experienced wheelbuilder. On the surface, it might seem as though wheel systems could put traditional wheelbuilders on the endangered species list. This isn't quite the case. With all that wheel systems have going for them, traditional hand-built wheels still hold a very important trump card: consistency. All manufacturers of wheel systems wish to create one-of-a-kind brand images for themselves, resulting in a fiercely competitive market where innovations are not shared. So Shimano's wheel system hub won't work with Campagnolo's wheel system rim, and neither one's spoke is interchangeable with Spinergy's, and so on. Conversely, if you buy a well-built traditional 32-spoke wheel in Tucson and break a spoke in London or need an axle in Marseilles, chances are you'll be rolling again in no time. So, for ultimate performance, wheel systems could be the way to go; but for a balance of performance and serviceability, traditional wheels still come out on top.

WHEEL MAINTENANCE AND REPAIR

The best way to obtain outstanding wheel performance is to make sure that the wheels are appropriately designed for your riding, constructed from top-quality components, and expertly built. From then on, avoiding damage is the biggest challenge. Unless they become damaged, well-built wheels don't need periodic maintenance apart from hub lubrication. Moreover, quality tires will last for many thousands of miles if kept properly inflated and free of glass, metal, wire, and other debris. Unfortunately, many wheels are not expertly designed or built. Such wheels demand more time and effort for maintenance and need to be repaired more frequently. These routine maintenance tasks will help you avoid repairs.

Maintain proper spoke tension. Wheels built too loose, as the mass-produced ones can be (more of a problem on road than mountain bike wheels), can loosen even further with use. Wheels plagued by many limp spokes are dangerous and deteriorate rapidly. On road wheels, this can lead to sudden collapse or spoke breakage, because every time a wheel is used the spokes accumulate fatigue. Tight spokes last much longer than loose ones, though they all eventually wear out.

Spoke wear occurs when spokes are loose and can move inside the hub, flexing slightly as you ride. Then, similar to what happens when you flex a piece of wire back and forth repeatedly, the spoke eventually fatigues and breaks. Tightness enables each spoke in the wheel to remain fixed and avoid the flex that leads to breakage problems. A tight wheel is also able to resist severe loads more successfully than a loose wheel.

Besides much longer life, a tight wheel is less likely to have individual nipples rattle loose from vibration. If you find one loose spoke and the rim isn't dented at the spot, the culprit is a wheel that's simply too loose. The remedy for the problem is to lubricate all the nipples, tighten the loose one, and then add tension all around, perhaps one-half turn to each. Go easy on the general tightening—as spokes reach their optimum level of tension, small twists of the nipple add tension very rapidly. Occasionally, nipples need to be glued tight (with thread adhesive), but adequate overall tension normally keeps a wheel free from further loosening.

Be aware that excessive tension can create instability and make a wheel susceptible to sudden collapse. To be on the safe side, find a well-built wheel to use as a model. When plucked, similar-gauge spokes will make a musical note that is proportional to tension. Higher is tighter, lower is looser. Make your wheel approximately as tight as the one you're using as a model, but no tighter. Your aim isn't to make the wheel as tight as possible, just tight enough to prevent any spokes from loosening during use. It takes a good bit of experience to be able to sense when a wheel has reached this optimum level of tightness, so don't expect to automatically get it right the first time you try.

Properly inflate tires. Air-filled, pneumatic tires were one of cycling's great breakthroughs. They provide traction, comfort, and protection for the rim. To deliver these advantages, tires need to be properly inflated. The number-one reason that wheels are rebuilt is rim damage, and the number-one cause of rim damage is underinflated tires, especially on road bikes, which have much less air volume than mountain bike tires. Yes, owner laziness or inattention to proper tire pressure is an even greater threat to tires than ruts, roots, potholes, curbs, and other hazards.

Before every ride, check the tire pressure on your road bike and inspect the tread for cuts. Setting off with underinflated tires is a terrible financial risk if you're riding on expensive wheels. With no warning, a minor road hazard can cause $100 worth of wheel damage.

Because mountain bike tires hold so much more air than road models, inflation is less critical. Still, check pressure regularly because even with fat tires, low pressure can cause problems. Besides rim damage, the other big cost exacted by underinflated mountain bike tires is tube pinching. When the tire is collapsed by a rock or curb, the tube is caught between it and the rim, and the rim often cuts the tube. You'll recognize a puncture caused by pinching by the telltale pair of "snake bite" holes that it typically produces.

Bypass road hazards and rim damage. Even when your wheels are appropriately tight and your tires are properly inflated, you can still easily ruin a rim. Hitting a deep pothole, wiping out on a rut that catches and twists your wheel, or ramming something hard enough are just a few rim-damaging possibilities. Prevention is the key. On a road bike, it's important to avoid hazards as much as possible. An easy way to soften blows to the wheels is to get off the seat when you spot bumps ahead. Bend your knees and arms like a jockey riding a horse and let the bike float over the rough stuff.

Attention to the road surface has many payoffs besides wheel preservation. Debris or moisture on the road could cause a crash, especially if you hit it while turning. Crossing railroad tracks at an angle other than 90 degrees is treacherous, especially if you're riding on tires with little or no tread. Be alert and learn to make quick maneuvers to dodge major obstructions and to thread your way carefully through water or debris that can't be completely avoided.

Obviously, you won't avoid every hazard off road (what fun would that be?). The key for keeping the wheels safe here is proper tire pressure. It's amazing what a good pair of mountain bike wheels can handle if you maintain the correct tire pressure.

Despite all your precautions, you may find that your wheels receive occasional dents. If so, try one of the following solutions.

Pump it up. Increase air pressure to the maximum after first inspecting for any tread or sidewall cuts.

Go to larger tires. Many riders can't use the very smallest tires without experiencing costly rim injuries. Tiny road tires are best for small riders or near-perfect pavement surfaces.

Modify your riding habits. Avoid particularly bad roads, and reduce speeds where pavement trouble is unavoidable.

Keep your eyes open. Learn to spot risky terrain early so you can rise off the seat and take the hit in your knees and elbows, which will help keep hard jolts from reaching the wheels.

Punctures, headwinds, and dirty chains are facts of life. Wheel damage need not be. Spared from crashes, underinflation, and hazards, an appropriately designed and well-built wheel should deliver many years of trouble-free service.

Avoid spoke damage. If you have quality spokes (a brand-name spoke made of stainless steel, such as DT or Wheelsmith spokes, for instance) and the wheel is adequately tensioned, spoke damage should be rare. Spokes are usually damaged in two ways. Something gets caught in them, or you shift into low gear (your easiest gear) and the chain overshifts and lands on the spokes, cutting them. (The most likely cause of overshifting is a bent derailleur.) Common sense can minimize the chances of either problem. However, if you discover that one of your wheels is inexplicably out of true, check for bent spokes or chewed up spokes.

One thing to remember when riding any bike is to always ease off your pedaling effort when shifting onto the largest cog (your lowest gear). That way, if the derailleur is bent and the chain jumps over the top cog into the spokes, you'll be able to stop pedaling immediately, before any real damage is done. This is especially important after a wheel change or when riding a bike with improperly adjusted derailleurs.

Test the gear before you reach a steep section. When adjusting the derailleur, don't allow it to move closer to the spokes than necessary. It's better to just barely get into low gear than to occasionally throw your chain into the spokes because once drive-side spokes get scratched, they are much more likely to break.

After crashing, dumping your bike on its side, or jamming your bike into a car with its right side down, shift gently through the gears to ensure that the rear derailleur has not been bent. If it has, shifting into low gear may cause spoke damage—and if you're really unlucky, the wheel might grab the derailleur, pull it into the spokes, and ruin the derailleur, too.

REMOVING AND REMOUNTING WHEELS

You have to master this operation because without it you won't be able to repair flat tires, the most common bicycle breakdown. It's also essential for putting your bike on certain car racks or disassembling it to store it in a small place. The key to easy wheel removal and installation is proper fit. Whether your wheel is fastened to the frame with nuts or a quick-release, the removal and remounting procedure should be as easy for you as putting on or taking off your shoes. After all, wheels are your bicycle's shoes.

To practice, remove the wheels while the bicycle is supported. Use your repair stand or hang the saddle's nose over a branch, fence, or loop of rope suspended from a rafter, or bribe a buddy to hold the bike while you remove the wheels. With practice, you'll learn to remove a single wheel while supporting the bike yourself.

Open the brakes. Because brake pads are usually adjusted so that they are close to the wheel rims, the first step in wheel removal is finding a way to spread the brakes. Forget this step and the tire will jam in the brake, making it hard to get the wheel off and on. It's true that you can take off a wheel with a totally flat tire without opening the brake, but you'll have to open it when the tire is fixed and inflated, or it won't fit through.

Fortunately, most bikes equipped with quick-release hubs also have quick-release built into the brakes for slackening the brake cable, which allows the calipers to spread enough for tire removal.

Most road bikes have sidepull brakes. To open these, look for small levers on the brake caliper (the U-shaped part over the wheels), near where the cable is clamped. For recent Campagnolo brakes, look for a button on the brake lever. Open the levers or push the buttons to spread the brakes and get the wheels off easily.

Cantilever brakes, which are what you'll find on many mountain bikes, are opened by releasing the transverse cable (the wire that runs from one side of the brake to the other). Squeeze the brake pads to the rim with one hand to create slack, and lift one end of the transverse cable out of its pocket. Let go of the pads, and the brake will spring open.

On direct-pull cantilevers such as Shimano V-Brakes, squeeze the pads to the rim, then pull back on the L-shaped "noodle" and lift to release it and the cable from the stop.

Disc brakes don't require any sort of release mechanism to ease removal and installation of your wheels. Take care, however, when installing wheels to not force the disc into the caliper. If the disc does not slip easily into the caliper, a brake pad may be out of place. Forcing the disc at this point could cause severe damage to a piston or to the disc itself. Also be careful to not squeeze the brake lever of self-adjusting hydraulic disc brake models when the wheel is removed. This can cause the caliper pistons to fully distend, locking up the system.

Get the wheels off. The next step for derailleur-equipped bikes is to shift onto the smallest outside cassette cog (on the back). This puts the chain and the derailleur in a position with enough slack to ease wheel removal.

Front wheels are the simplest to remove. First, loosen the axle. If it's held with nuts, use a wrench to loosen one side a bit, then the other, and back to the first. Nuts should be tightened or loosened gradually. If you try to loosen one side all at once, you might loosen or tighten the hub-bearing adjustment, which can cause bearing problems.

Open quick-release levers by pulling the lever away from the frame until it points straight out, and then rotate it around until it's parallel with the frame again. In some cases, this 180-degree rotation will, like loosening the nuts, allow the hub to come free from the front forks.

Deal with wheel retention devices. Most modern bikes have forks with wheel retention devices built into the dropouts. Usually, these are ridges that prevent the wheel from falling off even if the quick-release is mistakenly left loose. While these are a nice safeguard, they make it a little trickier to use the quick-release because when you swing the lever 180 degrees, the release doesn't open far enough to clear the stops on the fork. To remove the wheel, hold one end of the quick-release after swinging it open, and unscrew the other end enough to get the wheel off.

Loosen the axle nuts gradually, or the quick-release all at once. Check to see that the brakes are widened to permit tire clearance. Now give the wheel a sharp blow from behind. If it's ready to be removed, this blow will jar the axle in the dropout slots, hopefully freeing it.

Free the rear wheel from the chain. Once the axle is out of the dropouts, the wheel is free. With derailleur bikes, it helps to grab the rear derailleur and twist it back (clockwise) so the wheel can exit. Now the only encumbrance is the chain, and it must be unlooped from the wheel. Lift it off by hand if you don't mind getting dirty. Or learn to jiggle it off by shaking the wheel, which will keep your hands clean.

Make sure it fits right. Most of the difficulties encountered when replacing wheels are caused by a mismatch between frame and wheel. It's worthwhile to let an expert adjust your frame with alignment tools if necessary to allow your wheels to fit properly. Otherwise, every time you dismount or replace a wheel, you'll find yourself caught up in a first-class wrestling match.

TIRE MOUNTING AND TUBE REPAIRS

Tire removal is a deceptively easy task, well within the abilities of anyone who can ride. Because punctures are largely unpreventable, it's vital that every cyclist learn how to remove a tire, repair the tube, and replace both. It's considerably easier to remove and install mountain bike tires than road tires. But with both, success depends on four factors, the last and most important of which is correct procedure.

1. Rim and tire size. These must, of course, match. A difficult fit is rarely caused by mismade rims and tires. Rim makers almost never err by more than 1 percent in diameter. Major tire companies are scrupulously careful to match their tires to prevailing rim designs. The most likely mistake you'll make is to try to use a too-narrow tire. Although its diameter might be correct, the tire's inadequate width will make installation difficult (unless you replace your tube with a supernarrow model). And the narrow tire may be susceptible to pinch-flats and may allow rim damage because its profile isn't tall enough.

2. Rim design. Some rims are easier to put tires on than others. There's no easy way to second-guess how a tire will fit, though. The biggest factors seem to be overall diameter and the difference between the rim's inner trough and its upper edge. When you install a tire, the mounted bead sits in the center trough of the rim, while the remainder is lifted over the rim edge. The difference between these two provides the slack needed for installation and removal. The larger the difference, the easier the fit. To get the most benefit from this slack, use the thinnest rim strip possible. Almost all rims require a rim strip or liner to protect the tube from the ends of the spoke nipples. (The only exceptions are a few one-piece composite aero wheels that don't use conventional spokes.) The thinner the material used for this liner, however, the simpler it is to mount tires.

3. Tube size. Whenever possible, use a tube that is one size smaller than the tire. For instance, use a 1-inch tube with a 1⅛-inch tire, and a 1½-inch tube in a 2-inch mountain bike tire. The more compact the tube, the simpler it is to insert and the less crowding will occur as the tire's last tight section is lifted onto the rim.

4. Procedure. The last critical factor is procedure. Without skillful procedure, even the best-matched components refuse to cooperate. As with any endeavor, attitude plays an important role. Tire mounting often catches us at bad moments, especially after unwelcome flats. The embarrassment of delaying a group ride or the disappointment of being late to work is enough to make most people cross-eyed with impatience. Work smoothly and efficiently and you'll soon be rolling again. For complete step-by-step instructions for tire and

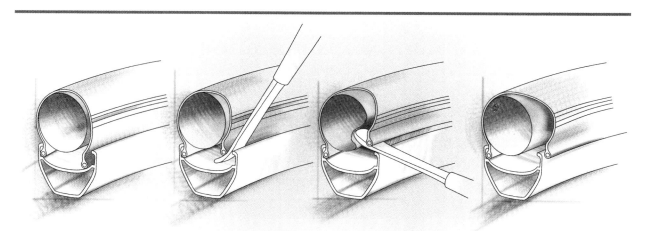

When removing a clincher tire, deflate the tube and push the tire bead off the bead seat and into the center trough of the rim. Use a tire lever to pry the bead over the side of the rim.

wheel mounting and tube repairs, see the repair sections at the end of this chapter.

Removing the tire. After the wheel is removed, ensure that the tube is completely flat. Unscrew and depress the tip of a presta valve or poke the tire lever into a Schrader valve and squeeze the tire to push all the air out of the tube. Once the tube is deflated, press the beads of the tire together and away from the rim edge, down into the center trough, as shown in the illustration. That's how you get some slack to lift one section of tire over the rim edge with tire levers. Use one lever to pry the bead over the edge of the rim and then hook its end onto a spoke. Then place another lever a few inches away on the same side of the tire and pry the bead off. Repeat with a third lever and slide it around to pop off that side of the tire. Now reach in and pull out the tube. To remove the valve stem, the loose bead must be lifted over the valve hole. Leave the other half of the tire on the rim.

Finding and marking the hole. Inflate the tube. With luck, you'll hear a hissing sound. If so, mark the spot. Either make index marks above and next to the hole but ½ inch away or so (because the glue will hide the ink if it's directly on the hole); or if you don't have a pen, tear the hole to about ¼ inch to mark it (don't worry, the patch will still work perfectly).

If you don't hear hissing, it's either a slow or fast leak. The latter is easy to find because there's usually a huge hole in the tube—you'll see it if you look a bit. Slow leaks can be tough. The best test is to submerge the tube in water and look for telltale bubbles. Take your time because a small hole will release air slowly. Linger on each section for a few seconds as you inspect, and mark the hole immediately so you don't lose it again. Still can't find a hole? If it's a Schrader valve tube, it may be a valve leak. Put a little spit or water on the valve and watch for a few seconds to see if a bubble forms. If so, use a valve tool to tighten the valve and test it again. Still leaking? Remove the valve core, put a drop of oil on the rubber piece on the core, and reinstall. Or replace the core.

Patching the tube. Start by scuffing the area around the hole with the sandpaper or metal scraper included in the patch kit. Scuff an area a little larger than the patch you plan to use. After scuffing, brush away the rubber dust with your hand.

There's a type of "glueless" patch designed for quick repairs that simply sticks to the tube. Park Tools makes one. Speed Patch is another brand. With these, once the tube has been scuffed, just peel off the backing, stick the patch over the hole, and reinstall the tube. These patches are designed to be temporary, but they'll get you home and they require less effort than a proper patch job because no gluing is required.

If you prefer to permanently repair the tube, use a normal patch kit such as one by Rema, Tip Top, Schwinn, Trek, or Specialized. These kits contain patches, glue, a piece of sandpaper, and instructions. The patches are so effective that it's possible to patch a tube many times with no bad effects.

The glue in these kits comes sealed. To open it, unscrew the cap, flip the cap over, and press to push the spike inside the cap into the top of the glue container. Apply plenty of cement to the tube. The glue should be thin and runny. If the solution is thick and gummy, it will barely work. Smear the cement over a generous area, larger than the patch you plan to use. Once the shiny, wet surface of the cement dulls, it's ready. On a dry day, it usually takes about 5 minutes for the glue to dry completely. Wait longer if needed. Don't apply the patch until the glue is completely dry, or it won't stick.

Applying the patch. Most patches come with a protective top layer of cellophane and a bottom layer of foil. Hold the cellophane and pull slowly to separate the patch from the foil (discard the foil piece). This exposes the sticky side of the patch. Don't touch this surface because you'll contaminate the glue. Place the patch onto the tube (make sure you cover the hole), and press firmly so it bonds to the tube. Leave the cellophane in place because it'll help keep the glue from sticking to the inside of the tire.

Before you reinstall the tube (an efficient time to do this is while the glue is drying), check the condition of the tire by running your fingers—or a rag, which is safer—around the inside. Remove any bits of wire, thorns, or glass before inserting the repaired tube, or else you'll probably have another puncture right away.

If you're working on a composite aero wheel, the tube usually includes a valve extender, a plastic or brass screw-on valve lengthener that ensures there's enough valve showing above the rim to attach a pump. This is usually screwed on to the presta valve after you've unscrewed the tip of the valve. Leave it on the tube during tire installation. And when you install a new tube, be sure to move the valve extender to the new tube.

Installing the tube and tire. Before installing the tube, inflate it just enough to round it out and remove wrinkles. Just blow into presta valve tubes to inflate them. Use a pump on Schrader valves. However you do it, this little bit of air is the key to avoiding getting the tube stuck under the tire bead, a glitch that will complicate tire installation.

First, fit the tube's valve by lifting the tire bead back and away, exposing the valve hole. (If you had to remove the tire completely, start installation by putting one side of the tire on the rim.) Get the valve in place, then work the rest of the tube into the tire. After it's inside the tire all the way around, go around again, working the tube up and onto the rim. When done, the free tire bead should be flat against the rim and the tube should be completely tucked up inside the tire and onto the rim.

Now is a good time to double-check whether you have the tire on right. Some mountain-bike tires are directional, meaning the tread should face a certain way. Look for arrows on the tire sidewalls that show which way to install the tread for top performance. An extra little trick that may seem insignificant but can save time in the future is to always install your tire with the label adjacent to the valve stem. When you get your next flat (and it will happen, trust us), you can quickly and accurately locate an offending object in your tire by matching the distance from the valve stem to the puncture from the label on your tire. Now you've got two spots to check, rather than the entire circumference of the tire.

It's best to reinstall the tire by hand because tire levers can pinch and cut the tube, repuncturing it. Begin remounting the bead at the valve stem. Once both beads are in place on either side of it, push the valve stem up into the tire to ensure the tube is not caught under either bead. Hold the wheel on your lap and work your hands away from each other around the wheel, popping the tire bead on to the rim by pushing down with your thumbs or the heels of your hands (with your fingers resting on the back side of the rim). When you get to the last section, opposite the valve stem, it gets tough. Don't give up.

The Schrader valve (*left*) is similar to valves found on automobile tires, whereas the presta valve (*right*) is thinner and has a small nut that must be loosened prior to tire inflation. The core of a Schrader valve can be removed with a special valve cap or removal tool. This is handy to repair valve leaks. Some presta valves have replaceable cores, too. If so, there are wrench flats on the sides of the valve.

Crouch and put the section of the wheel you're working on on top of your right knee if you're right-handed, or on your left knee if you're left-handed. Hold the tire bead on the rim on one side with your weak hand so it can't come undone as you work on the other end of that last tough section of tire. Using your stronger hand, work about an inch of the section onto the rim. Pop it on by pushing down and forward with the heel of your hand (now that you're pushing against your knee you have plenty of leverage). When you get an inch on, push another inch on, and so on. When the last bit pops into place, you're done. Good job.

Seating the tire on the rim. With the tire replaced on the rim, take a breather. Start inspecting the bead seat by pushing the tire away from the rim, one side at a time, and looking down into the rim. Make sure the tube isn't visible. If the tube is caught under the bead, the tire isn't seated on the rim correctly, and it won't inflate evenly and may blow later. Wiggle the tire to work the tube under it, or gently poke the tube inside the tire with a tire lever (be careful, or you'll cut it). One last time, push the valve stem up into the tire and pull it back down, snugly.

Inflating the tire. If everything looks right, add 20 to 30 pounds of pressure. If you're using the pump on your bike, attach it to the valve carefully. Schrader valves are nearly bulletproof, but metal presta valves can break if you're rough. Press the pump head on and flip up the lever (if applicable). To prevent too much pressure on the valve while pumping, hook a thumb over the tire and put your fingers behind a spoke and around the pump head on the valve. This technique will ensure you never break a valve while pumping.

When it's inflated a bit, rotate the wheel to see that the tire is sitting uniformly. Bulges at low pressure can be explosive at high pressure. If the tire looks straight, inflate to full pressure. If not, lubricate the beads with soapy water and reinflate, or simply dismount everything and try again.

TUBELESS (UST) TIRES

Many mountain bikes now benefit from a tire-and-rim combination that eliminates the need for an inner tube. This system, called Nagesti or Universal System for Tubeless (UST), relies on a rim with a special internal shape and a tire with a butyl rubber liner molded right into the casing. UST can save a marginal amount of weight (there is no inner tube, but the liner in the tire makes it slightly heavier than a similar non-UST model) and reduces the risk of pinch-flats. The real magic of the tubeless system, though, is traction. By running about 10 percent lower air pressure than you normally would, a UST tire's tread can spread out wider, yielding a larger contact patch on the trail. With a typical tube-type tire, inflation pressure must be kept higher to minimize the risk of pinch-flatting and to reduce rolling resistance caused by friction between tube and tire as the tire tries to deflect and adapt to changes in the terrain. Here are the steps for changing UST tires.

Remove the tire. Once deflated, pinch the tire's sidewalls toward one another until you feel and hear one of the beads pop out of its channel. This may take some force.

Get a grip. If pinching isn't enough, grip the tire firmly from the top with your strong hand and the rim from beneath with your weak hand. Pull with your weak hand and push the tire with the heel of your strong hand. Few tires should be able to resist this technique. Determine which side has come free and continue pushing this bead out of its channel all the way around the tire.

Tuck the bead into the center of the rim, where the rim's diameter is smallest. You should then be able to carefully pry the first tire bead over the rim wall by hand. Tire levers can rupture the airtight lining of the tire or scratch the sealing surface of the rim, so it's best to avoid their use entirely. Some tires, of course, will defy even the strongest of fingers. Reach for a lever only as a last resort.

Good things come in threes. For those exceptionally tight tires, get three of the widest, flattest plastic tire levers you can find. Pry the tire with a lever and use the lever's hook to hold it in place on a spoke. Repeat this with a second tire lever, and then a third. Remove the middle tire lever and "leapfrog" past the third, repeating this step until the tire bead is sufficiently loose to release the rest of the bead by hand. Pop the second bead free of its channel in the same manner you did the first. Once out of its channel, the second bead should come off the rim with relative ease.

Flat repair. Patching a UST tire is done in much the same way that you would patch an inner tube, but the patch is installed on the *inside* of the tire, not the outside. First determine the nature of the leak. A simple puncture from a thorn, shard of glass, nail, etc., can be patched using a vulcanizing glue patch like those used for patching inner tubes, or with a tubeless-specific patch like the one manufactured by Hutchinson. Most tubeless tire manufacturers recommend against glueless patches.

Cleanliness is next to airtightness. Locate and remove the cause of the puncture from the outside of the tire. While you're at it, check the whole tire for other debris that could cause trouble farther down the trail. On the inside of the tire, clean the area around the puncture, ensuring that it is free of debris.

Go ahead, be rough. Using a coarse piece of sandpaper or other abrasive material, deeply scuff the butyl liner in the area surrounding the hole slightly larger than the patch you will use. Apply a dot of glue and spread it around the abraded area.

Be patient. Let the glue set up for several minutes—and don't let one of your know-it-all buddies convince you to burn off the evaporating fumes with a match or lighter to speed the process! When the glue has gone from clear to cloudy, it's ready for the patch.

Stick it. Peel the foil backing from the patch, exposing the colored side (usually orange), press it firmly into the glue, and hold it there for at least 60 seconds. Press on the edges, ensuring that the patch has completely bonded to the tire's liner. It's not necessary to remove the clear plastic from the patch you've just applied, but doing so will tell you whether you've done a thorough job of bonding the patch. If the patch begins peeling away as you try to remove the clear film, the edges may not be fully glued. You can touch up loose edges by spreading a small amount of glue with the tip of your finger.

PINCH-FLATS

Though less common with tubeless tires, pinch-flats can and do happen. Unfortunately, patching a pinched UST tire is almost never successful. As such, it's a good idea to carry a spare inner tube even though you may be riding tubeless. Even if you never need it, you just might make the day of one of your more old-fashioned-but-unprepared riding partners. After removing the valve stem according to your wheel manufacturer's method, installing a tube in a tubeless tire is no different than with any standard tube, tire, and rim combination.

MOUNTING A UST TIRE

A tubeless tire installs in a manner very similar to any tube-type clincher tire.

Hey, slick. Start by spraying the inside of the rim with a diluted soap-and-water solution—about ½ teaspoon of dish soap to 32 ounces of water works well. If you don't have a spray bottle, apply the soapy water solution with a soaked rag or paper towel.

Mount up. Align the tire label with the valve stem, and mount the first tire bead into place on the rim. Work the second bead onto the rim. Pushing the bead into the centermost, deepest portion of the rim will make the last portion of the bead slip easily over the rim's wall.

Extra leverage. Use plastic tire levers for the last short section of the bead if it proves too much for your thumbs to handle. Be gentle, and use the widest, flattest levers available. There's no tube to pinch, but remember that you don't want to damage that liner.

Air up. Check once more that all of both beads are nestled in the center of the rim. Getting the beads to move into their seats is the trickiest part of UST mounting. Compressed air works best, a floor pump is next best, and a handheld mini pump is little more than 12 inches of frustration. Quickly pump the tire to about 20 psi. At this point the tire should take shape and the beads should form a loose seal, making the rest of the process easier. Slowly continue adding air until the beads begin to audibly "pop" into the bead seats. Stubborn tires can sometimes be coaxed into place. Grip the inflated tire with your palms near the point where the bead will not seat and rotate your hands forward.

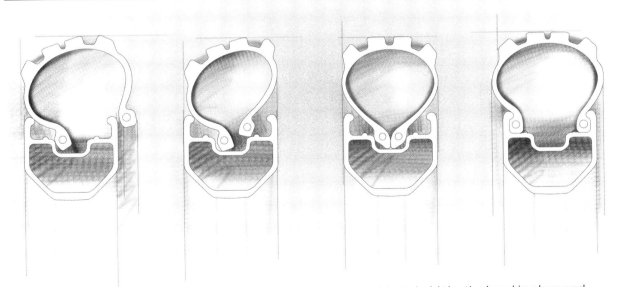

Tubeless mountain bike tires rely on a specially shaped rim or rimstrip to hold the tire bead in place and create an airtight seal.

Keep a sharp eye. Inspect the sidewalls for uniform seating and keep adding pressure (up to a maximum of 60 psi) until the bead-seat indicator (a textured ring that extends about ⅛ inch above the rim wall on most tires) is equally exposed all the way around on both sides of the tire. From here, lower the pressure to your riding preference and you're done.

MOUNTING AND REPAIRING TUBULAR TIRES

Tubular, or sew-up, tires used for road, track, and sometimes cyclo-cross racing are glued to the rim with a special contact cement. This bond is critical because if a tubular comes off the rim, a crash is almost guaranteed. Proper gluing is the key, and the first step is cleaning the rim. Sand it lightly with emery cloth to scuff up the surface and give the glue a little more purchase. Using acetone or alcohol, clean the rim of any oil or other contaminants.

For a new tubular, it's best to first put it on a rim without cement, inflate it, and let it sit. This stretches the tire and makes mounting easier when you're gluing it on. Start by putting a bit of air in the tire so it has a shape but no pressure. Then set the wheel vertically on the ground in front of you, with the valve hole on top. Insert the valve through the hole and grasp the tire on either side with your hands. Place each section onto the rim, and advance down the sides, lifting each section of the tire onto the rim.

Bending over the wheel, continue to mount the tire while watching the valve to see that it remains straight. If it becomes crooked, pull the tire harder with one hand to correct. As your hands near the bottom of the wheel, the tire will become tight. Use your body weight to stretch the tire into place. Pop on the last difficult section by lifting the wheel off the ground and rolling that tire section away and then onto the rim with your thumbs.

Move around the wheel, straightening the tire, and then add full air pressure. Let the tire sit for a while—preferably overnight, but at least 10 or 15 minutes—to give it time to stretch (the longer you wait, the easier it'll be to mount after gluing).

When the tire has stretched, remove it from the rim. Place the wheel in the bike, suspend the bike, and dab the tubular cement between each spoke hole on the rim. Put your index finger inside a plastic baggie, then hold it on the rim as you slowly turn the wheel with your free hand and smear the glue to create an even coat that reaches from sidewall to sidewall. Then apply a bead of glue to the centerline of the tire's base tape. Spread this glue to cover the entire base tape using an old toothbrush or a flux brush—something that you don't mind tossing out afterward.

Allow the first glue coat to dry for an hour, and then add a second coat. Wait about 15 minutes for this coat to get tacky. Then mount the tire exactly as before. Work carefully so you don't get glue all over the sidewalls of the tires. You'll know you did a good job of gluing if, when eventually punctured, the tire is nearly impossible to remove from the rim.

When mounting a tubular tire on a used rim, you'll be faced with a buildup of old glue on the rim. It's not necessary to remove this old glue, but it's important to have a smooth surface for the tire, or it won't sit properly when installed. You also don't want any loose bits of dried glue that can prevent the new glue from holding the tire to the rim.

To prepare the rim, place it in the bike frame (the tire should already be removed) and turn it while scraping with a tool that fits the shape of the tire seat on the rim. Cone wrenches often fit nicely here, but anything that fits the rim's shape and has a good scraping edge will work. Spin the wheel while you hold the scraper's edge against the rim to chip off the loose glue and smooth the rim's surface. It doesn't have to be perfect, just smooth and flat enough for a good glue purchase and for the tire to sit properly on the rim. When the rim is prepared, glue it as directed and mount the tire.

Patching tubular tires. Repairing tubulars is slow but fairly easy work. When possible, locate the puncture while the tire is still on the rim. Inflate the tire and listen for leaks. If you don't hear air escaping, hold the tire near your face and turn it, trying to feel the air (this sounds nutty, but the skin on your face is very sensitive). Look closely for a hole or cut in the casing that is the point of the puncture. Once you locate it, mark the spot so you can find it again quickly after you get the tire off the rim.

Unfortunately, some leaks are difficult to pinpoint. If you can't locate the precise point of the problem by one of the above methods, pull the tire off the rim and try another method.

If you have a slow leak, try pumping up the tire and immersing it in water, watching for bubbles. Unfortunately, air bubbles sometimes travel inside the tire casing before emerging into the water, so this method isn't foolproof.

The most certain way of pinpointing the tire leak is to isolate one section of the tire at a time and see if any air escapes from the rest of the tire. If not, the problem lies in the isolated section. Try blocking off a section of tire by squeezing it between your hands. A more elaborate method is to clamp a couple of short 2×4-inch blocks around the tire, section by section. Once you've located the source of the problem, begin your repair.

A tubular tire has protective tape called base tape over the stitching that holds it together. This tape is bonded to the tire with liquid latex, not rim cement. Cut the tape and pull it back to expose about 6 inches of stitching at the location of the puncture. Mark the stitches with a permanent marker so you can tell which holes line up across from each other after the thread has been removed.

Use a sewing seam ripper or a knife to cut the stitching threads. Pull the tire open and remove the thread remnants. Carefully pull aside any protective gauze or tape to expose the tube. Lift out the tube and look for the leak. Patch the leak using the same methods used for ordinary tubes. If it's a latex tube (very thin and flesh-colored), it's possible to patch it with a piece of latex cut from a discarded tubular tube. Just apply glue to both the tube and the patch, wait for the glue to dry, and press them together.

While you have the tire open, look inside to see if any pieces of the object that caused the puncture are embedded in the casing. Remove any offending material. Usually there'll be a visible black mark if an object has penetrated the casing, and it's easy to see because the casing is light-colored. Also check to see if any casing threads are cut. Reinforce any damage with a casing patch. Cut your own patch out of a piece of old tire or strong canvas or nylon. A generous size is best; overlaps of 2 inches or more are suitable. Sheer pressure will keep the casing patch (or "boot") in place, so there is no need to cement it.

Sprinkle a little talc into the casing to help the tube slide back into place. If necessary, wiggle the tire to help the tube position itself properly, then straighten the inner gauze or tape. You're now ready to restitch the tire around the tube, but take special care to use the exact same holes as were originally used for this. You don't want to weaken the casing by poking new holes through it. A simple overhand stitch works fine, or use a sewing awl of the type used by leather workers to reconstruct the original cross pattern. Use strong thread or, in a pinch, dental floss, overlapping generously at the ends to prevent unraveling.

It's very important not to pull the thread too tight as you stitch. Doing so can pinch the two edges of the tire casing together, creating a ridge on the bottom of the tire, which causes a problem. The bottom of the tire must retain a flat profile so the base tape will stick and the tire will sit flat when re-installed on the rim. If the casing edges are pinched, they will form a ridge that prevents the tire from sitting flat on the rim. To ensure this doesn't happen, while stitching, pull the thread just tight enough to bring the two edges of the casing together. Check the tire while stitching occasionally to make sure the finished seam will lay flat when you're done.

Another common problem is stitching the tire using the wrong holes. This is possible even if you mark the holes and are very careful. If you make this mistake, you'll end up with an S-shape in the tread of the tire, so check for this after resewing tubulars. If you find that the tread now has an S in it, cut the threads you just put in and restitch the tire using the correct holes. Any time you cut a tire for surgery, mark the holes in such a way that you can't possibly stitch the tire back up with the wrong ones.

Glue the rim strip back in place with liquid latex. This is the same material used to coat and protect the tire's sidewalls after extended use dries them out. Now you have a perfect spare tire.

The residue of rim cement left on the tire means it will achieve a decent bond with the rim when installed on the road. A brand-new, never-cemented spare tire is dangerous, so use a repaired tire as your spare. Or, if you must use a new tire as a spare, put a proper layer of glue on the base tape first. It's best to fold the spare four or five times and keep it in a simple pouch or old sock to protect it from wear and tear and exposure.

WHEEL BASICS

All wheel maintenance and repair can be done with your wheel mounted in your bicycle or on a truing stand. To work on a bike-mounted wheel, suspend the bike from the rafters, fasten it in a repair stand, or simply upend it so the wheels can turn freely.

At least once a month, clean the wheels with a rag or with soap and water (keep it away from the hub bearings and brake discs). Inspect the tires for cuts and bruises. If they're grimy, wipe down the rims, hubs, and spokes with a clean cloth lightly dampened with a solvent such as kerosene. (Again, keep the solvent away from the hub's bearings.) Brake pad material that accumulates on the rim can interfere with braking performance and is tough to dislodge. Use an abrasive pad or mild-grade steel wool to remove this residue.

After extended exposure to the elements, spoke nipples may resist turning, making corrections in spoke tension difficult. Before adjusting your spokes, lightly lubricate the nipples with penetrating oil. Place oil on the spokes where they enter the nipples and between the nipples and rim.

Turn the wheel and wiggle each spoke to feel how tight it is to find any loose or broken spokes. These, of course, will require attention. Check the rim closely for bends, wobbles, or dents. A wheel can wobble for several reasons. You must identify the source of the problem before trying to fix it.

Loose hub bearings. If you push laterally on the wheel and feel play, the hub bearings have loosened. This makes truing nearly impossible. Adjust the hub bearings before truing the wheel. See Chapter 5 for instructions on hub adjustment.

Incorrect spoke tension. With experience, you'll be able to find loose spokes by feel. Generally, loose spokes cause the wheel to go out of true. The repair is as easy as retensioning the loose spokes, but keep the following points in mind whenever you begin to true your wheels.

• You need not remove the tire to true the wheel, but you ought to release most of its air pressure. Otherwise, the turning nipple may cut through the rim strip and puncture the tube.

• Beware of spoke wind-up while you turn the nipple. This can occur when damaged or inadequately lubricated threads cause the spoke to twist with the nipple instead of threading into the nipple. Check for this by feeling the spoke with two fingers while turning the nipple. Back off to unwind the shaft if necessary.

• Pliers and crescent wrenches are no substitute for the right spoke wrench (there are four basic sizes). A damaged nipple is undesirable and often can't be removed without cutting and replacing its spoke. A spoke with a frozen (rusted) nipple must be replaced.

• Work in small increments. Adjust nipples only one-quarter turn at a time to avoid making overcompensations in spoke tension. Larger adjustments can be made if you have enough experience to know when they're appropriate.

• The tension in neighboring spokes on the same side of a wheel should be similar. Pluck them to compare their sounds.

• If, to straighten a wobble, the correction calls for tightening a spoke that can't be further tightened or loosening one that is already slack, then you're probably dealing with a bent rim. If the spokes can't correct the bend, attempt to forcefully rebend the rim (maybe over your knee) and try truing again. Chances are the rim will simply have to be replaced.

Broken spokes. Broken spokes must be removed and replaced as soon as possible. It's usually best to replace the nipple as well. If the wheel is otherwise undamaged, the replacement will be very easy. With a rear wheel, the gear cluster (cassette) may need to be removed. Thread a new spoke (get the right length) through the hub and up to the nipple, copying exactly the pattern of the other spokes. You may bow it considerably for installation, as long as you avoid sharp bends near the elbow and you make sure to straighten it afterward. Tighten the new spoke until its tension resembles its neighbors (pluck the spokes and compare their sounds).

Tighten further, if necessary, to straighten the rim at that point. This process is usually as simple as retuning a radio station after the dial is mistakenly brushed. Tighten and loosen only the new spoke until the rim runs true. On some very light or excessively tight wheels, a broken spoke leaves a kink in the rim that the new spoke can't correct. Sometimes the wheel is lost, though often it's salvageable.

Dents and bends. Small dents that widen a rim cause choppy braking action but can be eliminated by a gentle squeeze with a smooth jaw vise. Avoid overcorrecting by squeezing only a little at a time. Spoke readjustments can also help hide the damage. Small dents on narrow clinchers can often be remedied by grabbing the bent rim bead seat with a narrow-jawed crescent wrench, levering out and up.

Larger dents are serious business and require expertise. One way to undent a "flat" spot in a rim is to release the spokes at the point of damage and suspend the wheel off the ground with that position down. Slip between the spokes over the flat spot a 2×4 that's about 1 foot long. Strike the wood with a hammer, pounding the dent away from the hub. You may want to first carve the wood to the shape of the rim where they contact.

Keep pounding until the rim is very slightly bulging. Beware—it may take less force than you expect, so begin with light blows. Some lightweight rims will fail when subjected to this treatment, so don't assume success. If the correction is more than ½ inch or the rim ends up with cracks or wrinkles, the result may be unstable and therefore unsafe.

Sideways bends are tricky to fix. A typical cure for a small local bend is to release some of the spoke tension at the bend and then remove the wheel from the bike or truing stand. Kneel on the ground and lay the wheel on its side in front of you with the bent section facing down and positioned nearest you. Lean over the wheel and grasp the rim 8 to 10 inches to either side of the bent section, pressing it to the ground. By applying some of your body weight, you can force the rim back into shape. If you're lucky, you may be able to retension the spokes and reuse the wheel.

EMERGENCY WHEEL AND TIRE REPAIRS

So it looks like your wheel or tire is too far gone to be repairable.

Never say never. If a mishap disables your bike, it's time for emergency measures. Tire damage is the most likely inconvenience. When you discover that your tire casing has a cut that is so large that the tire can't hold the tube at pressure, use an internal reinforcing patch. In an emergency, such a "boot" can be made of scraps of clothing, high-fiber paper such as currency, or whatever is available. The less suitable the reinforcement, the less air pressure you can use before the tube bulges out. If the casing damage is near one of the tire's beads, wrap a long piece of cloth around the tube next to the inside of the tire and circle it around the tire's beads so that it will be held between the tire and rim when the tire is reinflated. Carry such a piece of reinforcement in your tool kit, something like a 5 × 10-inch rectangle of tough nylon.

A broken spoke must be removed as soon as detected or, at least, wrapped around a neighboring spoke to prevent tangles. If the damaged wheel won't clear the brakes or frame, some on-the-spot truing might help. A spoke wrench is almost essential, but other metal grabbers like crescent wrenches and pliers can do the trick in a pinch. Position the spoke to be adjusted near the frame stays or fork. Use your hand to pull the rim in the direction of the spoke that needs to be tightened, grasping the rim and frame together and squeezing. With such a deflection, the spoke will become slack and easy to turn.

Emergency spokes. A handy thing to have when traveling is a batch of special spokes that can be installed without removing the wheel, tire, or cassette. These are called emergency spokes and they're easy to make. Start by going to a shop to get a few spokes that match the thread of those on your wheels (usually 56 threads per inch) but are about ½ inch longer than yours.

You may want to take the wheel with you to see if the new spokes will thread into the existing nipples. If you have an odd thread, you'll need to purchase nipples to go with your emergency spokes. And when it comes time to install an emergency spoke, you'll need to replace the old nipple with a new one. The benefit of getting emergency spokes that match the thread of your existing spokes is being able to simply thread the emergency spoke into the old nipple, which saves deflating the tire, rolling the tire, tube, and rim strip back, and replacing the old nipple when you need to replace a spoke.

To turn the spokes into the emergency spokes, cut off the spoke elbows using a diagonal cutter. Bend the ends of the spokes into L-shapes. The tricky part is getting the bend at the correct point so that spoke length will match the spokes in your wheel. If you can't get it perfect, it's better to err on the short, not long, side.

When you're done bending, the end of the spoke should have two 90-degree bends in it, one at right angles to the long straight part of the spoke, and the other at right angles to the first bent section. If the spoke is held upright, it'll look like an L-shape was bent into the spoke end.

To use an emergency spoke on a ride, first remove the broken spoke. Then wiggle the L-shaped end of the emergency spoke into the hole in the hub any way you can get it to fit, weave it through the spokes and up to the nipple, and tighten the nipple until the plucked spoke sounds like the others. Check wheel trueness and adjust as needed. Then you're set to go, with none of the fuss of wheel, tire, and cassette removal.

Taco'd rim repair. In the case of complete wheel collapse, little can be done besides rebuilding. But it's sometimes possible to straighten even badly damaged wheels well enough to get you home by using one of a handful of brute-force techniques (sure to impress your ride partners). Two that we've found to be most successful are highlighted here.

If the wheel assumes a very symmetrical "taco" or "potato chip" shape, try bouncing it back to normal. Lay the wheel on the ground and kneel over it, holding opposite edges of the rim in each hand. Grab the high spots and press them down forcefully. Occasionally, this will cause the wheel to spring back to rideable condition. If so, consider yourself lucky. This procedure may get you home, but the wheel still needs rebuilding with a new rim.

If a skid or crash bends one section of rim badly out of true, try inserting that section in a narrow slot and bending it back into line by levering the rest of the wheel. Such a slot can be a doorjamb, sewer grating, or space between boulders or trees. Use your imagination.

Whether you use such drastic methods or simply phone home is your decision. But bicycles are tools of survival, and many irreverent and impromptu repairs have kept them on their way.

WHEEL CONSTRUCTION

Wheel building is impossibly complex unless you start with the right parts. It'll help a lot to have an expert select matching hubs, spokes, and rims. Arrange the parts and inspect them for flaws of any kind. Apply thread compound (a special lubricant), oil, or grease to the spokes. Then insert the spokes in the hub.

Lacing. Connect the spokes one "round" at a time. The wheel consists of four rounds, each inserted into the hub flanges from a different direction. In a 36-spoke wheel, each round contains 9

ROTATING DIRECTION OF WHEEL

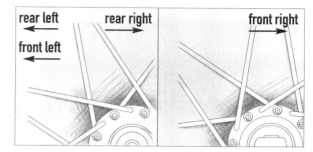

Shimano has recommended very specific patterns for lacing disc brake wheels to stress the spokes in a manner that maintains the structural integrity of the wheel.

spokes. Start by holding the hub in front of you, axle pointing down. If you're working on a rear hub, hold the cassette side down (the cassette gears must be removed). Drop 9 spokes into the top flange, using every other hole. Have a seat and hold the rim around the hub, either balanced on a bench in front of you or on your knees. Orient the rim so the valve hole is opposite your stomach.

Lift one of the spokes and stick it through the hole to the left of the valve hole, and attach a nipple loosely. This hole should be drilled a bit offset toward the top of the rim; it's intended for spokes from the top hub flange. If the holes are drilled some other way, then you're out of luck—you'll have to seek another lacing method. Luckily, 98 percent of all modern rims are drilled with the left hole offset up. Now take the spoke next to your first and insert it into the rim, leaving three rim holes empty between it and the first. Attach the nipple and proceed to insert and attach the rest of this round of spokes.

Rotate the hub counterclockwise so that the original spoke slants away from the valve hole in the rim. That's the direction in which the first round of spokes must slant in the completed wheel.

Flip the rim and hub over so the other flange is on top. Look carefully from the top to the bottom flange and notice that the holes are not drilled in line with one another. They're offset so that a spoke dropped straight through one hole will hit the other flange directly between two holes. Drop the first spoke in this second round into the hub hole that allows it to line up next to the first spoke in the first round (the spoke that's one rim hole away from the valve hole). Lift up this new spoke (the 10th, if you're lacing a 36-spoke wheel) into the rim hole that is next to spoke number one and that is two holes away from the valve hole. Attach a nipple and then insert the remaining spokes of round two, inserting the spokes into the next available hole to the right of each round-one spoke. This time, don't flip the wheel for the next round.

Drop the spokes set aside for round three through the remaining spoke holes in the bottom (first) flange of the hub. After this comes the only complicated part of the lacing procedure. Lift the rim up off your lap so it sits vertically, just as it does on the bike. The round-three spokes should all fall sideways, hanging loosely by their elbows. If they don't, help them to do so. Lay the wheel down flat again, flipping it so that the round-three spokes are on top. Holding the rim still, twist the hub relative to the rim, away from the valve hole. If you twisted correctly, then spokes number 1 and number 10 (for a 36-spoke wheel) will be parallel and will exit the rim moving away from rather than over the valve hole.

Each round-three spoke will travel in the opposing direction from the round-one spoke with which it shares the upper hub flange. Now is the time to arrange the correct cross pattern. In the case of the three-cross pattern, each spoke will pass over two and under one round-one spoke before entering its rim hole. The first spoke cross occurs right at the hub. Grab any loose round-three spoke and direct it over two and under one round-one spoke, then insert it into the first available rim hole. Loosely attach the nipple and go to the next. Don't worry if the spokes seem a tight fit in the hub. It's an inconvenient but healthy sign.

Round four is a repeat of three. Without flipping the wheel in your lap, drop the remaining spokes into the open holes in the bottom flange. Lift the wheel up vertically so the loose spokes can fall down. Then lay the wheel down the opposite way so the round-four spokes are now on top. Lace each to the remaining rim holes, following the same cross pattern as before.

Initial tensioning. With all the spokes attached, it's time to mount the wheel in a truing stand or bicycle so your hands will be free. Where the nipples enter the rim, oil them with some mild lubricant so they'll turn easily. Tighten each until three threads

are showing. While the wheel is still loose, bend the spokes near the elbows so they conform to their new directions. Press the outside spokes toward the hub with your thumb or a mallet so they'll rest flat against the flanges.

If you're using the correct spoke length, the spokes should be fairly loose at this point. Tighten each nipple one-half to one turn (when they're at the top of the wheel, turn the nipple clockwise) and check tension. Repeat this uniform tightening until the spokes begin to feel slightly snug. You need a little spoke tension to begin truing.

Truing. The wheel must be straightened in both radial and lateral directions until it's as true as you want it. Master wheelbuilders get the wheel round up and down and true laterally with as little spoke tension in the wheel as possible. We call this point of supreme straightness at minimum tension "ground zero." Once ground zero is achieved, the wheel is finished by adding layers of tension until the spokes are tight enough. If you get the wheel true at ground zero, tension can be added with little disturbance of the trueness. Any other procedure is full of risks and delays.

True away lateral wobbles first. If the rim is out to the left, loosen the left-side spokes at the wobble and tighten the right-side ones. If the problem is on the right, tighten the left-side spokes and loosen the right ones. Turn the nipples in one-half-turn increments. After getting one spot straight, move to the next until the wheel is as true laterally as you can get it.

When the side-to-side wobbles are gone, concentrate on roundness, turning the spokes in half-turn increments. Spin the wheel and watch for high and low spots. Usually, a high spot has a corresponding low spot on the other side of the wheel. Find the low spot and loosen the spokes. Then snug the spokes at the high spot. Move to the next low and high spot. Once you've made the rim as round as you can get it, go back to side-to-side truing (because the roundness adjustments probably affected the side-to-side). Alternate between trueness and roundness, patiently making small corrections. Like silver that is being polished, the wheel will begin to show the results of your patient efforts. Once the wheel is very true, it's time to add tension.

Sometimes you'll find a rim with a bad seam (usually the seam is opposite the valve hole). You'll notice it because it'll appear as a blip when you're truing. You want to fix bad seams because they can make the brake grab. To fix it, lay the rim on a vise or benchtop, and strike the high part of the rim with a mallet or hammer. Be careful not to bend it too far in. It should be flush with the other part of the rim. If that doesn't work, sand it smooth.

Before a wheel is done, you must ensure that the rim is centered over the hub. Otherwise, when you install it in the frame or fork, it may sit crooked. Use a wheel dishing tool to check. Or, put the wheel in your frame or fork, reverse the wheel, and sight to see if the rim is in the same place regardless of hub direction. A dished wheel will always present its rim at the same spot whether the hub is in forward or backward. Correct any asymmetry by tightening only one side of the wheel to draw the rim nearer to one or another of the hub's locknuts as needed.

Adding tension. A true wheel at low tension is a very cooperative subject. Go around the wheel, adding a layer of tension by turning each nipple one-half turn. On rear wheels, turn left-side spokes one-quarter and right-side spokes one-half turn, which will keep the rim centered. Check trueness and adjust as necessary, then add another layer of tension. Continue to add layers of tension until the total is similar to another good wheel. Pluck the spokes and listen. Remember that in a rear wheel, it's normal for the left side to be considerably looser than the right. Whenever you tighten a nipple, its spoke tends to wind up a bit. So after turning, back off a bit so the spoke can unwind. If you don't, the hidden windup will be released while riding, spoiling the wheel's straightness.

Prestressing. To begin the final step, grab parallel sets of spokes on opposite sides of the wheel, left and right, in each hand. Squeeze each pair firmly to stretch and stress the spokes. This technique will set up the elbows for greater fatigue life and stretch all the parts so that use won't cause loosening. If the wheel becomes unacceptably loose, add tension. If it goes wildly out of true, it's possible there is too much tension in the wheel. Retrue it and try again. If it's unstable a second time, try loosening it before a third stress step. The wheel is ready to ride when the spokes are sufficiently tight and the wheel doesn't go out of true when you squeeze the spokes. Getting the right tension is the hardest part to learn. If in doubt, show your wheel to an expert.

Remember that a builder's goal is to build a wheel that runs straight but also has a high uniform tension. The best wheel isn't necessarily the straightest but the most equally reinforced by its spokes. Don't just be a wheel truer, be a tension equalizer. If you're unsure of which adjustment to make, pluck the candidate spokes and loosen the tightest and tighten the loosest. Steps taken to equalize tension nearly always contribute to a better wheel.

Wheel repair and building is a vast and detailed science. The brief tips offered here ought to get you off to a good start. But never tire of asking questions and seeking additional information, and don't forget to enjoy the fruits of your labors. Good rolling!

TROUBLESHOOTING

PROBLEM: Every time you fix a flat, the tire goes flat again.

SOLUTION: Check the tube carefully. Are the holes in one area? If they're on the bottom, the rim strip may be out of position, allowing the tube to get cut by the spokes. If they're on top, there may be some small sharp object still stuck in the tire. Find it by running a rag around the inside of the tire, and get it out of the tire.

PROBLEM: The tire loses air slowly.

SOLUTION: Put some spit on the Schrader valve and watch to see if a bubble forms, indicating a slow leak. Tighten the valve, or remove it and apply a drop of oil on the rubber seal, then reinstall. If it's not the valve, remove the tube, inflate it, and hold it under water to find the hole.

PROBLEM: You keep getting pinch-flats.

SOLUTION: Put more air in your tires, or install wider tires.

PROBLEM: It's hard to install the tires because the tube gets in the way.

SOLUTION: Tire installation is easiest if you use a tube that's narrower than the tire. Switch to either thinner tubes or wider tires.

PROBLEM: You got the tire on but it won't sit right on the rim.

SOLUTION: Let the air out, wiggle the bad spot around, reinflate to about 30 psi, and roll the bad spot into place with your hands. Then inflate fully. If this doesn't work, try letting the air out, applying a soapy solution to the tire, and reinflating.

PROBLEM: The patch won't stick to the tube.

SOLUTION: Put on enough glue and let it dry completely (about 5 minutes). Never touch the sticky side of the patch with your fingers. Don't blow on the glue to get it to dry faster because you may get water on the glue.

PROBLEM: You can't get air in your aero wheels.

SOLUTION: Get tubes with long enough valves (they must protrude enough to get the pump on) or get valve extenders. Be sure to leave the presta valve unscrewed when installing the valve extenders.

PROBLEM: Your tubeless tire loses air slowly.

SOLUTION: Remove the tire and check the rim for foreign matter in the bead channel. Ironically enough, one manufacturer's quality control sticker has a nasty habit of sliding into the bead channel and causing a slow leak.

A dent or nick in the rim can also cause slow air loss. Aside from rebuilding with a new rim, there is no way to repair this. If the rim is still able to hold a tire, you can use a standard tire and tube on a UST tubeless rim.

PROBLEM: You finish repairing a tubular tire and find that you've created an S shape in the tread.

SOLUTION: You stitched the tire up using the wrong holes. Cut your stitches and try again. Next time, mark the casing so you'll know which holes to use when restitching.

PROBLEM: You keep breaking spokes.

SOLUTION: Usually this is because the wheel is built of poor-quality spokes. Replace them with better-quality spokes, such as DT or Wheelsmith stainless-steel models.

PROBLEM: It's always a struggle to install the wheels after removal. The wheel doesn't seem to want to fit into the frame.

SOLUTION: Remember to place the chain on the same cog it was on when you took the wheel off (usually the smallest cog). If you're doing that and it's still difficult, the frame dropouts may be bent, which can make wheel installation a pain. Have a shop check and align them with special tools.

PROBLEM: The wheels won't stay true.

SOLUTION: True them and make sure that the spoke tension is sufficient and uniform. If the spokes continually loosen, add a round of tension to the spokes, which should stabilize the wheel.

PROBLEM: You're about to head out on a ride when you realize your only spare tube has a presta valve. Trouble is, your bike is set up with Schrader valves.

SOLUTION: Take the tube along. The valve will fit loosely in the Schrader-size hole in the rim, but it will still work fine. In fact, you can get rubber inserts to downsize the rim's valve hole if you want to switch to presta valves permanently. Or, if you have presta-drilled rims and want to switch to Schrader, just drill the rim holes with a ¼-inch drill bit to enlarge them.

PROBLEM: You're trying to upgrade wheels and you discover that the new wheels won't fit into the frame. It seems like they want to go but something is getting hung up.

SOLUTION: In order for any wheel to fit in a frame, the over-locknut distance on the hub (measured from locknut to locknut on the axle) must match the dropout-to-dropout distance (the distance between the inside faces of the front or rear dropouts) in the frame. Most front wheels are 100 mm, while rears can be 120, 125, 126, 127, 130, 135, or 140 mm. If you're trying to fit a too-wide hub, have the frame realigned by a shop so the wheel will slide right in (this works on steel frames only).

PROBLEM: You want to change a bike that has 27-inch wheels to 700C wheels because that's what everyone has today.

SOLUTION: Proceed carefully. Before you spend any money, try a friend's 700C wheels on your bike to make sure that your brake pads can be lowered enough and adjusted to strike the 700C rims properly. The brakes may not reach because 700C rims are smaller in diameter than 27-inch rims. If your brakes don't reach, stick with 27-inch wheels. There's no big advantage to 700C anyway.

PROBLEM: There's a creaking sound from the wheels.

SOLUTION: The spokes may have loosened. Tighten them slightly. If they're tight, the spokes may be moving slightly at the cross, causing the sound. Lubricate each cross of the spokes with light oil and wipe off the excess.

PROBLEM: You have a radial-spoked wheel (the spokes travel directly from the hub to the rim without crossing other spokes) on which the spokes continually loosen.

SOLUTION: Try adding tension to the spokes. If the spokes loosen again, it's probably because of the spoke pattern. Radial spokes take shocks more directly than spokes that cross others, so they're more apt to loosen. To keep them tight, loosen all the nipples, apply a light thread adhesive to the nipple, and retension the wheel. Your loosening troubles should cease.

Wheel Removal and Remounting

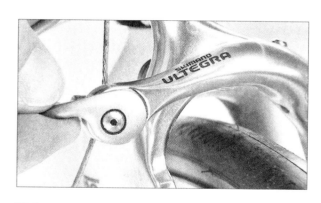

1 If your bike is equipped with quick-release hubs, removing the front wheel is quite simple. First, open the brake quick-release lever to spread the caliper arms wider so the tire can pass between the brake shoes without hanging up.

2 For cantilevers, squeeze the pads to the rim with one hand and lift the end of the transverse cable.

3 For Shimano V-Brakes or similar brakes, release the "noodle" out of its pocket in the brake arm (see photo).

When locked, quick-release levers should be parallel with the bike frame. Grab the lever and twist it in a 180-degree arc away from the frame and on around until it's parallel with the frame again (see photo 4). The wheel should now be loose enough to drop out of the frame. If not, give it a push or a tug to force the axle out of the dropouts.

If that doesn't do it, the fork is probably equipped with a wheel-retention device, which prevents the wheel from coming off even if it's loose. To remove the wheel, hold one end of the quick-release and unscrew the other end several turns to open the quick-release farther and allow it to clear the retention stops.

4 If your wheel is fastened in the bike frame with nuts, loosen one of the nuts slightly with a wrench. Then move the wrench to the other side of the wheel and loosen the other nut in the same way. Or put a separate wrench on each nut and break both free at the same time.

Loosen each nut just enough to allow the wheel to drop out of the frame.

Watch the axle as you rotate the nuts to make sure you're not altering the adjustment of the bearing cones and changing their position on the axle. When fastening the wheel back on the bike, the same amount of axle should protrude from each side.

If your bike isn't equipped with quick-release hubs, chances are it also lacks a brake quick-release. In this case, deflate the tire slightly.

5 Disc brakes can become very hot during a ride and are also very sensitive to oil contamination. The trace amounts of oil on your skin can sometimes be enough to ruin a pair of disc brake pads. To avoid unnecessary contact with the brake disc, consider mounting your quick-release levers on the side opposite the disc.

6 This enables you to squeeze the tire through the brake shoes to remove the wheel. Another way to create the room needed is to remove a brake pad (see photo).

A rear wheel is a bit more complicated to remove because of the chain and the cassette cogs. First, shift gears so that the chain is on both the smallest chainring and smallest rear cog. Spread the brakes and loosen the wheel.

Then, either lift the chain off the rear cog or pull the derailleur back to help free the chain from the cog (see photo 6). Strike the wheel to dislodge it, and move it down and out, disentangling it from the chain as you proceed.

Replace the wheels by following the same procedure in reverse order. Pull the rear derailleur back to take tension off the chain while you install the wheel.

7 Center each wheel in the frame and tighten it in place. If the wheel is fastened with nuts, tighten each the same amount until both are very tight. If the wheels are quick-release, push the levers into the locked position to ensure that they're very tight and can't loosen accidentally. Fine-tune the quick-release adjustment by turning the nut on the opposite end of the skewer before locking the lever.

Rotate the quick-release lever so that when open it points forward and when locked it points toward the back of the bike. This will eliminate the possibility of the lever accidentally catching on something and loosening while you're riding.

Lastly, make sure everything is in working order and the pads are centered on the rim. Make sure all bolts and fasteners are tight.

Clincher Removal, Repair, and Remounting

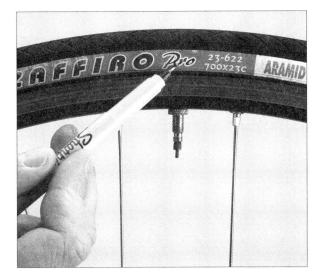

1 Whenever a tire goes flat and needs repair, don't ride on it any farther. Push or carry your bike to a safe spot, then remove the wheel from the bike to repair the tire.

Before taking the tire and tube apart, mark the tire next to the valve stem to establish the relationship between the tire and tube (or simply always place the tire label by the valve stem). This makes it easier later to locate any foreign matter that may still be embedded in the tire casing.

2 If any air remains in the tire, let it out by pressing on the valve (unscrew the tip of a presta valve first). Start your tire removal on the side of the rim opposite the stem to minimize chances of damaging the stem. Squeeze the sides of the tire toward the trough at the center of the rim to produce some slack, then hook a tire lever under the edge of the tire and pull it over the rim. (Make sure your tire levers have no sharp edges that could further damage the tube. There are good plastic tire levers available that are less likely than metal ones to damage a tube.)

Move a few inches along the rim, hook a second tire lever under the same bead, and pull it over the rim (see photo). If necessary, use a third tire lever. Once you get several inches of the tire diameter over the rim edge, pull the rest of it over the rim by hand.

3 When one entire bead of the tire is free from the rim, it's easy to remove the tube for repair. There is no need to take the tire completely off the rim at this point. Just push it over to one side while you remove the tube. Lift the tube's valve stem out of its rim hole, being careful not to damage it, then slip the remainder of the tube out of the tire and pull it away from the rim.

Pump some air into the tube and try to pinpoint the puncture by listening or feeling for the escaping air. If a container of water is available (use a puddle on the trail or road), immerse the tube in water and watch for air bubbles. When you locate a repairable puncture, mark the tube at that point (dry it first if it's wet).

4 Pull the tire off the wheel and lay it down. Spread the tube over the tire so the two are in the same relationship they were in the wheel. Line up the valve stem with the mark you previously made on the tire. Then check both the inside and outside of the tire casing at the point of puncture. Remove any offending objects.

5 If you're unable to locate a puncture in the tube, check the valve stem. Tubes on underinflated tires can shift position, allowing the rim to cut into the side of the stem. If the stem is cracked or cut, you'll need to replace the tube.

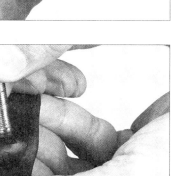

6 Spread the tube on a table. Use the piece of sandpaper or metal scraper from the tube repair kit to rough up the puncture area. Brush off any dust with your hand.

7 Coat the roughed area of the tube with a fine, even layer of glue that's a little larger in diameter than the patch you intend to use. Make sure there are no globs that would prevent the patch from sealing properly. After spreading the glue on your tube, allow it to dry completely (this usually takes 5 minutes).

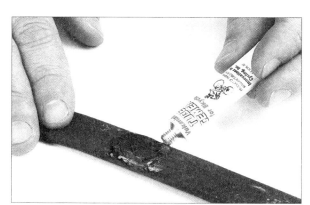

Clincher Removal, Repair, and Remounting *continued*

8 Take a patch out of your repair kit. Choose a size that will cover the puncture and make good contact with the area all around it. Peel off the foil from the sticky side of the patch and fasten the patch in place on the tube.

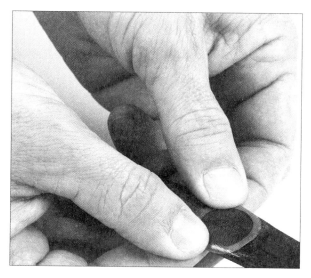

9 To make sure you get a good seal, press down hard to force out any air bubbles. Inflate the tube enough to give it shape.

Push one bead of the tire back onto the rim, leaving the other bead and most of the casing hanging off the rim while you replace the tube. Temporarily push the second bead of the tire over the rim at the valve hole and roll it back over the first bead to uncover the hole.

10 Fit the valve stem of the tube through the hole, then pull the compressed section of the second tire bead back over the tube and off the rim. Starting in the area of the valve stem, work your way around the rim, tucking the tube back inside the tire.

Once the tube is in place, let the air out of it while you work the second bead of the tire onto the rim. Begin at the stem. With the first few inches of the bead in place, push the valve stem up into the tire to ensure no part of the tube around the stem is caught under the bead. Then continue your way around the rim.

11 Try to avoid using tire levers to put the tire onto the rim. You should be able to do it with your hands alone. If you use tire levers, you risk pinching the tube and damaging it. To get the slack you need for the final part of the process, go around the tire and squeeze the two beads together so they will drop down into the trough in the middle of the rim.

When you get to the last section of tire, you may find it quite difficult to force it onto the rim.

12 Make sure you have given yourself all the available slack, then grasp the tire with both hands and, using a vigorous twisting motion of the wrists, try to roll the stubborn bit of bead over the edge of the rim (see photo). If this technique does not work for you, push the bead onto the rim bit by bit with your thumbs or the heels of your hands.

13 Once the tire is on the rim, push the valve up into the tire and pull it back down to be sure the stiff portion of the tube surrounding the valve is not trapped beneath the tire bead. Then, work around each side of the rim, rolling the tire back and looking to see if the tube is trapped beneath the tire bead anywhere else. If it is, the tube will get pinched and the tire won't seat properly when you inflate it (use a tire lever to poke the tube into the tire). If everything looks okay, pump 20 to 30 pounds of pressure into the tube. If the stem is still straight and the tire is seating properly, continue pumping up to the recommended pressure (usually printed on the tire label).

UST Tubeless Tire Removal, Repair, and Remounting

1 UST tire service is remarkably similar to any other clincher. In the case of a flat, stop riding and walk your bike to a safe spot to make the repair and remove the wheel from the bike. Pinch the sidewalls together firmly to get one of the tire beads to pop out of its channel. Then determine which bead has dislodged and work your way around the wheel, pushing the rest of this bead into the center of the rim.

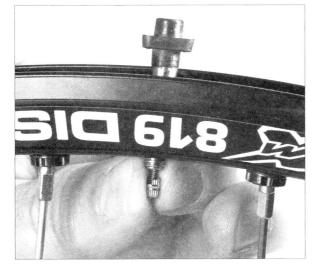

2 The rim's diameter is smallest in the center. With the bead in this position, you can now pull the tire up and away from the rim on one side, freeing the bead from the rim. Avoid the temptation to use tire levers except as a last resort. Using tire levers on a tubeless tire or rim can be damaging and render the system no longer airtight. If you must use tire levers, be extremely careful and use broad, flat plastic levers.

3 Check the tire inside and out for the cause of the puncture, mark it, and remove it. On the trailside, the quickest way to get back rolling is to remove the valve stem from the rim and install a tube in the same manner you would any other clincher tire (as described in "Clincher Removal, Repair, and Remounting" on page 74). You can then continue with the rest of these steps in the comfort of your home shop.

4 Push the second bead free of its channel in the same manner you did the first. Once the second bead is dislodged and in the center of the rim, the tire should easily come off the rim.

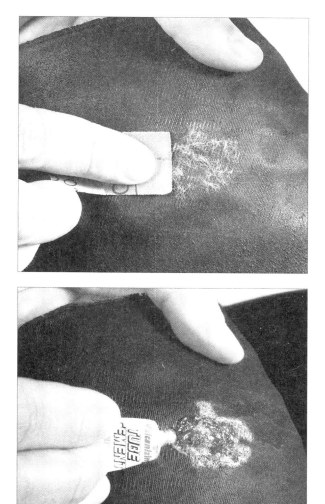

5 Turn the tire inside out at the point of the puncture and scuff it heavily with the coarse sandpaper or rasp included in your patch kit. Scuff an area on the inside of the tire around the hole slightly larger than the patch you plan to use.

6 Apply a gob of glue and spread it around the rough area. Let the glue set up for several minutes. You're ready for the next step when the glue goes from clear to cloudy.

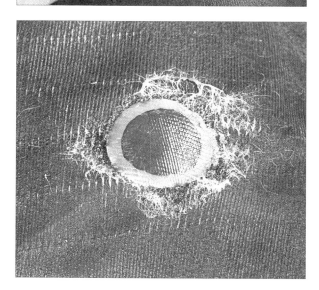

7 Remove the foil backing from the patch and firmly press the colored (usually orange) side of the patch into the glue. Keep constant pressure on the patch for 2 to 3 minutes, then carefully peel the clear plastic from the patch. Though it can be left in place, removing this film will help you be sure the patch is completely vulcanized to the tire's lining. If the edges of the patch peel up, spread a small amount of glue over the top of the patch and smooth the edges down from the middle outward.

8 While the patch dries, reinstall the valve stem and prepare the rim. Clean the rim out with a clean cloth to ensure a good seal with the tire. Spraying a diluted soap-and-water mixture (about ½ teaspoon of dish soap to 32 ounces of water) into the rim will make the tire's beads pop into their respective channels more easily and help to maintain a good seal. If you don't have a spray bottle for this purpose, use a clean rag or sponge soaked in the same mixture.

9 When the patch is dry, mount the tire. The first bead should slip into place easily. The starting point of the second bead is less important than with a tube-type tire, but it's slightly easier to start opposite the valve stem. Hold the wheel in your lap with the free bead facing up. Set the bead into the rim's center opposite the valve and then work the bead over the rim wall little by little with your thumbs, moving away from each other around the wheel.

10 As the last section of exposed bead becomes tight, recheck that the rest of the bead is settled into the center of the rim. Hold the wheel into your waist with the last section of bead away from you and grip the tire firmly on both sides of the still exposed section of bead. Roll your hands forward to stretch the last bit of bead over the rim. Though some tires may prove difficult, give it your absolute best shot to finish without using levers. Remember: There's no tube to pinch, but you don't want to compromise an expensive UST tire. Got it? Good!

11 With the tire mounted, check once more that both beads are set down in the rim's center. Using a floor pump or compressed air, quickly pump the tire to about 20 psi. The UST system requires a quick burst of air to create the initial seal between tire and rim. It's possible to achieve this with a mini pump, but it's more likely to only cause aggravation. Once the initial seal is created, pump the tire steadily, listening for the beads to pop into place. When this begins, inspect the tire every few strokes until the bead is seated evenly all the way around the wheel. Once the tire has reached about 40 psi, you can help the process along by gripping the tire with the heel of your hand near a section that hasn't popped into place and pushing away with steady, even pressure. If necessary, keep inflating the tire up to (but not beyond) 60 psi. When the bead seat indicator (a textured line that extends about ⅛ inch beyond the rim wall) is fully and evenly exposed, that's it. Set the tire to your chosen riding pressure, reinstall the wheel, and go for a ride.

Tubular Removal, Repair, and Remounting

1 When a tubular tire goes flat, stop riding on it immediately. Take the wheel off and pump a little air in it to try to locate the puncture while the tire is still on the rim. If you find the leak, mark the spot and proceed with the removal of the tire from the rim. If not, you'll have to pull the tire off the rim.

If the tire was glued on properly, it won't come off the rim easily. Try gripping one section of the tire with both hands and rolling it over the side of the rim, pushing on its underside with your thumbs or palms. Once you get a section loose, it will be easier to get a good grip for pulling the rest of the tire off the rim.

If you weren't able to find the puncture while the tire was on the rim, pump some air back into the tire, then hold it near your ear and listen for a leak. Even if you can't hear anything, you may be able to feel the escaping air hitting your face.

2 If you couldn't locate the escaping air otherwise, immerse the tire in a pan of water and watch for escaping air bubbles. Once you see, hear, or feel escaping air, search for evidence of a puncture in the tire. Until you actually locate a cut or puncture, you can't be certain where the problem lies because air can travel out of a hole in the tube and move several inches inside the tire before emerging.

The most foolproof way of isolating a leak is to clamp off a small section of tire, then pump air into the tire. If air escapes from the tire, loosen the clamp and move it along to another section. When no air escapes from the unclamped part, you know the problem lies within the clamped section. Take off the clamp and inspect that section to discover the source of the leak. Make clamps using a couple of pieces of 2 × 4 lumber. Tighten them around the tire using a large C-clamp or the jaws of a vise (see photo).

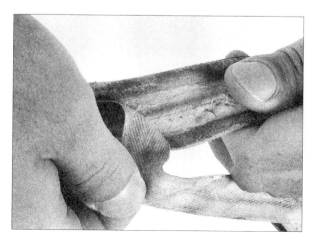

3 The smaller the pieces of wood used, the more frequently you'll have to reposition them, but the more narrowly you can pinpoint the source of the leak.

It's important to know precisely where the tube needs repair before cutting the stitching because you want to keep to a bare minimum the area you have to cut and later restitch.

Once you've located the puncture, lift up a few inches of base tape in that area (see photo). The base tape covers the tire's stitches and is bonded to the tire with latex glue. This is different glue than the glue used to mount the tire to the rim. When the stitching is exposed, make a distinct mark across the seam to help you line up the edges of the tire for later restitching.

4 Use a sharp knife, razor blade, or (best of all) sewing seam ripper to cut enough stitches to allow you to pull out the section of tube needing repair.

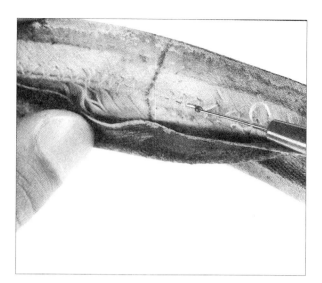

5 Pull out that section of tube and rough up the punctured area with fine sandpaper. Spread a layer of patch glue over the area and let it dry completely (it'll lose its glossy appearance, usually after about 5 minutes).

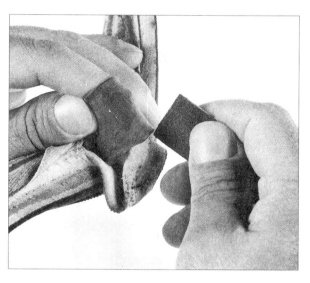

6 Find a patch of the appropriate size and peel off the protective backing from its sticky side. In order to get a good seal, place one edge of the patch on the tube first, then roll the remainder of the patch over.

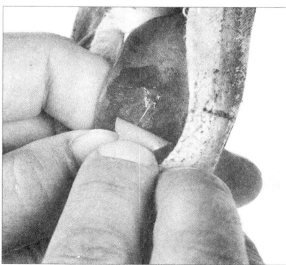

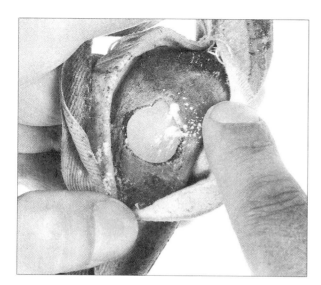

7 Sprinkle a bit of talc over the patched area to prevent the tube from sticking to the tire. Check both inside and outside the tire to locate and remove any remaining foreign material that may repuncture it once it's inflated and back in use. If any threads of the tire casing have been severed, cut a piece of strong canvas, nylon, or old tire casing and insert it inside the casing over the damaged area. When the repaired tube is inflated, it'll hold the patch in place.

Push the tube back into place inside the tire. Straighten the inner tape over the tube, then pull the edges of the casing together, lining up the two halves of your mark.

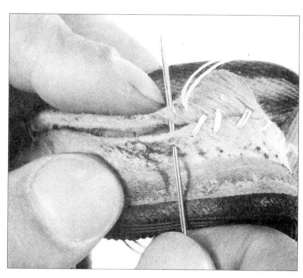

8 Restitch the tire using the original holes. (Creating new holes will weaken the casing.) Be sure to begin by overlapping the old thread for several holes on either side of the repair area. If you're a talented sewer, you may want to try to duplicate the original thread pattern in the tire. However, a simple overhand stitch will work adequately (see photo).

Tubular-tire repair kits provide thread, but any strong thread should work. Some people prefer dental floss to the type of thread found in most kits. Just tie a small knot in the end of your thread as if you were sewing on a button, and tie off the other end when you complete the stitching. Fasten the base tape with liquid latex.

9 Carefully scrape dried old glue off your rim as well as possible (you needn't get it all off). If it's a new rim, sand it lightly with emery cloth, clean it with acetone or alcohol, and add a layer of glue. If you've never put a tubular tire on a rim before, you may want to practice putting it on without glue first.

Set the rim down on a clean floor with the valve hole at the top. Insert the valve through the hole, and, beginning at that point, stretch the tire around the rim, working in both directions at once.

10 When you get to the last difficult section, lift the rim off the floor and simultaneously stretch and roll the final part of the tire over and onto the rim (see photo).

Work your way around the rim, checking to make sure the tire is on straight. When it looks right, inflate it. If the tire was difficult to get on, let it sit for a while, perhaps overnight, to let it stretch a little. Then deflate the tire and remove it from the rim for gluing.

11 Apply a dab of tubular cement between each spoke hole on the rim. Then run a bead of glue all the way around the rim. Apply a lighter coat to the base tape of the tire.

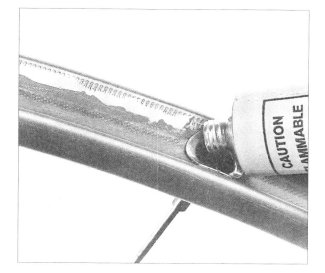

12 Put a small plastic baggie or a piece of plastic over your fingers and spread the glue around. After an hour, apply a second coat of glue in the same way.

When the second coat is tacky, proceed with the tire mounting. When you set the rim down, be sure the floor is clean because you don't want to contaminate the glue (or floor).

Roll the tire onto the rim as you did before, then spin the wheel and sight the tread to make sure the tire is on straight and that it's properly centered. If necessary, work it straight with your hands. Partially inflate the tire and put it on your bike. If everything looks fine, inflate the tire to full pressure and let it sit overnight before being used.

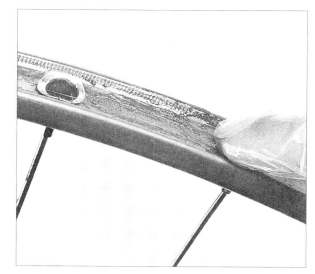

Rim Maintenance and Repair

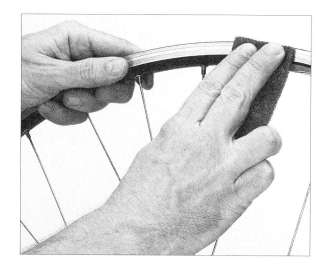

1 Basic wheel maintenance includes cleaning your rims regularly because the road grime that builds up interferes with good braking performance.

Wash rims with soapy water, as you would a car. To break up the residue that remains on the rims, use a solvent such as kerosene and fine steel wool or an abrasive pad made of material that won't scratch metal.

Take care not to get the kerosene on your tires or brake pads. Use a milder solvent such as alcohol to clean the grime off your brake pads.

2 Not only do rims get dirty but they also frequently get scratched or dented. If the dents are not too severe, you may be able to squeeze them out. Remove the tire from the rim and fasten the dented section of the rim between the jaws of a smooth jaw vise. Tighten the vise to squeeze out the dent.

You may be able to straighten a minor bend in the edge of the rim with the help of a small adjustable wrench. Screw the jaws of the wrench down snugly against the rim and lever the rim in the direction needed to straighten it.

3 Large dents or bends that result from a crash are more of a challenge to correct. There's no guarantee you'll be successful, but it's usually worth the effort to try to salvage an expensive rim.

First, remove the tire from the wheel and loosen the spokes in the affected area, then choose whether to go for push or for pull. If it's push, then tie the rim to a limb of a tree or hang it from a rafter with the bent section pointing down. Lay a block of 2 × 4 lumber across the smashed-in area and hammer down on it to force the rim back out into its proper shape.

The alternative approach is to set the rim vertically on the ground and run a heavy stick or a length of lumber over the dented-in area. Position your feet on the stick, one foot to either side of the rim. Bend your knees, grasp the upper part of the rim with your hands, then straighten up, pulling the rim back into shape (see photo).

4 Sideways bends can be handled in a similar manner. However, in this case you may not need to remove any spokes; you can simply ease the tension off those found at the trouble spot. If you have a big bulge at one spot, set the edge of the rim on a workbench and try pounding it out with a mallet.

If the bend is over a fairly large area, place one hand 8 to 10 inches on either side of the problem area, then push the rim down against a piece of lumber or against a tree trunk to try to eliminate the bend.

This process can also be reversed. Hold your knee against the bulge in the rim and your hands several inches to either side. Pull back on the rim to pop it back into round (see photo).

If you're lucky, one of these techniques will eliminate the unnatural tension in the rim, and you can use spoke adjustment to bring it back into usable shape. But if not, at least you tried. Replace the rim with one that is dependable, keep your rims strong through proper spoke tension, and try your best to avoid potholes and trees.

5 Take extra care with high-performance, low-spoke-count wheels. Wheels such as these rely on extra-high spoke tension to maintain strength. Too great a disparity in spoke tension on these wheels can make them very unstable.

They are not drastically different to work on than conventional wheels, but if you are uncertain about your abilities, it may be best to leave them to a professional.

Spoke Maintenance and Replacement

1 The spoked wheel is a marvelous invention. When properly built and maintained, it's incredibly strong; when improperly adjusted, it's very vulnerable to damage.

Spokes don't demand a lot of maintenance. Primarily, your job is to make certain they're properly tensioned. Periodically, work your way around each wheel, plucking each spoke to make sure that it's not loose. You'll spot a loose spoke both by the way it feels and by the way it sounds when plucked (see photo).

When you locate a loose spoke, use a spoke wrench to bring it up to a level of tension that is similar to that of its neighbors. After you've tightened the loose spokes, check the wheel for trueness and make further adjustments as needed. Consult the instructions beginning on page 94 for more details on this process.

Wheel truing is made easier and more precise when it's done in a special truing stand. If you don't have access to such a stand, use your brake calipers to help you check your wheel, or rest a thumb on a brake pad and sight the gap between the rim and your thumbnail. Sighting between the brake pads or your thumb and the rim will allow you to see whether the wheel needs side-to-side truing.

2 Vertical trueness can be checked by fastening a straightedge to the frame or the brake just above the wheel or by resting your thumb above the rim. Spin the wheel and sight to see if it's out of round.

When a spoke breaks, it's best not to ride any farther on the wheel. Instead, push your bike to a place where it's safe to replace the spoke. If you must ride the bike, first weave the loose spoke end around an adjacent spoke, and then ride slowly to your destination.

Replace the spoke with one of the same size. If you need a new nipple, roll the tire back, lift up the rubber strip that covers the tops of the nipples, and take out the old nipple. Drop a new one in its place.

Remove the broken spoke and run the new one through the hub flange in the same direction as the old one.

3 Pull your new spoke through the flange until its curved end is seated, then weave it through the other spokes, following the pattern of the old one. If in doubt, follow the pattern of the second spoke to either side of it.

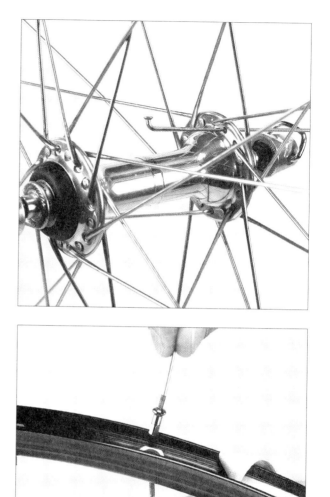

4 Before threading the new spoke into its nipple, apply a small amount of oil to its threads. This will make it easier to thread the spoke into the nipple and will help prevent it from freezing in the nipple over time (see photo). Then thread it on and use a spoke wrench to bring it up to tension.

When working on spokes, it's important to use a wrench of the correct size. If the wrench flats on a nipple get worn round, you'll have a difficult time adjusting that spoke. Also, before adjusting any of the old spokes, it's a good idea to spray a little penetrating oil at the points where the spoke enters the nipple and the nipple enters the rim. Rotate the wheel so that the oil will flow down into the threads after you spray it on.

Building New Wheels

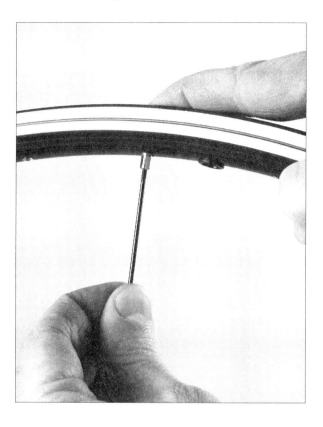

1 Whether you're building a 28-, 32-, 36-, or 40-spoke wheel, begin by dividing your spokes into four equal groups. Sit down and hold the hub in front of you with the axle pointing down. If it's a rear hub, turn the cassette side down (the cassette cogs should not be on the hub). Drop the first group of spokes down through the upper flange, inserting one spoke through every other hole.

Pick up the rim and suspend it between your lap and the edge of a bench in front of you or balance it on your knees, then twist it around so that the valve hole is opposite you. Drop a nipple through the spoke hole immediately to the left of the valve hole and fasten one of the spokes to it.

2 Moving left (counterclockwise) around the rim, skip three holes and put a nipple in the fourth spoke hole. Look back at the hub to locate the spoke immediately to the left of the first one attached, and fasten that spoke to the nipple in the fourth hole (see photo). Continue in this manner all the way around the rim until the entire first group of spokes is attached to the rim, with a spoke in every fourth hole. Screw each nipple only a little way down each spoke, just enough to securely hold it.

3 Rotate the hub counterclockwise so that the original spoke slants away from the valve hole in the rim. That's the direction in which the first round of spokes must slant in the completed wheel.

Flip the wheel over and sight down from what is now the upper flange to the flange below that contains the spokes. Notice that the spoke holes in the two flanges are not directly in line but offset from one another, so that a spoke pushed straight down through a hole in the upper flange will hit between two holes in the lower flange.

Locate the hole in the upper flange that is immediately to the right of the hole containing the original spoke in the lower flange. Drop your first spoke in the second group down through that hole. Now, skipping one hole between each spoke, drop the remaining spokes in round two down through the upper flange.

4 Drop a nipple through the rim hole immediately to the right of the one containing the original nipple used; that is, the second hole to the right of the valve hole. Fasten the first spoke in round two to that nipple. Working clockwise around the rim, drop a nipple through every fourth hole and fasten the next available spoke to it (see photo). Continue clockwise around the hub and rim until all the spokes in round two are fastened to the rim.

Before flipping the wheel over again, drop the third group of spokes down through the remaining holes in the bottom flange so that they enter and exit the flange in the opposite direction from the spokes already present there. Start to turn the wheel over, but stop when it's vertical, and force the new group of spokes to turn sideways on their elbows so they won't fall back out of the flange when you lay the wheel down.

Lay the wheel down with the loose spokes on top. Each spoke in this round will run to the left, in the opposite direction from those installed in the first round. This is the time when you must commit yourself to a cross pattern. If you choose to use the popular three-cross pattern, each spoke in this third group will cross over two round-one spokes and then under a third spoke before being fastened to the rim.

5 Grasp any loose spoke and pull it to the left across the first two adjacent spokes and under the third one, then fasten it to a nipple inserted through the first available rim hole (see photo). Notice that the first crossing of spokes occurs right at the edge of the hub flange and that the second crossing is still quite near the hub. Don't worry about the fact that you have to bend the spokes as you lace them or that they feel stiff when you're fastening them. Just flex them gently so that you don't put a crimp in them. After the wheel is laced and tensioned, the spokes will straighten out and find their proper place.

6 After you've finished lacing all the spokes in round three, drop the final set of spokes through the remaining holes in the lower flange. Raise the wheel up into a vertical position while you seat the spokes in the hub flange and bend them at their elbows toward the rim. Then turn the wheel the rest of the way over and lace up these spokes, following the same pattern as you did in round three (see photo).

Once all the spokes are fastened to the rim, begin to bring them up to tension. Fasten the wheel in a truing stand and put a little oil on all the spoke threads to help the nipples turn easily.

At the outset you want to treat all the spokes equally, so begin by turning all the nipples down until only three threads of each spoke are visible. At this stage, you'll find it easier and faster to turn the nipples with a screwdriver inserted into their heads.

Press on the spokes with your thumbs or tap them with a mallet so they sit flat against the hub flanges.

7 Start working your way around the rim, turning the nipples with a spoke wrench to tighten the spokes. Work in increments of one-half turn of the nipple each time (see photo).

As tension begins to build in the spokes, check to see how well they're seated in the hub flanges. When the spokes begin to feel snug, you're ready to true the wheel. See the following repair section for details on this process.

Once the wheel is true, your next task is to bring it up to optimum tension. Unfortunately, there is no way to precisely describe what this is. An expert wheel-builder can sense when that point has been reached. To learn the feeling, locate a well-built wheel and compare the sound and feel of its spokes when plucked to those on the wheel you're building.

As the wheel gets tighter, turns of the spoke wrench have an increasingly dramatic effect on the level of spoke tension, so work in increments of one-half turn at a time. Each time you complete a round of tensioning, check your wheel again for trueness and make any adjustments needed. As you turn the nipple, the spoke tends to twist a little. After each turn of the wrench, back it off a little to eliminate this spoke windup.

8 The final step in building a tight wheel is to grab parallel sets of spokes, one pair in each hand, and squeeze them to prestress them (see photo). If this causes the wheel to become too loose, then add more tension. If the wheel goes badly out of true, you may have too much tension on the spokes. Retrue the wheel and try again. If it won't stay true, reduce the overall tension in the wheel, true it, and stress it a third time.

Truing Wheels

1 Wheel truing can be done most accurately with the tire off the wheel so the outside perimeter of the rim can be closely checked for roundness. If the tire is on the rim at the time you wish to true your wheel, simply let out most of its air to minimize your chances of puncturing the tube while twisting a spoke nipple.

Mount your wheel in a truing stand and adjust the calipers so that their tips are close to the sides of the rim. Spin the wheel and readjust the calipers to move them as close as possible to the rim without hitting it at any point in its revolution.

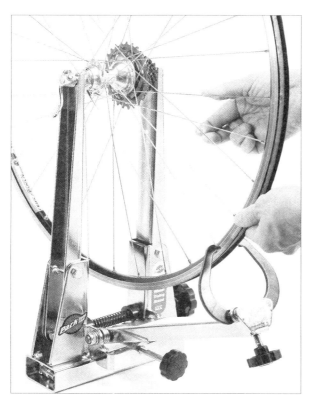

2 Start the truing process by working your way around the wheel, beginning at the valve or some other reference point, and plucking each spoke in turn to see if any are unusually loose (see photo). Bring each loose spoke up to a level of tension similar to that of its neighbors.

Spray a little penetrating oil where the spoke enters the nipple to help the nipple turn, and use a spoke wrench of the proper size so you don't round over the sides of the nipple. As you tension each spoke, place one or two fingers on it to make sure it does not turn along with the nipple. If it does, back off the adjustment to eliminate this windup and try again. Tension caused by spoke windup will be released when you use your wheel, ruining your adjustment.

Spin your wheel to check for horizontal trueness. To pull the rim to the right at any point, loosen the spoke or spokes that run from the left side of the hub to that point on the rim and tighten the spokes on the right side. Reverse the procedure to pull the rim to the left.

3 Tighten and loosen opposing spokes the same amount, and work in small increments of one-quarter to one-half turn each time (see photo). After working all the way around the wheel once or twice, you should have the wheel fairly true horizontally.

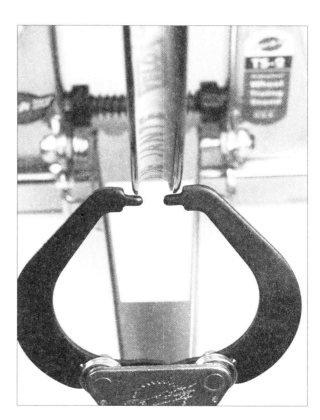

4 Check for vertical roundness in the wheel. If your tire is on the rim, check this by hooking a caliper over one of the inside edges of the rim, spinning the wheel, and looking for high and low spots. If the tire is off the rim, set the caliper (or other gauge provided on your truing stand) near the outside edge of the rim, then watch for changes in the distance between the gauge and the rim as it spins (see photo).

To eliminate high spots in the rim, tighten the spokes that meet the rim at those spots. To eliminate low spots, release some of the tension on the spokes in those spots. This time, tighten or loosen the spokes in pairs, one right-side and one left-side spoke in each pair.

Remember, when you add or subtract tension from any section of the rim, you're affecting the tension on other parts of the rim as well. So work in small increments and recheck the trueness of the rim frequently. Alternate between horizontal and vertical truing until you see only very minor variations in the rim's movement in either direction as it spins.

5 HUBS

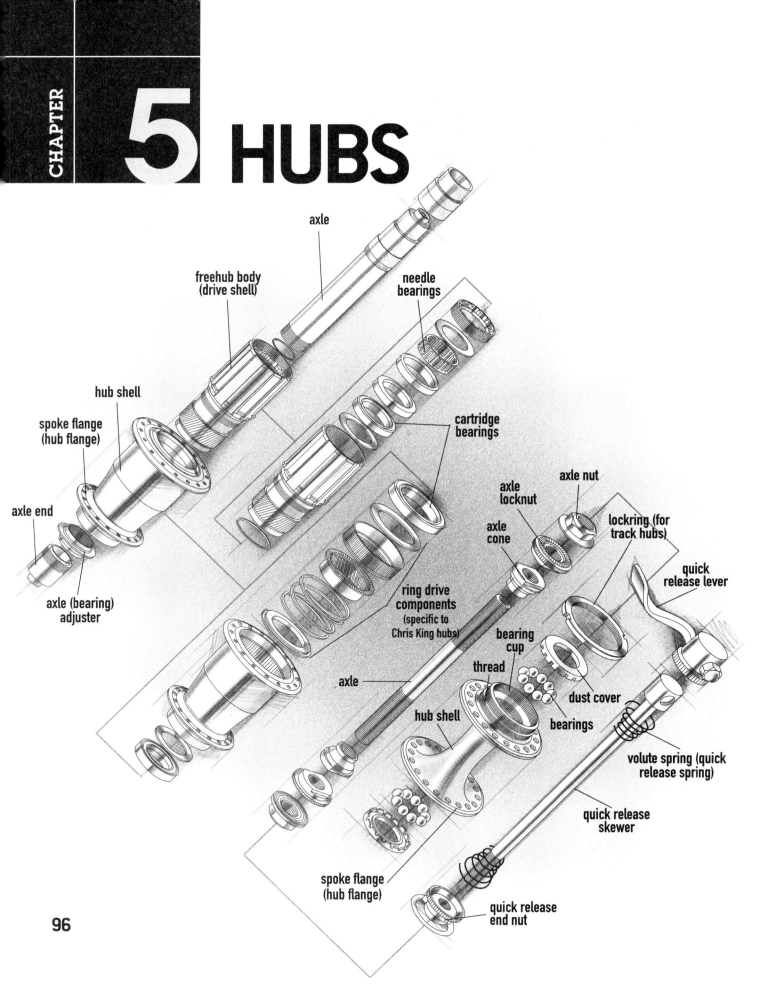

axle

freehub body
(drive shell)

needle
bearings

hub shell

cartridge
bearings

spoke flange
(hub flange)

axle nut

axle
locknut

axle end

axle
cone

lockring (for
track hubs)

quick
release lever

axle (bearing)
adjuster

ring drive
components
(specific to
Chris King hubs)

bearing
cup

axle

thread

dust cover

hub shell

bearings

volute spring (quick
release spring)

quick release
skewer

spoke flange
(hub flange)

quick release
end nut

While some may argue the point, many more would agree that the single most significant upgrade you can make to any bike is a pair of smooth-spinning, high-quality hubs. The hub occupies the center of your wheel and is the foundation of a well-built wheelset.

Hubs perform two critical functions. They house the axles and bearings on which your wheels spin, and they anchor the spokes that hold your rims round and true. With regular maintenance, a quality hubset can outlive several pairs of rims, sometimes even several framesets (we've seen 50-year-old hub sets still spinning smoothly).

Though the hubs may appear intimidating because the parts are hidden inside, the mechanisms are pretty basic. With a little practice and the right tools, anyone can service most types.

HUB CONSTRUCTION

Before beginning to disassemble a hub, it's important to understand how it is put together. Most are of the conventional adjustable cone-and-race variety. Hubs of this design come in all price ranges and are easily serviced. Replacement parts are available at most bike shops.

The largest part of a hub is the shell. The shell is the part to which the spokes are attached, and it encases the working parts—that is, the axle and bearings. The part of the shell that holds the heads (the flared ends) of the spokes is called the flange.

Flanges come in different sizes, depending on the purpose of the wheel. Though it's hard to discern through a fat mountain bike knobby tire, generally speaking, the larger the flange, the stiffer the wheel. Road sprinters often want stiff wheels because they like the rigid feel when they stand to explode to the finish line. Mountain bikers often use medium-flange hubs for a nice mix of stiffness and comfort.

The flanges to which spokes are anchored differ in size on different hubs. They are usually referred to as "low-flange," "medium-" or "mid-flange," and "high-flange."

For most applications, the following rule applies: If you want a comfortable wheel, consider using a smaller-flange hub; for a stiffer wheel, use a larger flange. The actual strength of a wheel, however, is determined more by the type of spokes, rim, and spoking pattern employed than by the size of the hub flange.

Hubs are also sometimes described by mechanics by the type of flange they have—high- or large-flange, medium-flange, and low- or small-flange.

Inside the hub shell are two bearing races, one at each end. The bearings roll on the surfaces of the races and are held in place by the cones, which screw onto the axle. The bearings also roll on the surfaces of the cones. Because of the special shapes of the races and the cones, the bearings roll in a circular path. The cones fit on the axle and are held in place by a series of washers and a locknut.

The axle on a front wheel hub fits into slots cut into the tips of the front fork; on a rear hub the axle fits into slots in the rear fork, called dropouts. A hub is held in place on a bicycle frame either by means of an axle and a pair of axle nuts or by a quick-release unit consisting of a hollow axle, a skewer, springs, a cam lever, and an adjusting nut. Nuts must be tightened and loosened by means of a wrench, whereas a quick-release mechanism permits wheels to be locked in place or removed without any tools.

Downhill and freeride bikes often come equipped with a new design of axle called a through-axle. A through-axle is a large-diameter axle that passes through substantial fork leg ends or rear dropouts (for lack of a better term) and the hubshell. The through-axle is firmly clamped in place, creating a strong, stiff connection. The purpose of through-axles is first to resist independent movement of the fork legs or rear triangle halves on long-travel suspension designs. Additionally, by clamping the axle all the way around, through-axle forks are able to fight the force of powerful disc brakes that can try to pull the axle out of a conventional fork dropout. The standard dimension for front through-axles is 20 mm in diameter and 12 mm for the rear (with a few exceptions that use 24 mm front axles or 15 mm in the rear). Fortunately, frames and forks that do not conform to the accepted standards usually come equipped with hubs that fit.

CHECKING HUB ADJUSTMENT

To check hub adjustment, remove the wheel from the bicycle. The front wheel is easy to remove. Unbolt the axle or flip the quick-release lever to the open position and drop the wheel out of the fork.

If you have sidepull brakes, you may have to open the caliper arms a bit to get the tire past them.

Axles can be held in place in several ways. Most common on modern bicycles are quick-release (QR) axles that use a cam-action skewer to grip the frame or fork dropouts on the axle. Solid axles use nuts to achieve this goal, while through-axles have a large-diameter axle that is clamped in place on specially designed forks.

Most sidepulls have a quick-release mechanism—a small lever that, when thrown, opens the caliper to permit the tire to go past. Most cantilever brakes have a transverse cable (the wire that runs from one side of the brake to the other) that can be released from one side of the brake to spread the pads for tire clearance. For direct-pull brakes, release the metal noodle from its holder to open the brake. If your brakes don't have these features, deflate the tire until it is soft enough to squeeze past the brake pads.

Removing the rear wheel means dealing with the gears and chain. Open the brake for tire clearance as described above. Then shift the chain onto the smallest cog on the cassette and the smallest chainring on the crankset. Loosen the axle nut or the quick-release lever. While holding the rear of the bicycle off the ground, pull back on the body of the rear derailleur and push the rear wheel down and forward to get it out.

Once the wheel is off, grasp one end of the axle with the thumb and index finger of your dominant hand. Turn the axle slowly for a few revolutions. Does it feel rough and seem to catch in pits as you turn it? If it does, it's too tight or the hub is full of dirt or corrosion. If your hub doesn't feel too tight, check it for looseness. Grab the axle again, only this time wiggle it up and down and from side to side. If the axle moves in these directions, causing a slight knocking feeling, it's too loose.

If the hub is too tight or too loose, adjust it. To continue to ride it while it's out of proper adjustment will subject its parts to unnecessary wear and will limit how well the bike can perform. For instance, a loose rear hub can affect shifting, while tight hubs may make clicking sounds.

ADJUSTING THE HUB

Adjust the hubs with the wheels off the bike. Don't even think about removing the hubs from the wheels, though. The only time that's necessary is when you're replacing a hub, a rim, or a set of spokes.

You'll need only a couple of tools to make a hub adjustment: a wrench to fit the axle locknuts and a special wrench for the cones. A cone wrench is a thin wrench that fits into the narrow wrench slots on cones while a regular wrench is on the adjacent locknut. Regular wrenches are too wide to fit side by

side in this way. Cone wrenches are available from some bicycle shops. They range in size from 12 mm to 19 mm and often come in sets.

Usual measurements are 17 mm for axle locknuts, 13 mm for front cones, and 15 mm for rear cones, but always check to be sure. It's also possible to use an adjustable wrench for the locknut. Some hubs may require two cone wrenches because the axle locknuts are slotted like cones and accept cone wrenches, not regular wrenches. Before you buy an extra cone wrench, check the hubs to be sure you really need one. For these instructions, we'll assume you're using one cone wrench and one regular wrench.

To adjust a rear hub that has a freewheel, remove it. (See page 160 for instructions on freewheel removal.) Once the freewheel has been removed, you can begin the adjustment.

If you have a cassette rear hub (one where the freewheel mechanism is built into the hub), you may not need to remove the cluster of gears to adjust the hub. It's a good idea, however, to check the gears for tightness because they can loosen with use, and this can affect shifting.

Follow the hub-adjustment procedure recommended here, but don't be intimidated if you don't get it perfectly right on the first try. Almost nobody does.

For ease of handling, lay the wheel flat on a workbench. Put the cone wrench on the upper cone and another wrench on the axle locknut above it. Tighten the cone and the locknut against each other by turning the cone counterclockwise and the locknut clockwise. This locks one side of the axle so that it can't accidentally loosen while you are adjusting the hub or riding the bike. You may lock either side of the front hub in this way, but you should do this on the derailleur side of the rear wheel so that fine-tuning your adjustment can be done at later times with the freewheel/cassette in place.

This is easy to do on freewheel-equipped wheels because once the freewheel is removed, the cone and locknut are exposed. This is not true with wheels equipped with cassettes. On these, you must first remove the left locknut, lockwasher, and cone, and then push the axle toward the right to expose the right-side axle parts so that you can tighten them against each other. Then push the axle back into the hub and reinstall the left-side axle parts.

After locking the cone and locknut on one side of the hub, turn the wheel over and put your wrenches on the cone and locknut of the other side. While holding the cone, turn the locknut counterclockwise to loosen it.

Before you make the final adjustment to your hub, there are a few points you should note.

• If you have bolt-on axles, there should be no play in the adjustment prior to tightening the wheel in the frame.

• If you have quick-release axles, you must make allowance for the pressure of the quick-release skewer. The adjustment of the cones will initially need to be a little loose because when the quick-release skewer closes and compresses the axle, it makes the adjustment slightly tighter. So there must be a little play in the axle when it's wiggled.

Once the locknut is loose, begin final adjustment by gently turning the cone clockwise until it comes into full contact with the bearings. Back off the adjustment slightly, then tighten the locknut while holding the cone in place. Check the adjustment of the hub in the same manner as before.

For quick-release hubs, check to be sure the hub is not excessively loose after the quick-release has been closed. The only way to check is to put the wheel in the bike, lock the quick-release, and then try to move the rim from side to side. Feel any play (it sometimes feels like a clunk)? If so, the hub adjustment is too loose. If the hub is not properly adjusted, repeat the procedure until it is.

If, after repeated tries, you simply cannot find the magic line between loose and tight, leave the adjustment slightly on the tight side. It may loosen a bit when you ride. But don't settle for less than perfection in the adjustment until you've made careful and repeated attempts to get it just right. The time spent learning to make sensitive adjustments to the hubs will pay off because similar techniques are used on headsets and some bottom brackets and pedals. Look at attempts at hub adjustment as valuable training in general bicycle repair and maintenance.

HUB OVERHAUL

Check hub adjustment and make any needed changes about twice a year. To ensure long hub life, perform a complete hub overhaul at least every other year for road bikes, and at least annually for mountain bikes ridden off road. Or, if you rack up 3,000 miles a year or so, figure that the hubs ought to get a good cleaning and relubing annually. Also, if for some reason the hubs are completely submerged in water, overhaul them at the first opportunity—water can rust the bearings and races, ruining the hub.

Only hubs that don't use precision or sealed bearings need this periodic overhaul. Hubs that use seals to protect the bearings from contaminants may be able to go much longer without an overhaul.

To overhaul hubs, use the same cone wrench and regular wrench as in the hub adjustment. In addition to that, find or buy a large flat-head screwdriver or tire iron, medium-weight grease that's not vegetable-based, and new bearings of the appropriate size and number (there are usually 18 of the ¼-inch ball bearings in rear hubs, and 20 or 22 of the ³⁄₁₆-inch bearings in front hubs).

Bearings are not very expensive to replace, so avoid the hassle and use new ones. Be certain to install bearings of the same size and number as you are currently using (take samples to the shop to match the new ones with the old).

Begin hub overhaul in the same way as an adjustment. Follow these basic steps.

1. For hubs with freewheels, place the wheel horizontally on the floor or workbench (the freewheel should be removed; see page 160). If your hub is equipped with a quick-release mechanism, thread the adjusting nut off the end of the quick-release skewer and pull the skewer out of the axle. Be careful not to lose the cone-shaped spring that had to come off the skewer when it was pulled out of the axle. Put that spring back on the skewer and partially thread on the nut so these parts won't get lost. Set the quick-release assembly aside before doing the hub overhaul. If you have an ordinary nutted axle, remove at least one of the nuts so you will be able to remove the axle from the hub.

2. On the derailleur side of the rear hub, use the hub wrenches to tighten the cone and locknut against one another. (Either side of the front hub will do.) This locks one side of the axle so that it cannot accidentally loosen later while you are adjusting the hub or riding the bike. Leaving this locknut and cone in place on the axle during the overhaul also makes it easy to re-assemble the hub later.

This is also necessary for cassette hub overhaul, but you must first remove the axle to gain access to the right-side parts; start hub adjustment or overhaul with Step 3.

3. Flip the wheel over to reach the cone and locknut on the other side of the hub. Use the cone wrench to hold the cone still while turning the locknut counter-clockwise to loosen it.

4. Remove the locknut, the lockwasher under it, and then the cone. It's best to do this with the other end of the axle resting on a tabletop to prevent it from falling out, which usually means the bearings will fall on the floor, too.

5. Carefully remove the axle assembly. Do this over a rag or paper towel to catch the loose bearings. If it's a cassette hub, now is the time to lock the right locknut and cone in position with cone wrenches. (If the axle can't be pushed out, remove the cassette; see page 158.)

Use the large flat-head screwdriver or the tire iron to remove the dustcaps. These are the caps that fit into the openings at the ends of the hub shell. Their function is to surround the cone and thus prevent dirt from getting into the bearing. It's possible to leave dustcaps in place during a hub overhaul, which eliminates the need to correctly reinstall them later. The drawback is that it makes it more difficult to clean the races (where the bearings sit inside the hub).

6. Thoroughly clean all the parts in solvent. Inspect the cones and the races for pitting (cavities in the sur-faces) or cracks. Roll the axle on a smooth countertop to see if it wobbles. If it does, it's bent. Replace it, being sure to get a matching model. Also replace any parts that are cracked, pitted, or that have other signs of excessive wear.

7. If the cone that was left on the axle is ruined, re-move it the same way as the other one. Before re-moving it, measure and note how much axle was protruding past the end of the locknut. When in-stalling the new cone, grease the axle threads first. This not only helps get the cone on but also prevents the axle from rusting under the cone. When locking the cone and locknut together, try to get the same amount of protruding axle as there was before.

8. Now that all the parts are cleaned and the broken ones have been replaced, start reassembly. First, heavily grease the hub races. Don't worry if a little grease gets into the axle shaft or on the dustcap lip. Reset the dustcap. Try to get the edge of the dustcap even with the edge of the hub shell lip. If the dustcap is crooked, it may rub on the cone when the wheel is spinning. Be careful with the caps because they bend easily.

Some dustcaps fit so loosely that they won't stay in place. An easy fix for metal dustcaps is to gently grip the edge with the jaws of a diagonal cutter and pull it out very slightly. Repeat at two other spots so that there are three points, each about one-third of the way around the dustcap, that are slightly pulled out. Then the dustcap will be a press fit and will stay put.

9. Install the bearings in the races. The grease should hold them in place. Be sure to get the proper number (usually 9 per side for rear hubs and 10 per side for fronts) and correct size of balls (usually ¼ inch for rears and ³⁄₁₆ inch for fronts) in each side.

10. Grease the entire axle shaft and the cone and in-sert it into the hub. Be careful not to knock any bear-ings off the races when placing the axle.

11. Grease the cone and thread it on the axle. Slide the lockwasher onto the axle over the cone and thread on the locknut.

Now that the hub is back together, adjust it. Re-member the differences between bolt-on and quick-release axles that were mentioned earlier. There should be no play in the adjustment on a bolt-on axle after the locknut has been tightened, but because of the pressure exerted on the axle by a quick-release, there should be a slightly looser adjustment on this type of axle.

In both cases, while the locknut is still loose, turn the cone down on the bearings until it comes into full contact with them. Then back it off as needed for the correct adjustment—between one-eighth and one-quarter turn for bolt-on axles; more for axles of the quick-release type. As we said before, don't be sur-prised if it takes several tries to get it just right.

Also remember, for quick-release hubs, check to be sure the hubs are not excessively loose after the wheel is back on the bike and the quick-release lever is shut. If there's play when you wiggle the rim from side to side, remove the wheel and alter the adjust-ment, then replace the wheel and check it again. Be patient, and before long, you'll develop a good sense of what the proper adjustment is, even with the wheel off the bike.

Let's say that, after a number of attempts, you can't seem to get the hub adjustment right. It's always either too tight, too loose, or it clicks when you spin the axle. Don't smash the wheel to bits in a fit of frustration. Take a break and try again. One possible explanation is that the grease got contaminated with grit during the rebuild. (Sometimes the parts look clean but crud is still on them.) Try disassembling the hub, cleaning everything one more time, putting fresh grease in, and reassembling and adjusting.

If you've done all this but still can't seem to find a happy medium between tight and loose bearings, run the adjustment a little on the tight side. The bearings might loosen a bit after a few rides, but they won't tighten. And remember to check periodically to make sure that none of the locknuts has worked its way loose, thus allowing the adjustment to loosen.

SPECIAL HUB TIPS

To make hubs more resistant to water and dirt, slip rubber O-rings over the ends of the axles and push them up against the openings around the cones. O-rings are available at hardware or auto parts stores. Other "poor-man's seals" that work well are pipe cleaners and butcher's twine. Simply wrap a pipe cleaner or tie a piece of twine around the area next to the cone to keep out contaminants. (Add one of these seals only after completing the hub-adjustment process.)

If the hubs have small holes in the dustcaps or hub bodies, use the holes as a quick way to repack the hubs with fresh grease. You'll need a grease gun with a needle injector to get grease into the holes. Stick the end of the injector into each hole and pump grease in until the dirty grease is forced out of the bearing through the opening around the cone. When clean grease starts to appear, simply wipe away the dirty grease, and the hubs are ready to roll.

If you purchase new quick-release hubs that feel silky-smooth, with no play in the axle, they're probably adjusted too tight for actual use. The adjustment you feel is actually for the manufacturer's quality-control checks. It's important to add some play to compensate for the compression caused by the quick-release skewer when the wheel is mounted

on the bike. Skip this step and the hubs will spin with extra resistance and suffer premature wear.

SHOPPING FOR NEW HUBS

When purchasing new hubs, consider these factors.

Flange height. The flange height affects the feel of the bicycle a little bit. On road bikes, the larger the flange, the more road shock you may feel, though this is usually a problem only on long, bumpy rides. For shorter rides, there's no need to consider this factor. Due to fatter tires that offer some shock absorption, flange height isn't that important on a mountain bike.

Sealed or conventional bearings. Both are excellent. We recommend purchasing well-tested, established designs. Ask ride partners and shop personnel, and get hubs that have a good reputation. Conventional bearings are usually easier to service, but sealed models usually require service less often. Before purchasing sealed-bearing hubs, inquire about special tools and techniques, along with the warranty.

Availability of replacement parts. It doesn't do much good to buy expensive hubs if 3 years later you have to replace them because replacement cones aren't available.

Cassette versus freewheel. There are two main hub types: cassette and freewheel. These are named according to how the gear cluster attaches to the rear hub. Cassette hubs, the most common today, have freewheels built into the hubs. Freewheel hubs, with threaded-on gear clusters, were the norm for years but are now rare on new bikes. The advantage of the cassette system is that the hub bearings are farther apart, which increases axle strength. On freewheel hubs, any gear cluster that fits your hub will work. Today, however, fewer and fewer manufacturers are making freewheels. At this point, the best bet is to go with cassette-style hubs.

Axle width. Cassette hubs come in six-, seven-, eight-, nine-, and now ten-speed models. Each is equipped with the proper-length axle. For freewheel hubs, a different width (length) of axle is needed for five-, six-, seven-, and eight-speed freewheels because the more cogs on the freewheel, the more space it takes up on the axle. This means that, when purchasing freewheel hubs, it's necessary to tell the shop the number of cogs on the freewheel, so they can install a different axle if necessary.

Learning to overhaul and adjust hubs is not difficult and is a good way to get started maintaining and repairing a bike. Once you experience the payoff from your effort—smooth-rolling wheels—you'll want to move on and master other areas of bicycle maintenance as well.

TROUBLESHOOTING

PROBLEM: The wheel pulls out of the frame when you're climbing hills.

SOLUTION: Loosen the axle nuts or quick-release, center the wheel in the frame, and tighten the axle nuts or quick-release tighter than before.

PROBLEM: You clamp the quick-release but it doesn't hold the wheel tight in the frame.

SOLUTION: The axle has to be just the right length for the quick-release to work. Leave the wheel in the frame and remove the quick-release. Look at the axle ends. Do they protrude past the outside faces of the dropouts? If so, remove the wheel, file the axle down until the ends are within the dropouts, and reattach the quick-release.

PROBLEM: There's play in the hub when you push laterally on the wheel, but the hub is adjusted right.

SOLUTION: You may have broken the axle. Remove the quick-release and pull on the axle to see if it's broken in two. Replace the axle if it is.

PROBLEM: You've reassembled the hub after servicing it, and you can't get the adjustment right. It's either too tight or too loose.

SOLUTION: You may have put too many or too few bearings or the wrong-size bearings in the hub race. There are usually 9 bearings of the ¼-inch size in each side of the rear hub and 10 bearings measuring ³⁄₁₆ inch in each of the two front races.

PROBLEM: Your sealed-bearing hub has a trace of side-to-side play when you push the wheel sideways.

SOLUTION: Don't worry about it. This is acceptable.

PROBLEM: Your sealed-bearing hub has developed a lot of lateral play that you feel when pushing sideways on the rim.

SOLUTION: The cones may be worn. Replace them if possible. Or have the hub checked by an expert or the manufacturer.

PROBLEM: It's harder than usual to close and open the quick-release.

SOLUTION: Remove the quick-release and lubricate it with a penetrating oil. If this doesn't help, the quick-release may be worn out. Replace it.

PROBLEM: After a hub overhaul, the wheel won't sit straight in the bike.

SOLUTION: Make sure that the springs on the quick-release are installed correctly. The narrow end should always face in.

PROBLEM: After a hub overhaul on a nutted wheel, the rear derailleur doesn't shift right.

SOLUTION: Nutted wheels should always have a washer between the nut and frame. If this washer mistakenly gets between the frame and hub, it'll change the spacing and ruin the shifting. Remove the wheel and put the washer where it belongs.

Adjusting Cone-and-Locknut-Type Hubs

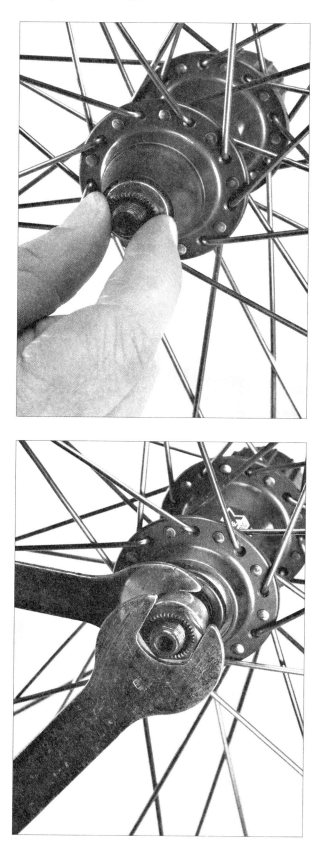

1 Cone-and-locknut hubs are the most conventional type of bicycle hubs, even today. Ball bearings ride between a hardened steel cup fitted in the hubshell and a hardened steel cone threaded onto the axle. The adjustment is maintained by a locknut that threads against the cone, preventing it from simply spinning out of place.

Whether front or rear, freewheel or cassette, all cone-and-locknut hubs adjust in the same basic manner. Adjusting rear hubs can require one additional series of steps relating to the cassette or freewheel, so we'll focus on those types here.

To start, remove the wheel from the bike (see page 72). Lay the wheel flat on a workbench. Remove the axle nuts or quick-release. Grab the axle with your fingers and turn it back and forth (see photo). If there's any binding in the bearings, the cone adjustment is too tight.

If binding is not a problem, check for looseness. Try to move the axle back and forth while holding the hub steady. If you feel any play, the adjustment is probably too loose. If the wheel has a quick-release mechanism, however, take into account the compression it places on the axle. A hub that feels a little loose off the bike might feel okay on the bike. The only way to be sure is to remount the wheel, then check to see if the axle still seems loose.

2 A hub that is either too tight or too loose should be adjusted. Before adjusting any hub, one set of cone and locknut must be locked in place on the axle. On front hubs, this can be done on either side, while on rear hubs, it should be done on the right (drive) side of the hub. If you're not sure if the locknut and cone are properly secured on a rear hub, don't chance it. The process to check this adjustment is a little involved, but it will save you the frustration of an adjustment that won't keep.

First, you must remove the cassette (see page 158) or the freewheel; otherwise, you won't be able to expose the right-side cone and locknut. Now, remove the left-side locknut, lockwasher, spacers (if there are any), and cone, and push the axle just far enough to the right to expose the right-side cone (be careful not to disturb the bearings—if you dislodge any, just poke them back into place in the race).

3 When the axle can be pushed to the right, hold the cone with a wrench, grip the right locknut with another wrench, and tighten the two against each other to secure them in place on the axle (see photo).

4 Push the axle back into the hub and screw on the left-side cone by hand until it rests against the bearings. Then add the spacers, lockwasher, and locknut, and snug the pieces in place by turning the cone counterclockwise while turning the locknut clockwise with the wrenches. Twirl the axle between your fingers to check the adjustment. If it binds, the adjustment is too tight. Loosen it slightly by holding the right-side locknut with a wrench and the left-side cone with a cone wrench (see photo). With the tools on either side of the hub, you should be able to back off the left-side cone slightly to fine-tune the adjustment.

If the hub is too loose, hold the right-side locknut with a wrench while turning the left cone clockwise until the play disappears. Still holding the right locknut with a wrench, snug the left locknut against the left cone. Secure the left side by placing wrenches on the cone and locknut and tightening them against each other.

It may take a few tries to get a perfect adjustment, but with practice it'll become simple. If it's difficult to make a good adjustment, it may be a sign that the hub is damaged or just full of dirt and needs to be overhauled and inspected for wear.

Cone-and-Locknut-Type Hub Overhaul

1 If your hub is equipped with a quick-release mechanism, thread the adjusting nut off the end of the quick-release skewer and pull the skewer out of the axle. Be careful not to lose the cone-shaped spring that had to come off the skewer when it was pulled out of the axle. Put that spring back on the skewer and partially thread on the nut so these parts won't get lost. Set the quick-release assembly aside before doing the hub overhaul. If you have an ordinary nutted axle, remove at least one of the nuts in order to remove the axle from the hub. Fit a properly sized cone wrench onto the axle cone and another on the locknut (this must be done on the left side of cassette-type rear hubs). Turn the cone clockwise and the locknut counterclockwise to separate the two. For overhauling a freewheel rear hub, remove the freewheel as well.

2 Remove the locknut, spacers, and cone from the axle, keeping them in order. The axle will now slide out the other side. If you're careful about how you do this, grease in the hub may hold the bearings in place. Hold the wheel horizontally over a rag while removing the axle from the top to ensure that bearings don't bounce across your shop if they fall out. Leave the cone and locknut on the other end of the axle in place to simplify hub reassembly. This way, you'll be sure to end up with the proper amount of axle on each side of your hub.

3 Remove the bearings from the cups and set them aside. You won't be reusing them, but once they're cleaned, they serve as a good initial indicator of the condition of the hub's bearing cups and give you a reference of the correct number and size of replacement bearings you should purchase. Spray a light solvent or degreaser into the cups to break down the grease, and then wipe them clean with a rag. Rinse the cups with rubbing alcohol and let them air-dry. Visually inspect the cups for pits, cracks, or irregular wear. Pitted or otherwise compromised cups on inexpensive hubs may be your cue to replace the hubs or wheels altogether. Some higher-quality hubs may be salvageable with the installation of new replacement cups. Check with your local shop to inquire about the possibility of this solution.

4 If there is a significant amount of dirt contamination inside the hub, it may be easiest to pry the dust seals out of the shell. These seals are generally delicate, so proceed carefully. Gently pry at the cover from several angles using a flat screwdriver. Once the covers are out, clean and inspect the cups and covers as described above.

5 If you have a Shimano freehub body that requires replacement, this is the time to do it. Insert a 10 mm hex key inside the freehub body and turn it counterclockwise to remove the hollow retaining bolt. The retaining bolt may be very tight. Clamping your hex key in a bench vise and using the wheel for leverage can ease removal.

Fit a new freehub body on the hubshell's spline. Clean and grease the threads of the retaining bolt and reinstall it into the freehub body and hubshell.

6 Clean the axle and roll it on a level surface, like the edge of a countertop, to see if it wobbles. If it does, that indicates that it is bent and needs to be replaced. Take the axle to the bike shop to get the proper replacement.

If the cones are excessively worn and need to be replaced, you must remove the one remaining on the axle. Before loosening the locknut, measure and record the position of the cone on the axle so that the new one can be threaded to the same location.

If all is well, use your cone wrenches to ensure that the cone and locknut are tight against one another.

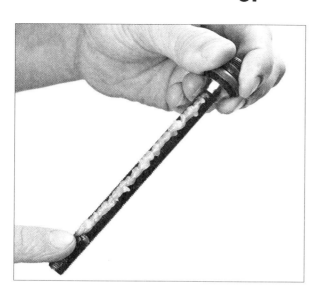

7 Grease the axle well. If both cones came off the axle, put one of them back on and carefully thread it down to its proper position. Replace the lockwasher and the locknut, and lock the nut against the cone as previously explained.

8 When you have all the replacement parts you need, reassemble the hub. Fit the dustcaps back on the hub shell, taking care to seat them properly so the cones can be correctly adjusted. Some metal dustcaps fit so loosely they won't stay in place. An easy fix is to gently grip the edge with the jaws of a diagonal cutter and pull it out very slightly. Repeat at two other spots so that there are three points, each about one-third of the way around the dustcap, that are slightly pulled out. The dustcap will be a tight fit and will stay put.

Apply a thick bead of fresh grease into each of the bearing cups. Insert the correct number (usually 9 per side on rear hubs and 10 per side on fronts) and type of new ball bearings into side of the hub (drive side on freehubs). The grease will hold the bearings in place for the moment.

Slide the axle partway into the hub to secure the bearings in the cup. Insert the new bearings into the other cup. Once they are all in place, slide the axle the rest of the way through the hub.

9 Thread the cone onto the axle until it makes contact with the bearings. Lift the wheel up into a vertical position to check the bearing adjustment. Twirl the axle a bit to make sure the bearings are properly seated, then adjust the cone until there's no tightness or play in the hub.

10 When the adjustment is right, slide on the spacers in the correct order, followed by the locknut. Hold the adjustable cone still with a cone wrench while you tighten the locknut against it. Slide the quick-release skewer back through the axle and thread on its nut. If you have a nutted axle, replace the axle nuts. Remount the wheel on the bike.

Overhauling and Adjusting a Campagnolo Hub Equipped with an Oversize Axle

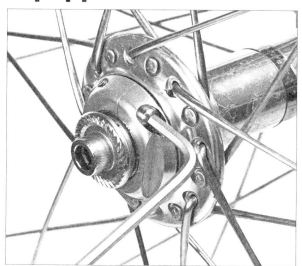

1 Newer Campagnolo hubs use a very large-diameter axle for stiffness and weight savings. Along with this new axle, Campagnolo has devised a simple new method for overhauling and adjusting their hubs. Front and rear hubs follow the same steps, with the difference that the freehub body on the rear hub will stay in place on the axle through all the steps. Campagnolo's new freehub bodies use cartridge bearings and don't require regular maintenance.

Begin by laying two rags or paper towels on your workbench. One can be dirty; the other should be perfectly clean. You'll put your parts on the dirty rag as you remove them from the hub and move them to the clean one as you prepare them for reinstallation. Remove the quick-release skewer and set it and its springs aside. The left side of the hub has a pinch bolt on the adjusting ring. Loosen this using a 2.5 mm hex key.

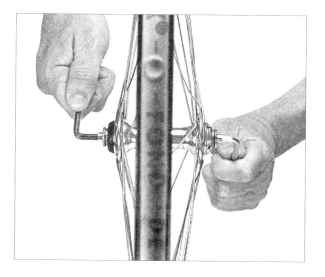

2 Remove the left-side axle cap using a pair of 5 mm hex keys, one in each axle end. Turn them counterclockwise and the axle cap will thread right out. Be sure to keep track of the thin washer between the axle cap and axle.

3 The adjusting ring will now thread off the axle. It may require a wrench to start.

4 Lightly tap the end of the axle with a plastic or rubber hammer to free the axle from the collet that holds the cone in place. The axle is made of aluminum, so under no circumstances should you use a metal hammer for this step. In the absence of a plastic hammer, use the handle of a screwdriver or a block of wood between the hammer's head and the end of the axle. Pull the axle out from the right side and remove the collet and axle from the left. On rear hubs, you may need to slowly rotate the freehub body counterclockwise as you pull it out to let the ratchet pawls snap free.

5 Carefully pry the white seals out of the hub using a pick or small flat screwdriver. Be gentle: Too much force could deform the seals, rendering them less effective or even unusable. Remove the bearings and retainers from the hubshell. Pay close attention to the orientation of the retainers in the hub; you'll need to reinstall them facing the same way. You can discard the retainers if you have a complete new set. If not, pop the old bearings out, clean the retainers thoroughly with degreaser, then with rubbing alcohol, and press new bearings into place.

6 Clean everything. Do this first with degreaser and a rag. After degreasing, use rubbing alcohol and a fresh clean rag or paper towel to rinse everything spotless. Lay all the cleaned parts out on the clean rag. Apply a bead of fresh grease covering both cups in the hubshell, and then put the bearing retainers in place with retainers facing in, and exposed bearings facing out.

Overhauling and Adjusting a Campagnolo Hub
Equipped with an Oversize Axle *continued*

7 Press the seals back over the bearing retainers in their cups. They should pop easily into place with just a little pressure from your thumbs. Slide the axle in from the right, then slip on the left-side cone and collet. On rear hubs, you may need to slowly rotate the freehub body counterclockwise to allow the ratchet pawls to slip into place. Thread the adjusting ring into position, but don't tighten it yet. Using your two 5 mm hex keys, tighten the axle cap and washer back onto the axle end.

8 Bearing adjustment of this system is independent of quick-release tension, unlike most other quick-release hubs. Thread the adjusting ring down by hand until you feel the cone make contact with the bearings. Use an adjustable wrench to turn the adjusting ring down just a fraction of a turn to properly preload the bearings. Turn and wiggle the axle with your fingers. It should spin smoothly and not bind, and have no looseness like you want with conventional quick-release hubs. If your adjustment is too tight, you will need to back the adjusting ring off and tap the axle end with a plastic hammer to release the collet's grip on the axle. Then start your adjustment again. When the adjustment feels right, tighten the pinch bolt on the adjusting ring.

9 Well done. Put the quick-release skewer back through the axle, and you're ready to roll. Don't forget to properly orient the volute springs on the skewer—with the narrow end toward the hub.

Lubricating Sealed-Cartridge Bearings

1 There are a number of hubs available, often called sealed-cartridge bearing hubs, that use precision-bearing cartridges instead of the conventional race-and-cone system. The bearing assembly is a premanufactured unit and is fitted into the hub shell with bearing adjustment preset.

   Many of these hubs have to be sent to the manufacturer or to bicycle shops with special tools for maintenance. Hubs with this kind of sealed bearing usually don't have any place to attach a wrench to the axle. If you suspect that you have hubs of this kind, consult your bicycle dealer before attempting to service them.

   Still, there are some that use cartridge bearings that aren't too tough to service. If, after you've removed the locknut and cone, you see a flat plastic seal (see photo), your hub has cartridge bearings.

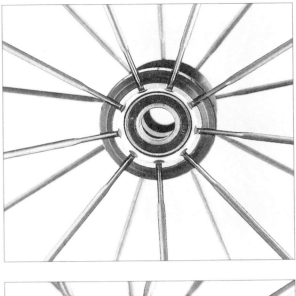

2 These bearings are easy to service and generally hold up quite well, which is why they're common on upper-end mountain bikes. Although the seal protects the bearings, it also allows moisture to be trapped inside, which is why it's important to regrease the bearings. To service this type of hub, first wipe off any dirt that has accumulated on the seal. Gently slide the tip of a sharp knife or utility knife under the edge of the plastic seal, and pry the seal off the bearing cartridge (see photo). Be careful: Don't bend the seal.

3 Once you've removed the seal, you'll see the bearings beneath. Charge them with fresh grease by squeezing in enough to cover all the balls (see photo). Then simply press the seal back in place with your fingers until you feel it seat in the cartridge. Repeat for the other bearing, and reassemble the axle.

   To adjust bearings, screw the cone in until it rests against the bearing (or dustcap), snug the locknut against it, and, using two wrenches, one on the cone and another on the locknut, turn the parts against each other to lock the adjustment. When done, there should be no play in the axle and the hub bearings should feel smooth and not tight when you turn the axle.

   Some hubs have this type of serviceable cartridge-sealed bearing but employ clever axle designs that seem impossible to disassemble. In some cases they are; in others, they only look hard to take apart. It might take some detective work to find the secret, but if you can figure out how to get the hub apart, regreasing the bearings is easy. If it's a particularly challenging design, contact a shop or the manufacturer for instructions or advice.

6 CRANKSETS

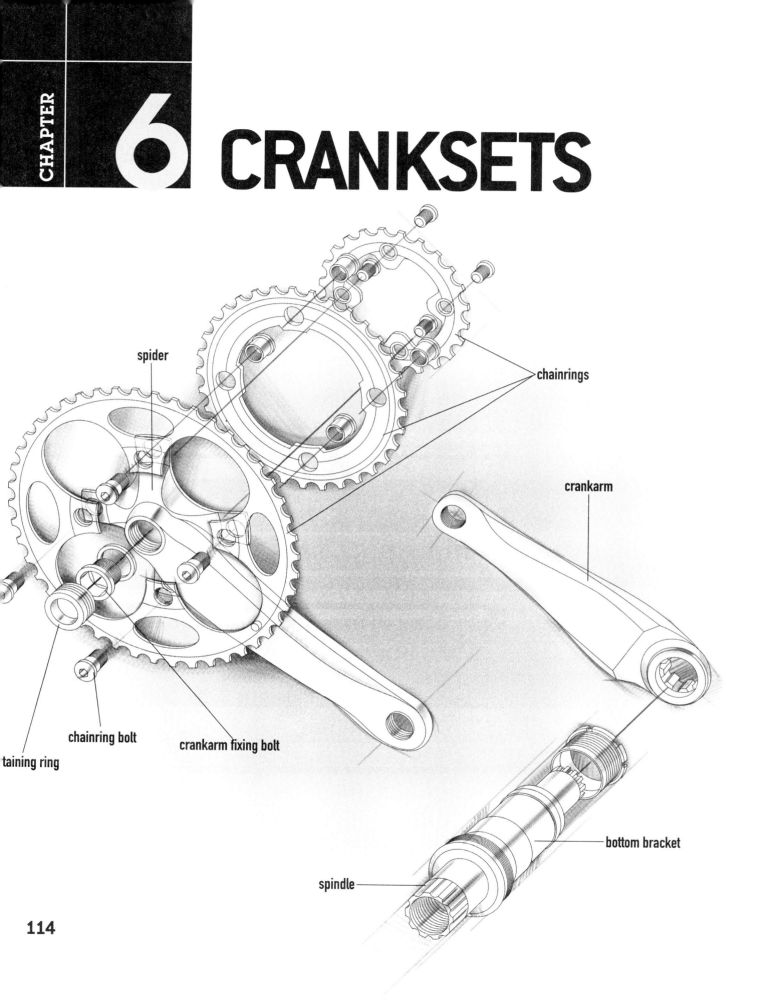

spider

chainrings

crankarm

chainring bolt

crankarm fixing bolt

taining ring

spindle

bottom bracket

The crankset, like most parts of the bicycle, is designed first and foremost to do its job in the most efficient manner possible—a textbook case of form following function. As such, what is one of the bicycle's largest components is also one of the most recognizable. The designs differ slightly, but all cranksets do the same job: They serve as the point where human power becomes mechanical motion by taking leg power from the pedals and transferring it to the chain and ultimately to the rear wheel. The crankset also must support the weight of the rider when standing—or landing—so it needs to be very strong.

Most cranksets consist of a right and left crankarm, a bottom bracket assembly (this includes the spindle, cups, and bearings held inside the frame), and one or more chainrings. The right crankarm is the one that has the chainrings, or sprockets, attached to it. These chainrings attach to arms built into the crankarm or a plate that attaches to the arm. This part of the crankarm or piece is the spider.

The spider's arms radiate outward from the base of the right crankarm. Some cranksets integrate the spider with the chainrings, while others make the spider part of the right crankarm, with the chainrings as separate pieces. The ability to separate the chainrings from the spider makes them easy to replace when worn or damaged.

There are three general kinds of cranksets: one-piece cranksets, cottered cranksets, and cotterless cranksets. One-piece cranksets, sometimes called Ashtabula cranksets, are found primarily on juvenile bicycles and inexpensive adult bicycles. These cranksets integrate the bottom bracket spindle and the crankarms into one piece. One-piece cranksets are generally made of steel, which makes them very durable, but they are also quite heavy. All it takes to service this type of crankset is a pair of water-pump

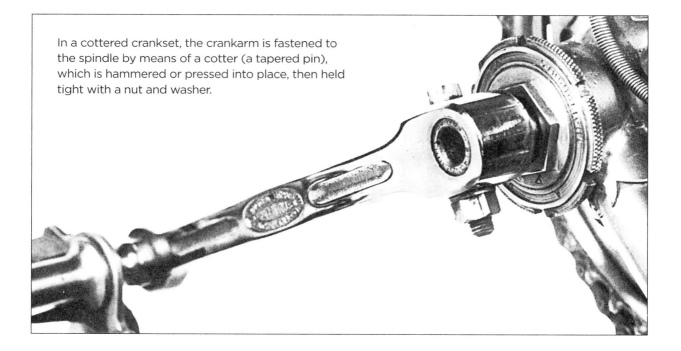

In a cottered crankset, the crankarm is fastened to the spindle by means of a cotter (a tapered pin), which is hammered or pressed into place, then held tight with a nut and washer.

There are two types of square-taper crankarm spindles. One has a hollow axle end that is threaded to receive a bolt (*top*), and the other has a threaded stud on the end that receives a nut (*bottom*).

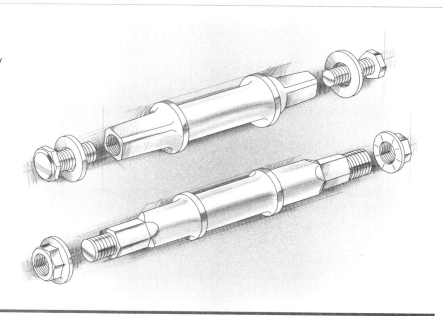

pliers that are large enough to grab the nut on the left side. Keep in mind, though, that this nut and the cone beneath it (it's sometimes covered by a washer), which is used to adjust the bottom bracket, are reverse-thread. Turn to the left (counterclockwise) to tighten and to the right (clockwise) to loosen.

Cottered cranksets use two separate crankarms that mount onto a spindle. These cranksets are held on the spindle by means of cotters, tapered metal pins inserted through holes in the crankarm that are lined up with grooves on the ends of the spindle. Generally, either a hammer or a special press is used to seat the cotters firmly, and nuts fastened to their ends hold them in place. Most cottered cranksets are steel, though some have aluminum alloy chainrings.

Cotterless cranksets are the most popular cranksets for use on high-quality bikes, and it is this

Axle? Spindle? Which Is It?

Two terms exist for seemingly similar components—axles and spindles. It's easy to confuse the two, but there is a difference—and it has to do with how the part moves or doesn't move. Simply put, an axle remains stationary while something rotates around it—like the axle of a wheel—and a spindle revolves inside a stationary bracket—like the spindle of a crankset.

type that is pictured in the illustration. Most cotterless crankarms have square tapered holes that fit onto the end of a spindle, which is also square and tapered on the ends. In recent years, new designs for fitting crankarms to spindles have emerged that employ a larger, splined hole and spindle. All cotterless crankarms are held in place with either a nut or a bolt (see illustration on this page), depending on whether the spindle ends have threaded studs on their tips or are hollowed out and threaded on the inside. Most cotterless cranksets and chainrings are made of aluminum. Cotterless cranksets come in a multitude of styles and offer a wide selection of crankarm lengths, chainring sizes, and bottom brackets.

THE BOTTOM BRACKET

The bottom bracket consists of the spindle (which may have cone-shaped bearing races near each end), two cups, and two sets of bearings that are mounted in the bicycle frame and support the crankarms. Currently, the most common type of bottom bracket on quality bikes is designed as a one-piece cartridge that requires little, if any, service.

The part of the bicycle frame in which the bottom bracket is installed is the bottom bracket shell. The bottom bracket is held in the shell by cups that thread in. These, along with the bearings, support the spindle and the crankarms attached to it and allow them to spin.

The main function of the bottom bracket is to spin. However, while the spindle spins, it must also carry the torsional and lateral loads produced when the bicycle is pedaled. To minimize power losses and wear, the bottom bracket bearing adjustment must be properly maintained. A bottom bracket spindle should spin smoothly, without binding or looseness, on bearings that are properly protected. Grease is used not only to lubricate the bearings but also to protect them from both dirt contamination and moisture that can cause rust.

Sealed-bearing systems are the latest word in bottom brackets. Shimano currently produces only this type of bottom bracket, and most of Campagnolo's are also sealed. These units require little or no service because the bearings are protected with seals that prevent the grease and the bearings from becoming contaminated with grit. If you have a good-quality bike manufactured after 1992, it probably has a sealed bottom bracket, which will require little service. In fact, most of these bottom brackets are designed to be replaced if they wear out or fail. Fortunately, they hold up nicely and aren't that expensive when it's time to replace them. Because the bearing is preadjusted and prelubricated at the factory, it's impossible to damage the unit by maladjustment, and because it's sealed, it's unnecessary to lubricate it.

Other less-common sealed-bearing bottom brackets can sometimes be serviced, but they may require special (and sometimes expensive) tools. Some units, however, can be serviced with standard tools. Because each is a unique design, consult your owner's manual to find out how to service the unit. As a general rule, if you can access the bearings, it's usually possible to add grease, which in many cases is all the service that is required to keep these sealed units operating smoothly.

MORE IS BETTER

Two major new developments made in recent years have all but taken over the market of high-performance cranksets and bottom brackets—spline interfaces and external bottom brackets. Tried and true, square spindles have been around for decades, and they are entirely adequate. They make contact

Cotterless crank bottom brackets now come in several different configurations. When replacing crankarms or bottom brackets, be sure of which system you're using.

with each crankarm at four points and maintain their grip by slightly stretching the aluminum crankarm over the tapered spindle. The endless search for greater performance, more strength, and less weight, however, knows no bounds. Progression in the realm of freeride mountain biking, too, has strained the capabilities of the trusty square spindle.

There are three spline interface designs that are common on the market today. Shimano developed both the Octalink V-1 and Octalink V-2; the third design, ISIS (International Spline Interface System), was born of a cooperative effort between Chris King Components, RaceFace, and Truvativ. The Octalink V-1, Octalink V-2, and ISIS are in no way cross-compatible, so be sure of what you have before spending your money.

There are two key benefits to the design of these spline-fit bottom brackets. First, by using several splines rather than a square as the interface, the contact area between crankarm and spindle is increased, reducing the risk of mashing the relatively soft aluminum of the crankarm on the steel of the spindle under heavy torque or impact (which ultimately results in a poor fit between spindle and crankarm and requires replacement of the arm). The second benefit is the larger diameter of the spindle. This makes it possible to manufacture a hollow spindle with thin walls, saving weight while maintaining the same level of strength. Or the spindle can be made thick, yielding more strength than a traditional spindle ever could.

THE PRICE

Since the diameter of the bottom bracket shell remained the same and the spindle got larger, it became necessary to use smaller ball bearings. Smaller ball bearings need to rotate more times per revolution of the spindle and thus, they wear out more quickly. Don't throw out your spline-fit cranksets just yet, though. These bottom brackets still last many thousands of miles, and the benefits to most riders in terms of strength, rigidity, and weight savings far outweigh the shortcoming of marginally reduced bearing life.

THE NEXT LEVEL

Not ones to rest, both Shimano and RaceFace have raised the bar again with new cranksets that address the issue of how to fit a large spindle and full ¼-inch ball bearings without enlarging the frame's bottom bracket shell. In the sort of move that is obvious only after someone else has thought of it, they figured out that putting the bearing cups to the outside of the bottom bracket shell would give them all the space

The most recent trend in performance cranksets is the two-piece design, where one crankarm is permanently or semi-permanently attached to a large-diameter, hollow spindle. The bottom bracket bearings for these systems ride outside the bottom bracket shell, allowing for larger, more durable bearings and increased drivetrain rigidity.

they needed and even produced another benefit—a wider bearing stance that makes the drivetrain even a little bit stiffer.

These new outboard bottom brackets require specific cranksets, but what cranksets they are! The cranksets are built with a spindle that is permanently or semi-permanently attached to one of the two crankarms. With one arm and the spindle making up one piece and the other arm as the second piece, these cranksets have come to be known, logically, as two-piece cranksets. On top of the leaps made in the categories of weight, strength, and service life, installation has become incredibly simple and straightforward, as well.

Both manufacturers have a slightly different approach to installation. Shimano's spindle is permanently fixed to the right crankarm, and the left arm attaches by means of a preload cap with a pair of pinch bolts to hold the arm firmly in place. Conversely, RaceFace semi-permanently fits the spindle to the left arm (meaning the spindle or left arm can still be replaced individually if the need ever arises) and affixes the right arm in the same manner that their ISIS splined spindles and crankarms are mated. Oddly enough, though, these two fiercely competitive manufacturers arrived at a common spindle diameter and bearing stance, making it possible to use a RaceFace crankset with a Shimano bottom bracket, and vice versa.

IDENTIFYING THE BOTTOM BRACKET TYPE

Cup-and-cone-style bottom brackets, unlike sealed models, require regular maintenance. To determine if your frame has this bottom bracket type, look for a notched and possibly knurled lockring on the left side (the side without the chainrings). Also look at the cup faces. Modern sealed-cartridge-style bottom brackets (see photo on page 117) employ cups that are splined inside to accept the installation and removal tool. Other sealed bottom brackets have notched rings on both the right and left sides. If you see the notched ring only on the left side and notice that the cup faces are flat, your frame probably has the older cup-and-cone-style bottom bracket.

To function properly, this type of bottom bracket requires periodic maintenance. How often maintenance is performed depends on the number of miles ridden, the environment, and the kind of bottom bracket. Road bicycles ridden only on sunny weekends at distances of 30 miles or less may require a bottom bracket overhaul every 2 or 3 years. Bicycles that are used every day, regardless of the weather, should be overhauled at least once a year. Mountain bikes ridden in the muck may require it twice a year or more. This preventive maintenance can save the cost of a new bottom bracket by catching minor problems before they ruin the bottom bracket.

Bottom Bracket Threading

BRACKET TYPE	THREADING
English	1.37" × 24 tpi*
French	35mm × 1.0mm
Italian	36mm × 24 tpi*

* threads per inch

Note: All left-side cups (nondrive side) are turned clockwise to tighten/install. English right-side cups are reverse-threaded (turned counterclockwise to tighten/install). French and Italian right-side cups are turned clockwise to tighten/install.

CHANGING CRANKS

To change the crankset, consider these factors.

What kind of bottom bracket do you have? If your frame has an oversize bottom bracket shell used for one-piece cranksets, such as on older Schwinn road bikes and some bikes sold at department stores, you can use only one-piece cranksets unless you buy a conversion bottom bracket assembly. However, these conversion kits are hard to find and are intended primarily for BMX (bicycle motocross) bicycles, and you may have trouble fitting a double- or triple-chainring crankset to them since they were intended for single-chainring use.

Cottered and cotterless bottom brackets, on the other hand, thread into the bottom bracket shell the same way. So if you have a bike with a cottered crankset, you can change to a cotterless unit, as long as you change everything. That is to say, you can't use a spindle from a cottered bottom bracket assembly with a set of cotterless crankarms. The spindle and the crankarms won't match.

The major consideration when changing bottom bracket assemblies is the threading of the bottom bracket shell. Most bottom brackets come in English, French, or Italian threadings. You must get the correct one for your frame; they are not interchangeable. To complicate matters, the frame's origin isn't always a true indicator of its type of bottom bracket threads. But with a set of calipers and a thread gauge, it's possible to measure the cups. Check them against the table on this page to determine the threading and type of bottom bracket needed. Otherwise, take one of the cups or the entire bicycle to a bicycle shop to find out what kind of threads it has.

Another factor to consider when replacing bottom brackets is the width of the bottom bracket shell. The two most common sizes are 68 mm and 70 mm. Some mountain bikes have 73 mm bottom brackets. Most French- and English-thread bicycles have a bottom bracket width of 68 mm, while 70 mm is standard for most bottom brackets equipped with Italian threads. Sometimes the spindle is stamped with a 68 or 70 to tell you the bottom bracket width for which it was designed, but the only way to be certain of the width of your shell is to measure it. Use a small ruler to measure from one side to the other. Don't include any part of the bottom bracket—just measure the bottom bracket shell width.

Most cranksets have a bottom bracket that is designed specifically for them. If you want to mix the crankset of one manufacturer with the bottom bracket of another, check with one of the manufacturers as to the compatibility of such a match-up. Sometimes it works and sometimes it doesn't. Or ask your bicycle shop to check *Sutherland's Handbook for Bicycle Mechanics* (or buy a copy and check it yourself). This handbook is a standard reference tool in most bicycle shops.

Most replacement cranksets are made of aluminum, which makes them quiet, light, durable, and trouble-free when installed correctly. When purchasing a crankset, be sure to get a model with interchangeable chainrings. Look for aluminum chainrings when possible. Some inexpensive cranksets come with steel chainrings, but compared to aluminum, steel rings are heavy and very noisy when shifting. The exceptions are on some mountain bike cranksets. On these, you'll sometimes find steel used for the smallest chainring because an aluminum model could wear quickly.

Generally, the higher the price of the crankset, the higher the quality. Inexpensive aluminum cranksets sometimes have the right crankarm swaged on to the spider. A swaged fitting is similar to a rivet; one piece of metal is bent in such a way that it holds firmly to another piece of metal. A fitting of this type can loosen with age. In better cranksets, the arm and the spider are forged from a single piece of metal or bolted together.

As you go up the price scale in cranksets, you find systems made of lighter and stronger materials. The machining processes get more precise, which translates into systems that allow better and quieter shifts and chainrings that last longer. Weigh the benefits against the costs to determine the level of quality you are willing to pay for.

Also decide what chainring sizes to buy. Some cranksets offer a wider range of possibilities than others. For more information on an individual crankset's range, ask a shop that sells the crankset or check the manufacturer's literature. For advice on how to determine the chainring sizes that best suit your riding ability and needs, consult Chapter 17.

One basic decision is whether you want a double- or a triple-chainring set. The double is standard fare for road racers and most road sport riders, but many people prefer the gearing flexibility that is gained with a triple. Triples are standard on mountain bikes, and they can add a low range of gears that are well suited to loaded touring and steep climbs. If you don't expect to do much of this type of riding, the third chainring may be useless, so think carefully about your gearing requirements and decide accordingly. Just be sure before purchasing that the crankset you select accepts the chainring sizes you want.

There's also the matter of crankarm length. The standard mountain bike length is 175 mm, and on road bikes it's 172.5 mm. While these are the most readily available and most commonly used, crankarms are available in 2.5 mm increments, from 165 mm to 185 mm. Crankarms are measured from the center of the pedal hole to the center of the crankarm dustcap, but the length is usually stamped on the back.

There are a few theories concerning crankarm length. Most relate the length of the crankarm to the rider's leg length. Longer arms aid uphill riding because they offer greater leverage, but they're more difficult to spin, so they limit leg speed. For a long-legged rider this isn't a problem because longer thigh muscles benefit from the added crankarm length. For shorter riders, this can hamper riding form on the bike. Long arms may enhance the climbing ability of such riders, but the rest of the time their riding will suffer.

If you're tall (over 6 feet), climb a lot, and tend to push big gears rather than spin, long crankarms are for you. Otherwise, you should stick to 172.5 mm—or shorter, if you have short legs.

Interestingly, mountain bikes come stock with 175 mm crankarms. This is because when riding off road, there's more climbing and the speeds are slower. For most riders, this length is perfect. Only riders under 5 feet tall need to consider swapping for shorter crankarms. Consider longer arms only if you're 6 feet, 4 inches or taller. Before buying, make sure that you'll still have sufficient ground clearance if you ride technical trails.

PREPARING A BOTTOM BRACKET SHELL

Before installing a bottom bracket in a new frame, have the frame tapped and faced by a shop that has the special tools required. This is especially impor-

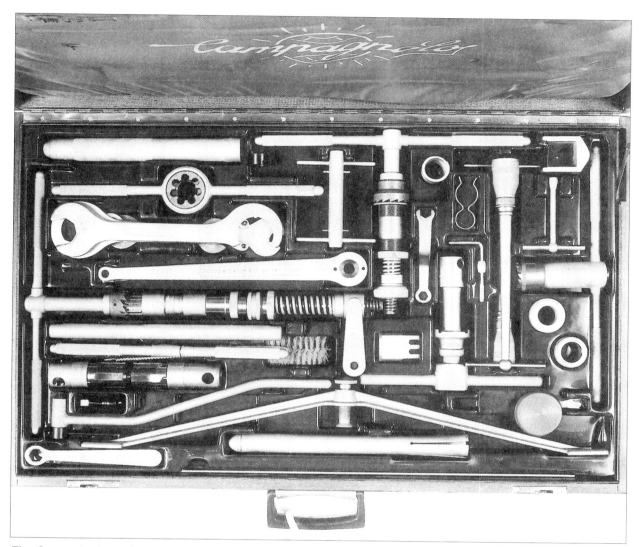

The Campagnolo tool kit has all of the tools necessary to properly dress the head tube and bottom bracket shell of most road frames and many mountain frames.

tant for cup-and-cone-style bottom brackets because the cups tighten against the sides of the bottom bracket shell. In order to make a proper bearing adjustment, the sides of the frame's bottom bracket shell must be made nearly perfectly parallel, which is what tapping and facing tools are for.

Most modern bottom brackets are sealed-cartridge designs that are threaded into the frame's bottom bracket shell but do not rely on parallel surfaces to achieve a proper adjustment (the adjustment is set at the factory). It's still important that the threads in the frame are prepared properly so that the cartridge and cup will thread in properly. Some-

times, new frames arrive with too-shallow threads, which make bottom bracket installation difficult. If the bottom bracket cartridge won't thread into the frame easily, have the threads tapped (also called "chased") by a shop.

Tapping prepares the inside of the bottom bracket shell. A special thread-cutting tool called a tap is run through the threaded parts of the shell. The tap cuts the threads to the proper shape and depth and also makes the threads on the left side concentric with the threads on the right side.

Facing tools are used to prepare both ends of the bottom bracket shell. These special cutting tools smooth the outer edges of the bottom bracket shell and make them parallel to each other as well as perpendicular to the centerline of the threads. This allows the cups on cup-and-cone-style bottom brackets to tighten properly against the frame so that they won't back out as you're pedaling.

We recommend having a shop do the tapping and facing of the bottom bracket because the tools required to do it are quite expensive and rarely needed. The traditional standard tool set used to prepare a frame is the coveted Campagnolo tool kit, which sells in shops for more than $4,000. The kit is a selection of mills, dies, taps, and other special hand tools needed to completely prepare the frame. It's ideal for most road frames. Mountain frames usually require other tools since the dimensions are slightly different. There are less-expensive frame-tool kits available, but they still have price tags that discourage ownership by a single individual as opposed to a commercial shop.

Of course, it takes some bucks to have this work done in a shop. Should you spend it? For modern sealed bottom brackets, do it only if the threads in the frame won't allow easy installation of the bottom bracket. For cup-and-cone-style bottom brackets, have a shop prepare the frame if it's a high-quality bottom bracket and if the frame's bottom bracket shell looks as if it's never been prepared (look for paint on the sides of the bottom bracket). The good thing is, it's a one-time expense (per frame), and it'll extend the life of cup-and-cone bottom brackets.

OVERHAULING A CRANKSET AND BOTTOM BRACKET

Special tools are needed for cotterless crankset and bottom bracket overhauls, depending on the type of crankset and bottom bracket. For all types, you'll need a crankbolt wrench and crankarm extractor to remove the crankarms.

Most sealed-cartridge bottom brackets are removed and installed with splined tools that fit inside the cups. Get the model that matches your bottom bracket (usually Shimano or Campagnolo). Cup-and-cone-style bottom brackets require a lockring spanner, a pin tool for the adjustable cup, and a wrench for the fixed cup.

To overhaul cup-and-cone-style bottom brackets, get some medium-weight grease and purchase new

ball bearings of the appropriate number and size (usually 22 of the ¼-inch size).

Remove the pedals. If the crankset is grimy and you plan to clean it with solvent, remove the pedals to prevent solvent from getting inside the pedal bearings. First, shift the chain onto the large chainring to minimize the chances of getting cut by the teeth while removing the pedals.

Pedal removal usually requires a 15 mm pedal wrench. Some newer clipless designs from Time, Crank Brothers, Shimano, and others will need a long 6 mm or 8 mm hex key, like one of Pedro's Pedal Drivers, while older French pedals fitted into French-threaded crankarms require a 16 mm open-end wrench. The right pedal, the one on the side with the chain and sprockets, has a right-hand thread and threads out counterclockwise. The left pedal has a left-hand thread and threads out clockwise.

To remove either pedal, rotate the crankarm until the pedal is at the front of the bike. Fit the wrench on the pedal so that it runs back alongside the crankarm, then push down. Keep the bike from moving and the wheels will provide the resistance needed to keep the crankarms from turning while loosening the pedals. Shift the chain to the large chainring before doing this to prevent the chainring teeth from biting into your knuckles should you slip.

Once the pedals are off, remove the crankarms from the bottom bracket spindle. The left crankarm should be removed first.

Remove the cottered crankarms (often found on old bikes). If you have an old-fashioned cottered crank, remove the arms by loosening the cotter nuts and forcing out the cotters. Use a wrench to loosen the nuts, a hammer and punch to drive out the cotters, and a block of wood to support the crankarms while you're pounding on them. Commercial cotter-pin presses are available, but they cost more than individual bike owners generally want to pay. Some people have created homemade presses with such things as locking pliers and heavy-duty C-clamps, but the hammer approach is the one most commonly used. Whatever method you use, plan on buying new cotters because the removal process usually damages the originals.

Remove the cotterless crankarms (modern style). A specialized tool is needed to remove cotterless crankarms, though the process is much easier than driving out cotter pins. Don't try to remove

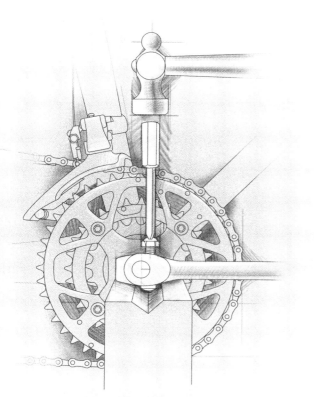

The traditional method for removing cotters from a crankarm involves using a hammer and punch. Support the crankarm with a wooden block or length of pipe to transmit the force of the hammer blows directly to the cotter, or the hammer blows may simply smash the cotter, essentially fusing it into the crankarm and making it nearly impossible to remove.

crankarms by any method other than using the tool made for the job. There are universal crankarm removal tools on the market that work, but the wisest choice is to use the tool made by the manufacturer of the crankset because it will be the one most certain to fit. Some crankset manufacturers make a tool that has a bolt wrench at one end, a crankarm extractor at the other, and wrench flats in the middle for gripping and turning the tool.

There are three common ways that crankarms are attached. Most new bikes have hex key bolts securing the crankarms. Removal is simple: Just turn the bolts counterclockwise with the appropriate hex key. On other bikes, there may be dustcaps covering the crankarm bolts. Remove them to get at the bolts. There are also cranksets equipped with

one-step removal systems. In these systems, the dustcap is left in place during the crankarm removal process. A hole in the dustcap allows you to insert a hex key into the head of the bolt. As you unscrew the bolt, it pushes against the back of the dustcap, forcing the arm off the end of the spindle (so you don't need a crankarm removal tool, just the hex key).

Dustcaps that cover crankbolts are simply protecting the threads inside the crankarms, into which the crankarm extractor will fit. Such a dustcap has either a narrow slit in it or a hole that is shaped to receive a hex key. If it's the latter, remove the dustcap with the appropriate wrench. If it's the former, use a wide, flat-blade screwdriver or a quarter. If the slit is on the dustcap edge, pry the dustcap off. If the slit is centered, unscrew the dustcap. Don't damage the dustcap.

Once the dustcap is off, remove the fastener that's holding the crankarm on the spindle. Square-taper bottom bracket spindles come in two types (see the illustration on page 116). One type has a threaded hole in each end, and bolts, aided by washers, hold the crankarms in place. The other type has a threaded stud at each end and serrated nuts that need no washers to hold the crankarms in place. Use a crankarm bolt wrench or a thin-wall socket to remove the crankarm bolt or nut. Be sure to remove the washers, too (if there are any).

Before you thread the crankarm extractor into the crankarm, make sure that the center section of the extractor is backed all the way out. Also double-check that the washer is not inside the crankarm because it will prevent removal. Thread the extractor in until the threads of the tool have gone all the way into the threads of the crankarm.

Turn the center section of the tool clockwise (use a wrench if necessary) until it begins to push against the spindle. Continue turning the tool to force the crankarm off the end of the spindle.

Check the bottom bracket and clean the chainrings. Once the crankarms are removed, grab the end of the spindle and turn and wiggle it to check the adjustment. Is there play? Does it spin smoothly, or does it bind? Does it turn with a hydraulic-like resistance? How much dirt is clinging to the area around the spindle? These are indicators of problems that may mean you should replace the cartridge (if it's a sealed-cartridge bottom bracket), or that you should overhaul the unit (if it's a cone-and-cup type).

With the crankarms off the bike, wipe the dirt from around the bottom bracket area of the frame (be careful not to push dirt into the bottom bracket bearings, unless you're replacing or overhauling them). This is also a good time to disassemble the right crankarm, remove the chainrings, and clean them. Do this with a 5 mm hex key. If a bolt turns but won't loosen, hold the back of the bolt with a chainring nut spanner, a special tool that fits in the groove on the back. (Try a wide-blade screwdriver if you don't have the tool.) Grease the bolts before re-assembly and tighten them securely. Otherwise, your crankset may drive you bonkers with annoying clicking sounds when you're out on the trail.

If the bottom bracket is a sealed-cartridge model, the spindle should turn with a hydraulic re-sistance. A sealed bottom bracket is shot when the spindle spins effortlessly and feels and sounds dry. Also, look for signs of rust near the spindle, which indicate that water has penetrated the seals and con-taminated the bearings. Oddly enough, it's possible to ride on a wasted sealed-cartridge bottom bracket, but expect some crunching noises and don't count on it lasting too long. The bearings may disintegrate and jam the spindle.

Sealed-bearing bottom brackets are available in a wide price range, so it's always best to simply buy and install a new one if yours is worn out. Installa-tion is easy; just be sure to purchase the correct re-placement bottom bracket. The new one must match the length of the old one. The folks at the bike shop can select the right one if you take the old one in.

If you're checking a cup-and-cone-style bottom bracket, feel the spindle for roughness and play. If it turns smoothly with a slight hydraulic resistance and no play, it doesn't need to be overhauled. Always check the tightness of the fixed cup (on the left side) and lockring with tools.

The fixed cup is tricky. It probably tightens by turning to the left, but if that loosens it, turn it to the right. Get it as tight as possible. (If the loos-ening repeats, back out the fixed cup so that several threads show, apply thread adhesive, and tighten.) Then snug the lockring before reinstalling the crankarms.

INSTALLING CARTRIDGE-STYLE BOTTOM BRACKETS

Before installing a new cartridge-style bottom bracket, you'll need to remove the old one, of course. It might be as easy as turning the cartridge out with the splined removal tool. Turn the left-side cup first, counterclockwise, until it comes out of the frame. Then turn the right side clockwise to remove the cartridge.

If the cups won't turn, don't force them initially, especially if they're made of plastic. Instead, apply Liquid Wrench to the cup edges and tap the bottom bracket shell with a hammer to vibrate it, which works the solvent into the threads. Wait a while and try to turn the cups again. Repeat this procedure until the cups unscrew, or take the bike to a shop for professional help with removing the frozen cartridge.

Cartridge-sealed bottom brackets come packed with grease and adjusted from the factory. Before in-stalling the new cartridge, turn the spindle by hand to feel how it turns—how the factory adjustment feels. Later, when it's installed, the spindle should turn ap-proximately as easily as when it's out of the bike.

Cartridge bottom brackets usually have one cup preinstalled on the drive side of the cartridge. If the bottom bracket is being installed in a titanium frame, coat the threads with an anti-seize com-pound. Finish Line Ti-Prep is a titanium-specific anti-seize available at most bike shops, but if you can't find it, Permatex anti-seize is close to the same thing and is available from hardware or auto-supply stores. This will prevent chronic clicking noises from the bottom bracket area and inhibit galvanic corrosion that could freeze the bottom bracket into the shell. Another solution is to wrap plumber's Teflon tape around the threads before installing the cartridge and cup. (Grease is usually adequate for steel and aluminum frames.)

Start threading the cartridge into the drive side of the frame by hand-turning it counterclockwise. Be careful not to cross-thread it. When it gets tough to turn, install the splined tool and continue turning until the cup is snug and fully screwed into the frame (it'll only go so far because of the built-in lip on the cup's edge).

Install the other cup (be careful not to cross-thread it), turning it clockwise with the splined tool. Check how things are going by turning the spindle by hand. If it's a lot tighter than it was before installation, it's likely the cup is going in crooked. Remove it and start it again, making sure it's straight. Turn the cup until it bottoms against the cartridge. When the cup is secure, check the installation by putting the splined tool on the drive side again and making sure it's tight, then double-checking the tightness of the left-side cup. Finally, grab the spindle and turn it. It should feel smooth, like it did before installation. If not, try again.

There are many different sealed-bearing bottom bracket designs today. The preceding directions apply to common types. If yours seems different, follow the manufacturer's installation instructions. If you don't have them, get them from the dealer who sold you the bottom bracket, contact the manufacturer, or check its Web site.

OVERHAULING CUP-AND-CONE MODELS

To disassemble cup-and-cone-style bottom brackets, remove the lockring (on the left side) with a lockring spanner. Some spanners are unique to a particular brand of bottom bracket, while others, such as hook spanners and plier-type spanners, are more universal. Once again, tools made to match with a particular brand of component are generally the surest fitting, but not all manufacturers have such tools. You may have to use the universal kind. If you don't have a lockring spanner, a hammer and punch, used with care, can be used to drive the lockring off. Some lockrings have peculiar notch spacings and may require a hammer and punch since even the universal tools won't grip the part adequately.

Remove the lockring by turning it counterclockwise. Work cautiously—the threads of the ring and the cup are prone to producing metal shards that can jab your fingers.

Turn the adjustable cup (what the lockring was holding in place) counterclockwise to remove it. Usually a special spanner is needed for this also. Many of the better bottom brackets match a pin spanner with a series of six pinholes in the adjustable cup. Some cups have notches, and a few have a hex fitting that is suitable for an appropriately sized wrench. Here again, some companies make special spanners for their adjusting cups, and these will en-sure the best fit, but there are also a variety of universal pin-and-notch spanners available.

When removing the adjustable cup, be careful in case the bearings are not in a retainer. Place a rag or a piece of paper under the bottom bracket to catch any bearings that may drop out. Once the adjustable cup is out, remove the spindle, bearings, and dust sleeve. Not all bottom brackets have the latter, which is a plastic sleeve that prevents dirt and debris in the frame tubes from entering the bottom bracket shell and contaminating the bearings.

For the time being, leave the fixed cup in the frame. Clean and examine all the bottom bracket components that you removed, as well as the bottom bracket shell and the fixed cup. Use solvent and either a rag or a small brush to remove any contaminants and as much grease as possible.

Look at the adjustable cup race for any pitting or excessive wear on the scored line around the surface of the race. This is the bearing path. Carefully check the spindle at the shoulders for the wear line and examine it closely. Inspect the fixed cup also, possibly with a flashlight. Look at the ball bearings. Check to make sure that none have cracked or broken. See if the retainer (the metal or plastic ring that holds the bearings) is intact. If either a bearing or the retainer is damaged, make sure that no broken part is clinging inside the frame in such a way that it may drop into the bottom bracket after reassembly.

If any of the components are heavily worn or damaged, replace them. They'll ruin the bottom bracket adjustment and cause additional wear to the other bottom bracket components.

Replace all the bearings, even if they don't appear worn. Good bearings are inexpensive and will make adjusting the bottom bracket easier.

If the fixed cup is worn and needs to be removed, it's best to have the task performed at a bicycle shop that has a special fixed cup tool. In some cases, it's possible to lock the fixed cup in a vise and spin the frame off it. This method will work if the flats of the fixed cup are large enough to grab. However, proceed very carefully. If you slip, you may damage the cup or your frame. The fixed cup may be locked down very tightly to keep it from working loose. Most home mechanics cannot get enough leverage to remove this part. If the special fixed cup tool is needed to remove your fixed cup, you will

125

also need it to properly lock the cup or its replacement back into your frame.

If you must remove the fixed cup, remember that English-thread bicycles (found on most bicycles) use left-hand threads on the fixed cup, meaning that the fixed cup spins out clockwise. All others, except for some rare Swiss threads, unscrew counterclockwise. When installing a fixed cup in a steel frame, apply thread adhesive to ensure that it stays tight.

Tapping and facing cup-and-cone bottom brackets. If you have removed both cups from the cup-and-cone-style bottom bracket, you may want to have the bottom bracket shell tapped and faced (this is not usually needed on sealed-cartridge bottom brackets). As described earlier, tapping cleans and cuts the threads to the proper dimension, making threading in the cups easier. It also makes both sets of threads concentric, that is, cut on the same axis, which allows a finer bearing adjustment than is otherwise possible. The facing tool shaves the bottom bracket shell's outer edges so the lockring and the fixed cup seat are parallel to each other and perpendicular to the axis of the spindle.

Custom framebuilders tap and face bottom brackets as a matter of course, but many fine stock frames have never been faced. If you have such a frame, you may want to have a bicycle shop tap and face it for you. It is a one-time expense that will provide you with years of easier and more precise bottom bracket adjustments. It's usually needed for a cartridge-sealed bottom bracket only when the frame threads are so poorly manufactured that the cartridge can't be threaded in (this is a rare occurrence).

INSTALLING CUP-AND-CONE BOTTOM BRACKETS

Now that you have removed, cleaned, and replaced any worn parts of the bottom bracket, reinstall everything.

If you removed the fixed cup, grease both its threads and those in the bottom bracket shell before threading the cup back in. Be sure that the fixed cup is locked down very tightly, preferably using a tool designed for fixed cups. If you've had problems with this cup repeatedly loosening, don't grease it or the frame. Instead, apply thread adhesive before installing and tightening it.

Apply a liberal amount of medium-weight grease to the fixed cup's bearing race. If medium-weight grease is unavailable, lightweight grease is preferable to heavy. To apply the grease, reach through the bottom bracket. Be careful not to let any dirt or metal from the bottom bracket contaminate the grease. Once the race is greased, install the bearings. If the bearings are in a retainer, pack the retainer with grease and insert it into the cup. If the bearings are loose, stick each bearing into the cup individually, relying on the grease to hold the bearings in place until the spindle is installed.

Caged bearings versus loose bearings. Bearings come two ways: loose, and in retainers. Both work fine. The retainer conveniently holds the bearings while you work with them, so if your bottom bracket has balls in retainers, use them. Some folks argue that retainers add friction, but it's so little that it's not worth worrying about. Fact is, when cup-and-cone-style bottom brackets were the main type, most racing team mechanics used the retainers because they sped up bottom bracket overhauls.

One of the most difficult things to do is to explain which way a retainer fits into a cup. Only one way works. Assembling the bottom bracket with the retainer in backward prevents proper adjustment and, if the bottom bracket is used that way, will ruin something. Many a mechanic has been distracted just long enough to slide a retainer on backward only to discover the error when he tries to eliminate the side-to-side play later while adjusting.

Look at a retainer. There are two common types: One has rounded edges and a fingertip-size hole, and the other has a flat profile and a smaller hole. The rounded style is most common. On both retainer styles, the metal frame that holds the balls looks like a C in cross-section. On flat-style retainers, the open side of this C should face in toward the shoulder of the spindle. Thus, the open sides of the two retainers will face each other when properly installed in the bottom bracket. Round-style retainers are installed the opposite way.

After the bearings are installed, insert the dust sleeve. It prevents contaminants from falling into the bottom bracket shell from the frame tubes. These sleeves are available at bike shops for about a dollar, or you can fabricate one out of a flexible piece of plastic that is cut to the proper width and rolled to fit into the bottom bracket. Make sure that the sleeve is wide enough to meet the inner edge of each cup, but not wide enough to interfere with the bearings. Also, allow a little extra length so that once the piece of plastic is rolled up, the ends overlap slightly.

Apply a liberal amount of grease to the whole surface of the spindle, especially at both bearing shoulders. Grease applied to the inner section of the spindle will serve to retard corrosion. Take a close look at the spindle. Most likely one tapered end is slightly longer than the other. If so, insert the longer end into the bottom bracket first so that it emerges through the fixed cup on the drive side of the bike.

Pack grease into the adjustable cup as you did the fixed cup, and install its set of bearings. Then grease the threads and screw it into the bottom bracket shell until you feel the bearings pressed snugly against the spindle shoulders. Thread the lockring onto the adjustable cup and lightly tighten it by hand.

Adjusting cup-and-cone-style bottom brackets. Now that it's back in the frame, spin the bottom bracket spindle to make sure the bearings are not binding. Also, try moving the spindle up and down to check for looseness. If necessary, fine-tune the adjustment by backing the lockring off a little and using the wrench or spanner to turn the adjustable cup until the spindle spins smoothly but without play. Once the adjustment is right, use the lockring spanner to turn the lockring down very tight.

When tightening the lockring, watch the adjustable cup. It may start to turn along with the lockring. If so, try holding it still with a pin spanner. However, if you must use a pin spanner, it may not be able to resist the force of the lockring without breaking off a pin. If that looks like a possibility, try another approach. Loosen the lockring and adjustable cup together, then hold the lockring still while you back the cup off a little farther. Tighten them both together and see if you end up with the correct adjustment.

Be patient. You may have to experiment to find the best method to get the adjustment right. Just remember, when fine-tuning the adjustment, don't try to move the adjustable cup with your pin tool without first loosening the lockring. If you try to do so, it's possible that you'll break the tool.

Put a crankarm on the spindle to check for any looseness in the spindle adjustment. It'll give the extra leverage needed to detect very small amounts of play. If the adjustment always seems to be either a little too tight or a little too loose, and you simply cannot find the magic place in between, don't scream. Just leave it a little on the tight side. Once the excess grease works its way out of the bearings, it should be about right.

INSTALLING THE CRANKARMS

Reinstall the crankarms. Cottered crankarms should have the cotters running opposite each other. If viewed while sitting on the saddle with the crankarms at 6 and 12 o'clock, one cotter nut should be facing forward and the other should be facing to the rear of the bike. If, after installing the cotters, the arms are not exactly straight, try putting the cotters in the other way. Or purchase new cotters (take an old one to the shop to purchase ones that match).

Tighten the cotters with a cotter press (a special tool) or a hammer. Trying to fully tighten them by means of the nut on the cotter will strip the threads, ruining the cotter. If you're using a hammer, give the back end of the cotter several sharp blows, then tighten the nut until it's snug. Give the cotter a couple more raps with the hammer and retighten the nut. Then, after the first ride, check to see if the nut is still tight. Check again after a couple hundred miles.

To reinstall a cotterless crankarm, put the arm on the spindle, thread on the nut or bolt, and tighten fully. Expect to use a good bit of force. Don't put all your weight behind it, but snug the nut or bolt down firmly. If you have a torque wrench to gauge your force, tighten it to between 25 and 30 foot-pounds.

One common practice you should avoid is greasing the spindle tapers before installing the cotterless crankarms, unless the crankarm manufacturer specifically prescribes it. Most crankset manufacturers recommend that the spindle tapers be free of lubricant. Exceptions to this rule include RaceFace and a few late-model mountain bike crankarm sets manufactured by Shimano. If you're unsure, play it safe and keep everything clean. Greasing a spindle taper for a crankarm set not intended for greased tapers can result in the crankarms working their way up the flats until the arms bottom out against the ends of the spindle.

Another rare exception to this rule is crankarms that develop a chronic creaking noise. It's usually caused by corrosion between the steel spindle and the aluminum crankarm, and it usually occurs on cranksets with bottom brackets that use a nut-style spindle. It's okay to apply a trace of grease to this type of crankset to eliminate the creaking because the tapers on the spindle are long enough to make bottoming the crankarm unlikely.

Retighten the crankarm bolts after your first ride, and check them periodically thereafter.

Remove chainrings. Most cranksets have removable chainrings. Get them off by loosening the bolts that hold them in place (there are usually five). Sometimes, these bolts require a 10 mm or 11 mm wrench, but these days, most require a 5 mm hex key. Sometimes, you'll also need a special wrench, called a chainring nut spanner, to hold the nut on the back side of the chainring. These are available through bicycle dealers, but if you can't get one, a large flathead screwdriver will sometimes work in its place. You also might find that the chainring bolts are very tight and that you have to slide a small piece of pipe over the hex key to get enough leverage.

CRANKSET MAINTENANCE

There's very little maintenance that can be done on a crankset, short of a complete overhaul, but there are a few preventive measures worth taking. We've already suggested checking the tightness of cotters and crankarm bolts at the end of the first ride after their installation. It is also good to recheck it at least monthly because riding on loose crankarms will usually ruin them. It's good to check pedal tightness, too, because loose pedals can also damage the crankarm if they're ridden enough.

When you check the crankarms, tug on them to see if the bottom bracket adjustment has loosened. If yours is a cup-and-cone-style bottom bracket, remove the play by adjusting the bottom bracket (it's not necessary to remove the crankarm for this). If it's a sealed-cartridge model, don't be concerned if

there's a trace of play. Lots of play, however, indicates that something is wrong, possibly a worn-out bottom bracket.

If the crankarms get bent (in an accident, for example), only steel ones can be safely bent back. Bent aluminum models should be replaced because they usually break when straightened (sometimes well after being straightened). Bent spiders can be straightened in many cases, even on aluminum cranksets. The same is true for aluminum or steel chainrings. Straightening a chainring is not too difficult. However, straightening a bent crankarm is a job best left to a bicycle shop. Without the proper tools and knowledge, you might further damage the components. Inspect each crankarm thoroughly for cracks that may cause it to fracture under hard pedaling pressure.

To straighten a chainring, it's best to leave it on the crankset and bike. Straighten it by tapping on it with a hammer in the direction in which it needs to go. Sight from above as you turn the crankarm by hand. Use the front derailleur cage as an indicator to determine where the ring is out of true. Hit the ring lightly at first, then harder, until you get the feel for what it takes to bend it. To get at a hard-to-reach spot, place a screwdriver on the warp and hit the screwdriver's handle with the hammer. To pry out a bent tooth or an extreme bend in a ring, use an adjustable wrench after tightening the jaws enough so they just slip over the ring.

If you misuse the crankarm removal tool, the result is usually stripped cotterless crankarm threads, which means it'll be impossible to remove the crankarm with the tool. It may seem like there's no way to remove the crankarm, but there is. Remove the bolt and ride around for a while. Eventually, the crankarm will loosen and come right off.

Another possible glitch is stripped pedal threads in the crankarm, usually the result of forcing the wrong pedal into an aluminum crankarm. Sometimes it's possible to repair this problem, though it's a job for a shop with the right tools.

TROUBLESHOOTING

PROBLEM: The large chainring flexes, causing the chain to rub against the front derailleur cage all the time.

SOLUTION: Learn to pedal faster (about 90 rpm is a good goal), which will put less pressure on the chainring and flex it less. Check for loose chainring bolts. Get the chainring straightened if it's bent.

PROBLEM: There's a trace of play in the sealed bottom bracket.

SOLUTION: Tighten the retaining cup/ring; it may have loosened slightly in the frame.

PROBLEM: There's a creaking sound when you pedal.

SOLUTION: Tighten the crankarm bolts. If the arm still creaks, remove it, apply a trace of grease to the spindle, and reinstall the arm.

PROBLEM: You removed the chainrings to clean the crankset and now the front derailleur doesn't shift right.

SOLUTION: You may have installed a chainring upside down. Remove the rings and put them on correctly. Usually, the crankarm bolts fit in indentations on the chainrings. Sight from above, too, to make sure that there's even spacing between the rings.

PROBLEM: You're trying to remove the chainring bolt but it just spins.

SOLUTION: Hold the back half of the chainring bolt with a wide flathead screwdriver or get a chainring bolt wrench.

PROBLEM: After you overhaul the bottom bracket, the adjustment is either tight or too loose.

SOLUTION: The bearing retainer(s) are installed upside down. Remove and reassemble correctly.

PROBLEM: You bent the bearing retainer when you took the balls out to clean them.

SOLUTION: Try to straighten it, or replace it. If that's not possible, toss the retainers and install loose ball bearings in the bottom bracket.

PROBLEM: There's a knocking sound when you pedal.

SOLUTION: If you have a sealed cartridge bottom bracket, moisture may have penetrated the threads between the bottom bracket and the shell, causing light corrosion. This is especially common with aluminum frames. Remove the crank and bottom bracket, clean the threads of both with a wire brush, wrap plumbers' Teflon tape over the threads, and reinstall the bottom bracket. For those with a non-sealed bottom bracket, this sound usually comes from a loose fixed cup (the right-side one). Tighten it securely by turning it counterclockwise.

PROBLEM: The fixed cup on a nonsealed bottom bracket continually loosens.

SOLUTION: Back it out (on modern bikes it's usually turned clockwise), clean the threads, apply thread adhesive, and reinstall tightly.

PROBLEM: You stripped the crankarm threads and now you can't remove the crankarm.

SOLUTION: Ride the bike around the block a few times. The crankarm will loosen and you'll be able to take it off.

PROBLEM: You crashed into a rock and bent the chainring.

SOLUTION: On the trail, try pounding it straight with a rock. At home, use an adjustable wrench (make the jaws just wide enough to grab the ring) to pry the ring back into place. If it's really bent up, replace it.

PROBLEM: You broke a tooth off the chainring.

SOLUTION: Don't worry about it. It should still work okay. If it's causing the chain to run rough, file down any protruding pieces.

Crankarm Adjustment

1 From time to time, grab the crankarms on your bike with your hands and tug on them to check for looseness either in the crankarms themselves or in the bearing adjustment inside the bottom bracket (see photo). If you discover that the crankarms are loose, tighten them immediately. Even if they never feel loose, at least once every 2 months give them a preventive tightening.

Cottered crankarms are held in place by cotters that have nuts threaded on one end. To tighten these crankarms, give the head of each cotter a sharp rap with a hammer, then use a wrench to tighten the nut (don't overtighten because the threads on cotters are delicate).

2 Tighten cotterless crankarms by turning the bolts clockwise. Modern cranks have hex key bolts. On older models, you might have to remove a dustcap. To remove a dustcap with a slit across its face, use a wide-blade screwdriver or a large coin, such as a quarter. Other types are can be removed with a hex key. A dustcap with a slit near the edge can be pried out with a screwdriver (see photo).

3 Once the dustcap is out, tighten the fixing bolt or nut that holds the crankarm on the end of the spindle. Special crankarm bolt spanners are made for turning these bolts. A thin-walled socket wrench of the correct dimension will also work. Some crankarm removal tools are also designed to double as crankarm bolt spanners (see photo). Such tools must be turned with the aid of an ordinary open-end wrench. Use the appropriate tool to snug up the crankarm fixing bolt, then, if necessary, replace the dustcap.

4 When you tug on the crankarms, if there's play in the bearings and it's a cup-and-cone-style bottom bracket, adjust it. You can do this without removing the crankarm. However, it'll be easier if it's out of the way. To remove the crankarm, follow the instructions on page 122. To adjust cup-and-cone bottom bracket bearings, the lockring does not have to be removed, only loosened. Use a lockring spanner to turn it counterclockwise (see photo). Don't spin the lockring all the way off; just loosen it enough so that it doesn't hinder the movement of the adjustable cup.

5 Some adjustable cups have pinholes, others have notches or wrench flats. Use the appropriate tool to turn the cup clockwise to eliminate the play in the bearings (see photo).

Work carefully. You may need to move the cup just one-eighth turn or less to get the adjustment you need. Check frequently by grabbing a crankarm and moving the spindle around. When there's no binding or play in the bearings, retighten the lockring to hold the cup in that position.

As you tighten the lockring, watch the adjustable cup. It may try to move along with the lockring, spoiling your careful adjustment.

6 If the adjustable cup moves, hold it still with your spanner or wrench while tightening the lockring (see photo). If your cup tool is a pin spanner, it's possible to break the tool by putting too much pressure on the pins. Pay attention to how much pressure it takes to prevent the cup from moving along with the lockring. If a lot of force is involved, you should resort to a different technique. Calculate how far out of adjustment the cup moves when you tighten the lockring, then loosen both the lockring and cup. Hold the lockring still while backing off the cup adjustment enough to compensate for its expected later movement. Then when you retighten the lockring, the cup should end up in the right place.

If you removed a crankarm, replace it. Tighten the crankarm bolt, then reinstall the dustcap (if there is one).

Bottom Bracket Overhaul

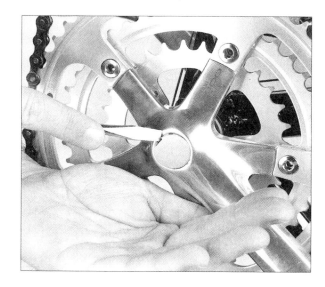

1 Get together the tools and supplies needed (see page 122). You'll also need, at the most, 22 of the ¼-inch bearings.

Decide now if you will want to have the pedals off the crankarms anytime during the overhaul. If so, remove them now, while the crankarms are still on the bike.

Modern crankarms are held in place by hex key bolts. Remove these by turning counterclockwise. Be sure to remove any washers beneath the bolts.

Older crankarms may have dustcaps protecting the threads that are used in the crankarm removal process. Dustcaps are easily damaged, so treat them gently. Pry the dustcaps free with a screwdriver if they have slits near the edges (see photo).

2 If there's a slot or hexagonal hole in the center, turn the dustcap counterclockwise to remove it, using a screwdriver, a coin, or a hex key (whichever fits best).

There's either a nut or a bolt holding the crankarm on the spindle. If your crankarm extractor has an end made to fit this fixing bolt, use that, along with a wrench, to turn the bolt counterclockwise (see photo). Otherwise, use a crankarm bolt spanner or a thin-walled socket.

Extract the fixing bolt all the way out of the spindle and set it aside, along with its washer. If you have the type of crankarm that's held on with a nut rather than a bolt, there is no separate washer because the nut has a serrated edge that acts as a built-in washer. If a hex key bolt holds on the crankarm and it won't loosen, go to step 4.

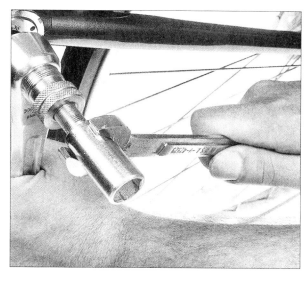

3 Study the crankarm extractor. As you twist the movable part, a rod that runs down the center of the tool moves either in or out. Adjust the tool so that the rod retreats as far back inside as it can. Thread the end of the tool inside your crankarm.

As you begin to insert the tool, make certain that its threads mesh with those inside the crankarm. Thread the tool in as far as you can, then place a wrench on the wrench flats and advance the inner rod forward until it butts against the end of the spindle (see photo). Continue turning in the same direction, pushing the rod against the end of the spindle, which will pull the crankarm off the spindle.

4 Cotterless crankarms with a built-in system for crankarm installation and removal with a single hex key are now quite common. In this design, the dustcap and crankarm fixing bolt are both used in the crankarm removal process. A hex key is inserted through the dustcap into the head of the crankarm fixing bolt. As the bolt backs out, it pushes against the dustcap, forcing the crankarm off the spindle (no special tools required).

Remove both crankarms from the spindle. Use a lockring spanner and loosen the lockring found on the left side of the bottom bracket by turning it counterclockwise (see photo). Spin the lockring completely off the bike.

5 Use your pin spanner to turn the adjustable cup counterclockwise until it is threaded almost all the way out of the bottom bracket shell.

6 Unless you know that your bearings are held in a retainer, turn the bike on its side and spread paper towels or rags under it to catch any of the bearings because they're inclined to roll away. Though you'll be replacing these bearings, keep track of them to inspect them for signs of wear that indicate potential damage to other parts. Also, that way you can count them to make sure you have the right number of replacements (usually there are 22 of the ¼-inch bearings).

Hold the spindle in place with one hand to trap the fixed cup bearings while removing the adjustable cup with the other hand.

Bottom Bracket Overhaul *continued*

7 Once the adjustable cup bearings are out, remove the plastic dust sleeve, if one is present, along with the spindle and the bearings from the fixed cup side. Don't remove the fixed cup (on the drive side of the bike) unless it has loosened (look for a gap between the cup's lip and the frame). Remember: Some cups turn clockwise for removal.

8 Clean the metal parts with a solvent and a rag or stiff brush. Don't forget to thoroughly clean inside the fixed cup and the bottom bracket shell.

After you've cleaned all the parts, inspect them closely for signs of damage or excessive wear. Look at the adjustable cup. You'll see a score line running in a circle where the bearings made contact with the race (see photo). Look for any irregularities in the surface of the race along this line. Is one part of the line worn more heavily than another? Are there any pits along the line that might cause a bearing to snag?

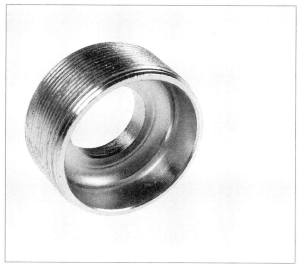

9 Inspect the fixed cup. Since it's still in place on the bike, a flashlight may help.

Study the spindle. Look along each shoulder for the wear line where the bearings make contact. Are there any pits or signs of excessive wear?

Clean and examine all of the old ball bearings. Are any of them cracked or chipped? If the bearings are caged in a retainer, is the retainer still intact and free of damage?

If there are any broken parts, check inside the bottom bracket shell again to make sure no metal fragments are clinging to the frame. You don't want them hanging around to do damage after you've reassembled the bottom bracket. Replace any excessively worn or damaged parts.

10 If in doubt, take the part to a knowledgeable bike mechanic for a second opinion. If your fixed cup needs replacing, have it done at a bike shop. It's very difficult to adequately tighten a fixed cup without a tool too specialized and expensive to be worth your purchasing (see photo). Try tightening it with a wrench after applying a few drops of thread adhesive. If it loosens, however, have a shop mechanic tighten it professionally.

If you haven't already purchased new bearings, collect and count the old ones to know how many to buy. Take a sample to the bike shop to match the size. If you have caged bearings, take one of the old retainers to the shop to get two new ones to match. Or gently pop out the old bearings and press in new ones to reuse the retainers.

11 Begin reassembling the bottom bracket by packing plenty of medium-weight grease into the fixed cup. Push the ball bearings into the grease, which should hold them in place until the spindle is in place.

Caged bearings must be installed in the correct way. To determine what that is, take a close look at a set. Note that individual balls are separated from one another by small metal fingers that form a sort of C shape. There are two retainer types: one with a round profile, and another with a flatter profile. The latter is correctly installed when the cup shape or open side of the C formed by these fingers faces in toward the center of the bottom bracket. Or, to put it another way, the individual metal fingers of the retainer curl toward the inside of the bottom bracket (see photo). The former type goes the opposite way.

12 Once the bearings are in place inside the fixed cup, the spindle can be replaced. This too has to be turned in the right direction since the ends of most spindles are asymmetrical. The difference may not be obvious at first glance, but on most spindles the distance between the tapered end and the adjacent bearing race is slightly greater on one side than on the other (see photo). If the manufacturer's name is on the spindle, install the spindle in such a way that if your bottom bracket were transparent you could read the name while sitting on the bike. Otherwise, make sure the longer end is on the drive side, where the extra length is needed to compensate for the space taken up by the chainrings.

Bottom Bracket Overhaul *continued*

13 If you have a plastic dust sleeve, clean off all the old grease and grime. Hold the spindle in place on the fixed cup side while sliding the sleeve in over it.

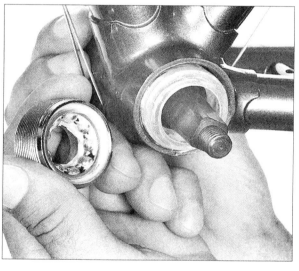

14 Pack the adjustable cup with grease and insert the bearings. Once again, if using caged bearings, be sure to put them in the correct way. Put a little grease on the threads, then carefully screw the adjustable cup back into the bike frame by hand (see photo).

15 Thread the adjustable cup clockwise into the frame until you contact the bearings. Back the cup off about one-eighth turn, then grasp the spindle and twirl it back and forth to check the adjustment. If you feel any binding in the bearings, the adjustment is too tight. Use your pin spanner to back the cup out a tiny bit, then check the adjustment again (see photo).

After you're sure the adjustment is not too tight, try moving the spindle up and down. If there's any play in it, the adjustment is too loose. Twist the cup clockwise a short distance and check again. When you feel neither looseness nor binding in the bearings, screw the lockring back on.

16 Try tightening the lockring down without using a tool to hold the cup still. If the cup insists on turning with the lockring, try holding it still with the pin spanner while turning the lockring (see photo). If you feel a lot of force being put on the pin tool, quit using it or it may break. Loosen the cup and lockring together, then hold the lockring still while you back the cup out a bit more. Now tighten both together and see if your adjustment is correct.

Even if you had no problem with the cup turning, check the adjustment again after tightening the lockring, since that procedure may alter your cup adjustment. When you're satisfied with the adjustment, replace the two crankarms. Be sure you do not put any grease on the end of the spindle.

17 Push a crankarm onto the end of the spindle, then tighten the nut or fixing bolt to pull the crankarm into place (see photo).

When both crankarms are tight, tug on them laterally to check again for looseness in the bottom bracket and twirl them to check for binding. If you are not satisfied with your adjustment at this point, you may be able to alter it without removing a crankarm again. Loosen the lockring, adjust the cup as needed, then retighten the lockring. Once everything is okay, replace the pedals (if you removed them earlier) and lift the chain onto the chainring.

Finally, don't forget to replace the dustcaps (if necessary). They protect the threads inside your crankarms, which you'll need to use the next time you overhaul your bottom bracket.

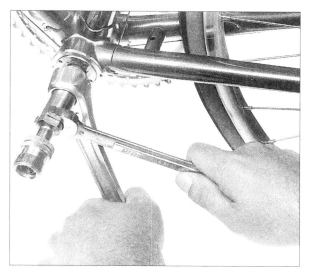

Removal and Installation of a Shimano Octalink Crankset

1 Shimano's Octalink design was the first widely accepted, spline-fit crank and bottom bracket standard. There are now two Octalink standards— Octalink V-1 and Octalink V-2. In recent years, a consortium of smaller manufacturers including Chris King, RaceFace, and Truvativ developed a competing standard called ISIS (International Spline Interface Standard). None of the three designs are cross-compatible, so it's important to know what you have before replacing parts, even though all adhere to the same procedure for installation and removal. If you're lucky enough to have self-extracting crankbolts, removal will be as simple as loosening the crankbolts with an 8 mm hex key.

2 If your crank arms are not equipped with self-extracting bolts, remove the crankbolts and washers, then extract the crankarms using a crankarm removal tool similar to, but not the same as, the one used for tapered crankarms. Because Octalink and ISIS spindles are larger and have a larger bolt hole in the spindle end than square-taper types, you will need a crankarm extractor with a larger tip such as the Park Tools CCP-4. If you already have an older cotterless crank puller, it's sometimes possible to find a steel slug that will fit on the end of large spindles, allowing the use of your older tool.

3 If you have self-extractors, reinstallation begins with the removal of the self-extracting hardware. Using a small pin spanner or a crank dustcap remover (often integrated as the opposite end of a chainring nut spanner) turn the dustcaps counterclockwise. Keep all the parts of the extracting hardware in order.

4 Cover the splines on the spindle and inside the crankarm with grease, and then carefully line up the splines. Tightening the arms in place without the splines properly meshing can cause permanent damage, ruining an expensive crankarm.

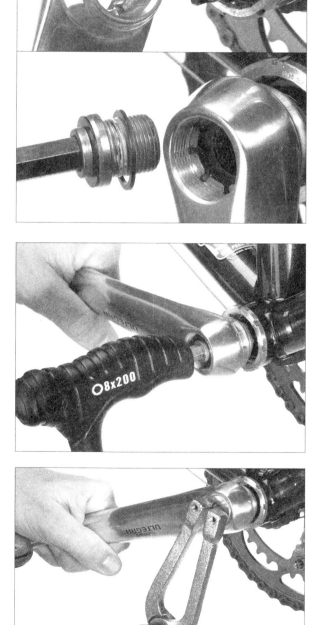

5 Install the crankarm fixing bolt and steel washer with your 8 mm hex key. The recommended tightening torque for this bolt is generally between 300 and 400 inch-pounds. Your crank manufacturer will have specific numbers in mind, but in plain terms it translates to tight, tight, tight. With these new spline systems, you tighten the crankarm until it bottoms out, taking a lot of the guesswork out for those who don't have a torque wrench available.

6 If you don't have self-extractors, you're done. Those that do need only replace the plastic washer and retaining ring that complete the self-extracting system.

Chainring Maintenance

1 It's a good idea to keep chainrings clean. A lot of grease mixed with road grime is passed on to the teeth of the chainrings by the chain. The abrasives in this grime cause the chain and chainrings to wear out at a faster rate than they otherwise would.

Therefore, at least once a month—preferably more often, especially if you do a lot of riding on wet and dirty terrain—take a rag and wipe your chainrings clean. Dampen the rag with a little solvent, if you need to, or use a stiff brush to loosen the grime so it can be wiped away (see photo).

Of course, it does little good to clean chainrings if you never bother to clean your chain. The two work together, get dirty together, and wear out together, though not necessarily at the same rate. Thus, whenever you clean your chainrings, you should also give your chain a thorough going-over. For details on chain cleaning and lubrication, see page 170.

2 Sometimes a chainring gets bent in a crash, or two chainrings are so close together that when the chain is on the smaller one it rubs against the larger one. The solution to the first problem is obvious: Straighten the bent area. To solve the second problem, you need to bend the larger chainring slightly away from the smaller all the way around its circumference.

Both these repairs can be accomplished with a hammer or with the help of a chainring bending tool (see photo). This is a simple tool, one that is less expensive than most specialized bike tools. However, bending a chainring is one of those jobs that you may prefer to leave to an experienced bike mechanic. If the problem is quite severe, you are better off just replacing the chainring.

If you see shiny cuts on the sides of the chainring teeth, it's a sign that you are riding in gear combinations that force the chain into extreme angles. One extreme occurs when you ride with the chain on the large chainring and the largest inner cog. Another results from the chain being shifted onto the inner chainring and the rear cog. Such gear combinations should be avoided.

3 When you start riding with a new chain and new chainrings, the teeth of the rings should mesh perfectly with the links of the chain. Over a period of time, the teeth on the rings will gradually become thinner as they wear down. Meanwhile, the plates on the chain will gradually cut into the sides of the pins or rivets, causing the chain to increase in length slightly. As long as the chain and chainrings wear at the same rate, their performance should be satisfactory. However, this is not likely to be the case. Eventually, both will wear out and need to be replaced.

Replacing chainrings is usually an easy process. Normally, they're attached with hex key bolts to a five-armed spider that radiates out from the base of the right crankarm. Simply remove the five bolts (if they're stuck, hold their backs with a flat-blade screwdriver) while holding the ring in place, then slide it off the crankarm (see photo). Slide on a new ring and bolt it in place (always grease the bolts first).

4 As a preventive measure, check periodically to make certain that all the chainring bolts are tight. You may even wish to carry the necessary wrench along with you in a small tool kit when you travel on your bike.

141

Sealed-Bearing Cartridge-Style Bottom Bracket Installation

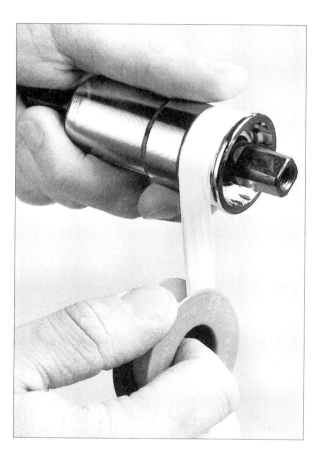

1 Before installing a new cartridge-style bottom bracket, remove the old one. It might be as easy as turning the cartridge out with the splined removal tool. Turn the left-side cup first, counterclockwise, until it comes out of the frame. Then turn the right-side cup clockwise to remove the cartridge.

If the cups won't turn, don't force them. Apply Liquid Wrench or a similar penetrating lubricant to the cup edges and tap the bottom bracket shell with a hammer to vibrate it, which should work the solvent into the threads. Wait a while and try to turn the cups again. Repeat this procedure until the cups unscrew, or take the bike to a shop for help.

Cartridge-sealed bottom brackets come packed with grease and adjusted from the factory. Before installing the new one, turn the spindle by hand to feel how it turns—how the factory adjustment feels. Later, when it's installed, the spindle should turn approximately as easily as it does now that it's out of the bike.

Cartridge bottom brackets usually have one cup preinstalled on the drive side of the cartridge. If the bottom bracket is being installed in a titanium frame, coat the threads with Finish Line Ti-Prep or some other anti-seize compound. Wrapping plumber's Teflon tape around the threads of the cartridge and cup is also acceptable (see photo).

2 Treating the threads will prevent chronic clicking noises from the bottom bracket area and will fight galvanic corrosion, which can freeze the bottom bracket into the shell. (Grease is usually adequate for steel and aluminum frames.)

Start threading the cartridge into the drive side of the frame by hand-turning it counterclockwise (see photo). Be careful not to cross-thread it.

3 When the cartridge gets tough to turn, install the splined tool (see photo) and continue turning until the cup is snug and fully screwed into the frame (it'll only go so far because of the built-in lip on the cup edge).

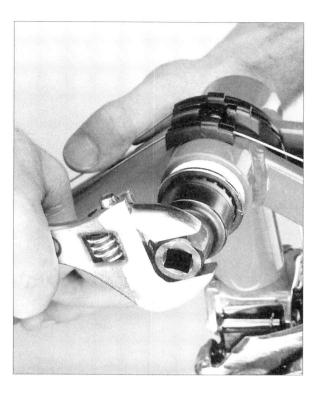

4 Install the other cup (be careful not to cross-thread it), turning it clockwise with the splined tool until the cup bottoms against the cartridge (see photo). Check how things are going by turning the spindle by hand. If it's a lot tighter than it was before installation, it's likely that the cup is going in crooked. Remove it and start again, making sure it's straight. When the cup is secure, check the installation by putting the spline tool on the drive side again and making sure it's tight, then double-checking the tightness of the left-side cup. Finally, grab the spindle and turn it. It should feel smooth, like it did before installation. If not, try again.

When the bottom bracket is installed correctly, attach the crankarms. Remember to snug the bolts after the first ride and monthly thereafter.

There are many different sealed-bearing cartridge-style bottom bracket designs today, with more coming along almost daily. The preceding directions apply to the common types. If yours seems different, follow the manufacturer's installation instructions. If you don't have the directions, get them from the dealer who sold you the bottom bracket, contact the manufacturer, or check its Web site.

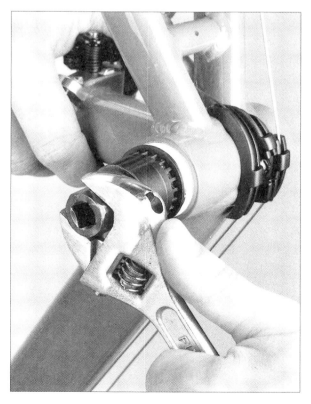

Removal and Installation of Two-Piece Cranksets

1 Shimano and RaceFace two-piece cranksets are removed and installed in very similar manners. Since Shimano's procedure is slightly more involved, we will focus on that system here and point out where RaceFace's procedure differs.

The first step in removing a Shimano two-piece crankset is to loosen the two pinch bolts on the left crankarm with a 5 mm hex key. These bolts clamp the arm in place on the spindle.

2 Next, use Shimano's crank arm installation tool (TL-FC16) to remove the preload cap by turning it counterclockwise. Park Tool also makes a tool that can be used for this (BBT-9). The left crankarm will slip easily off the spindle.

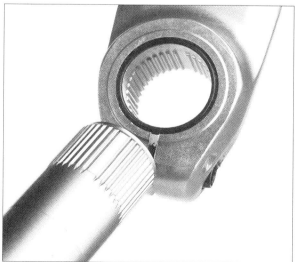

3 Notice that there is a broad spline on the spindle and inside the crankarm, making it nearly impossible to misalign the left crankarm when you reinstall it. There will also be a thin, black rubber O-ring on the spindle between the bearing and crankarm. Remove this from the spindle and set it into its seat on the crankarm to keep track of it.

RaceFace cranks forego the use of pinch bolts and preload cap. Instead, the right-side arm is affixed to the end of the spindle in a fashion typical of other spline-interface cranksets. Turn the crankarm fixing bolt counterclockwise with an 8 mm hex key to pull the right arm off the spindle on its own.

4 The spindle will now smoothly slide out of the bottom bracket. If it's not cooperating, there may be some trace amounts of corrosion on the spindle. Give the end of the spindle a few light taps with a rubber mallet.

5 Remove the bottom bracket cups from the shell using an appropriate spanner. Shimano's part number for this tool is TL-FC32; Park Tool's BBT-9 will also work. Most road and mountain bikes today will have an English-thread bottom bracket shell, so the left-side cup will come out when turned counterclockwise, but the right-side cup must be turned clockwise to remove it.

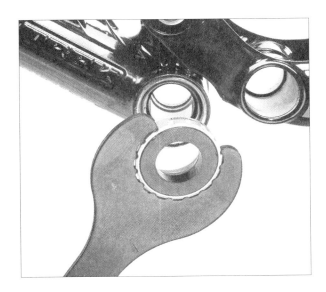

6 Installation is as simple as reversing these steps. With Shimano cranks, don't overtighten the preload cap that holds the left crankarm in place. This cap is intended only to snug the crankarm in place and should be only slightly more than finger-tight. Last, tighten the pinch bolts incrementally to be sure they are both properly and evenly torqued.

FREEWHEELS & CASSETTES

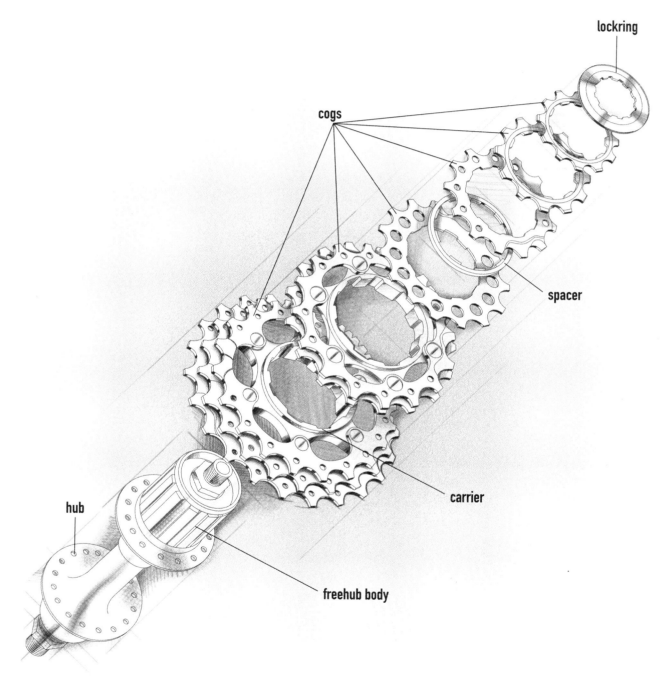

lockring

cogs

spacer

carrier

hub

freehub body

In the mid- to late nineteenth century, people rode bikes called velocipedes and high-wheelers. The former had equal-size wheels like most of today's bikes, except that the crankset was rigidly attached to the front wheel. The high-wheeler, which was invented after the velocipede, shared this trait; however, the front wheel was huge (up to 60 inches in diameter) because inventors realized that with an increased wheel size, riders could go faster.

High-wheelers had a dangerous drawback. Bringing the bike to a stop too abruptly would result in the rider getting pitched over that tall front wheel. With legs trapped behind the handlebar, the common result would be the rider landing squarely on his head (almost all riders were men in these, the days before the women's suffrage movement). "Taking a header" was all-too-often fatal, and so a safer design was sought. In the 1880s, the idea of a chain-driven rear wheel was developed and the Safety bicycle was born. Safety bicycles most resemble the bicycles of today, except that they had a fixed drivetrain, which meant that whenever the rear wheel was in motion, so were the crank and pedals. Though this "fixed gear" system allowed you to contribute the strength in your legs to the braking process by resisting the forward movement of the pedals, it never made for very comfortable or very safe riding. Fixed gear drivetrains still can be found today on track bikes (one-speed road bikes raced on an oval track called a velodrome) because of the added control that it offers track racers, whose machines do not have brakes.

With the exception of the track bike, modern bikes are equipped with a ratcheting mechanism and cogs that connect the rear hub, via the chain, to the pedals but allow you to coast when you stop pedaling. This makes bikes safer and much more comfortable to ride, thanks to the various gearing it provides. This device is called a freewheel because it frees the rear wheel from the connection to the crankarms.

The ratcheting mechanism is made up of bearings, a gear, and pawls. The pawls are angled one way and rest on springs. When coasting, the gear spins past the pawls, which trip over the gear teeth, making the fast clicking sound you hear. When you pedal, however, the pawls engage the gear teeth, driving the bike.

The cogs—or sprockets, as they are sometimes called—are disks with teeth on them. The number of teeth on the cog combined with the number of teeth on the chainring determines the gear ratio of the bicycle's drive system at any given time. The larger the cog, the easier it is to pedal; but the larger the chainring, the harder it is to pedal. Cogs and chainrings are commonly referred to by the number of teeth on them (they're usually stamped with the number, so you don't have to count to determine size). The more cog and chainring combinations you have, the greater the number of available gear ratios and the greater the variety of terrain on which you can ride. A cluster of different-size cogs and the spacers that divide them is known as a freewheel or a cassette, depending on the type of ratcheting mechanism to which it is connected.

THE DIFFERENCE BETWEEN FREEWHEELS AND CASSETTES

When derailleur drivetrains were first invented, there had to be a way to attach multiple cogs to the rear wheel of a bike to provide different gears. For the gearing, inventors came up with the freewheel, which is an integral unit comprising the cogs (usually five, six, or seven) and spacers attached to a ratcheting mechanism in the center that drives when you pedal but allows coasting (freewheeling) when you stop pedaling. This center section that includes the bearings, gear, and pawls is called the freewheel body. There are threads in the center of the freewheel so that it can be screwed onto the rear wheel's hub.

To remove the freewheel, a special tool is needed called (naturally) a freewheel remover. Each brand of freewheel has its own remover. Freewheels can be difficult to remove because pedaling pressure tightens the freewheel on the hub. If it's not adequately lubricated or if a strong, powerful rider has been racing the bike, the freewheel can become very tight. Another tricky thing with freewheels is cog removal. This varies from brand to brand, but on most freewheels, there are cogs that thread on and those that slide on. It's important to know what you're dealing with before attempting to replace a cog.

Another interesting thing about freewheels is how they affect the design of the hub. Because of the spacing requirements of the freewheel, the hub bearings on either side of the hub can be only a certain distance apart.

It's precisely these shortcomings that led to the development of the cassette system. You can still get freewheels today on certain bikes, but the vast majority of new models are equipped with cassettes—and have been since the late 1980s.

At a glance, cassettes look just like freewheels, but there are significant differences. The basic one is that the ratcheting mechanism on a cassette system is part of the hub (called a freehub or cassette body). It's not screwed onto the hub, it's built into the hub. (Remember that on a freewheel system, the freewheel is threaded onto the hub, not built into it.) This provides one of the main advantages of cassette hubs: It allows the bearings on either side of the hub to be placed farther apart, which increases support for the axle, strengthening it and preventing it from breaking in most cases.

Another big advantage is simple cog removal. All that's required is unscrewing a lockring or the bottom cog or cogs (depending on model), and the cogs can be lifted off the hub as a unit or as a cassette. Then you can simply slide on a replacement cassette (or one of a different size if, for example, you're changing cogs to make the gearing easier).

It's important to understand the differences between cassettes and then determine which type is on the bike you're working on. Cassettes are found on most modern bikes and can be identified by looking for a flat lockring on top of the smallest cog. The lockring is splined in its center. Freewheels are

Freewheels and cassettes are built up with a combination of different-size cogs and spacers that separate the cogs evenly.

mostly on older bikes. Usually freewheels have two notches built into the freewheel body or a splined pattern just visible inside the freewheel body. There is no lockring. If you're in doubt, a shop mechanic can quickly identify the type if you bring in the wheel. Once you know what you have, both are easy enough to work with.

SELECTING THE RIGHT FREEWHEEL

Today, only a few companies make freewheels. If your bike has one and you need to replace it, with luck you should be able to find one that matches closely enough to work.

Over the years, there have been many manufacturers of freewheels. Campagnolo made what were perhaps the most exotic ever built. Constructed completely of aluminum, Campagnolo freewheels were only 25 percent the weight of ordinary free-wheels—which are made of steel—but strong enough for the rigors of bicycle racing. These freewheels are marked "Campagnolo," so they're easy to identify. They're not very practical for everyday use because aluminum wears quickly. Also, special tools are required to work on them.

Maillard marketed the Helicomatic freewheel/hub system, which appeared on many Trek brand bikes in the 1970s and early 1980s. The Helicomatic freewheels and hubs can be used only with each other because they incorporate a set of helical splines in place of the usual threads. Thus, if you have a Maillard Helicomatic freewheel and you need to replace it, your options are quite limited. Maillard also produced an exotic, very light, all-magnesium freewheel.

Normandy made a freewheel system that was popular on European bicycles. Very durable, it was found on many French, Italian, and English as well as American-made bicycles.

Regina freewheels are found primarily on older Italian bicycles. The Regina system used to be as popular as the Normandy, but it began to be displaced somewhat in the late 1970s and early 1980s by inexpensive Japanese freewheels.

Shimano, the world's largest bicycle parts manufacturer, made several lines of freewheels. The quality and durability of all the Shimano freewheels are excellent.

SunTour is another notable Japanese manufacturer of bicycle components. The SunTour Pro-Compe and Winner freewheels were extremely popular due to their simplicity and durability. The Winner freewheel system was especially popular because it could be built with ratios ranging from 12 to 34 teeth in five-, six-, and seven-speed combinations. All this could be done on the same freewheel body simply by changing the combinations of cogs and spacers. Unfortunately, it's difficult to find these SunTour freewheels and cogs. If you're lucky, you might still find some shops with old stock.

A note about cogs: You have to match the manufacturer and type of your old cogs when selecting replacements. For example, Shimano cassette hubs will accept only Shimano cassette cogs. Ditto for Campagnolo. And if you have an older SunTour freewheel, you'll need to find SunTour freewheel cogs.

If you have a bike that needs a new freewheel, your best bet may be to replace the rear hub with a cassette hub rather than searching endlessly for replacement parts. You can either replace the rear wheel as a unit or purchase a cassette hub and rebuild your rear wheel on the new hub (think of it as a chance to polish wheel-building skills). You'll also have to purchase the cassette cogs, as they're not included with the wheel/hub. Once you've upgraded, you'll be able to get the parts you need in the future.

Getting the right gearing. The combinations of cogs possible on cassettes and freewheels vary from model to model and manufacturer to manufacturer. Whether you are buying a stock combination or building up a custom one, check the manufacturer's literature or speak to your local bicycle dealer to find out what combinations are available and possible for the model you're considering.

Some companies furnish cog boards to dealers. These boards hold all the sizes of cogs available and provide instructions on how to build up the gear combination you desire.

These days, most cassettes come in a range of stock sizes to suit particular drivetrains. The cog sizes are selected by the manufacturer to provide a decent ratio of gears and to ensure a smooth transition between cogs, which best accommodate the derailleur and shifter design. This suits most riders because the eight-, nine-, and even ten-speed cassettes found today have wide enough gear ratios to handle most types of riding. It's rarely necessary to modify the gearing significantly.

Still, if you have an older five- or six-speed drivetrain with a thread-on freewheel and you don't want to upgrade to a cassette system, you may wish to customize the gearing to suit the type of riding you do. You will need to determine what high and low gears you need and how you want to space the in-between gears. You'll also need luck to find the parts to do it. Although this information applies mostly to older bikes, you'll find complete instructions on designing gear ratios in Chapter 17. Plan several options, then consult your bicycle dealer. If you can't find the gearing you like, it's probably best to take the plunge and upgrade to a modern drivetrain.

Freewheel threads. On cassette hubs, the freewheel is part of the hub, and it's difficult (and usually unnecessary) to remove it. Freewheels, however, attach to wheel hubs by threading onto them. Thus, it's most important to get the correct replacement.

Over the years, freewheels and hubs were available with three thread patterns: English, French, and Italian. Most modern bikes that have freewheels employ English threading, which keeps things simple because the only replacement freewheels available are English-threaded. Things get trickier if you're working on an older bike. French-threaded freewheels are unique and are compatible only with French-threaded hubs. If you find that your worn freewheel has French threads, you'll need to upgrade to either an English-threaded hub or replace the hub and freewheel with a cassette system. English and Italian threads, on the other hand, are similar enough to be interchangeable.

To determine the freewheel threading, look first at the identity of the manufacturer. Ninety-nine percent of all Japanese hubs and freewheels are English-threaded. Italian hubs are almost always either Italian or English in threading. The threading on freewheels made elsewhere should be checked.

You can do this two ways. On some freewheels, the thread type is marked on the back side of the freewheel body. Remove the freewheel to look for this. Some manufacturers label the freewheel by country—England, France, or Italy. Others mark the dimensions of the threads—34.7 mm × 1.0 mm for France, 1.370" × 24 tpi (threads per inch) for England, and 35 mm × 24 tpi for Italy. If the freewheel is simply marked "metric," this means it's French-threaded. The other way to check the threading is to measure the threads using a thread gauge. Thread gauges are usually available through stores that sell tools.

CLEANING AND LUBRICATING A CASSETTE OR FREEWHEEL

Most of the time when you clean a cassette or freewheel, you clean only the outside. This is because the outside gets the dirtiest. You don't have to remove the cassette or freewheel to clean it, so it's an easy job. Just wipe it down with a rag.

When the cogs are clean, give the cassette or freewheel a spin. If it feels or sounds dry, drip some medium-weight oil into it through the crack in the body. Phil Wood brand Tenacious Oil is a favorite for this purpose.

Use an axle nut or quick-release skewer to hold the cassette lockring tool or freewheel remover in place and prevent damage caused by the tool slipping free. Remember to remove the nut or skewer; otherwise, the lockring or freewheel won't unthread all the way.

There's little need to overhaul a cassette hub or freewheel body because the moving components work only when they're not under a load. If the body produces a grinding sound, as if it has sand or dirt in it, all that's usually required is to flush the body with oil to remove the dirt.

To clean the cogs, lift the chain off and remove the rear wheel from the bike. Take a rag and wipe the dirt from the surface of the cogs. Use the edge of the rag to clean between the cogs, or use a small screwdriver to dig out dirt or debris that may have gotten jammed in, then wrap the rag around one finger to clean in the troughs of the teeth.

It's usually possible to lubricate the cassette hub or freewheel body by squirting some medium-weight oil into the opening between the inner and outer bodies. To find this opening, rotate the cogs counterclockwise with the wheel sitting horizontally on a table or the floor. The outer body will rotate while the inner body remains stationary. Usually, you can see the separation between the two (although sometimes you'll have to remove the cogs to see it). That's the opening to put in the oil. Rotate the outer body while applying the oil so that it works its way into the internal parts of the body.

After applying the oil, wrap the rag between the cassette or freewheel and the spokes to catch any excess that drains out. If, after you've done this, the cassette or freewheel still makes grinding sounds while coasting, repeat the lubrication process. This time, however, you may wish to first use a light oil and solvent mixture like WD-40 to try to carry out the dirt. Then lubricate the body with medium-weight oil, as before. If you use a stronger solvent, like kerosene, you may have to lubricate your cassette or freewheel several times before all the parts get coated with oil again.

There's a special tool designed for cleaning and lubricating cassette hubs, which makes this job easier. It's called the Morningstar Products Freehub Buddy and sells for about $25. It fits into the right side of the hub and allows you to pump cleaners and lubes directly into the cassette bearings. Also offered by the same company are a special dustcap and a tool for removing the original dustcap. This is a great system for maintaining a cassette.

REMOVING THE FREEWHEEL

There are four reasons to remove a freewheel: to replace a worn one, to change a worn cog, to overhaul the hub, and to replace a broken spoke (because the freewheel makes it difficult to push the spoke into the hub flange).

To remove a freewheel, you need a freewheel removal tool. These tools fit into special notches or splines on the freewheel and allow its removal. Almost every type of freewheel requires a different tool, one made especially for it. You can damage the freewheel by trying to take it off with the wrong tool, so it's very important to get the correct one. You'll probably have to order it from a tool supplier because freewheels are no longer the norm.

In addition to the freewheel tool, you'll need a large adjustable wrench or a bench-mounted vise to fit the freewheel tool's wrench flats.

Before removing the freewheel, remove the rear wheel from the bike. Once the wheel is off, completely remove the axle nut or the quick-release skewer nut from the freewheel side of the wheel. Fit the freewheel removal tool into the slots or splines made for it in the freewheel body, then tighten the axle nut or the quick-release skewer nut down over it to hold the tool securely in place. You'll be using a lot of force to remove the freewheel. If the freewheel tool slips, it could break the freewheel removal notches or the tool itself, so make sure it's properly seated and firmly fastened to the freewheel before you apply pressure to it.

Set the wheel upright on the floor, with the freewheel side pointing away from you. Fit a large adjustable wrench on the flats of the freewheel tool so that as you bend over the wheel you can push down hard with your right hand to break the freewheel loose from the hub. If you prefer to use a bench-mounted vise, bring the wheel down horizontally over the vise and lock the freewheel tool in its jaws.

If you use the wrench, you must hold the wheel stationary while applying force to the freewheel tool. If you use the vise, the tool will be held stationary, so you must turn the wheel to apply leverage on the tool. In either case, you must twist the wrench or the wheel in a counterclockwise direction to unscrew the freewheel from the hub. Because of the constant tightening action that results from pedaling, it may take a lot of force to break the freewheel free. If your freewheel proves quite stubborn, you may have to get a bigger wrench or slip a length of pipe over the handle of your wrench to get extra leverage.

Once the freewheel begins to unscrew, loosen and remove the axle nut or quick-release skewer before continuing to turn the freewheel removal tool. At this point, you may be able to unthread the freewheel by simply turning the removal tool with your fingers. If that's the case, take the entire quick-release assembly off the wheel and set it aside.

If you still need the leverage of a wrench or vise to unthread the freewheel, it's best to keep the tool fastened in place while you turn it so that it cannot slip out of its grooves. In this case, you'll have to continually unthread the fastening nut or quick-release as you spin the freewheel off the hub. Do this by holding still the axle or quick-release skewer on the left side of the hub while you spin the freewheel, the removal tool, and the fastening nut counterclockwise on the right side of the hub. Whenever the nut becomes too tight against the tool, loosen it a bit by twisting the axle or skewer from the other side of the hub.

REMOVING COGS

One of the advantages of cassettes is that they're easy to work with, so jobs requiring cassette removal, such as replacing a spoke or installing a new cassette or cog, take less effort. Once the cog or lockring that holds the cassette on the cassette hub is removed, the cassette is easy to take off the hub because it's not threaded on. It's attached via splines, which makes cassette removal and installation easy.

There are two types of cassettes: those held on the hub by the first cog(s) and those held on the hub by a lockring. Determine which type you have by removing the rear wheel and looking at the center of the smallest rear cog (remove the axle nut or quick-release skewer first). If there's a splined shape inside the center of the rear cog, the cassette is a modern model requiring a splined tool (lockring remover) that fits inside the lockring. If there's no spline, the cassette is an older design requiring two chain whips to remove. A chain whip consists of a steel handle with a piece of chain attached.

If you have the tools and new cogs are available, you can remove your old cogs. There are two reasons to replace a cog. One is to get a different gear ratio. To accomplish this, you change the cog to one with more or fewer teeth. The other reason is simply because the old cog is worn out.

Cogs wear due to the friction of the chain against their teeth. If a cog is worn out, you'll know it when you ride on it. When you put a lot of pressure on the pedals, such as when accelerating or climbing, the chain will skip over the worn teeth of that cog. You can easily feel and hear this when it happens. The smaller the cog size, the quicker the wear, because there are fewer teeth to share the load.

Replacing a cog is not particularly difficult, but you do need the appropriate equipment. For modern Shimano and Campagnolo cassettes, you'll need a lockring remover, a large adjustable wrench, and a chain whip. For older cassettes and for freewheels, you'll need two chain whips. If you remove the freewheel from the wheel, you'll need two chain whips and a freewheel vise.

The freewheel vise is a special tool that has prongs to clamp onto the largest cog of your free-

Though both Shimano and Campagnolo use spline-interfaces to fit cogsets onto their freehub bodies, they are not compatible.

wheel. This small vise must then be held immobile between the jaws of a bench-mounted vise while you use the chain whips to apply force to the cogs.

If you don't plan on changing your cogs very often, it might be a good idea to let a bicycle shop remove the cogs for you, since that will probably cost you less than the price of the tools needed to do the work. Also, before you attempt to replace a cog, check with your local bicycle shop to see if spare cogs of the type you need are available.

For modern Shimano and Campagnolo cassettes, disassembly is simple. Hold the large cog with a chain whip to keep it from turning, place the appropriate lockring remover in the splines of the lockring, and turn it counterclockwise with a large adjustable wrench. Remove the lockring, and the cogs can slide off the hub.

If you're working on a freewheel and have a freewheel vise, lock the freewheel in it. Remove the smallest cog by wrapping the chain whip around it and using the handle to turn the cog counterclockwise.

If you're using two chain whips, use one to hold the freewheel steady and the other to remove the cog. Set the tools on the cogs in such a way that you are able to squeeze their handles together. This will give you good leverage while preventing skinned knuckles. Be careful when you're using the chain whips: If you don't keep the exerted force in line with the cog, you can warp the cog and ruin it.

Look closely at the chain whips. Each has two sections of chain: a short section attached at both ends to the handle, and a long section with one end free. When you fit the tool onto a cog, keep the gap between the two pieces of chain as small as possible. This will minimize your chances of twisting the handle out of line and warping a cog.

The most reliable method of all is to immobilize the freewheel in a freewheel vise and use two chain whips. This gives you maximum control and leverage for the job.

Depending on the brand and how many speeds your freewheel has, you will usually have to remove between one and five threaded cogs (on cassettes without lockrings, one or two cogs are threaded, and the rest slide on). The remaining cogs are notched and slide onto the freewheel body. (There are a few exceptions—such as Regina freewheels, on which all the cogs are threaded on—but they're pretty rare today.)

As you remove each of the cogs, lay them out in the order and orientation they came off. This will ensure getting the cogs back on properly. Before you put the cogs back on the body, check the order against the manufacturer's chart, if it is available. Make sure the threads are clean and lubricated with a light oil.

As you install the cogs, make sure that you don't put any of them on backward. There's no risk of this with modern cassette cogs, which fit on the hub only one way. It's easy to make mistakes with older freewheel and cassette cogs, though. Remember that the

side of the tooth that is sloped (chamfered) usually faces the spokes. Most likely, you will discover that some cogs have no threads; they are held in place by adjacent cogs. When replacing a cog that is threaded, hand-tighten it first, then tighten threaded cogs with a chain whip so that each threaded cog is snug against the cog below it. The cogs will tighten fully when you ride.

The first time you use this cassette, start out riding on the largest cog, pedal a few feet, shift to the next cog, and pedal a few feet. Do this until you've seated all the cogs.

INSTALLING A FREEWHEEL

No tools are required to install a freewheel. Be sure the threading on your freewheel and hub match before attempting to put the freewheel on, and thoroughly clean the threads on both the freewheel and the hub, then lubricate them with a medium-weight grease before trying to put them together.

Be careful while threading on a freewheel—its threads are steel, and the hub threads are usually aluminum. If you cross-thread the freewheel, you may strip the hub threads, which will ruin it.

Apply grease to the threads inside the freewheel, then hold it in one hand and steady the wheel in the other. Put the freewheel against the hub and turn it counterclockwise at first. This unscrewing action will align the fine threads of the freewheel and hub to prevent cross-threading. Once you feel the threads drop into alignment, reverse direction to begin threading the freewheel clockwise onto the hub.

Spin the freewheel on carefully for the first few turns. If you meet any resistance, you've probably cross-threaded it. Stop, remove the freewheel, and try again. Once the freewheel has been threaded down three or four full turns, you can safely assume that you have it right; continue until it's tightly threaded all the way on.

SPECIAL MAINTENANCE SITUATIONS

Cassette hubs combine the inner workings of the freewheel and the hub into one unit. In this system, the freewheel mechanism and hub can usually be separated with a 10 mm hex key. Replacement freewheel mechanisms are not always easy to get and

Though you hardly ever see them today, the Maillard Helicomatic hub and freewheel were of an ingenious design. The freewheel slid onto splines on the hub, rather than threading, and was held in place by a lockring.

rarely fail, though, so this procedure is usually best left to a shop mechanic.

The Maillard Helicomatic freewheel body requires a special hub. Due to the special helical splines, the freewheel body is held in place with a small lockring. A special tool easily removes the lockring. Once that's off, the freewheel body can be lifted straight off the threads, making spoke replacement easy. Don't expect to find replacement cogs for a Helicomatic system, though, because it's been obsolete for some time.

Generally speaking, all types of freewheels and cassettes are very dependable. Basic maintenance requires only that you wipe away any surface dirt and drop a little oil into the bearings periodically. Developments over the last several years of indexed shifting systems and increasing numbers of cogs—nine or ten fit into about the same space that once held seven or eight—have lead to thinner cogs with short, radically shaped teeth and slender chains to improve shifting. Add the use of

exotic materials and the practice of combining multiple cogs of a set on alloy carriers to save weight, and you will find that a cluster of cogs will wear much more quickly than five- or six-speed cogs ever did. As a result, replacing individual cogs has all but become a thing of the past. You can maximize the life of your modern cassette by replacing your chain periodically—every 750 to 1,000 miles on the road, and more often when mountain biking or riding through bad weather. Any but the lightest of us putting more than 1,500 to 2,000 miles on a single chain and cogset will most likely need to replace the entire cassette and chain at the same time.

TROUBLESHOOTING

PROBLEM: When installing a cassette, it won't fit onto the cassette hub.

SOLUTION: Cassettes fit onto hubs only one way. Inspect the cassette closely and match its spline to the hub's spline and it'll slide on.

PROBLEM: The cassette is getting rusty.

SOLUTION: A little rust won't damage the cogs quickly, so it's not a major concern. Usually, using a little more lube will prevent rust, and riding will cause the chain to wear away the rust while you're pedaling.

PROBLEM: A tooth or teeth got bent or broken on a cog.

SOLUTION: Usually, it's possible to lever the tooth back into alignment with a screwdriver. Place it between the damaged cog and its neighbor, and apply a little bit of leverage to straighten the tooth. A broken tooth usually won't prevent the cog from working adequately. If it does, replace it.

PROBLEM: Shifting is not as accurate as it once was. When you shift, the drivetrain is noisy, as if the chain isn't quite in gear.

SOLUTION: Check that the cassette lockring is tight. It may have loosened, allowing the cassette cogs to move slightly and rattle around on the hub.

PROBLEM: When you ride an older bike with a freewheel, the freewheel doesn't coast. Instead, it drives the pedals around. If you stop pedaling, the chain gets bunched up, causing a racket.

SOLUTION: The freewheel has probably rusted inside. Free it by dripping some oil with penetrating qualities into the body.

PROBLEM: When pedaling in certain gears, there's a disconcerting skipping feeling and sound.

SOLUTION: This occurs when a cog is worn out. If you have a five-, six-, or seven-speed freewheel and individual replacement cogs are readily available, figure out which is worn and replace it. Users of seven-, eight-, nine-, or ten-speed cassettes may in some cases be able to replace individual cogs or sets of three, but most often this skipping is a sign that it's too late and the chain and complete cogset will need to be replaced. Skipping can also be caused by debris getting jammed between two cogs. For this, clean out the gunk with a small screwdriver.

PROBLEM: Once in a blue moon, you feel and hear a loud metallic pop coming from the cassette hub or freewheel body.

SOLUTION: This is the pawls inside the mechanism slamming into place after getting hung up. If it happens only on rare occasions, don't worry about it too much. Clean and relubricate the freewheel or freehub internals. If it becomes chronic, there may be permanent damage inside the mechanism. In this case, replace the freewheel or the freehub body.

PROBLEM: You hear a creaking sound coming from a rear wheel.

SOLUTION: Remove the cassette cogs, grease the splines that the cogs sit on, reinstall the cogs, and tighten the lockring.

PROBLEM: Pedaling feels crunchy and rough.

SOLUTION: Either the chain has gotten dirty, or dirt has gotten inside the cassette or freewheel bearings. Flush it out with a light lube such as WD-40, and then apply a medium-weight oil like Phil Wood Tenacious Oil. Repeat until it runs smoothly.

PROBLEM: You were going to build a new wheel, so you cut the spokes out of the wheel, but you forgot to take the freewheel off first. Now you can't use the hub.

SOLUTION: This can be tricky. Install the freewheel remover and clamp the hub (by the remover) in a sturdy bench vise so that the left flange is pointing up. Wrap a piece of inner tube around the right-side hub flange (the one closest to the freewheel) to protect it. Then grab the flange with large water-pump pliers or a large monkey wrench and turn counterclockwise. If you're lucky, the freewheel will unscrew. Don't worry about it if you slightly mar the flange.

PROBLEM: The shifting isn't as precise as it was before you disassembled and cleaned your freewheel or cassette.

SOLUTION: Check to see that the spacers are installed correctly and that all of the spacers were reinstalled. There should be same-size gaps between each pair of cogs. If not, the shifting won't work correctly.

PROBLEM: The derailleur refuses to shift onto one of the larger freewheel cogs.

SOLUTION: At some point, you may have reversed the freewheel cog. Most cogs are directional. When installed backward, the ramps on the teeth can't pick up the chain when you shift. Try disassembling the freewheel and flipping over the cog.

PROBLEM: When installing a cassette, it fits too tightly on the hub.

SOLUTION: Sometimes manufacturers build the cassette body on the hub slightly oversize because they want the most amount of purchase for the cogs, which can dig into the body during pedaling. (This is often the case when the hub has an aluminum cassette body.) To install the cassette, lubricate the body and gently press the cassette onto the body. It'll go on if you rock it and work it on gently.

Basic Cassette and Freewheel Maintenance

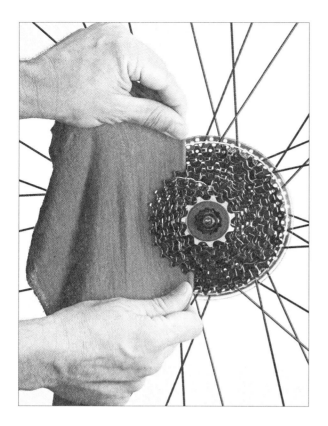

1 Cassette and freewheel maintenance consists basically of cleaning and lubrication. We recommend that this be done at least monthly. If you ride in a heavy rainstorm, clean and lubricate both your chain and cassette or freewheel afterward.

A thorough job of cleaning is best done with the wheel off the bike. Lift your chain off the cogs, release the axle, and remove the wheel. Lay the wheel down on a workbench or other flat surface to free both your hands for cleaning.

Use a rag to wipe the grease and road grime off the surface of the cogs. You may want to moisten the rag with solvent, or spray some solvent directly on the cogs, to help loosen grime. After cleaning the outer surface of the first cog, hold the rag with both hands. Pull it taut and slide it between successive cogs, cleaning both sides of each one with a shoe-shine motion.

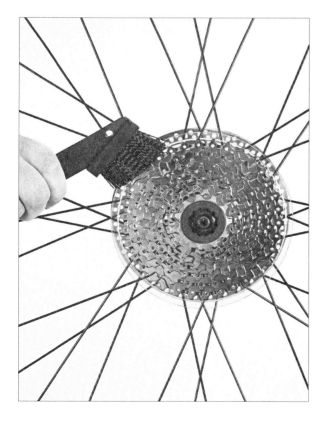

2 In addition to cleaning the sides of the cogs, make sure you clean the troughs between adjacent teeth. If you have difficulty getting the cogs clean with a rag alone, use an old toothbrush or other stiff brush to loosen the foreign matter, then use the rag to wipe it away (see photo).

Make a special effort to clean the teeth of the cogs as well as you can. When the chain pulls against those teeth, any gritty matter that is there serves as an abrasive, causing both the chain and the cogs to wear at a faster rate than would otherwise be the case. Cleaning the chain and cogs not only prolongs their life but it improves shifting quality as well.

3 Now that the cogs are clean, attend to the inner parts. Spin the cassette or freewheel around a few times. If you hear only the familiar sound of the ratcheting mechanism, you can proceed with lubrication. However, if you hear grinding sounds, as if there are little particles of sand partying inside, try to clean out this grit.

Don't try to disassemble a freewheel body or cassette body. They're not meant to be serviced, and replacement parts aren't available. To clean them, it's usually possible to flush out foreign matter by dripping oil or some type of solvent through the mechanism.

On cassettes, look for a crack between the outer and inner cassette bodies by spinning the cassette and watching for where they are separated. Usually, you can find this without removing the cassette from the hub. Spin freewheels, too, to locate the line between the outer and inner bodies (between the part that moves and the part that stays still).

Drip bicycle oil or medium-weight motor oil into the mechanism, spinning the freewheel to help the oil work its way around (see photo). Put a rag underneath to catch any excess that drains through. For cassettes, there's a handy tool available called the Morningstar Products Freehub Buddy that allows you to flush and lubricate cassette bodies.

4 If your cassette or freewheel still feels or sounds gritty, try flushing out the foreign matter with the help of a penetrating oil-and-solvent mixture such as WD-40. Rotate the cassette while you spray the solvent mixture into it (see photo). Wipe away any excess, then lubricate the cassette or freewheel once again with oil.

Some people use more potent solvents, such as kerosene. However, after using such a substance, you may have to oil your cassette several times before the lubricant is adequately replaced. A penetrating oil should be able to do the job satisfactorily.

Cassette Removal and Cassette Cog Disassembly

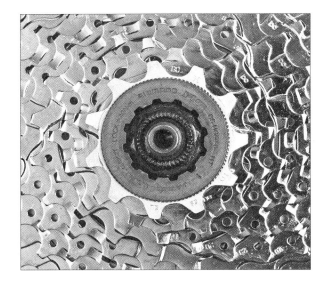

1 To replace a broken spoke, lubricate the cassette body, change gear ratios, or replace worn cogs, it's necessary to remove the cassette from the rear hub. This is easy to do with the correct tools. For modern Shimano and Campagnolo cassettes, it requires one chain whip, the appropriate cassette lockring remover, and a large adjustable wrench. For older cassettes (ones without lockrings), two chain whips will do the trick.

Start disassembly by removing the rear wheel from the bike. If it's a modern Shimano or Campagnolo cassette, you'll see a spline pattern at the center of the small cog; this accepts a special lockring remover.

2 Unscrew the quick-release mechanism, insert the cassette lockring remover into the spline, and reinstall the quick-release (remove the springs first) to hold the remover in place. This step, though not crucial, will prevent the tool from rocking and getting damaged when you apply force.

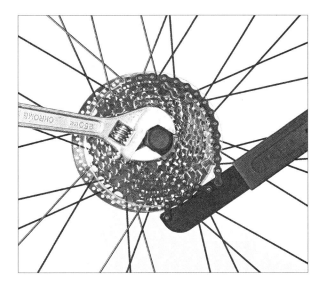

3 Stand the wheel up, hold it or lean it against something, and wrap the chain section of one chain whip around the largest cog, placing the handle forward (in the drive direction). Then place a large adjustable wrench on the flats of the lockring remover with the handle facing the other direction (see photo). Holding the chain whip handle, push down on the adjustable wrench to loosen the lockring.

4 Once it's loose, remove the quick-release, and while holding the chain whip, unscrew the lockring completely, turning the remover by hand. Once the lockring is removed, the cogs will then slide off the hub.

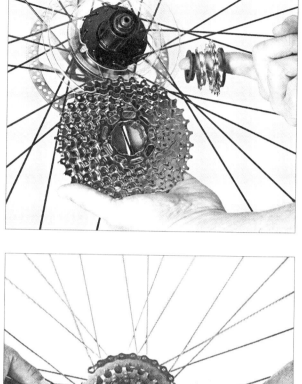

5 If you don't notice splines at the center of the small cog, you probably have an older style Shimano cassette system, which doesn't require a lockring remover. To remove the cogs, stand the wheel up, and place one chain whip on the large cog with the handle facing forward (in the drive direction) and another on the smallest cog with the handle facing backward. Push down on the chain whip on the small cog while holding the freewheel with the other chain whip to remove the cog (see photo). Once the bottom cog is off, the rest of the cogs will follow.

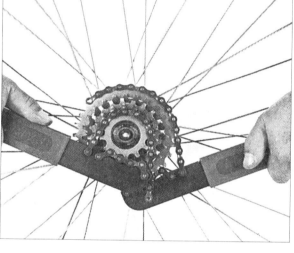

6 Some cassette gear clusters are assembled with bolts or screws (see photo), or are attached to a carrier, which you'll see when you remove the gear cluster. In order to separate the cogs on these, it's necessary to remove the hardware. Just be sure to keep everything in order as you remove it so that you can reassemble the cogs correctly.

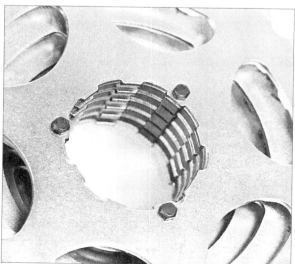

Freewheel Removal and Replacement

1 There are several reasons to remove the freewheel. The most common is a broken spoke. You may also have discovered the convenience of setting up separate freewheels with distinct cog combinations for use in different riding situations. Then again, you may take the freewheel off your bike to make cleaning it easier or to replace cogs. Before you attempt to remove your freewheel, make sure that you have a removal tool made to fit your particular brand of freewheel.

Begin freewheel removal by taking the rear wheel off the bike. Thread the axle nut or quick-release skewer nut completely off the freewheel side of the axle. Slip the removal tool over the axle and into the body of the freewheel (see photo).

2 Make sure you have good contact between the prongs or splines on the removal tool and the grooves of the freewheel body. Hold the tool securely in place by threading the axle nut or inserting the quick-release and screwing the quick-release skewer nut against it.

3 Set the wheel upright on the floor with the freewheel facing away from you. Lean over the wheel and fit a large adjustable wrench on the wrench flats of the removal tool (see photo).

You'll turn the freewheel counterclockwise to remove it, so fit your wrench on the tool in whatever position will give you the most leverage—it may take considerable force to break the freewheel loose from the hub. If you wish to use your right hand, set the wrench on the right side of the hub so you can push down on it. Flip the wheel for left-hand work.

Grasp the wrench in one hand and steady the wheel with the other. Take a deep breath and push down hard to break the freewheel loose.

4 An alternative to using a wrench for freewheel removal is to lock the wrench flats of the removal tool in the jaws of a bench vise. Grab the wheel and twist it in a counterclockwise direction to loosen the freewheel (see photo).

Once the freewheel begins to move, stop and loosen the nut or quick-release holding the tool in place (to give the freewheel room to thread its way out of the hub). You may be able to dispense with the wrench at this point. If so, remove the axle nut or quick-release skewer and turn the removal tool by hand to extract the freewheel. Or continue with the wrench until the freewheel comes off by hand.

5 Mounting a freewheel on a hub is easier than removing one. First, make sure that both sets of threads are clean, then lubricate both with a thin coat of medium-weight grease (see photo). Thread the freewheel carefully on the hub, beginning in a counterclockwise direction to align the two sets of threads.

6 Reverse direction and screw the freewheel on as far as you can by hand. Riding the bike will take care of any further tightening that might be needed, but pedal gently at first so that the freewheel can gradually tighten on the hub.

Freewheel Cog Removal and Replacement

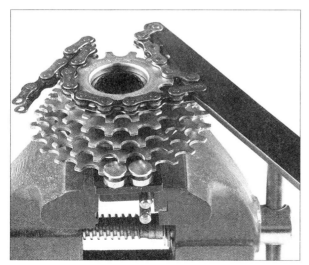

1 Cogs occasionally wear out, especially the smaller ones that have fewer teeth to share the load placed on them. Sometimes you'll want to remove cogs to make room for a different size. Cog removal is not particularly difficult and can prolong the life and expand the usefulness of a particular freewheel, but with freewheels rapidly falling out of fashion, before buying any tools or doing any work, check that the cogs that you want or need to replace are available.

As is true with many other bicycle repair jobs, having the right tools is the key to successful cog removal. The right tools in this case consist of a freewheel vise and at least one, but preferably two, chain whips. A chain whip consists of a metal bar and two lengths of chain, one long and one short. Both ends of the short piece of chain are attached to the bar. One end of the long piece of chain is attached to the bar, while the other end remains loose so it can be wrapped around a cog.

2 A freewheel vise consists of two small pieces of angle iron that slide back and forth on parallel metal rods. Each piece of angle iron is topped by a pair of metal studs sized to fit between adjacent teeth of a freewheel cog. Once closed around a cog, this little vise is locked between the jaws of a bench vise to prevent the cog from moving.

3 To remove the small, outside cog of a freewheel, immobilize the freewheel in the freewheel vise. Fit the chain whip on the right side of the cog, wrapping the loose length of chain underneath and around the cog in a clockwise direction. Push on the handle of the tool to twist the cog in a counterclockwise direction to loosen it.

It is possible to use a second chain whip in place of a freewheel vise to immobilize the freewheel while loosening one of its cogs. In this case, place the second chain whip on the opposite side of the freewheel from the first and wrap it in the opposite direction.

4 Try to set up the chain whips in such a way that the handles of the tools are crisscrossed. Then, by squeezing the ends of the two tools together, you can get the leverage needed to break one cog free (see photo).

When you attempt to remove a cog with a pair of chain whips, it is important to keep the tools fairly close together. This means that you should allow no more than one cog to separate the two cogs against which pressure is being applied. The farther apart the tools are, the harder it is to channel their force in the right directions. If you twist a tool sideways, you may damage some cog teeth.

The most reliable method of all is to immobilize the freewheel in a freewheel vise and use two chain whips. This gives you maximum control and leverage for the job.

5 As you begin removing cogs, pay attention to how they come off (see photo). You may find separate spacers between some cogs. Other cogs may have a built-in spacer protruding from one side. Attention to how the freewheel comes apart will aid later reassembly.

When in doubt, look closely at the cog teeth. The chamfered (or sloped) side usually faces the spokes. Before removing the cogs, check the chamfer orientation so you will know the proper way to put the new ones on.

6 Most likely, you will discover that some cogs have no threads but are held in place by adjacent cogs. When replacing a cog that is threaded, hand-tighten it first (see photo). Snug it up further with a chain whip, but expect the cog to tighten fully when you ride on it.

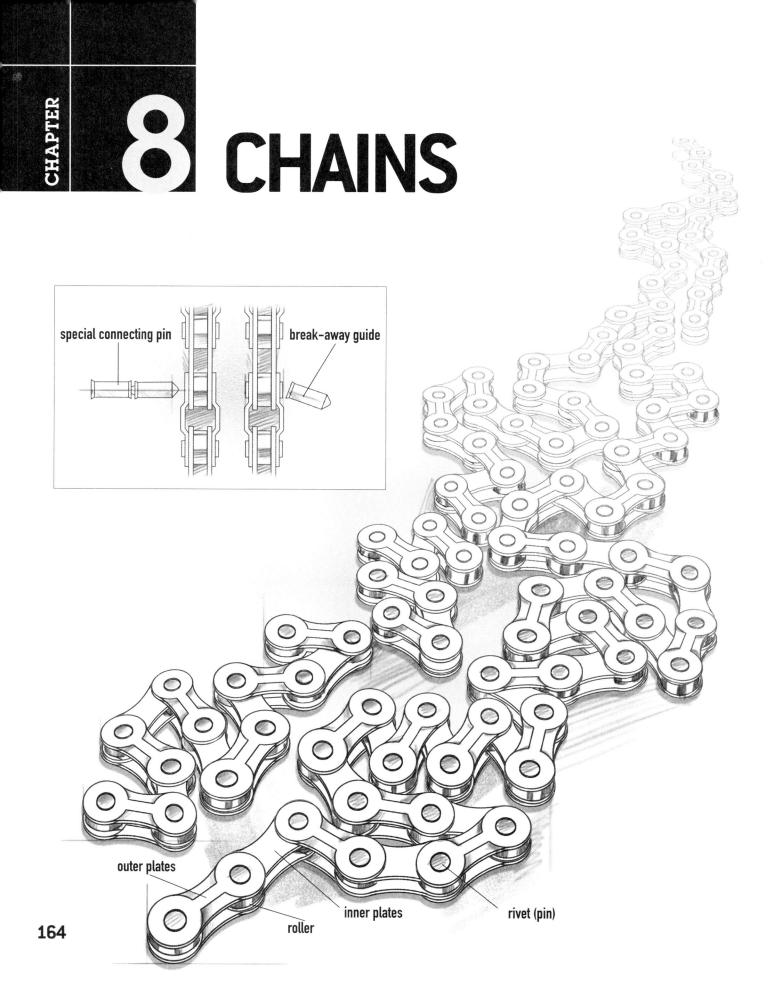

CHAPTER

8 CHAINS

special connecting pin

break-away guide

outer plates

inner plates

roller

rivet (pin)

Chains are all too often mistreated and poorly maintained, largely due to the common misconception that all you need to do to take care of your chain is keep it covered in oil. This practice then furthers the bad reputation chains have for being dirty, grimy, nasty things that no one would ever want to touch. Well, it's time to turn this all around.

Caring for your chain is easy—and it gets easier the more frequently you do it. Better still, a chain that is kept clean and properly lubricated benefits you and your bike in several ways. It will shift more smoothly and last longer; it will inflict less wear on other parts like derailleurs, chainrings, and cogs; and best of all, a clean, properly lubricated chain will work more efficiently. That means for every pedal stroke, you waste less energy fighting the chain, so more of it goes into moving you forward!

If you like the sound of all this, it's time to start paying attention to the chain. Before you begin working on your chain, you should know what kind of chain you're dealing with.

CHAIN IDENTIFICATION

There are two common sizes of bicycle chain: ⅛-inch width, which is used on most BMX bikes and all 1-speed and 3-speed bikes; and ³⁄₃₂-inch width (also known as derailleur chain), which is used on all 5-, 6-, 7-, 8-, 9-, 10-, 12-, 15-, 16-, 18-, 21-, 24-, 27-, and now 30-speed (!) derailleur bikes. The width referred to is the thickness of a compatible gear tooth. The span between the two inner plates of a chain link must, by necessity, be slightly wider than the teeth that will fit into the space.

If you can't identify the chain size of your bike from its type of drivetrain, measure the thickness of one of your bike's gear teeth. It should be either ³⁄₃₂ inch or ⅛ inch. If your bike has a ⅛-inch chain, you're all set. If your bike is equipped with ³⁄₃₂, or derailleur chain, you must determine what type.

Chains come in different widths to correspond with different drivetrains and their different numbers of cassette cogs. If you're replacing a derailleur chain, it's important to correctly identify its type. The easiest way to do so is to count the number of cogs on the rear cassette. The more cogs, the narrower the chain. Shops will be able to select the appropriate chain if you can tell them how many cogs are on the cassette and what type of derailleurs and shifters you have (or just take your bike in and show them). Pay attention because a mistake here will, at the very least, diminish your bike's ability to shift smoothly. At the worst, it may no longer shift at all.

Standard width. Standard-width chains are no longer standard. They're usually found on older bikes with five and six cogs, and they won't work properly on modern 7-, 8-, 9- and 10-speed drivetrains. With practice, you may be able to distinguish standard-width chains by their slightly greater width. If not, look first at the surface of the inner plates. Most standard derailleur chains have straight-edged plates or sometimes plates bulged to the outside. In addition, standard-width chain pins protrude about ¹⁄₃₂ inch beyond the sides of the outer plates.

Narrow width. Narrow-width chains are appropriate for seven- and eight-speed drivetrains. Complicating matters, the new 9- and 10-speed drivetrains each take a different ultra-narrow chain. The designs are similar, though. The inner links of most narrow-width chains have slight bulges on their edges. This is to help counteract the slightly smaller opening in the narrow chain that the gear teeth must fit into. That narrower opening makes shifting less accurate. So, even though a narrow-width chain will work with a standard-width freewheel, don't try it. That combination just doesn't shift as well as a properly matched chain and freewheel.

Another visual tip-off to narrow chains is their flush chain pins. The ends of these pins barely protrude beyond the surface of the chain's outer links.

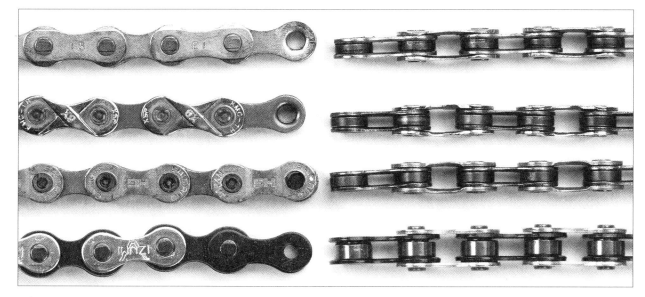

Close inspection reveals subtle differences in the shapes of different bicycle chains. Bulging and flared side plates help make derailleur chains shift quickly and quietly, while the straight sides and broad rollers of track chains give them strength and help them stay on the chainring and cog where they belong.

The extra side clearance that the flush pins provide allows the narrow chain to settle down onto the teeth of a narrow freewheel's cogs without interference from each cog's neighbors. If you ever try a standard-width chain on a narrow cassette, you'll see firsthand how necessary that clearance is: The standard-width chain doesn't engage any of the cogs.

WHEN TO SERVICE CHAINS

There are three common reasons to service a chain: dirt buildup, poor shifting, and component changes.

Dirt can have several harmful effects. Mixed with the oil often found on chains, it can permanently stain clothing (now you know why so much bicycle clothing is black). The same mixture also greatly accelerates chain, cog, chainring, and derailleur-pulley wear. Finally, dirt trapped between chain links and pins can degrade your bike's shifting ability by reducing the chain's flexibility.

Worn chain. Do you ever find yourself overshifting your rear derailleur almost to the next cog to complete rear shifts, and reducing pedal pressure to finish front shifts? A chain that has too much lateral, or sideways, flexibility can cause these problems. Although it's often called chain "stretch," the

problem is not caused by actual lengthening of the chain's steel links but by wear on the chain pins and bushings. As the chain wears, or "stretches," the distance between its chain pins increases. This condition won't cause problems as long as the sprockets on which the chain works wear at the same rate.

However, if you're a sensitive rider, you may notice the changes in performance. Besides slow and imprecise shifting, a worn chain may make more drivetrain noise when you're pedaling. You may hear a metallic rattle caused by the parts of the chain, which have worn and now are loose, vibrating against each other (although if the chain is heavily lubricated, it may still run quietly). Also, because the links and rollers have changed shape due to wear, they do not seat properly on the cassette cog and chainring teeth. This can cause a rough pedaling feeling. Where once pedaling felt silky-smooth, it now feels like there's gravel in the drivetrain, and no amount of chain cleaning will restore the smooth pedaling feeling (in fact, cleaning usually worsens things because it removes the lube and allows metal-to-metal contact).

When you hear or feel these things, it's time to inspect the chain closely and replace it if it has become worn.

Usually, chains and cogs wear at the same rate. By the time a chain is worn out, the most-used cogs have also worn out and will need to be replaced at the same time as the chain. You can't see cog wear. The teeth actually take on a slight hook shape, but it's difficult to see even if you could compare a worn cog side by side with a brand-new one. Unfortunately, the best test for worn cogs is test-riding the bike in the cog you think is worn out and pedaling hard to see if the chain skips in that gear. Pedal carefully—the skipping can cause a loss of control.

As a stopgap if you're on a tight budget or can't get to a shop right away, it's often possible to install a new cassette cog or chainring and continue using the old chain. It might not even skip. We don't recommend this, however, because the worn chain will rapidly wear the chainrings and cogs. (Plus there's always the danger of a worn chain breaking.) In fact, one way to get the cogs and chainrings to last as long as possible is to replace the chain regularly, say at the first signs of wear or every 750 to 1,000 miles. Doing this prevents the chain from ever having a chance to wear the cogs past a certain point. Just when the chain is starting to wear and cut into the cogs and cassettes, you'll install a new chain, which eliminates the wear because the new rollers and links are in perfect condition.

When you wear a cog or chainring out, the chain links no longer settle down snugly over the teeth and you usually experience chain skip, a disconcerting lurch in the pedal stroke as the chain rides up and jumps forward one tooth or more, making a clunking sound, and possibly throwing you forward, causing an accident. It can happen consistently or only occasionally, but it's guaranteed to annoy you to no end. It's even more likely to occur when you replace an old chain, but keep the old cassette (if the cassette is worn).

Stiff links and skipping. If your bike begins to skip in a gear, check first to see if the chain is excessively dirty (mud or sticks stuck between cogs can cause skipping) or has a tight link. That's a joint in the chain that doesn't bend easily and, consequently, doesn't run through the rear derailleur or settle onto the cogs easily. To find a tight link, watch your rear derailleur's jockey cage closely while you turn the crankset slowly backward. A tight link won't lie snugly on the pulleys and you'll be able to spot it passing through them.

If the drivetrain is clean, there's no tight link, and your bike skips in only one gear, replace the offending cassette cog (it's worn out). If it skips in more than one gear, weigh the cost of replacing the individual cogs against the cost of a new cassette. The cassette as a unit is frequently cheaper than a set of replacement cogs. If your bike skips in all gears and your drivetrain is old, you may need both a new chain and a new cassette.

Even if your bike isn't skipping in any gear, it's worth checking the chain periodically to make sure that it's still in good shape. To check a chain, lean the bike against a wall or some other object that will hold it upright and immobile. Tension the chain by pressing lightly on the right pedal while you hold a 12-inch ruler against the top half of the chain. On any new chain, 12 full links (measuring from pin to pin) measure exactly 12 inches long. When the same number of links measures 12⅛ inches or more, replace the chain.

Chainsuck. This chain glitch occurs on heavily used mountain bikes. It's the annoying tendency of the chain to get sucked up and jammed between the small chainring and the chainstay. It usually happens when you're trying to shift onto the small chainring. When it happens, it jams the pedals, forcing you to stop. Once you experience chainsuck, you won't want it to happen again.

To prevent the problem, always use a chain that's in good condition and keep it clean and lightly lubed. Replace the small chainring if it's damaged from chainsuck or if it's worn excessively. Perhaps most important, remember to ease off a bit on pedal pressure when shifting to lower gears. And if you ever hear or feel a crunching sensation while shifting, stop pedaling immediately or you'll jam the chain badly and damage the components, causing a worse chainsuck problem.

A common cause of chainsuck is mud. As it builds up on the chain and chainrings, the shifting gets sluggish and eventually chainsuck develops. Fortunately, there's something you can try to fix it. If you have some water to spare, try washing away the mud on the rings and chain. If you have a water bottle, spray water at the crank while you're riding. That's sometimes enough to blast off the mud sufficiently to end the chainsuck.

If you're out of water, find a puddle or creek you can use to wash the mud out of the drivetrain. Lay the drivetrain side of the bike down in the water and use your hands to splash and scrub the mud out of the drivetrain. This will take a few minutes, but it'll be worth the hassle and slight delay because the bike will shift again and you'll prevent component damage caused by the chain getting jammed.

It can be tricky to extract a chain that's gotten sucked between the chainring and frame. First try pulling it out, but don't jerk or twist the links too much. You don't want to bend the chain or chainring. Sometimes a combination of pulling the chain and turning the crank will work the chain out. If these steps don't work, you'll need to either separate the chain and rejoin it, or remove the crankarm. Both are easy enough if you have the tools handy.

Don't panic when you see how the chain has scratched the frame. Usually, it's just nasty looking. If the chain gouged the metal, remove the right crankarm so you can get at the chainstay. Then lightly sand the damaged area smooth with emery cloth before repainting the area. The only cause for concern is if the chain got jammed on a carbon or aluminum frame and cut into the chainstay. Carbon and aluminum can break when notched, so this damage could lead to a broken chainstay (worst-case scenario). If you have a carbon or aluminum frame

Certain derailleur chains have special connecting links (such as the SRAM Power Connector chain shown here) that make chain installation and removal easier because you can do it by hand.

and the chainstay gets deeply scratched, have the damage checked by a professional mechanic.

Correct chain length. The final reason for working on a chain is to achieve correct chain length after component changes. The changes that may affect chain length include the replacement of your cassette with one that has a different range of cogs, the installation of a wider-range or triple-chainring crankset, and a change in rear derailleurs.

A general rule for chain length is that there should be enough chain to permit shifting onto the largest cassette cog while also on the largest chainring. This will prevent damage to the derailleurs in the event that you unintentionally shift into this normally unused combination. With a triple crankset that has a "granny," or small inner chainring, this may mean that the derailleur will double over onto itself when your chain is on the smallest chainring and any of the outer, or smaller, freewheel cogs. However, it's considered acceptable practice to use the granny chainring only with the three to five largest inner freewheel cogs. In those positions, the rear derailleur shouldn't double over onto itself.

Modifying chain length provides you with the opportunity to use those seemingly useless scraps of chain that were left over from your last chain installation. Don't throw away any short lengths of new or usable chain until you have a substantial collection. You never know when you're going to need to lengthen a chain or replace a tight, damaged, or broken link. Smart mountain bikers and touring cyclists carry a few links and a chain tool along on

Chains are separated and put together with chain rivet or chain pin extractors (commonly known as chain tools).

rides—if you have a chain mishap far from help, you usually have to repair only one or two links, not an entire chain.

SEPARATING A ⅛-INCH CHAIN TO REMOVE IT

If your bike has a ⅛-inch chain, that chain can be disconnected, or "broken," at its special master link. This link is fatter than the others and you can usually find it by watching closely for it while pedaling. There are two types. One has a spring clip (it looks like an elongated horseshoe) holding the link together. On the other, the link is held together by the pins, which have notches in them.

If the master link is the clip type, use a small screwdriver or a pair of needle-nose pliers to pry off the spring clip, then pull off the outer link on that side of the chain. Slide either end of the chain off one of the exposed pins of the master link. Reverse the procedure to put the link together.

If the master link is the pin type, simply bend the chain sideways at this link to close the pins slightly. In this position, the inner plate of the link will slip off the ends of the pins, allowing the chain to be separated. You may have to loosen the rear wheel of the bike to get the slack you need to give

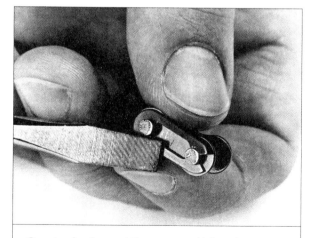

Coaster brake and three-speed bikes have chains that are connected at a master link, a special link that can be disassembled for removing the chain. There are two types. One is opened by flexing the chain and lifting off the sideplate; the other (see photo) is removed after prying off a spring clip.

The right tool in the wrong hands is the wrong tool. Chain tools are simple to use, but it takes experience to use one well. Don't learn on the chain that's on your bike—if you get it wrong, the chain could break during a ride. Instead, pick up a short length of discarded chain and practice disassembling and reassembling the chain until you feel comfortable with the whole process.

the chain lateral flex. Otherwise, it's a simple and quick procedure. Replace the plate in the same manner you took it off.

SEPARATING A ³⁄₃₂-INCH CHAIN TO REMOVE IT

The fatter master link found on single-speed coaster-brake bikes and 3-speed bikes would create problems if found on a ³⁄₃₂-inch, or derailleur, chain. It would lead to chain snags on the front derailleur cage and the rear derailleur pulley. That's why master links have traditionally not been used on these chains.

In order to separate and reassemble a ³⁄₃₂-inch chain, you'll probably need what is commonly referred to as a chain tool. Buy an inexpensive, screw-type chain tool for at-home maintenance—and consider carrying one on rides. Certain chain types are easier to service with particular tools. Make sure that the chain tool you purchase is compatible with the type of chain on your bike. A bike shop or tool supplier should be able to advise you if you tell him what type of chain you're working on.

All current Shimano chains and Campagnolo 9- and 10-speed chains require a special replacement pin for reassembly. To remove these chains, press a pin completely out. When it's reassembled, insert the new Shimano pin until it clicks, and break off the end that protrudes by bending it sideways with a pair of pliers.

For other derailleur chains, it's important not to push the pin all the way out of the link, because doing so will make reassembly difficult. When pressing the pin with the chain tool, the object is to have the inside end (the end nearest the bike) of the pin protrude a little on the inside of the outer plate of the link (the plate nearest you when you face the chain). If you're using a screw-type chain tool (there are also plier-type tools), take the time to unscrew the tool and periodically check progress before you've gone too far and pressed the pin all the way out. If you do it right, you will have to grab the chain on either side of the link you're separating and bend it a little to wedge the link apart. The little bit of pin that is still in the link will help hold the two ends of the chain together while you get the chain tool aligned to press the pin back in.

If you do extract the pin all the way, a trick to help reconnect the links more easily is to get a Shimano special replacement pin, put that in to hold the chain ends together, and then push the original pin back in. Otherwise, if you can't get the pin in, remove that link and the one next to it and replace them with another pair. Press the new pin out the way you wanted to do on the first one, and replace the damaged link from your supply of extra links.

You'll note that our description assumes that you will break the chain by pressing the chain pin out toward you, rather than in toward the bike. This may seem a bit awkward, but if you do it this way, it means that when you're ready for the more difficult task of rejoining the chain ends, you'll be working on the pin from your side of the chain instead of from the hard-to-reach back side.

QUICK CONNECTORS

Chain tools do their job well enough if they are used carefully. Still, the job of separating a de-

railleur chain is a lot easier if it has a master link. SRAM's Power Connector chains include just such a link. There's also an aftermarket link made by KMC called the Missing Link that comes in versions to work with most seven-, eight-, nine-, and ten-speed chains. These special links are easy to spot because they look different than the other links on the chain.

The SRAM Power Connector and the KMC Missing Link come apart by pinching the side plates inward, and then sliding the pins toward each other. The force of pull on the chain makes it impossible for these quick connectors to separate unintentionally.

CLEANING AND LUBRICATING CHAINS

Sometimes it seems that every mechanic has a different idea of what is the best way to clean and lubricate a chain. But all would agree, I think, that the key words are "lightly and frequently." This simply means that it's better to wipe your chain down and apply a little lubricant every few rides than it is to soak the chain in oil a couple times a year.

Unless your chain is equipped with a quick connector, think twice about removing it to clean it. If it's not too grimy, it's easy to clean the chain while it's still on the bike by wiping it with a rag moistened with solvent. Spray a few links at a time with solvent to loosen the grime. Put on gloves to protect your hands, then wipe off the gunk on the sideplates and rollers and repeat until all the links are clean.

This is the best way to clean mountain bike chains and 9- and 10-speed road chains because removing and reinstalling them can lead to weakening the links and worse—possible chain breakage when you're riding. If you wipe the chain regularly, it'll also reduce the amount of grime buildup on the cassette and chainrings.

The other thing to consider is how worn the chain is. It's always best to measure a chain before cleaning it, as there's no sense in cleaning a worn-out chain. Replace it instead.

If the chain is in good condition but is so filthy that you feel you must remove it for cleaning, take it off and immerse it in a solvent, such as a commercial degreasing/cleaning fluid or kerosene (put rubber gloves and goggles on first for protection). Pour enough solvent into a container (a 2-liter plastic soda bottle is handy because it'll keep the fumes down and you can shake it to clean the chain) to cover the chain.

If the chain is particularly dirty, let it soak for a while to allow the worst of the dirt to float off. Then carefully pour off the upper, cleaner layers of solvent into another container and leave the grit from your chain behind. Transfer your chain into the container with the clean solvent and brush it clean. When you're done cleaning with the solvent and brush, dry the chain thoroughly with an old rag and hang it somewhere to dry. Don't try to lubricate the chain until all of the cleaning solvent has evaporated.

There are varied opinions of what is the best lubricant. Some prefer dry lubes that consist of a light lubricant in a volatile carrier, which are usually applied from an aerosol can. Because they end up dry to the touch, these lubricants attract and hold a lot less road dirt than lubricants like motor oil that remain moist. After cleaning the chain and allowing it to dry, apply one of these specialized lubricants to reduce dirt pickup on the chain while maintaining good lubricating properties.

You can also use the same type of spray lubricants to help minimize the number of times you have to remove your chain for cleaning. Every few rides (depending on the conditions), spray a wet coat of lubricant on the chain and wipe away the excess and whatever dirt you can. From time to time, you will still need to thoroughly clean and relubricate your chain or replace it, but this type of treatment can help you stretch out the time between major cleanings.

Also popular today are wax-based lubes that are applied and left to dry. These need more frequent application but are among the cleanest lubes available. They're not the best for wet riding, but they work well in dry climates.

Of course, there are also those who prefer using oil on chains. It's only natural. Oils do a better job of fighting corrosion and don't wash away when wet, making them a good choice for early spring or for rainy climates.

Because there are so many types of lubricants designed for different uses (new ones come along almost monthly), you may want to experiment to find the best one for the type of riding you do and the climate you ride in. For advice, ask local shop mechanics or friends you ride with.

Sometimes, after a thorough cleaning with a potent solvent, a chain will squeak even after a light lube has been applied. To stop the squeak, apply a light coat of bicycle oil or an oil-based chain lubricant to the chain. Wipe it as clean as possible, and then maintain the chain with your spray, nonaerosol drip, or wax lubricant.

Whatever you do, don't use three-in-one oil: It's vegetable-based, which means it will gum up your chain, and it doesn't protect against wear as well as a lubricant that is mineral-oil based. Also, though it might seem like a frugal way to reduce waste and spending, avoid the temptation to lubricate your chain with used motor oil. Used motor oil contains fine particles of metal and acids formed from the heat of combustion that can attack the chain—potentially causing more wear than it prevents.

REASSEMBLING A CHAIN

When installing a chain, don't place it on the chainring, but be sure it passes through the front derailleur and rear derailleur cages correctly. Leaving it off the chainring during installation will provide slack in the chain, which makes aligning the ends easier.

If you're putting together any modern Shimano chain or a Campagnolo 9- or 10-speed chain, you must have the special replacement pin. Both work in a similar way. Align the ends of the chain, start the pointed guide end of the pin in by hand (for Shimano, the guide is integrated; for Campagnolo, the guide is a separate piece), put the chain tool in place, and turn the handle until the pin is seated. You should hear or feel a slight click when the pin is fully inserted. Remove the tool and remove the guide. You will need to break the guide off a Shimano pin with a pair of pliers, or you can just insert it in the end of the chain tool and twist.

Flex the newly joined link in your fingers to make sure it isn't tight. If it doesn't pivot as freely as the other links, hold the chain on either side of the link and flex the chain sideways to loosen the tight link.

To install other types of chains, run the end of the chain that does not have the pin sticking out (remember, the pin should protrude toward your side of the bike) through the rear derailleur cage, over the freewheel, through the front derailleur cage (but not over the chainring teeth), around the bottom bracket, and back to the other end of the chain. If you do place the chain over the chainring at this point, there will be tension in the chain and you may find it difficult to keep the two ends of the chain together while you attempt to rejoin them.

Wedge the inner-link end of the chain into the outer link. The little bit of pin protruding inside the outer link should hold the two ends together. Use your chain tool to press the pin back through the links until the pin protrudes equally from each side of the outer link.

Usually, a chain will be tight at the newly rejoined link. There are two ways to free it. First, if your chain tool has an alternate position for holding the chain, unscrew the tool enough to move the chain into the other position so the chain will be held in place by its inner link instead of by its outer one. That means that if you press on the pin just a little more, the outer link will be free to move away from the inner link, freeing the chain.

The second, cruder method involves grabbing the chain firmly on either side of the tight link and

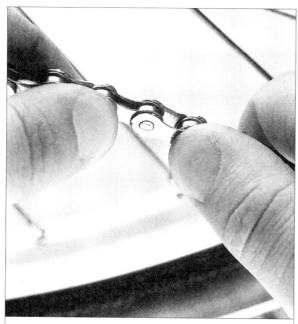

Loosen stiff links by holding the chain in your hands and flexing it back and forth and sideways. This should work on a newly installed chain. If the tight link is on an older chain, especially one that's rusty, you may have to replace the bad section with a new section.

bending it sideways, back and forth, a few times. If the link doesn't free up, bend the chain again a little harder. Don't overdo it or you may permanently bend the chain.

Once your chain is back on your bike, take the time to wipe it off occasionally and lubricate it when it starts to look "dry." Regular preventive maintenance will reduce the number of times you have to go to the trouble of a major cleanup. It will also help you maintain good shifting and minimize the number of chain stripes you end up wearing. Once you discover how nice it is to have a clean, smooth-running chain, you'll never take this valuable part of your bike for granted again.

TROUBLESHOOTING

PROBLEM: The chain is always a black, grimy mess.

SOLUTION: Clean it, and use less lube or a lighter lube.

PROBLEM: The chain breaks on a trail and you don't have a tool to fix it.

SOLUTION: Find a piece of wire (from a fence maybe) or string (use a shoelace if you have one) and try tying the chain ends together. Then pedal gently (walk up hills) and you ought to be able to "limp" home.

PROBLEM: The chain squeaks when you pedal, even though you've lubed it.

SOLUTION: Try a type of lube with better penetrating qualities. After applying it, let it sit a bit. Be sure to wipe off excess lube because it will attract dirt.

PROBLEM: When you pedal hard, the chain skips.

SOLUTION: If it skips on only one cog, it's probably a worn-out cog. Replace it. If the chain skips on all or most of the cogs, it's a tight link. Find it by pedaling backward and watching for it to bind as it passes through the derailleur pulleys. Then flex the chain sideways to free the link. If the link is rusted tight, replace it. Replace the chain if there are several stiff links in different locations.

PROBLEM: The chain runs rough when you pedal.

SOLUTION: Replace it if it's worn out, or try a different model of chain if yours is relatively new but it runs rough. Some chains run smoother than others. It may also be a worn chainring (if the teeth are smallish and hook-shaped, it's worn).

PROBLEM: While you're shifting your mountain bike, the chain gets sucked up and jams between the chainring and frame.

SOLUTION: This is called chainsuck. Keeping the chain clean and lubed helps prevent this. It's also crucial to shift with light pedal pressure. When chainsuck is chronic, it's often necessary to replace the chainring.

　　If you get the chain stuck, try pulling it out. You may need to turn the crank while pulling on the chain. If this doesn't work, either remove the crankarm or separate the chain to get the chain out.

PROBLEM: A few chain links got bent.

SOLUTION: Try straightening them by twisting the chain with pliers. Or replace them with new links (be sure to use the same type).

PROBLEM: The chain runs noisily.

SOLUTION: If the chain is lubed and not worn, it's probably a derailleur adjustment problem.

PROBLEM: The chain falls off all the time.

SOLUTION: This is usually a derailleur adjustment problem.

PROBLEM: When you shift, the chain gets jammed between the chainrings.

SOLUTION: Make sure that the chain is the right width for the drivetrain. If it is, check the chainring bolts for tightness. Make sure that the chainrings are straight. Check the spacing of the chainrings. Replace any worn chainrings.

Assembly and Disassembly of Quick-Connect Derailleur Chains

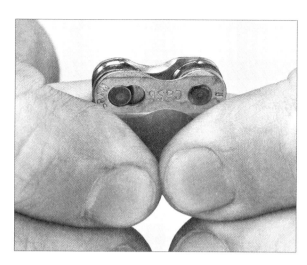

1 Quick-connect chains like SRAM's Power Connector models make it simple and convenient to remove your chain for cleaning without the use of tools.

To begin, find the special connecting link. Some manufacturers make this link a different color than the rest to make locating it easy. In all cases, the connecting link can be identified by elongated holes in the side plates.

Pinch the side plates toward each other with your fingers. This frees the ends of the pins from recesses in the side plates.

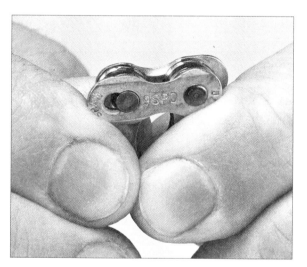

2 With the side plates pinched together, slide the pins toward each other. Each pin will shift through the elongated hole in the opposite side plate to the release position.

3 The connecting link can now be separated by moving the side plates away from one another. Reconnecting the chain is as simple as reversing these steps.

Despite their uncomplicated design and ease of assembly and disassembly, quick-connect links can be as strong or stronger than traditional press-fit rivet connections. This is especially true after several uses.

Chain Maintenance and Repair

1 Frequently clean and lube a chain to keep it operating well. Especially wipe down the chain and relubricate after it has been subjected to muddy water.

Modern mountain bike chains and ultra-narrow 9- and 10-speed road chains are best cleaned while they are on the bike; moisten a rag with solvent and wipe the chain clean weekly.

Since many chains found on derailleur bikes are not equipped with master links (there are exceptions; see page 168), the customary method of removal involves the use of a special tool to separate a link.

To separate a chain, slip it off the front chainring to remove tension from the chain. Wind the center rod of the chain tool back far enough for a link of chain to slip into the slot provided for it, then screw the rod forward against the pin (see photo).

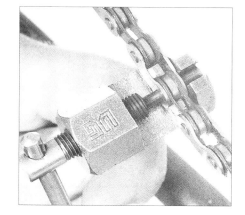

2 Make sure that the rod and pin are properly aligned, then continue to wind the rod forward to push out the pin.

When the pin appears to be most of the way out of the link, remove the tool and see if the link can be separated. If not, replace the tool and drive the pin farther out. Be careful: Stop when the pin end against which you are pushing is still visible on the inside of the outer plate (see photo).

A pin that is pushed all the way out of a chain link can be put back in, but the process is so difficult that it's simpler to move the tool to the next pin and work on it, completely removing and discarding the first link. The exception is Shimano's modern chain. On this, the pin must be pushed all the way out, and after cleaning is finished, the chain is rejoined with a special hardened steel pin made for the purpose.

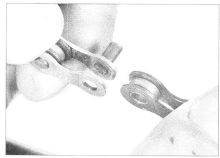

3 After separating the chain, pull it off the front and rear sprockets and soak it in a can of solvent (or put it in a plastic soda bottle with some solvent, and shake it up). Once the grease and grime have begun to loosen, use a brush to clean inside the bearing areas (see photo).

Wipe off the chain with a clean rag and hang it up until all the solvent has evaporated, then reassemble it on the bike, making sure to run it through the front and rear derailleur cages (but don't put it on the chainring yet). Align the ends and use the chain tool to force the pin back in. If it's the Shimano or Campagnolo special pin, it will make a slight clicking sound when it's seated, and you'll need to remove the guide end of the pin (break it off with pliers if it is a Shimano version).

If the rejoined link is stiff, flex it back and forth sideways to loosen it.

4 Using a drip bottle of your favorite lube, or an oil can or aerosol spray can with a thin nozzle, direct some lubricant into the bearing areas of each link (see photo). When the entire chain has been lubricated, wipe off the excess with a clean rag. Oil left on the surface of the chain will only attract more dirt. If you favor a wax-based or dry lubricant like Pedro's Ice Wax or Finish Line Krytech, don't wipe it off. Allow it to dry before you ride.

9 SHIFT LEVERS

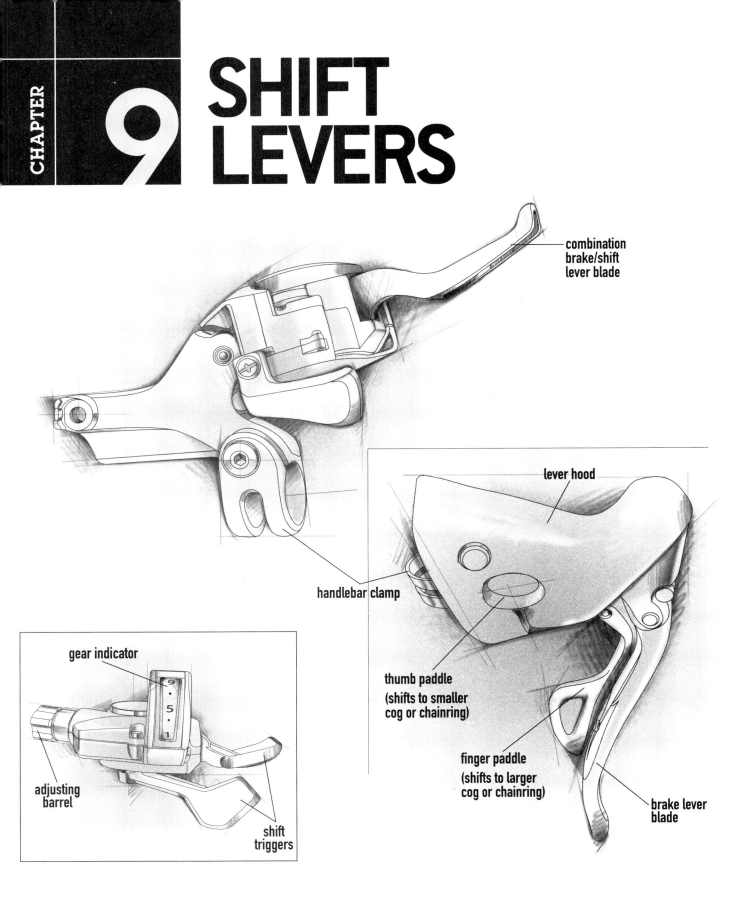

combination
brake/shift
lever blade

lever hood

handlebar clamp

thumb paddle
(shifts to smaller
cog or chainring)

finger paddle
(shifts to larger
cog or chainring)

brake lever
blade

gear indicator

9
5
1

adjusting
barrel

shift
triggers

The shift levers are the means by which you connect with the variable gearing of your bicycle. On a road bike, the shift levers are most often mounted on one of three different locations: the down tube on the frame, the stem, or the handlebar. In the last decade or so, the handlebar has become the most common location for the shifters, emphasizing convenience and control.

Shimano, Campagnolo, and Modolo all offer road shift levers built into the brake levers. For mountain bikes, shift levers are always mounted on the handlebars—near enough to the hand grips that gears can be shifted with the thumbs and/or forefingers while your hands remain on the bars. This is certainly most appreciated when the going is rough and removing a hand from the grip might result in an "off-of-bike" experience. Also in common use on mountain bikes are twist-grip shifters, such as those made by SRAM. Twist shifters replace a short section of the grip so your hands are always in place on the shifter, ready to make a shift. Three-speed bicycles use a type of shifter that has three distinct positions—the first indexed shifter.

Despite differences in size, shape, and location, all shift levers have much in common. On a three-speed bike, the single shift lever is connected by cable to a gear system housed inside the rear hub. Bikes of five speeds or more have one or two shift levers, each connected by cable to a derailleur. Moving these shift levers back and forth tensions or relaxes the cables, moving the derailleurs so that they can shift the chain from one cog or chainring to another to produce the various gears of the bike.

Because derailleurs are spring-loaded, they will always move quickly to the most relaxed position unless restrained by the shift levers. Thus, shift levers on modern derailleur bikes have a set position and the lever is "clicked" into each gear. Older bikes with down-tube shifters may be equipped with levers that do not click but are held in place by friction.

The levers are simply tight enough that they can resist the tension of the springs and hold the derailleurs in whatever gear you have selected. This tension resistance is sometimes done by means of a special ratcheting system.

SHIFT LEVER LOCATIONS

The most desirable road bike shifter among enthusiasts is the combination brake-and-shift lever (commonly referred to as a brake-shifter) because it allows shifting while climbing and sprinting. In fact, any time the hands are near the brake levers, it's possible to shift by pushing sideways on the brake levers or small built-in toggles. This ingenious design makes it so easy to shift that you actually shift more often, which helps keep your legs fresh on long rides. Manufactured by Shimano, Campagnolo, and Modolo, the dual-purpose levers are complicated, expensive, and heavier than down-tube levers but provide too much of a shifting advantage for many serious riders to pass them up. They now come standard with most component groups, though you can sometimes request that the company substitute down-tube or bar-end levers. (But why would you want to?)

For a long time, the down tube was the standard position for the lever on dropped handlebar bikes. To shift, you reach down to the lever. To some degree, this would lower your center of gravity, maintaining stability while you have a hand off the bar. Also, the cable runs are short and direct, resulting in very fast shifts. Moreover, many down-tube shift levers are designed to mount on braze-on bosses. These fittings are actually part of the frame and can't slip or break like regular band clamps. The bosses give the frame a clean look.

Handlebar-end (also called bar-end) shifters are a favorite of long-distance tourists. Their positioning at the ends of a drop handlebar is nearly as convenient as integrated brake-shifters. Their real

Twist shifters like SRAM GripShift are light and simple. With a turn of the wrist, a rider can shift through several gears at a time, as compared to lever-type shifters that sometimes only allow a gear or two to change with each press of a lever.

draw, though, is that they retain the ability to switch between indexed mode and friction. In the case of a topple or other situation affecting the rear derailleur's ability to accurately index from cog to cog, a simple twist of a D-ring puts the shifter into friction mode so the rider can make fine adjustments until a permanent repair can be made.

There are several types of mountain bike shifters. Thumb-operated shift levers are available, which attach to the top of the handlebar (old style) or under it (modern style). There are also popular shifters made by SRAM that are twisted-throttle style.

The top-mounted shifters are simple, having only one lever on each side that moves forward and back to shift gears. Under-the-bar shifters use dual levers: one for upshifts and another for downshifts. Some designs take two-finger operation: You push one lever with your thumb to shift to a larger cog or chainring and the other lever with your forefinger to move the chain to a smaller cog or ring. Although below-bar levers are a little more complicated to repair and are heavier than above-bar levers, they're pretty much standard now because they shift more quickly than above-bar models and allow you to keep a better grip on the bar during shifts.

The latest innovation from Shimano is integrated brake-shift levers for mountain bikes. The lever moves in three directions: Pulling toward the handlebar pulls the brake cable, pushing the lever downward with the fingertips pulls the gear cable, and flipping the lever upward with the backs of your fingers releases cable. Shimano has mated this system with a new-design rear derailleur with a reverse action, called low-normal. The return spring pulls the derailleur toward the largest cog, rather than toward the smallest as most derailleurs do.

Twist shifters are light and simple, containing fewer parts than modern lever-type shifters. Lots of mountain bikers and casual cyclists like them because they allow shifting with a full-fingered grip on the handlebar. Twisters can also be shifted through several gears with a single twist of the wrist, rather than several clicks of a lever or trigger.

As with all things, deciding which type of lever is right for you is a matter of personal taste. Try out everything you can wrap your fingers around, and don't dismiss anything based solely on someone else's opinion. You may not know what you're missing.

BASIC SHIFTER DESIGNS

There are three basic categories of shift levers: the friction type, the ratcheting type, and the index type (which is featured on all bikes sold today). The friction-type lever employs several friction washers to prevent the derailleur from moving in response to the pressure from the spring in the derailleur body.

The ratcheting shift lever resembles the friction type in its dependence on friction to hold the shift lever from moving in reaction to the spring. An added feature is a built-in ratcheting device that allows you to move the lever backward, shifting into lower gear without having to overcome the resistance of the friction washers. The idea behind this design is to equalize the force needed to move the lever in either direction.

Index levers click when you move them into set positions that correspond to each cassette cog. This feature makes it unnecessary to fine-tune each shift by moving the lever slightly. Instead, you simply click the lever once to move the chain up or down a cog.

Index levers are the easiest type to operate, and when working properly, they'll prevent you from missing a shift. Of the other two types of levers, the ratcheting system is more advanced than the simple friction system.

FACTORS THAT AFFECT LEVER PERFORMANCE

Most shift levers are designed to work as a set manufactured by the same company; the set includes the

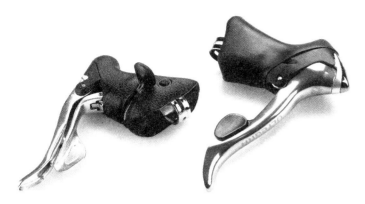

Integrated brake-shift levers like these from Shimano (*right*) and Campagnolo (*left*) keep all braking and shifting duties close at hand. Because systems like these have made shifting so convenient, you end up shifting more often, conserving energy on long rides.

front derailleur, the rear derailleur, and the two shift levers. You should try to maintain these sets. If you change to a different type of lever, it may negatively affect the way your derailleurs shift.

Shift levers do not ordinarily require much maintenance. The most common problem people have with them is allowing them to loosen and then losing parts. Sometimes the "clicks" of levers become less distinct. This is usually because the parts inside are dirty or worn. A good cleaning and lubrication may help. If the clicks still aren't crisp, small internal parts may be worn. One indication of this is when an otherwise well-adjusted system lands between gears frequently. In severe cases, the lever may be incapable of moving the chain to certain gears. Usually, worn levers should be replaced, although on some models you can purchase replacement parts from the manufacturer.

Expect your levers to shift poorly if they are mismatched to the derailleurs or if they are of poor quality. No amount of servicing will remedy these problems. Replacement is the best solution.

REMOVING SHIFT LEVERS

Most shift levers are held on either the stem, down tube, or handlebar of the bike by removable or built-in clamps, or they are fastened to braze-on bosses on the down tube. The removal method is similar for all these levers.

First, cut the cable end caps off if there are any, and release the shift cables from the front and rear derailleurs by loosening the cable anchor bolts on both.

Road bike clamp-on stem or down-tube levers. If the levers are clamped on the bike, loosen and remove the clamp nut and bolt. Gently bend the clamp wide enough to clear the down tube or the stem, and remove the lever unit.

For clamp-on and braze-on levers, use a screwdriver—or your fingers, if the tensioning bolt has a D-ring to grip—and loosen the tensioning bolt. The tensioning bolt is the part that holds the lever in place on the clamp. Gently wiggle the shift lever and pull outward, until it and the washers on both sides of the lever come off the fitting or the braze-on boss, depending on the way it is mounted. Make either mental or written notes on the order of the parts so you will be able to put the lever back together later.

Road bike handlebar-end shifters (Shimano/Campagnolo/SunTour). Release the shift cables from the front and rear derailleurs by loosening the cable anchor bolts on both.

On one side of the friction shift-lever body (the part sticking out from the end of the bar), there is a wide screwdriver slot in a cap-locknut. Insert a screwdriver and unscrew the cap. You'll see a recessed nut beneath the cap. Once the cap is removed, unscrew the screw on the other side of the lever, then pull the shift lever away from the body. Remove the lever by pulling the cable all the way out of the housing.

Index bar-end shift levers are attached with screws. On the right Shimano index levers, there's a D-ring that changes the lever from index to friction mode. Unscrew the center screw (the D-ring is attached to a ring outside it) with a screwdriver to remove the lever. For the left, the screw may have a D-ring directly attached—remove it either with a screwdriver or by hand, as appropriate.

Once the shift lever has been removed, you can remove the body. Inside the body, you will see a 6 mm hex bolt. Insert a wrench and turn it clockwise. After one or two turns, the expander should be loose enough for you to pull the lever body out of the handlebars.

Road bike brake-lever shift levers (Shimano STI/Campagnolo Ergopower). The inner workings of brake-shift levers can be incredibly complex. Shimano does not offer replacement parts for their shift mechanisms, so their brake shifters must be replaced when they fail. Campagnolo and SRAM both offer service parts, but performing a rebuild of a brake-shifter is tricky business, so it may be best left to a pro. It's fairly easy, however, to remove them from the handlebar should you need to replace a damaged lever or bar, and it's pretty easy to replace cables.

To remove the levers, unwrap the handlebar tape and loosen the 5 mm hex clamping bolts located on the sides of the lever bodies (look beneath the rubber hoods to find the bolts). This will loosen the clamps and allow you to slide the levers off the bar (it's unnecessary to remove the cables to do this).

To remove the shift cables, cut off the aluminum end caps (if there are any), click the shifter to its "normal" position (cable fully released), and loosen the anchor bolts on the front and rear derailleurs. The cables wrap around the shifting mechanism inside the lever. To find the ends, push the cables toward the lever. You may need to squeeze the brake levers to open them slightly and operate the shift lever to move the shifter into a position where the ends of the cable will come free, allowing you to extract the cables.

Internal gear hub three-speed thumb shifters (Sturmey Archer/Shimano). Three-speed thumb shifters are very simple to work with. If they don't work, replace them; there are no user-serviceable parts inside. Replace the cable by releasing it at the hub, freeing its upper end from the catch in the lever, and pulling it out. You may have to use a small screwdriver to lift a catch plate on the lever in order to do this. To reinstall the component, follow the removal steps in reverse order.

Mountain bike shifters (Shimano/SRAM/Sun-Tour). There are many kinds of mountain bike shifters, and the exact construction varies from manufacturer to manufacturer. Most types, including above- and under-bar thumb levers and twist shifts, are held on with a clamp that is loosened by turning a nut and bolt or a single hex bolt. Of course, to remove the lever from the bars, you must first remove the grips (and sometimes the brake levers).

One notable exception you might run into is an older above-bar thumb shifter model made by Sun-Tour. For this model, you must remove the lever to get at the nut. The lever is removed by unscrewing the tension bolt on top. Once the lever is off, the clamp can be removed or repositioned.

To reinstall mountain bike levers, follow the removal steps in reverse order.

SERVICING SHIFT LEVERS

As we discussed, Shimano Rapidfire shifters and STI brake-shift levers, whether for road or mountain bikes, cannot be serviced. They're designed to be replaced when they fail. Campagnolo Ergopower and SRAM Trigger shifters can be rebuilt and repaired by a qualified mechanic, but it's not a task to enter into lightly. All other lever types can be serviced by the home mechanic to one degree or another.

Road bike down-tube levers. Start by taking the lever apart and cleaning all its parts with a safe solvent. When working with index levers, do not completely dismantle the small parts inside unless they separate on their own. Most have factory-assembled inserts that are not designed for user servicing, and they won't work properly if this piece is misassembled. Make a note of the order of the parts as you remove them. Use alcohol on any parts made of plastic. Alcohol may be adequate for the metal parts as well. Allow all parts to dry before reassembling the lever.

If index levers still don't function after cleaning and reassembly, something inside is probably worn out or damaged. In that case, it's best to replace them. Usually, shift levers are sold in pairs.

When you reassemble the shift lever, only the metal-to-metal surfaces need lubrication. The nylon washers used in shift levers are normally self-lubricating, and grease or oil will make them too slippery. Remember, the main purpose of these washers is to generate friction, so you don't want them to be too slick.

If you're working on an older friction lever that slips all the time, you may need to replace its washers. Check with your local bike shop to see if washers for your particular lever are available.

If you can't find new washers, there are a few things you can do to make the old ones work better. To start with, turn the washer upside down and see if it works better that way. You can also rough up the surface of the washer with sandpaper to eliminate some of its slickness. Finally, you can fit a regular flat washer over the old washer.

Mountain bike twist-grip shifters. Usually, the cause of slow shifting is contamination in the cable and housing due to dirt that's gotten inside or corrosion caused by water running down the cable and entering the housing. Check the cable and housing first. Try lubricating it, or replace the cable and housing if necessary. If the shifter is still difficult to turn or doesn't work properly, it probably needs cleaning and lubrication.

When working with twist shifters, it's important to use only lubes and cleaners that will not damage plastic and rubber. Specifically, avoid petroleum- or citrus-based solvents. Products like Simple Green and Pedro's Bio Cleaner are both safe for plastics. In their absence, rubbing alcohol or a solution of dishwashing detergent and warm water work well. There are only a few lubricants that are factory-approved for use in plastic shifters like SRAM's Grip Shift shifters. SRAM Jonnisnot or Finish Line's Grip Shift–approved grease are the most widely available. Do not clean the shifters with high-pressure spray systems, such as those found at a car wash, because these can damage the parts and may worsen shifting by forcing dirt into shifters.

To clean twist shifters, disassemble them. Open older models by pulling outward to separate the twist grip from the shifter body, allowing access to the inside parts (move the grips or slide over the brake lever first). If the shifter doesn't open, try rotating it away from you fully first, or remove the triangular plastic cap by the cable adjuster and try again.

Mountain bikers have a choice in ways to change gears. GripShift (*center*) are the ultimate in simplicity and reliability. Triggers (*right*) guide your chain with the push of a thumb or the tap of a forefinger. Shimano's STI shifters (*left*) combine shifting and braking duties in a single, multidirectional lever blade.

SRAM's newest models are a little more complex inside and require a few more steps to disassemble and clean than older versions. The necessary techniques are detailed, with photos, on page 190.

When the shifter is open, wipe the interior clean with a rag or a cotton swab. If the insides are really dirty, clean them first with warm water and dishwashing detergent. Then let the parts air-dry, apply approved grease, and reassemble the shifter, being careful to locate the parts correctly.

INSTALLING SHIFT LEVERS

How you install your shift levers is largely dependent on what type of shift levers you've chosen to suit your bike and your needs. This is especially so on road bikes.

Mounting shifters on your mountain bike generally just involves sliding the grips and sometimes the brake levers off the handlebar, moving the shifters into place, and then reinstalling everything else. On road bikes, the processes can be even more simple, much more complex, or something in between.

Road bike braze-on levers. Gently slide the shift lever and the associated washers back on the bosses in the same order in which they were removed. Carefully fit index lever pieces together. The lever won't work if it is assembled incorrectly. Using a screwdriver or your hand, as appropriate, retighten the tensioning bolt.

Reroute the shift cables to the front and rear derailleurs and tighten the cable anchor bolt on each. If you are installing new derailleur cables, shift the derailleurs several times, then recheck the cable tension. If the cables stretch, loosen the anchor bolts, take up the slack, and retighten them.

Road bike clamp-on stem or down-tube levers. If you are replacing an old lever, reassemble the lever parts on the clamp in the same order in which they were removed. Gently bend the clamp wide enough to slide it around the down tube or the stem.

Insert and tighten the clamp nut and bolt on the stem or the down tube. Position a stem-mounted shifter assembly so that the tops of the levers are just a bit higher than the top of the stem. Position down-tube shifters so that they are located at the point where your hand naturally falls when you are sitting on the bicycle. Some frames will have a little stop to prevent the shifter from slipping down the frame. If you see one of these stops, set your shifter against it.

Reattach the shift cables to the front and rear derailleurs by pulling each cable taut and tightening the cable anchor bolt on each. If you are installing new derailleur cables, shift the derailleurs several times, then recheck the cable tension. These first few shifts may cause the new cables to stretch, requiring you to loosen the anchor bolts again, take up the slack, and retighten them.

Handlebar-end shifters. If you are installing handlebar-end shifters for the first time, you will also have to install the cable housing. Note that there are three ways to route the cable housing.

1. Externally, with a major loop. The cable housings run from the bar-end shifter along the bottom of the bar until the bar turns up toward the brake lever. Here, the cable stops following the bar and loops out and around to the cable stop on the down tube.

2. Externally, with no loop. The cable housings run from the bar-end shifter along the bottom of the bar and turn up toward the brake lever. They follow the shape of the bar, staying on the bottom side, until they exit from under the tape about 1½ to 2 inches from the stem, and then loop down to the clamp on the down tube.

3. Internally. It was once in fashion to run the gear cables inside the handlebars so riders do not feel them when they grip the bars. At this time in history, Pet Rocks and polyester leisure suits also seemed like a good idea. Sometimes, we live and learn.

Drilling holes in your handlebar is risky, at best. Most road handlebars today are carefully engineered to be exactly as strong as they need to be—without any extra holes in them. Even if the handlebar you are using is sufficiently overbuilt, it is unlikely that any manufacturer would endorse such a modification.

All three routes for the gear cables require that you wrap handlebar tape after the cable has been run. When you run the cable externally, you can hold the cable housing in place with a piece or two of electrical tape to make it easy to wrap the handlebars.

Some people like to cut a short section off the end of the bar to compensate for the extra length that is added by the shifter body. If you decide to do this, remove a piece of bar that is the same length as

the body of the shifter, so you will end up with bars of the same overall length as before.

When you are ready to install the shifter, insert the shifter body into the end of the handlebar and tighten the expander. (The expander is located inside the body.) You will see a hex fitting. Insert a 6 mm hex wrench and turn it counterclockwise. After one or two turns, the expander should be tight. Make sure that the body is oriented so that the lever moves vertically rather than off at some odd angle.

If the cable housing has not already been installed, install it now so that the opening of the housing lines up with the hole in the housing stop on the body of the shifter.

When both the shifter body and the cable housing are attached to the bar, run the cable through the shift lever, then through the hole in the body and through the cable housing. Fit the lever in place on the shifter body and bolt it in place. Friction levers are held on the body with a bolt and nut. The bolt passes through the body and lever and threads into a nut on the other side. On most models, the nut fits in a nut-shaped recess on the side of the body. There is a round, slotted locknut that should be tightened over the recessed nut to hold it in place.

Shimano index levers are held on by screws. Tighten the right lever into place by turning the screw in the center of the D-ring. The left lever is held in place by a screw that may either take a screwdriver to tighten or have a D-ring attached, allowing it to be tightened by hand.

Route the cables to the front and rear derailleurs. Run the cable ends through the anchor bolts, pull them taut, and tighten the nuts to hold them secure.

If you are installing new derailleur cables, shift the derailleurs several times to stretch them, then check the cable tension. If the cables stretch, loosen the anchor nuts, pull them taut again, and reanchor them.

Road bike brake-shift levers. Like handlebar-end shifters, brake-shift levers use long cables and housings. These attach in one of two different ways, depending on which brand you have.

Shimano STI models use housing sections that run from stops built into the side of the brake lever bodies to the down-tube stops. The housing sections are not wrapped under the bar tape, which simplifies housing replacement and lever installation.

Campagnolo Ergopower levers use housing sections that are wrapped under the handlebar tape. This gives the bike a cleaner look and shields the housing from wear, so it holds up longer. However, it adds an extra step if it's necessary to replace the housing.

Since brake-lever shift levers also operate the brakes, the brake cables should be hooked up before installing the levers on the handlebar (for advice on this procedure, see page 253). For Campagnolo Ergopower levers, however, it's necessary to unwrap the handlebar and rewrap it after you get the brake levers and cables connected and installed on the bar.

Once this is done, hook up the shift cables and housings. Start by shifting the right return button at least ten times, and the left three times. For Campagnolo levers, push down on the buttons located on the inside faces of the brake lever bodies. For Shimano models, push the smaller levers (located behind the main levers) to the inside. Also, shift the chain into the small freewheel cog/small chainring combination.

Now you can install the cables. Once they're in place, pull them taut with pliers to remove slack, and then tighten the derailleur anchor bolts. If you have installed new derailleur cables, shift the derailleurs several times, and then tighten the cables if you've created slack. On Campagnolo levers, rewrap the handlebar.

TROUBLESHOOTING

PROBLEM: You shift the bike to a comfortable gear and start pedaling, but the bike suddenly shifts on its own into a harder gear.

SOLUTION: This happens on older-style shift levers that don't click into gear. Look for a D-ring or screw to tighten (turn clockwise) on the side or top of the lever. That will increase friction and after a shift the lever will stay where you put it. When a lever has a D-ring, it can be tightened while riding.

PROBLEM: After installing a new cable, the shift lever doesn't click the derailleur into gear like it should.

SOLUTION: Loosen the cable anchor bolt on the derailleur. Pedal by hand to shift the derailleur to the smallest cog or chainring, and make sure the shift lever is in its starting position. Then reattach the cable.

PROBLEM: A shift cable breaks while riding.

SOLUTION: Try to tie a knot in the remaining cable so that it holds the bike in an easy gear so you can ride home. Or, if you have down-tube shift levers and a few inches of cable protruding past the derailleur anchor bolt, try this: Release the cable at the derailleur anchor bolt, push the cable through the lever a little bit, tie a knot at the lever, and tighten the anchor. Voilà. You can shift again.

PROBLEM: You've cleaned a twist shifter and replaced the cable, but it's still tough to shift.

SOLUTION: Replace the shifter; it's worn out.

PROBLEM: The shift housings are rubbing against the frame and wearing out the paint.

SOLUTION: Put tape beneath the housings where they rub. Or, if possible, run the housings to the opposite stops and cross the cables beneath the frame tube.

PROBLEM: You move the shift lever but the derailleur doesn't find the gear like it used to.

SOLUTION: Usually you can fix this by turning the adjuster barrel on the lever or on the frame counterclockwise, which adds tension to the cable, making the derailleur move a little farther.

PROBLEM: It's gotten very difficult to shift twist shifters.

SOLUTION: Clean and lubricate the cables. Still hard to shift? Clean and lubricate the shifter.

PROBLEM: You're trying to install a cable in Shimano STI or Campagnolo Ergopower brake-lever shift levers, but you can't find the end of the cable.

SOLUTION: Shift the lever to its starting position by pushing the return lever at least 10 times while pulling on the cable with your other hand. That will expose the end of the cable.

Braze-On Shifter Installation

1 A gear shift lever is an assembly of several separable parts. It is very important to pay close attention to the arrangement of parts while you disassemble a shifter so you will be able to put them back together correctly later.

Fortunately, when you buy a new set of shifters, they will already be assembled. If you buy braze-on-type road bike levers, they may come attached either to braze-on bosses or to plastic facsimiles. You will have to unbolt the lever assembly from the substitute boss in order to attach it to the boss brazed to the bicycle frame, but you can hold the internal parts of the lever together during this process to simplify the installation.

Fit the lever unit on its braze-on boss, making certain that all parts go on in the correct order. Thread the tensioning bolt into the boss to hold the unit in place (see photo).

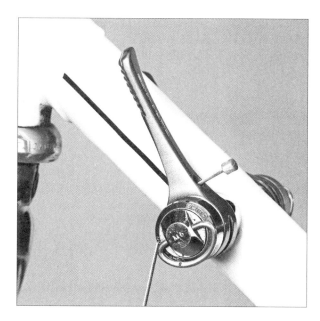

2 The head of the tensioning bolt will either be slotted to accept a screwdriver, recessed to receive a hex key, or fitted with a D-ring for hand tightening. The proper tightness of this bolt can be set only after the gear cables are in place.

If you're reusing the old cable housing, flush it out by spraying a light solvent like WD-40 or White Lightning Clean Streak through with a thin nozzle. Similarly, clean an old cable by spraying it down with WD-40 or Clean Streak, then wipe it down with a rag—or better yet, with a piece of steel wool or other abrasive cleaning pad like Scotch Brite. Nylon-lined cable housings and die-extruded cables available today work best when kept perfectly clean.

To install the cable, push the lever as far forward as it will go and thread the cable down through it from above. Pull the cable all the way through until the fitting on its end is seated in the lever (see photo). Then run the cable down toward the bottom bracket.

3 Some bicycles are equipped with cable guides that are either brazed or clamped on the down tube just above the bottom bracket area. These guides direct bare cables over the top of the bottom bracket on their way to the two derailleurs. On other bicycles, the cable guides are located on the underside of the bottom bracket.

4 Install the cables. If you're using a section of housing, set it in place and run the cable through it (see photo). Pull the end of each cable through the anchor bolt at the derailleur that it will operate.

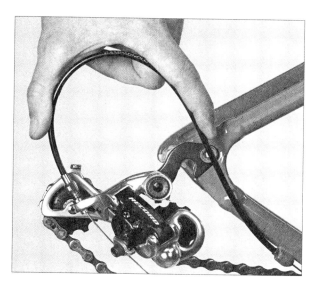

5 Hold the end of the cable with a pair of pliers to keep it taut while you tighten the anchor bolt with a wrench (see photo).

When new cables have been installed, move each shift lever back and forth a few times to prestretch the cables, then recheck the adjustment. If a lever must travel a ways before activating the derailleur to which it is attached, loosen the anchor bolt and make the cable more taut, then retighten the bolt. Leave about 1½ inches of cable beyond the anchor bolt. Trim away the rest with cable cutters.

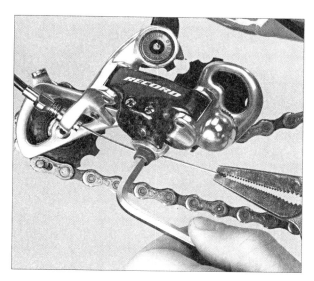

6 With the cables in place, the final step is to check the tension on the lever. Check the front and rear derailleur in turn, running through all the gears. This can be done on a repair stand but can more adequately be done while riding. If the lever is hard to pull down, there is too much tension on it. If it is easy to pull down but wants to upshift on its own, it needs more tension. Adjust the tension by loosening or tightening the tensioning bolt as needed. If the bolt is fitted with a D-ring, you can make the needed adjustment while riding the bike.

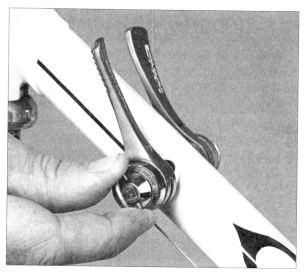

Bar-End Shifter Installation

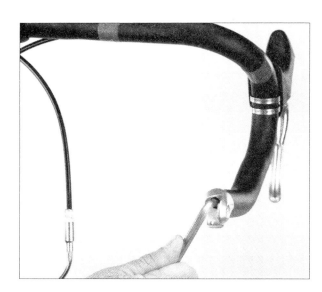

1 When installing bar-end shifters, the brake levers must be installed first because the brake lever's clamp won't fit over the shifter body.

Begin by fitting the shifter body into the end of the handlebar. Position them so that the cable housing stop is at the bottom of the handlebar and the flange the body is to the outside. Use a 6 mm hex key to turn the expander counterclockwise (the expander is located inside the shifter body).

2 Install the post and positioning washer onto the shifter body. The key of the positioning washer should point down (see photo).

3 Mount the shift lever onto the post, matching the keyway on the lever to the key on the positioning washer. The levers attach to the posts with screws. For Shimano, the screw used on the left (front) shifter has a broad head and the one used on the right (rear) shifter has a smaller head to fit into a recess in the shifter. Select the correct one and tighten it in place using a flat-blade screwdriver.

Trim the housing covers to match the length of the flat portion of the bottom of the handlebar, and tape them in place.

4 Fit a ferrule onto the end of a section of shift cable housing, and slide it into the housing cover until it seats into the stop in the lever body. Determine the proper length of the housing. Ideally, it will make a gentle arc from the point it exits the housing cover on the handlebar to the cable guide on the downtube of the frame.

5 Shift the lever up slightly. This will make a straight shot for you to insert the cable into the shifter and feed it through the shifter body and the housing.

Run the cable to the derailleur and anchor the end. Give the cable a few light tugs to seat the housing ends into the ferrules, and then take up any slack. Trim the cable about an inch from the cable anchor bolt and crimp it with a cable end crimp (or use some other manner of making sure the cable can't fray).

Repeat these steps for the other lever.

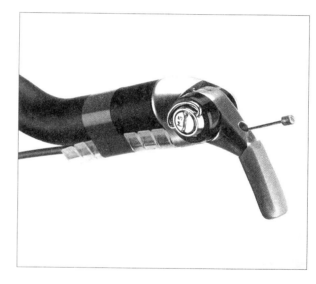

6 Wrap the handlebar from bottom to top, allowing the housing to emerge from the tape where the flat portion of the drop ends.

Check your shifting adjustment on the stand or by taking the bike out for a slow ride in an open flat area, where you can safely concentrate on watching the chain move across the sprockets.

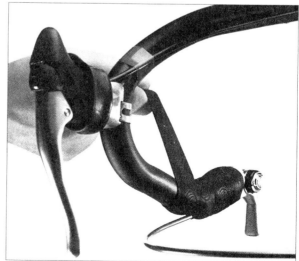

Brake-Lever Shift Lever Installation

1 Most everyone loves these dual-purpose levers because they provide several advantages: They can be reached from most hand positions, allowing more frequent shifts, which saves energy; it's possible to shift while standing and sprinting; and you can brake and shift simultaneously.

Because brake-lever shift levers also operate the brakes, the brake cables should be hooked up before installing the levers on the handlebar. To do this, follow the steps on page 253. For Campagnolo Ergopower levers, however, it's necessary to unwrap the bar tape after you get the brake levers and cables connected and installed on the bar.

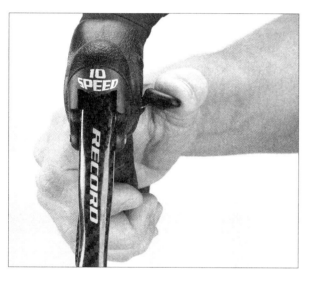

2 With the brakes set up and the levers attached to the handlebar, you can hook up the shift cables and housings. Start by shifting the right return button at least 10 times and the left one three times. For Campagnolo levers, push down on the buttons located on the inside faces of the brake lever bodies.

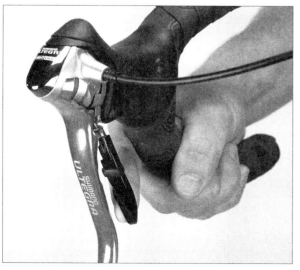

3 For Shimano, push the smaller levers (located behind the main levers) to the inside (see photo). Pick up the rear wheel and turn the pedals by hand to allow the derailleurs to shift the chain into the small freewheel cog/small chainring combination.

Shimano STI models use housing sections that run from stops built into the side of the brake lever bodies to the down-tube stops. The housing sections are not wrapped under the handlebar tape. Campagnolo Ergopower levers use similarly run housing sections, but they are wrapped under the bar tape.

4 Thread each cable through the hole (see photo) in the lever's shift mechanism (you may have to open the lever to spot it). Pull the cable to seat the barrel end in its holder.

5 Run the cables through the housing sections and back to the front and rear derailleur anchor bolts. Be sure the housing sections are seated in the lever and frame stops. Pull the ends of the cables (one at a time) with pliers to remove slack and tighten the derailleur anchor bolts. Trim the cables from 1 to 1½ inches past the anchors, then install aluminum end caps and crimp them in place with pliers or diagonal cutters to prevent fraying (see photo).

If you have installed new derailleur cables, shift the derailleurs several times to stretch them and seat the housing sections. Pluck the cables by the down tube. If you've created slack, loosen the anchor bolts, pull the cables taut, and retighten the anchors.

6 On Campagnolo levers, you'll need to wrap the handlebar. Hold the brake and shift housings in place on the bar with a few pieces of electrical tape. The bar is most comfortable to grip if you run the brake housings along the front of the bar and the shift housings along the back (see photo). When the housings are in place, rewrap the bar tape.

Twist-Grip Mountain Bike Shifter Removal, Installation, and Service

1 Twist-grip shifters (sometimes referred to as twisters) work by replacing a short section of each hand grip with a rotating sleeve. Turning this sleeve, or twist-grip, in your hand (like the throttle of a motorcycle) pulls or releases the gear cable, executing the shift. The simple design of twist shifters makes them light, durable, and easy to service. SRAM's GripShift shifters have gone through many evolutions over the years, making it difficult to cover all possibilities in this text. We'll cover the most recent incarnation of SRAM's shifters. If you have an older model, service instructions are readily available through your local bicycle dealer or SRAM's Web site.

To remove your twisters, start by shifting onto your smallest chainring or cog. Remove the cable-end crimp and release the gear cable from its anchor bolt on the derailleur. Pop the cable hatch open. On front shifters, the cable head will be secured beneath a small hex screw; on rears, it will be held in place by a small plastic clip. Remove the screw or push the clip aside and slide the cable out through the hatch. If you're replacing only the cable, you're halfway done: Just reverse these steps to finish. If your shifter needs a bit more care and feeding, read on.

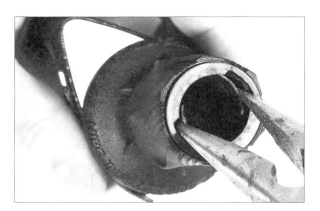

2 Slide the stationary grip off the handlebar and loosen the clamp bolt that locks the shifter body to the bar. The shifter will slide right off the bar. Separate the twist-grip from the shifter body by pinching the retaining clips inside the sleeve and sliding the twist-grip off.

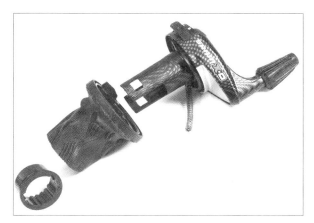

3 When you have your shifter apart, you'll see how simple its inner workings really are. To clean the parts, use a plastic-friendly cleaner/degreaser like Pedro's BioCleaner or Simple Green. Never use citrus or petroleum-based degreasers; they'll melt the plastic and ruin the shifters permanently.

4 Apply a bead of GripShift-approved grease like Johnnysnot or Finish Line GripShift Grease to all contact points within the shifter. The most critical points are where the twist-grip rides on the sleeve, the détente notches, and the grooves where the cable rides.

5 Slide the twist-grip about halfway onto the sleeve. Set the spring in place on the two pins, and twist the grip and body to slightly compress the spring as you mate the two parts. Before reinstalling the retaining clip, shift back and forth through the gears to be sure everything is seated correctly. With this established, snap the retaining clip into the end of the sleeve.

6 Reattach the shifter to the handlebar. The best location for the shifter's cable adjuster is just below and behind the brake lever—so it's protected in a crash but easily reached with your thumb and forefinger if you should need to make a quick cable adjustment while riding. Slide the stationary grip back on. It's easiest to do this after spraying a little rubbing alcohol into the grip. The alcohol lubricates the grip well enough to ease installation but evaporates quickly, leaving the grip tight on the bar. Replace the cable (along with the screw on the front shifter) and readjust the shifting.

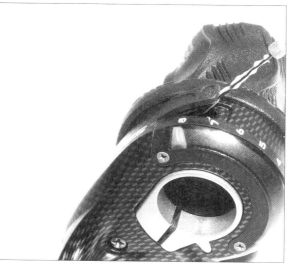

Mountain Bike Thumb Shifter Removal and Installation

1 Thumb shifters found on mountain bikes are mounted on handlebars in a location where they can quickly be reached by the rider's thumb.

Like down-tube shifters, mountain bike thumb shifters come in pairs, one for each derailleur. They are available as index (most common today), friction, or ratcheting types. Also, like their down-tube cousins, older thumb shifters use friction washers and tensioning bolts to regulate the level of friction.

Most thumb shifters can be moved after loosening the lever's clamp bolt. These are usually in plain view on top of or under the handlebar (see photo).

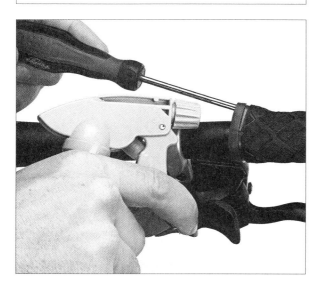

2 To remove the lever from the handlebar, slide off the grip and brake lever. Remove the grip by cutting it off if you're going to put on new grips. If not, lift up the edge with a screwdriver, and squirt some alcohol under it to make it slippery enough to pull off the bar (see photo). Once the grip is off, loosen the brake lever clamp bolt enough to slide off the brake lever, then loosen the shift lever clamp and remove the shifter. Usually it's not necessary to detach the cables.

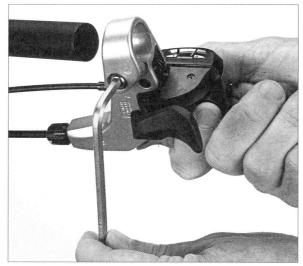

3 Some mountain bikes have shift levers that are built into or attached to the brake levers. On these, when the Allen bolt securing the brake lever to the handlebar is loosened, the shift lever will come off with the brake lever (see photo).

Older SunTour levers have yet another design. If your SunTour shifter has a D-ring on top, unscrew the D-ring completely to loosen or remove it. When it's free, lift the lever, bolt, and washers off the shifter base. Underneath you'll find a nut, which, when turned counterclockwise, loosens the clamping band and allows you to move the lever base.

Three-Speed-Type Shifter Removal and Installation

1 The thumb shifter on a three-speed bicycle is generally fastened by a removable clamp to the right side of the handlebar. The shifter is connected by cable to a set of gears located inside the rear hub of the bicycle. When a thumb shifter of this type goes bad, it must be replaced. It cannot be dismantled for repair or replacement of parts.

Begin the removal of a three-speed shifter by loosening the cable at the hub. This is done by unscrewing the fitting on the end of the cable from the fitting connected to the short length of chain that emerges from the rear hub.

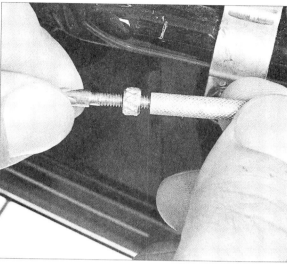

2 Use a screwdriver to loosen and remove the nut and bolt in the clamp that holds the shifter on the handlebar (see photo). Take out the bolt, gently spread the clamp apart just enough so it fits over the handlebar, and remove it and the shifter from the handlebar.

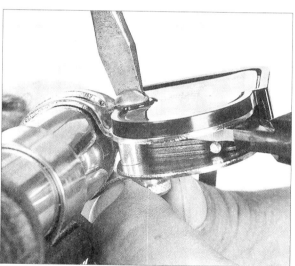

3 Free the fitting found on the upper end of the cable from the lever, and slip the cable out of the shifter. There may be a catch plate in the way that must be lifted before you can disconnect the cable. Or the entire body of the shifter may be enclosed in a plastic cover that must be slipped off before the cable can be freed (see photo).

Fit the end of the cable inside the new shifter and fasten it to the handlebar, reversing the steps of the removal procedure. Lubricate the shifter with a few drops of oil.

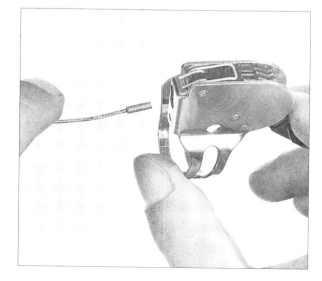

193

10 FRONT DERAILLEURS

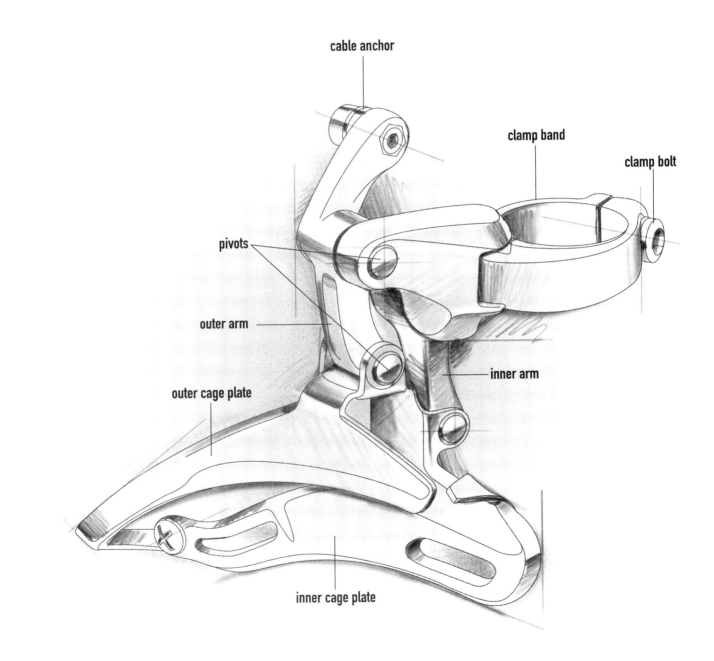

cable anchor

clamp band

clamp bolt

pivots

outer arm

inner arm

outer cage plate

inner cage plate

The front derailleur's simple appearance belies the complexity involved in its proper alignment and adjustment. The task of moving the chain from one chainring to another is handled by applying pressure to the side of the chain. While pedaling, the left shifter tenses or relaxes the cable, which in turn moves the front derailleur cage or allows a spring to return it to its normal position. Either of these actions forces the chain to climb off the teeth of one ring and onto the next. To do this is one thing; to perform the job consistently well is quite another.

Adding difficulty, the front derailleur must accomplish its task of moving the chain from one front sprocket to another while the chain is under tension, because it operates on the top or loaded part of the chain rather than on the slack lower run as the rear derailleur does.

In many cases, the derailleur moves back and forth between two chainrings, or what is known as a double chainring. The popularity of mountain bikes and their more casual offshoots, however, has made triple chainring sets commonplace. Triple chainrings require a front derailleur that can move over a wider range than is necessary for a double chainring. For this reason, derailleurs that are perfectly acceptable for doubles may not work well on triples.

Due to the subtle touch required to initiate a quick, clean, and positive shift, the front derailleur and its operation intimidate many novice riders. This is often due to a misunderstanding of the derailleur's operating principles. Understanding these principles will help you shift smoothly and should also provide you with the knowledge needed to service the front derailleur.

HOW FRONT DERAILLEURS WORK

Front derailleurs are designed only to push the chain from side to side, rather than to both push and lift it.

The speed at which they do this, or the speed of the shift, is determined by several design factors: the height of the cage plates (the two horizontal plates that push the chain back and forth), the width or distance between the cage plates, and the rigidity of the entire derailleur body. The distance between the derailleur and the chainring teeth and the type of chain used also affect the speed of the shift. For purposes of this discussion, we will let the chain be a constant.

The width of the cage plate is important because this determines how much of the chain is pushed. The wider the cage plate, the more area there is to push against the chain. However, the derailleur designer limits how wide the inner cage plate can be. The outer cage plate must be positioned to clear the outer chainring by only 1 to 3 mm, so if the inner cage plate is too wide, its bottom edge may strike the top of the middle chainring as you try to shift to the outer ring. Front derailleurs that are used on cranksets with half-step gearing (a seldom-used gear combination that usually has only a four- to five-tooth difference between chainrings) must have inner cage plates of normal width to avoid this problem. By contrast, front derailleurs designed for use on mountain bikes or other bikes with chainring steps of eight or more teeth often have very wide inner cage plates.

It was noted earlier that a wide cage plate has more area to push against the chain. You can also turn this around and say that the wider the plate, the greater the area the chain has to push against. This means that as the derailleur cage gets wider, its body must get stiffer to resist twisting because of the chain's extra leverage. The body of the derailleur and the arms that attach it to the cage must resist flexing or twisting during the shift. The stiffer the body of the derailleur, the faster the unit will shift.

The distance between the cage plates also plays a role in the speed of the shift. The closer the cage plates straddle the chain, the more control you will have over the chain and the speed of the shifts. The drawback to this is that the narrower the cage, the more you will have to adjust it as you shift the rear derailleur—as you shift in the rear, the angle of the chain changes, which can cause it to rub on the tail of the front derailleur.

THE WAVE

Because indexed shifters don't have as much capacity for trim as their older friction cousins, front derailleur cage shapes have been continually refined. They now incorporate ramps and twists that, along with small hooks and rivets on the sides of the chainrings, give the chain a little extra lift to make shifts from a smaller chainring to a larger one.

Precision like this comes with a price. Most front derailleurs today are designed to work as one part of a larger system that includes the rear derailleur, the shift levers, and a specific arrangement of chainrings. Generally, for best performance, you should stick to a set of levers, derailleurs, and chainring sizes that were made to be used together. This may sound draconian, but with the wide range of gearing choices available in modern 8-, 9-, and 10-speed cogsets, there is little need to make drastic changes to your chainring combination.

SELECTING A FRONT DERAILLEUR

When selecting a front derailleur, first consider the capacity you need. Most derailleurs specify the range in teeth (10 teeth, 14 teeth) that they can handle. This number refers to the difference in size between the small and large chainring. To find the range of your chainrings, subtract the number of teeth on the small ring from the number of teeth on the large ring.

Racing derailleurs usually have ranges from 10 to 16 teeth. Sport derailleurs can often handle differences of 20 teeth, whereas wide-range touring units can go as high as 26 teeth.

The numbers provided by derailleur manufacturers are usually conservative, and if you make a small compromise, you can often exceed them. The specified range is based on the calculation that if the chain length is correct and the correct rear derailleur is used, the chain will not drag on the front derailleur cage when you shift to the small-cog/small-chainring combination. When a chain drags, it does so across the lowest point of the derailleur, which is the spacer that connects the tail ends of the two cage plates.

Actually, you should not ride in the small/small combination even if your chain does not drag, since the extreme angle that this gear creates accelerates chain wear. By not shifting into this combination, you can use a slightly smaller inner chainring than would otherwise be possible without experiencing chain drag. In order to avoid chain drag with triple-chainring sets, it's often advisable to use the tiny inner chainring only with the three to five innermost cogs on the freewheel.

Front derailleurs designed for road racing usually have narrower cage plates than the mountain units. Road racing derailleurs will shift faster because of their narrow cages, but they need more correction as you shift in the rear. That is to say, to avoid rubbing the chain on the cage plates, the front derailleur will have to be moved slightly in or out as the chain moves in and out on the rear.

You must also consider the size of the large chainring as part of your selection process. The cage of the derailleur should match, as closely as possible, the curvature of the large chainring for optimum shifting performance. To prevent the tail from interfering with the chainring teeth, a derailleur designed for a large chainring of only 44 teeth will need to be set too high to be effective if used with a 53-tooth ring.

Be sure to find a derailleur that matches the requirements of your frame, as well. Look carefully at how it's mounted, or take your bike or old derailleur to the shop for advice. This is important because there are front derailleurs that mount in unusual ways, such as to a plate between the bottom bracket and shell.

When selecting a new front derailleur, look also at the routing required for its shift cable. Most derailleurs require an open cable that is routed through cable guides. Some older ones are designed to work with cable enclosed in one or more sections of cable housing that fit between housing stops, including a stop built into the derailleur. If your bike is equipped for a closed cable but you have chosen a front derailleur that requires an open one, you may have to put a cable guide beneath the bottom bracket to make everything work. You may also have to replace the shift cable because the new routing may be longer than the old one. If you are concerned about this, check with the dealer before buying the derailleur.

On mountain bikes, there are front derailleurs

known as top pull or bottom pull, based on which direction the cable comes from. It's important to select the appropriate style of replacement derailleur for it to work correctly.

Some road frames—usually chrome-moly models from small custom builders or carbon fiber frames with unusually large or oddly shaped tubes—have braze-on front derailleurs. This means that there is no band around the seat tube to hold the derailleur. Instead, a special fitting is permanently attached to the seat tube and the derailleur is bolted to that. If you have a braze-on fitting, be sure that the derailleur you want is available in a braze-on model. On steel frames, you can have the braze-on fitting removed by a frame builder, allowing installation of a clamp-on front derailleur. Removal of the braze-on, though, will require that your frame, or at least a section of it, be repainted.

REMOVAL, INSTALLATION, AND ADJUSTMENT

A front derailleur is easy to remove from a bike. Start by pushing the shift lever in the direction that will make the cable go completely slack. Use a wrench to loosen the anchor bolt that fastens the cable to the derailleur, and pull the cable free. Loosen and remove the nut and bolt that hold the cage plate spacer in the tail of the derailleur so the chain can slip through. If you have a late-1990s derailleur with a cage that can't be opened, you must break the chain to remove the derailleur. If you're going to replace the derailleur with a new one that has a cage that does open, cut the derailleur's cage with a hacksaw to extract the chain. (If your derailleur does not have a cage that opens, we recommend not removing it for cleaning. Instead, clean it with a brush while the derailleur is still attached to the frame.) Once the chain has been removed, loosen the derailleur clamp bolt and remove the derailleur from the frame.

For installation, remove the nut and bolt that hold the cage plate spacer, and remove the spacer to allow the chain to enter the cage. If yours is a derailleur on which the cage cannot be opened, you must rethread the chain through the derailleur and join the chain ends with a chain tool. Loosen and remove the clamp bolt from the new derailleur and fit the clamp around the seat tube in approximately the same position as the old unit. Install and tighten the

"E-TYPE" TRIPLE

ROAD TRIPLE

ROAD DOUBLE

TRADITIONAL "TRAPEZE" STYLE (OR BOTTOM SWING)

TOP SWING

Your frame's design, gearing choices, and shifter model all play a part in deciding what type of front derailleur you will need.

clamp bolt just enough to keep the clamp from sliding down the tube. Fit the chain between the cage plates, then replace the spacer and bolt it into position.

To set the derailleur at the right height, make sure that the cable is not anchored because tension on one of the lifting arms could pull the derailleur out of place. Also, be sure that the derailleur clamp bolt is loose enough to allow the derailleur to be moved up and down or sideways on the seat tube.

Slip the chain off the inner chainring and onto the bottom bracket shell to get it out of the way. Pull the derailleur cage out against its spring until the cage is over the outer chainring. Adjust the height of the derailleur clamp so the cage clears the highest teeth of the outer chainring by 1 to 3 mm when it moves across it, then tighten the derailleur clamp bolt slightly.

After the proper height has been set, align the derailleur. Replace the chain on the inner chainring of a double-chainring set or the middle chainring of a triple, then shift it onto the middle cog of the rear cluster. This should make the chain parallel with the bike. Align the front derailleur cage so that the chain bisects the cage plate and the outer cage plate is close to parallel to the chain. When that is done, tighten the clamp bolt fully. The derailleur is in its proper position on the bike.

The next step is to adjust the cable length. Operate the shifter to release all tension from the cable. Make sure the chain is on the smallest chainring. Fit the end of the cable through the cable anchor bolt and pull the cable taut. Hold the end of the cable with pliers while tightening the anchor bolt with a wrench. Leave about an inch of cable extending beyond the anchor bolt, and cut away any extra with a cable cutter. Crimp a cap on the cable end to prevent fraying. If the cable is new, move the lever back and forth a few times to get some of the initial stretch out of it, then take up any slack at the anchor bolt.

You can now set the inner and outer throw of the derailleur. The aim of this adjustment is to enable the front derailleur to shift easily onto both the inner and outer chainrings without overshooting either and dumping the chain.

Shift the chain to the largest rear cog and the small chainring. Find the low-gear adjusting screw (also known as the inner limit screw) on road or older mountain bike derailleurs (this is usually the innermost or uppermost of the two adjusting screws on the body). On newer "top swing" mountain bike derailleurs (they are easy to identify because they have a seat tube clamp below rather than above the top of the cage) the screws are reversed, but marked "high" and "low" to reduce confusion. Adjust it so that the inner cage plate clears the chain by about 2 mm. You may need to fine-tune this adjustment after riding the bike. If the chain rubs when you stand and pedal hard, readjust the inner limit screw so that the derailleur cage moves a little closer to the seat tube.

Once the inner throw is set, shift to the smallest rear cog and the large chainring. Now, adjust the high-gear adjusting screw (also known as the outer limit screw) so that the outer cage plate clears the chain by about 2 mm. Fine-tune the adjustment the same way as before. But take note: In no case should the derailleur strike the crankarm as you pedal.

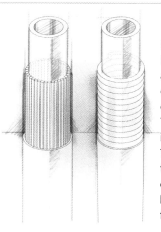

Spiral-wound cable housing (*right*) is strong and flexible, but it compresses slightly as the cable inside is pulled taut. The precision involved in modern 8-, 9-, and 10-speed indexed drivetrains makes linear or compressionless cable housing (*left*) necessary for accurate gear changes.

ADJUSTMENTS FOR SPECIAL PROBLEMS

If your derailleur is sluggish or shifts too far and the situation cannot be corrected with the adjusting screws, it often helps to custom-tailor the shape of the cage.

If the chain tends to overshoot the outer chainring, or if the derailleur shifts sluggishly from the large chainring to the small chainring, bend the nose of the outer cage slightly in toward the chain. However, do not bend it so far that the cage rubs the chain.

On the other hand, if the chain won't shift to the large chainring, look at the inner cage from the top. The nose of the cage plate should bend slightly in toward the chain. If it does not, then bend it, but not so far that the cage rubs the chain.

Check the cage plates from the front if you are still having problems. If the inner cage plate is not parallel to or slightly toed-in toward the outer chainring, bend it in until it is.

Finally, make sure that your shifting problem is not caused by a poorly adjusted gear cable. If your shift lever moves some distance before putting tension on the cable, there is too much slack in the cable. Push the lever all the way forward, and take up the slack at the cable anchor bolt. On some setups, you can take the slack out without tools by turning the adjustment barrel on the lever or frame stop counterclockwise.

MAINTAINING THE FRONT DERAILLEUR

A front derailleur has few working parts, but it is important to keep the unit clean. The grit that builds up on the derailleur body eventually works its way into the bearing surfaces. Once inside, the grit acts like sandpaper and cuts into the bearing surfaces, causing premature wear. This wear translates into play or slop in the mechanism, which causes the derailleur to shift poorly. Remember, stiffness is important for crisp shifting performance.

Clean the grit off the outside and out of the inner workings of the derailleur with the help of a solvent. Wipe the derailleur clean and allow all the solvent to evaporate, then lubricate the pivot points with a light lubricant. TriFlow or Pedro's Extra Dry works very well for this. Spray a little of the lubricant in the openings at the ends of the lifting arms, shift the derailleur, and spray a little more. Wipe away any excess or it will quickly attract new dirt.

CUSTOM DERAILLEUR MODIFICATIONS

If you are happy with your front derailleur except for the fact that you must adjust it after every one or two shifts of the rear derailleur, you can modify it to make the cage a bit wider. Loosen and remove the bolt holding the spacer in the tail of the derailleur, and slip a small washer between the spacer and the inner cage plate. Spreading the cage plates farther apart in this way allows the chain to move through a wider angle without rubbing.

By paying close attention to three simple but important matters—cleanliness, proper lubrication, and adjustment—you will provide your front derailleur with all the help it should need to perform its challenging task of crisply and accurately moving your bicycle's chain from chainring to chainring. The benefits in good performance will then be yours to enjoy.

TROUBLESHOOTING

PROBLEM: During a ride, the chain falls off while you are shifting to the small chainring.

SOLUTION: Usually, it's possible to just keep riding. Pedal very gently and shift the derailleur. With luck, the chain will shift back onto the chainring. If the problem is chronic, check the adjustment of the inner limit screw.

PROBLEM: When you stand to climb, the chain rubs the derailleur.

SOLUTION: Adjust the low-gear adjusting screw so there's more clearance between the cage and the chain when in low gear.

PROBLEM: When you stand to sprint, the chain rubs the derailleur.

SOLUTION: The chainring may be slightly bent. Sight it and have it trued if it's bent. Or adjust the high-gear adjusting screw to give more clearance between the cage and the chain when in high gear.

PROBLEM: The derailleur won't shift to the smaller chainring.

SOLUTION: Make sure that the cable is moving smoothly. Check that the angle of the cage is parallel to the chainrings, that the low-gear adjusting screw allows the derailleur to move far enough to the inside, and that the nose of the derailleur is slightly bent toward the chain.

PROBLEM: The derailleur won't shift to the large chainring.

SOLUTION: Check that the angle of the cage is parallel to the chainrings, that the high-gear adjusting screw allows the derailleur to move far enough to the outside, and that the cage's nose is slightly bent toward the chain.

PROBLEM: The derailleur won't shift to the middle ring on a triple chainring.

SOLUTION: Make sure that the chainring is correctly installed. If it's upside down or the spacers are incorrect, the chain won't be able to find the chainring.

PROBLEM: The anchor bolt got stripped when you tightened it.

SOLUTION: Try tapping it to a larger bolt diameter and installing a larger bolt.

PROBLEM: The chain rubbed a hole in the cage.

SOLUTION: If possible, install a new cage. Or replace the derailleur. When riding, be sure to not allow the chain to rub and wear out the new derailleur.

Front Derailleur Basic Maintenance

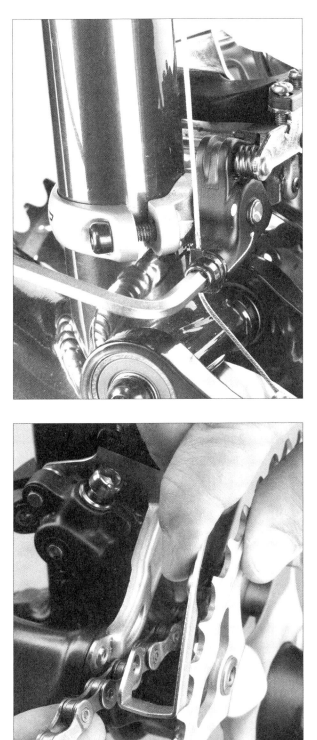

1 A front derailleur that moves sluggishly and is difficult to shift probably has grit and grime in its few moving parts. Most likely, a thorough cleaning and lubrication will dramatically improve its performance.

Lubrication of a front derailleur is most easily done with the derailleur on the bike. Leaving the derailleur in place allows you to shift it back and forth while the lubricant is being applied to its pivot areas. However, cleaning is another story. The best way to thoroughly clean a front derailleur is to remove it from the bike and soak it in solvent. Fortunately, removing a front derailleur is a simple process, one that takes only a small amount of time. First, shift the lever forward to take tension off the gear cable, then loosen the cable anchor bolt and disconnect the cable from the derailleur.

2 The main thing that now prevents you from removing the derailleur from the bike is the chain that is trapped inside its cage. The chain can be broken with a chain tool, but a simpler solution to the problem is to remove the pin that serves as a spacer between the tail ends of the two derailleur cage plates. Unscrew the bolt that holds the pin in place, remove the pin, and the chain will slip out of the cage. If you have a front derailleur with a nonopening cage (found on some late-1990s bikes), we recommend removing it only for replacement. For cleaning, brush it while it's on the bike. To remove the derailleur, you must break the chain. If you're replacing the derailleur because it's worn out, cut the cage with a hacksaw to extract it from the chain. Another option is to simply slide the derailleur down the chain to where you can clean the derailleur almost as easily as if it were free from the chain.

3 When both the cable and chain are out of the way, the derailleur can be removed from the bike. Locate the bolt that fastens the derailleur's clamp to the seat tube or the derailleur to a braze-on mount. Loosen and remove that bolt. Be sure to put it back in place in the derailleur (after the derailleur is removed) so that you won't lose the bolt.

4 If the derailleur is attached to the seat tube by means of a clamp, spread the jaws of the clamp and remove it from the tube (see photo). Soak the derailleur in a small container of solvent to loosen the grit in its bearing areas. While it soaks, give the lower part of your seat tube a cleaning and polishing, especially the area that is normally covered by the derailleur mounting clamp.

Use an old toothbrush or other stiff brush to loosen any grit or grease that is clinging to the derailleur. Rinse the derailleur in the solvent once more, then wipe it clean with a rag. Let the clean derailleur sit for a little while to allow time for the solvent to evaporate from its working parts.

Try to fasten the front derailleur back on the bicycle exactly where it was before. Then use the instructions on page 204 to properly adjust it. When the derailleur is properly located, reattach the gear cable to it. Squirt a little light oil or an appropriate spray lubricant into each of the derailleur's pivot points. Shift the derailleur a little bit and apply more lubricant. Shift the derailleur back and forth a few times to spread the lubricant around its working parts, then use a clean rag to wipe away any excess. Oil that is left on outer surfaces will only attract fresh contaminants.

Front Derailleur Installation

1 When installing a front derailleur, it is not necessary to break the chain if it is already on the bike. (A few late-model front derailleurs have cages that can't be opened. These require you to break the chain to install the derailleur.) Simply remove the spacer from the tail of the derailleur cage, drop the cage down around the chain, and replace the spacer. However, if the chain is already broken, there is no need to remove the spacer pin. Just install the derailleur, run one end of the chain through it, and rejoin the ends of the chain. If the derailleur is equipped with a clamp, take out the clamp bolt and spread the jaws of the clamp band. Fit the clamp band around the seat tube of the bike at approximately the correct height, and replace the bolt.

Tighten the clamp bolt to prevent slipping, but not so tight that it cannot be moved by hand (see photo).

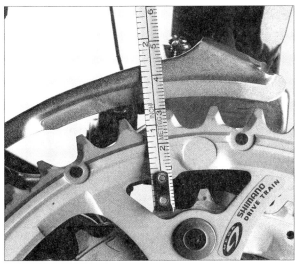

2 If the derailleur is a braze-on model, fasten it securely to the braze-on mount, then partially loosen the height-adjusting bolt.

Before reattaching the gear cable, set the derailleur to the right height and angle. Keep the chain out of the way during these adjustments by slipping it off the chainring to the inside and letting it rest on the bottom bracket shell.

Pull the derailleur cage out over the large chainring, watching the outer plate of the cage as it passes over the chainring teeth. Adjust the derailleur height so that the cage clears the tallest chainring teeth by 1 to 3 mm.

3 Let go of the derailleur cage and sight down from above. Make sure that the cage's outer plate is aligned parallel with the chainring (see photo). Once both the height and horizontal alignment are set, tighten the clamp bolt to hold the derailleur in that position.

4 Push the chain inside the derailleur cage and wrap it around the small chainring. Fit the spacer back into the tail and bolt it into place or rejoin the chain (see photo). Flush each section of derailleur housing with WD-40 or White Lightning Clean Streak, then thread a new gear cable through the shift lever and cable housing and route it to the front derailleur.

Be aware that some bikes are set up so that the cable runs above the bottom bracket on the way to the front derailleur, others run the cable below the bottom bracket, and still others route the cable from the top down. Also, note that some front derailleurs are designed to receive open cable; others have a cable housing stop and are designed to be used with a section of housed cable. If your new derailleur is not compatible with your bike, return to the shop and get the correct one.

5 Run the cable through the anchor bolt on the derailleur and pull it taut. Hold the end of the cable with a pair of pliers while you tighten the anchor bolt (see photo). Push the shift lever a few times to prestretch the cable, then loosen the bolt, take up any slack, and retighten.

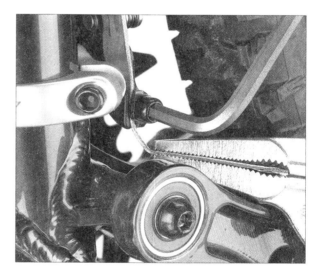

6 A new gear cable will almost certainly be longer than necessary. So after installing a new cable, leave approximately 1 to 1½ inches of wire extending beyond the anchor bolt, and use a sharp pair of cable cutters to trim away the rest (see photo). Crimp a cap on the cable end to prevent fraying.

After installing a front derailleur, follow the steps on pages 204 and 205 to make sure that it is properly adjusted before riding the bicycle.

Front Derailleur Adjustment

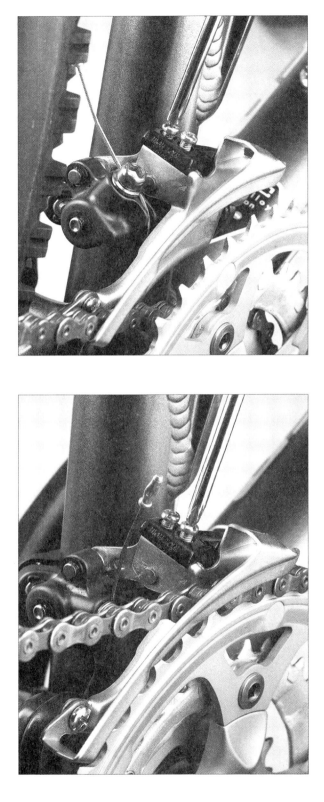

1 After installing a new derailleur, set its range of motion. This adjustment may need to be made periodically to an old derailleur as well. If you have trouble shifting onto any chainring or if a full shift in either direction tends to throw the chain past the intended chainring, it is definitely time for an adjustment.

Begin by shifting the chain to the inside onto the small chainring and largest freewheel cog. Locate the adjusting screw for setting the inner stop on the derailleur. Derailleurs with limit screws arranged horizontally come in two basic types: traditional and top swing. If the derailleur is a braze-on type or if the frame clamp is above the cage, this is a traditional derailleur, and the inner limit screw is the one closest to the frame. If the frame clamp is below the top of the cage, this is a top-swing derailleur and the screws are reversed. Fortunately, top-swing derailleurs usually have the screws labeled "high" and "low" to reduce confusion (see photo). If they are positioned vertically, it will probably be the one on top. Set the stop so that the inner plate of the derailleur cage is held 2 mm from the inside of the chain.

2 Shift the chain to the outside, onto the large chainring and the smallest rear cog. Set the other adjusting screw so that the outer plate of the cage is held about 2 mm outside the chain (see photo).

These settings should allow you to shift between chainrings and not be left with the chain rubbing the derailleur cage after the shift. Be sure to test the bike to check the adjustments. If the chain tends at all to rub on the inside with the first setting or the outside with the second, these limits will have to be slightly expanded. But don't set them so wide that the chain will come off the chainring during a rapid shift, and in no case should the derailleur move so far out that it strikes the crankarm.

3 If you're getting sloppy shifting performance with your front derailleur, look closely at its shape. Most manufacturers bend the front ends of the cage plates slightly in toward one another to create a narrow nose for more authoritative shifting. If your derailleur needs its nose narrowed, use a pair of pliers to gently toe-in the plates.

4 Often, when a shift is made with the rear derailleur, the change of chain angle causes the chain to rub the tail end of one of the front derailleur cage plates (see photo). This is especially common on a bike with a narrow derailleur cage and eight, nine, or 10 cogs. The rubbing will eventually wear out the derailleur. Usually, all it takes is slightly moving the shift lever, which is called trimming the derailleur.

5 If you want to eliminate or reduce chain rub after rear shifts, you can try to widen the back of your derailleur cage a bit. (This is not possible if you have a derailleur with a cage that cannot be opened.) Partially remove the bolt holding the spacer pin in the tail of the cage. Slip a small washer between the spacer and the inner cage plate of the cage, then retighten the bolt.

One final problem that you may encounter with a front derailleur is chain drag on the tail pin in certain gear combinations. For example, shifting the chain onto both a small chainring and small rear cog drops it low in the cage, which may cause it to drag. The solution is simple: Don't use the chain in this gear combination. Even if no chain drag occurs, such a gear combination puts the chain at an extreme angle and should be avoided.

Chain drag may also result from a mismatch between the front derailleur and the chainrings, such as using a tiny inner chainring with a derailleur designed for a sport touring bike (see photo). The solution here should be obvious: If you intend to use extra-small chainrings, equip your bike with a derailleur that is designed for them. No mechanical adjustment can compensate for mismatched chainrings and derailleurs.

11 REAR DERAILLEURS

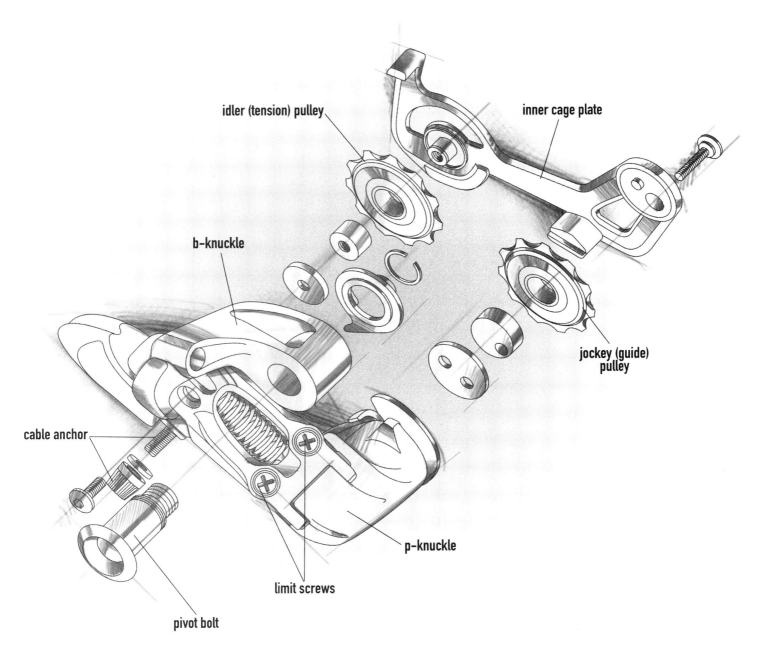

idler (tension) pulley

inner cage plate

b-knuckle

jockey (guide) pulley

cable anchor

p-knuckle

limit screws

pivot bolt

The broad range of gear selection made available through the advent and refinement of the rear derailleur has made cycling accessible and enjoyable to many millions throughout its history. In addition, the wide range of ratios availed by the rear derailleur is what made mountain biking—as we know it today—possible. Try as some might, there has yet to be a system of gear changing as light, effective, and efficient as that found on the now typical chain-driven, derailleured bicycle.

Unless you live on the plains of the Midwest or you ride your bicycle only along the beach on breezeless summer days, you know when your rear derailleur isn't working. It can be sluggish moving from one gear to another. It can misalign with a cog and cause your chain to jump back and forth between two gears—usually at the most inopportune time, of course. Or, worst of all, it can push itself and the chain right into the spokes of your rear wheel, ending your ride in a hasty fashion.

Hanging out in space on the right side of your bike is the rear derailleur's primary vulnerability. Contact with a rock on the trail, another rider on the road, or an unfortunate tumble on the sidewalk outside your favorite coffee shop can render your rear derailleur useless. But there are other enemies that lurk, and they aren't always so obvious.

Dirt, grit, corrosion, and wear all play major roles in hindering the performance of even the most robustly built derailleurs. A bit of careful cleaning and maintenance, though, can extend the life of a well-made rear derailleur almost indefinitely.

Derailleurs work—as the name implies—by "derailing" the chain from one sprocket to another. A cable, drawn by your shift lever, opposes a spring inside the derailleur. When you move the shifter to pull the cable, it overcomes the spring and moves the chain in one direction. When you move the lever to release the cable, the spring recoils and pulls the chain in the other direction.

In the early days of friction downtube shifters; short, direct cable routes; and five-speed freewheels; keeping a rear derailleur functioning properly was a relatively simple task. Close was close enough in many cases. The latest technology involving closely spaced cogsets in the double-digit realm and integrated brake/shift levers with precise, clockworklike internal mechanisms has added all-new levels of complexity to the proper care and maintenance of rear derailleurs.

TYPES OF REAR DERAILLEURS

There are two basic types of rear derailleurs: short cage and long cage. Cage refers to the two side plates that hold the derailleur pulleys apart. A short-cage derailleur is used primarily in conjunction with two-chainring drivetrains like those common on road racing bikes. Long-cage derailleurs allow for a greater difference in cogset and chainring combinations and so are most common on any bike with a triple chainring or a very wide-range cogset in the rear. There are also mid-cage or medium-cage rear derailleurs that are sometimes favored by cross-country mountain bike racers who use close-ratio triple drivetrains, but these are relatively uncommon and almost never seen as original equipment on any bicycle.

MAKING THE UPGRADE

Replacing a rear derailleur requires that you keep several compatibility issues in mind.

First and foremost, will the shiny, new derailleur in the glass case that has caught your eye work with the shifters and cogset that you have on your bike? Where indexed shifting is concerned, you can usually get away with using an eight-speed derailleur on seven cogs, a nine-speed on eight cogs, or a ten-speed on nine cogs, but not the other way around. You also need to know that Campagnolo doesn't

Rear derailleurs made for double-chainring road bikes have short chain cages (*bottom*), while those made for wide-range, triple-chainring bikes—such as mountain bikes—have longer cages (*top*) for greater amounts of chain wrap.

work with Shimano, Old Suntour doesn't work with anything else but new, Suntour works with Shimano, and some SRAM models work with Shimano and some don't. Start throwing around names like Sachs or Proshift, and it gets even harder to follow. It's a complex problem that could make you think you'd rather take up programming VCRs in your spare time. Luckily for you, there are knowledgeable people at your local bike shop who actually enjoy discussing and debating these subtle issues of compatibility. Let them help you determine what will work and what won't.

Most rear derailleurs are sprung so that the derailleur naturally returns to the small-cog position. Low-normal derailleurs, on the other hand, are sprung to return the derailleur to the large-cog position.

HOW REAR DERAILLEURS WORK: THE REST OF THE STORY

We discussed in fairly simple terms how derailleurs move the chain from one cog to another. The rear derailleur's second function, though no less important, is to maintain tension on the chain throughout your bike's entire range of gearing.

The cage of every rear derailleur is spring-loaded. The spring tension works to rotate the cage toward the back of the bike. When the chain is riding on the small-chainring/small-cog combination, the derailleur cage rotates back, taking up slack in the chain. Shift to a larger ring or a larger cog, and the cage is drawn forward, maintaining tension on the chain but allowing it to wrap around the larger gears.

Tremendous improvements in rear derailleur systems have occurred over the past several decades, so many moderately priced bikes sold today come with derailleurs that perform better than some systems used by racers in the 1970s and 1980s. Overall, differences in performance in the current models are not as dramatic as in the earlier period. Before, the range in quality was excellent to awful; these days it is excellent to acceptable.

DERAILLEUR ANATOMY

The body of the derailleur has a parallelogram form and is equipped with a spring to move it in one direction and a cable to pull it in the opposite direction. The spring is constantly pushing against the derailleur so that when tension is completely off the cables, the derailleur moves the chain out to the smallest cassette cog. The gear cable and shift lever must be able to overcome the resistance of the spring.

Attached to the derailleur body is a structure called the derailleur cage. The derailleur cage is the part that encloses the chain and actually moves it from cog to cog. The cage consists of two vertical plates (cage plates) and two small rollers. The chain follows a backward S-path around the rollers, which position it. The upper roller is called the jockey pulley; it guides the chain from one cog to the next. The lower roller is called the idler pulley; it keeps the chain tension constant. When the chain moves from one cog to a larger or smaller one, the derailleur cage pivots and moves the idler pulley for-

ward or backward to take up slack or feed out extra chain as necessary.

There are two basic derailleur body designs: the single pivot and the double pivot. SRAM ESP rear derailleurs are an example of a single pivot. In this design, the derailleur body sits at a fixed angle in relation to the cassette. The body of the derailleur stays at this predetermined angle throughout all the shifts. Only the cage changes its angle as it pivots forward and back to feed out chain or take up slack.

A double-pivot derailleur has a pivoting chain cage like the other type. It also has a spring in the upper end of the derailleur body that causes the derailleur body to move forward as the derailleur is shifted to the smallest cogs. This forward rotation allows more of the chain to wrap around the cassette cog for a more positive engagement between chain and cog teeth. This swinging action also allows the derailleur to move back and lower down when shifting the chain onto larger cogs.

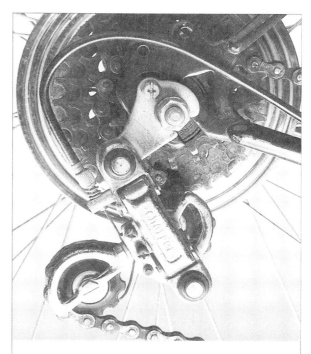

A less-expensive bike may feature a rear derailleur that is attached to the frame via a bolt-on hanger. It's a good idea to regularly check the nut that holds this hanger on the frame so it remains tight. Otherwise, the rear derailleur may come off when you remove the rear wheel, complicating reinstallation of the wheel.

The cage of the derailleur also affects the performance of the derailleur. The length of the cage contributes to the derailleur's ability to wrap up extra chain. The longer the cage, the greater the capacity of the derailleur.

Longer cages aren't necessarily the best solution for all bikes, though. A longer cage has difficulty maintaining as high a level of chain tension as a shorter one. This can result in slower shifting. So, in cases where top performance is the primary concern, it's best to use a derailleur with the shortest cage that is compatible with your desired cog- and chainring sets.

SELECTING A NEW REAR DERAILLEUR

When selecting a rear derailleur, you must first consider the capacity you need. Most derailleurs specify the range in teeth—20 teeth, 30 teeth, whatever—that they are designed to handle. This number refers to the difference between the small and large chainring plus the difference between the largest and smallest cassette cog. To find the range of your chainrings, subtract the number of teeth on the small ring from the number of teeth on the large ring. For the cassette, subtract the number of teeth on the smallest cog from the number of teeth on the largest cog. Add the two numbers together to find the number you need to know to select the proper rear derailleur.

Racing double derailleurs usually have ranges from 20 to 26 teeth. Wide-range mountain bike triple units can go as wide as 40 teeth.

The specified number is usually a conservative estimate on the manufacturer's part. It is based on the possibility that you might try to use all possible gear combinations. But it is never advisable to ride with your chain simultaneously on the smallest chainring and the smallest cassette cog. If you avoid this gear combination, as you should, you can probably exceed the stated range a little bit. On a triple-chainring set, the tiny third chainring is often usable only with the three to five innermost cogs on the cassette.

DERAILLEUR MOUNTING

Rear derailleurs mount on the bike frame in one of two ways: a bolt-on hanger or an integral hanger.

The bolt-on hanger is the least expensive and is found most often on bikes sold through department stores and toy stores, or on only the most inexpensive bikes sold through independent bicycle dealers. The bolt-on hanger is held in place with a small alignment bolt and the axle of the bicycle.

The integral dropout hanger is found on most bicycles today. In this case, the derailleur hanger is actually an extension of the dropout. An integral hanger is usually stiffer than a bolt-on hanger, which makes for better shifting. With bolt-on hangers, use the hanger supplied by the manufacturer.

Because aluminum can be bent and rebent only a few times before it fatigues and cracks, integral hangers on aluminum dropouts are designed to be easily replaced. To the untrained eye, replaceable hangers could be confused with bolt-on hangers. To tell them apart, bear in mind that bikes with replaceable hangers will generally have vertical dropouts, while bolt-on hangers work only on frames with horizontal dropouts.

The shape of the derailleur hanger is especially important when working with index derailleurs, all the modern types that are shifted via levers that click with each shift. The distance from the center of the rear axle to the center of the derailleur mounting hole should be 1¼ inches or less. If the derailleur is too far below the cogs, the indexing may function poorly.

It's also critical that the hanger isn't bent. If you suspect hanger or dropout damage, take your frame to a shop and have it checked.

Once properly adjusted, a rear derailleur that is correctly matched to a cassette should shift well and be quite dependable. Derailleurs made these days rarely stop working because they have gone out of adjustment. The problems they develop usually arise from crashes, dirt, and misalignment. To work properly, a rear derailleur must be kept clean, well lubricated, correctly aligned, and adjusted.

MAINTENANCE

If your rear derailleur fails to perform as well as you think it should, check the cable and housing first—corrosion, fraying, and dirt contamination are common problems. Try lubing the cable or replacing it if it's bad. If the derailleur still has problems, check it closely. Bend down behind the bike

Today's 9- and 10-speed systems require precise alignment of the rear derailleur hanger to function properly. With a tool like this one from Park Tool Co., you can get your derailleur hanger perfectly parallel to the cogs. In a pinch, you can roughly realign your derailleur by inserting a 5 mm hex in the pivot bolt for extra leverage to straighten it by hand.

and take a close look at the derailleur to see if perhaps it may have been bent. The pulley cage ought to be parallel to the centerline of the bike. If it's straight when sighted from behind, an imaginary line drawn through the cassette cog will bisect the pulley wheels. If the cage tilts in toward the wheel, either the cage, the derailleur body, or the hanger (possibly even the dropout tab to which the hanger is attached) may be bent. Check all three.

Precise hanger alignment is not necessary with friction-style rear derailleurs (those relying on shifters that don't click into position with each shift), so you can try to align a bent hanger with an adjustable wrench or a hex key. Unbolt the derailleur and remove it from the hanger. Leaving the wheel in place, use the jaws of the adjustable wrench to straighten the hanger. If the derailleur uses a hex key

mounting bolt, you can leave the derailleur mounted on the hanger. Simply insert the hex key into the head of the bolt and use it while also pulling out on the derailleur itself as a lever for bending the hanger back into line.

These measures won't suffice for index systems because the hanger must be exactly parallel to the cassette cogs. You can try aligning it with an adjustable wrench, but it takes a good eye to get it right. Also, using a hex key to align hangers works fine on friction derailleurs, but many index derailleurs have 5 mm mounting bolts, so a 5 mm hex key may not provide enough leverage. In general, it's worthwhile to take your bike to a shop and have the straightening done with professional alignment tools.

Bent cages on friction derailleurs can sometimes be straightened by hand well enough to work.

Bent index derailleurs should be replaced because they rarely work well once they've been damaged. If you try to straighten your derailleur, support the body so that it does not get twisted out of shape while the cage is being bent into shape. Work carefully; you don't want to overbend the cage. Bent derailleur bodies are the most troublesome. They're difficult to straighten. That's a job best left to a shop mechanic.

CLEANING

A rear derailleur has few working parts but it is important to keep the unit clean. The grit that builds up on the outside of the derailleur body also works its way into the bearing surfaces. Once inside, the grit acts like sandpaper and cuts into the bearing surfaces, causing premature wear. This wear can be seen as play, or slop, in the mechanism, which means poor shifting. Remember, with derailleurs, stiffness is important for good performance.

A dirty rear derailleur should be cleaned before lubricating. When a bike is being ridden often, it's a smart idea to occasionally give the chain and both derailleurs a thorough cleaning and lubrication. On mountain bikes, it might be necessary every month. Road bikes are ridden in a cleaner environment, so they don't pick up grime as quickly, and for them cleaning every 6 months is probably sufficient. Let appearance be your guide. If the drivetrain is covered with grease, grime, and dirt, it needs cleaning.

You can either clean the drivetrain parts on the bike or remove them for cleaning. To clean them on the bike, remove the rear wheel and insert a long screwdriver through the rear dropouts so that it supports the chain. Use a stiff bristle brush and some diesel fuel to clean the chain, derailleurs, and crankset.

If you want to disassemble the drivetrain to clean it, begin by loosening the rear derailleur's cable anchor bolt and pulling the cable free. Then remove the chain using a chain tool (see page 169). Unbolt the rear derailleur from its hanger and remove it from the bike. Put the rear derailleur and the chain in the solvent and let them soak briefly. Use a brush to clean the grit out of the chain and the working parts of the derailleur, then wipe them clean with a rag. Allow the solvent to dry completely before proceeding.

LUBRICATION

If you removed the derailleur and chain, reinstall them in that order. Flush dirt out of the last segment of the derailleur cable housing with a light aerosol solvent like WD-40 or White Lightning Clean Streak, and then apply a lubricant, such as Tri-Flow or Pedro's Extra Dry, to the derailleur pivots, cage pivot(s), pulley centers, and chain. Pedal backward as you lube the chain to allow the lubricant to work its way into the chain. After a few revolutions of the chain, wipe the excess lubricant from the outside with a dry rag. It's not important to apply lubricant directly to the pulley teeth, chainrings, or cogs. They will receive all the oil they need from contact with the chain. Shift through the gears to work the lube into the derailleur's moving parts. Once you are satisfied that the derailleur and chain are thoroughly lubricated, wipe off any excess oil with a clean rag before it has a chance to attract dirt.

CABLE AND CHAIN ADJUSTMENTS

When installing a new derailleur, you must make sure that the chain is the right size for your particular combination of derailleur, chainring, and cassette. Operate the shifter to put the derailleur in the small cog position. Place the chain on the smallest cassette cog. Loosen the cable clamp bolt at the derailleur, and thread the end of the cable through. Pull the cable to remove slack; pull it taut, but not tight. While holding the cable taut with a pair of pliers, tighten the clamp bolt to secure it.

Shift onto the largest rear cog and the large front chainring. The derailleur cage should be pulled forward almost as far as it is capable of traveling. Once you have done this, shift to the small-cog/small-chainring combination to see if there is any slack in the chain. If the derailleur is not near its limit in the first combination but the chain is loose in the second, shorten the chain by removing links. Judge how many to remove by how much slack you find in the chain.

Conversely, if the chain binds because it is not long enough to fit in the large/large combination, add chain links. You may find that you have to make a compromise between having plenty of chain for the large/large combination and avoiding excess slack in the small-cog/small-chainring position (or the small cog/middle chainring on a triple-chainring crankset).

If you have insufficient chain for the first combination and accidentally try to shift into it, you risk pulling the rear wheel right out of the dropout. On the other hand, if you have too much slack in the second combination and happen to shift into it, you risk having your derailleur bend back over on itself in an attempt to take up the slack. This could cause the chain to rub against itself and be damaged. The best way to avoid these problems is to provide enough chain for the large/large combination and use a rear derailleur capable of handling the slack when you shift into the small/small combination. Switching to a rear derailleur with a wider range will also give you the freedom to switch back and forth between wheels with different cassette cog combinations, should you desire to do so.

INSTALLATION

Most of what is involved in the installation of a new rear derailleur is identical to what must be done when installing and adjusting an old one after removing it for cleaning. However, some of the adjustments discussed are even more critical with a new derailleur than with an old one.

From the factory, the limit screws will almost certainly be set incorrectly for your frame and cogset, even if you've purchased the same model you had before. And since the body of the new derailleur may be different than that of the old one, the shift cable and cable housing may have to be lengthened or shortened to get a smooth bend where the cable goes from the stay stop to the rear derailleur.

ADJUSTMENTS

Because the location of the wheel can affect the derailleur's performance, the place to begin your derailleur adjustment is by considering the position of your wheel in the frame. Most modern bikes have vertical dropout on which the axle simply sits in the bottom of the dropouts.

You might have a bike with dropouts with horizontal slots on which the axle can be positioned in various spots. Index derailleurs work best if the axle is positioned toward the front of the dropout. This is also true of Simplex-type derailleurs (older type) with spring-loaded upper derailleur pivots. Friction rear derailleurs work well with the wheel centered in the dropout slots.

RANGE OF MOTION

Once the wheel is properly positioned, set the range of motion for the derailleur. Start by adjusting how far the derailleur can move to the inside (toward the spokes). Shift into low gear (large rear cog, small front chainring). Adjust the low-gear adjusting screw, also known as the inner limit adjusting screw (usually the upper or farthest to the rear of the two adjusting screws) so that the pulleys are centered beneath the largest cog. The adjustment is correct when chain noise is at a minimum and the chain shifts onto the cog without hesitating and without going over into the spokes.

Set the outer throw. Shift into high gear (small cog/large chainring). Adjust the high-gear adjusting screw, also known as the outer limit adjusting screw, so that the pulleys are centered beneath the smallest cog and the chain shifts quickly onto the cog. If the chain doesn't shift onto the small cog easily, loosen the adjusting screw to let the derailleur move a little farther out.

Finally, if you have a single-pivot derailleur with an angle adjustment screw, set the derailleur so there is about ¼ inch of clearance between the teeth of the jockey pulley and the teeth of the largest cog when in that gear.

INDEX BARREL ADJUSTMENT

With index (click) derailleurs you must fine-tune the derailleur so that it moves the chain to a new cog with each click of the lever. Otherwise, the chain will not land perfectly in gear and will run noisily.

Because index shifting is so dependent on precise cable adjustment, index derailleurs have an adjustment barrel that makes adding or releasing cable tension simple. The barrel is located where the cable enters the rear derailleur and has a knurled ring (usually plastic) to make turning by hand easy. Some shifters have adjusting barrels on the levers too, which makes adjustment easy even while riding. The same is true for brake-lever shift levers, which have adjusters on the downtube housing stops that can be used to adjust cable tension if needed.

Use your right hand to shift to the smallest cog while turning the crankarm with your left. Then shift one click to the second-smallest cog. The chain should instantly move to it and stay there. If it does not advance, turn the barrel adjuster counterclockwise a quarter-turn at a time until the system shifts quickly and precisely. If the chain moves too far, you'll hear noise as it brushes against the third-smallest cog. In that case, turn the adjustment barrel clockwise a quarter-turn at a time until the chain runs quietly. You can check the adjustment by shifting through all the gears.

If gear changes become less precise with time, the remedy is usually as simple as turning the barrel adjuster counterclockwise a quarter-turn or so to increase cable tension.

MODIFICATIONS AND ACCESSORIES

There are very few modifications that can be made on rear derailleurs. Some companies make special lightweight aluminum pivot bolts that replace the steel ones found in some of the more popular racing derailleurs. This does lower the weight slightly, but it also makes the derailleur a little more flexible.

Several manufacturers offer sealed-bearing derailleur pulleys. These pulleys offer low rolling resistance and are sealed so you don't have to service them.

Most rear derailleurs don't require spoke protectors. However, there is always the danger that if your bicycle falls on its right side, your derailleur could get caught in the spokes. Also, if the derailleur hanger gets bent inward, your derailleur could shift past the large cog. If the derailleur passes the large cog and gets caught in the spokes, it will probably ruin the derailleur and could damage the wheel and the frame. You can minimize this danger with a spoke protector.

Because of the conditions to which they are subjected, touring bicycles and mountain bikes are more likely than other types of bikes to suffer a bent derailleur. Spoke protectors are therefore recommended for these bikes. A plastic protector will not rust and makes less noise than a metal one. To install

a spoke protector, remove the cassette or freewheel, slide the protector over the cassette body or hub threads and up against the spokes, then replace the cassette or freewheel.

The rear derailleur is a marvelous invention, one that has helped make the bicycle into an incredibly efficient and enjoyable vehicle to operate. Install a derailleur model that is designed to fit your bike and its other components, keep it clean, well adjusted, and properly lubricated, and you will be rewarded by many miles of smooth shifting performance.

TROUBLESHOOTING

PROBLEM: You shifted into the rear wheel and trashed the rear derailleur. How do you ride home?

SOLUTION: Separate the chain with your chain tool (you did bring one along, didn't you?), extract it from the derailleur, and rejoin the chain on the middle chainring and cassette cog. Pull the derailleur out of the spokes, straighten the wheel, and ride home on your one-speed.

PROBLEM: You shift the lever, but the derailleur doesn't quite shift into gear and there are a lot of clicking noises as you pedal.

SOLUTION: The derailleur may be bent. Have it checked. If it's not bent, the cable tension has probably changed. If the shifting hesitates when moving to larger cogs, turn the adjusting barrel in quarter-turn increments toward the large cogs. If shifting to smaller cogs is the problem, turn the barrel toward them.

PROBLEM: You broke the shift cable and cannot shift into an easy gear to get home.

SOLUTION: Pedal so that the derailleur shifts onto the smallest cog. Pull on what's left of the shift cable to remove slack, and attach the upper end beneath a bottle-cage screw. Now you can shift by pulling on the cable (but you'll have to hold it to keep the bike in gear). Or you can pull the cable to shift into an easy gear and tighten the bolt to hold it in place.

PROBLEM: The rear derailleur makes a constant squeaking noise.

SOLUTION: The pulleys are dry and need lubrication. Try dripping some lube on the sides. If that doesn't work, disassemble the pulleys (one at a time), grease the bearing surfaces, and then reassemble.

PROBLEM: Shifting is difficult.

SOLUTION: Dirt may have penetrated the cable and housing. Shift onto the large cog, then move the shift lever back to create cable slack. Lift the housings out of the stops, slide them down to expose the cable, oil or grease the cable, and reassemble the housings.

Rear Derailleur Removal and Installation

1 The rear derailleur is positioned beneath the cassette and is fastened by a bolt to a hanger, which is suspended beneath the right rear dropout (see photo). The dropouts are the slotted metal pieces located at the junction of the seatstays and chainstays. Their function is to hold the axle of the rear wheel.

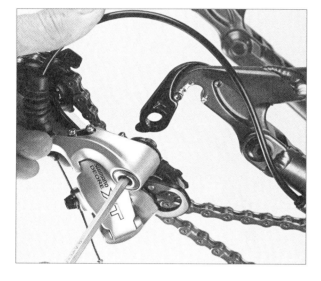

2 The derailleur hanger on an inexpensive bicycle is usually a separate piece held on the right rear dropout by means of the wheel axle and the axle nuts. A small bolt aligns this type of bolt-on hanger with the bicycle frame (see photo on page 209). The hanger on a higher-quality bike is usually integrated into the right rear dropout itself (see photo). An integral hanger contributes to better shifting by being stiffer than a bolt-on hanger. Some integral hangers, such as the one shown here, feature replaceable sections that prevent major frame damage if you bend the derailleur badly.

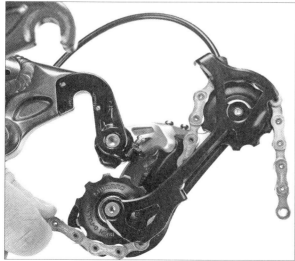

3 Before removing a rear derailleur for cleaning or replacement, you must free it from both the shift cable and the chain. Removing the shift cable is simple: Just loosen the bolt that fastens it to the body of the derailleur and slip it out.

Freeing the chain from the derailleur can be done in one of two ways. One way is to use a chain tool to break a link in the chain, then pull one end of the chain free from the derailleur cage (see photo). Do not try to pull through the derailleur the end of the chain with the rivet protruding from the broken link. The rivet will hang up on the cage. Pull the other end through. Removing the chain makes sense if it needs cleaning or replacement.

4 The simpler method of freeing the chain is to use a wrench to loosen the bolt that holds the idler pulley on the derailleur (see photo). Remove the idler pulley so the chain can be lifted off the jockey pulley and out of the way. You may need to move the derailleur cage plates apart to free the chain. The derailleur can then be unbolted from the hanger and cleaned or replaced.

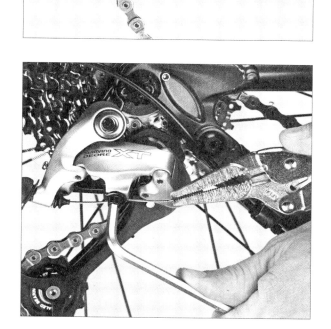

5 When installing a rear derailleur, follow the same procedure in reverse. Bolt it back onto the hanger, then replace the chain and shift cable. Before tightening the cable, however, put the wheel back on the bike and make sure that the chain is positioned on the smallest cassette cog so the derailleur is free to move to its outer limit.

Operate the shift lever to make sure it's in its starting position, which will give the cable all the available slack. Then thread the cable through the anchor on the derailleur body. Hold the cable taut with a pair of pliers while tightening the anchor bolt with a wrench.

6 After installing a new rear derailleur, check its range of motion and adjust it properly. Even if you are only remounting your old derailleur after a cleaning, it is a good idea to check the adjustment. Before fine-tuning the derailleur, make sure that the wheel is properly positioned on the frame. If the dropout allows, place the axle toward the front of the dropout, or just seat it fully in vertical dropouts. Some bicycles come with adjustable screws to stop the axle when it is in the proper position.

Rear Derailleur Cleaning and Lubrication

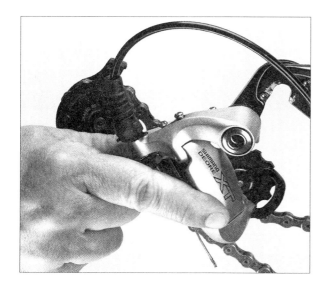

1 The various components of a bicycle's gearing system are subjected to a lot of stresses and strains, which are made worse by the accumulation of road or trail grime. The lubricants used to help keep moving parts working smoothly can also have the opposite effect by collecting dirt that clogs up and accelerates wear in those parts. This is why the chain, chainrings, cassette cogs, and both derailleurs need frequent cleaning and lubrication.

One way that you can tell when a rear derailleur is in need of a cleaning is by pushing it in with your hand (see photo). If it's difficult to move and sluggish about springing back out, assume that it has grit in its pivots and needs to be cleaned.

2 To give a rear derailleur a truly thorough cleaning, take it off the bike. While you're at it, remove the wheel and clean the cassette cogs. Also thoroughly clean the chain and the chainring teeth. All these components interact in such a way that grit accumulated on one is quickly passed on to the others.

To remove the chain from the derailleur without breaking a link, remove the idler pulley from the rear derailleur chain cage (see photo). One advantage of this is that it enables you to more easily clean the pulley and chain cage. In fact, you may want to remove the jockey pulley as well. This will make the cleaning and lubrication process easier and more thorough.

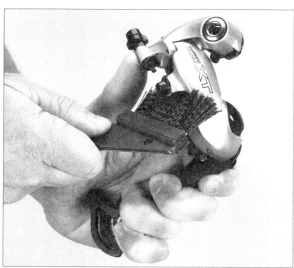

3 Loosen the shift cable and unbolt the derailleur from the bike. Soak the metal parts in a safe solvent to loosen the grime. Use soap and water or a mild solvent on the plastic surfaces of the pulleys.

Take the derailleur out of the solvent and scrub it with a small brush, such as an old toothbrush (see photo). Rinse off the residue with the solvent, and wipe the derailleur clean with a rag. Let it air-dry for a while so the solvent can evaporate.

4 Fasten the derailleur back on the dropout hanger. Before replacing the pulleys, coat their bushings with a light coat of grease (see photo). Replace the chain before putting the idler pulley back on.

Before hooking the shift cable back to the derailleur, wipe down the section of cable that runs through housing, and flush the dirt out of the housing with an aerosol solvent like White Lightning Clean Streak or WD-40. Thread the cable through the anchor on the derailleur and hold it taut while tightening the bolt.

5 Drip a small amount of general-purpose lubricant, like Pedro's Extra Dry or Tri-Flow, into each point where the derailleur pivots (see photo). Use the shift lever to move the derailleur back and forth. This will help spread the lubricant over all bearing surfaces and will help you tell when enough lubricant has been used (it doesn't take much).

6 After you have applied plenty of lubricant and worked it into the inner surfaces of the derailleur, wipe away any excess clinging to the outer surfaces—it will only serve as an unneeded trap for fresh grit (see photo).

Once the cleaning and lubrication is complete, replace the rear wheel and adjust the derailleur following the instructions on page 220.

Rear Derailleur Adjustment

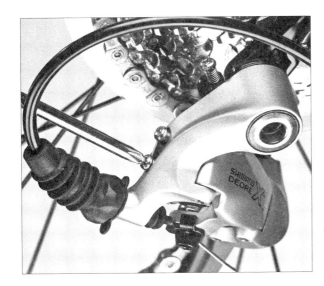

1 Place the bike in a repair stand. Check derailleur adjustment by pedaling with your right hand while pushing on the derailleur with your left. Adjust the inner throw of your rear derailleur first. Shift the chain onto the largest cog. It should seat quickly on the cog. If it hesitates or goes over the cog and into the spokes, adjust the derailleur with the low-gear adjusting screw. It's probably the upper one or the one nearest the rear (see photo). Counterclockwise turns allow the derailleur to move farther toward the spokes. Clockwise turns limit travel.

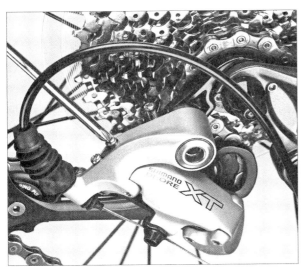

2 Shift the chain to the smallest cassette cog. Turn the high-gear adjusting screw until the pulleys line up beneath the small cog (see photo).

With your bike still mounted on the repair stand, spin the crankarms around and run through the gears. Pay special attention to how well the chain shifts onto the largest and smallest cogs (that you used to set the derailleur adjustments).

If there's any hesitation in these shifts or a lot of clatter in the rear after the shifts—or any sign that the chain may jump off the cogs—fine-tune the adjustments until the shifts become quiet and accurate. If you have no repair stand, take the bike out for a spin to check the adjustment.

3 Some derailleurs have a third screw called the B-tension screw or the B-angle screw (see photo). This adjusts the clearance between the jockey pulley and the cogs.

On single-pivot derailleurs like those manufactured by SRAM, the B-angle screw is used to directly adjust the distance between the jockey pulley and the largest cog. This distance should be about ¼ inch—close enough for quick shifting, but clear enough that the chain can pass freely from the second-largest cog to the largest.

Double-pivot derailleurs rely on a spring inside the B-knuckle to actively adjust the cog/jockey clearance for each gear. The ideal setting can be a bit elusive. Adjust the B-tension screw so the pulley rides as close to the cogs as is practical without making noise in any gear.

4 After installing a new rear derailleur or changing chainrings or cassette cogs, you may need to alter the chain length in order for the derailleur to shift properly.

The chain should be long enough so that it will go easily onto the largest chainring and the largest rear cog. (This is not a recommended gear because of the extreme chain angle it creates, but it is useful for checking chain length.) Conversely, when the chain is on the smallest chainring and the smallest cog (another gear that is not recommended), there should not be excessive slack in the chain.

5 Fine-tune the derailleur so that it moves the chain to a new cog with each click of the shift lever (unless you have an older bike with friction levers). Do this with the adjustment barrel. Use your right hand to shift to the smallest cog while turning the crankarm with your left. Shift one click. The chain should instantly move to the second-smallest cog and stay there. If it doesn't, turn the barrel adjuster counterclockwise a quarter-turn and try again. Continue to turn the barrel until shifts are quick and precise. If you go too far, the system will run noisily. In that case, turn the barrel clockwise a quarter-turn at a time as you pedal until the noise stops. As a final check, shift through all the gear combinations, making sure that the system works quickly and quietly.

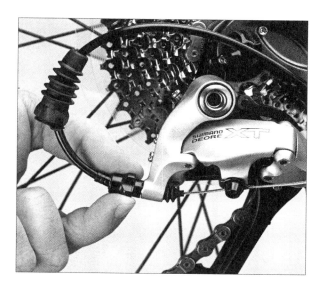

6 When a bike falls over or gets hit on its right side, the rear derailleur can be damaged. Fortunately, the most likely damage, a bent hanger, is not expensive to repair. You might even be able to fix it yourself. If your derailleur-fastening bolt has a hex head, insert a wrench into it and use it and the derailleur body to lever the hanger back into line (see photo). Relying on the hex key alone may cause damage to the derailleur pivot bolt or the key itself, so be sure to put a hand behind the derailleur and pull with it as you pull up on the bolt with your other hand. Have a pro mechanic perfect the "adjustment."

12 HEADSETS

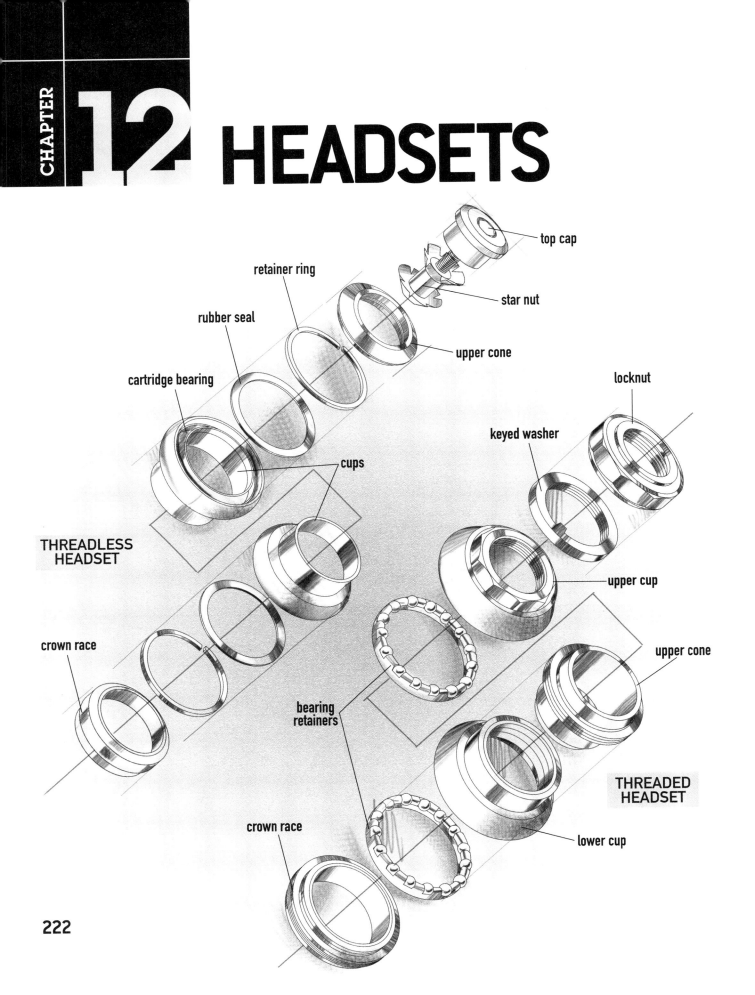

top cap

star nut

retainer ring

rubber seal

upper cone

cartridge bearing

locknut

keyed washer

cups

THREADLESS
HEADSET

upper cup

crown race

upper cone

bearing
retainers

THREADED
HEADSET

crown race

lower cup

eadsets are often overlooked when the time comes for regular maintenance. Maybe this is because headsets are so inconspicuous, but the fact is that a headset's function is so subtle that it often goes unnoticed only until something is drastically wrong. Unfortunately, when something does go wrong with your headset, precise steering can become difficult or even impossible.

A well-maintained, properly adjusted headset, on the other hand, will yield years of trouble-free service. Properly cared for, your headset will gladly let you sit back and enjoy the scenery while it sits quietly outside the spotlight, just getting its job done.

What exactly is a headset? Basically, it's the component that connects the fork to the frame and allows the fork to turn for steering. It's also forced to withstand the massive pressures encountered when the fork transmits shocks into the frame, such as on a rocky descent.

The headset must do all this without adversely affecting the handling of the bicycle. Certainly, the headset is not the only component that influences bike handling, but it's no less critical than the rest. A poorly installed, adjusted, or maintained headset can make even the finest bicycle difficult to handle.

Some symptoms of a neglected headset are a loose feeling in the handlebar or rattles and clunks coming from the fork when riding over bumps. Another problem is the inability to travel in a straight line when your hands aren't steering. Still another is when the handlebar turns but you feel it catch as if there were notches stopping the turning at various points through the fork's rotation inside the head tube. These problems indicate the necessity for headset maintenance or overhaul.

The most common sizes of headsets found on bikes today are 1- and 1⅛ -inch threaded, and 1-, 1⅛-, and 1½ -inch threadless. For a short time, 1¼ -inch, among other sizes, were experimented with by some manufacturers. Replacement parts for these are difficult to find now, but Chris King Components make it possible to use a 1⅛ -inch fork on frames built for the obsolete 1¼ -inch headset size.

TYPES AND BASIC PARTS

The most common kind of headset uses a cup-and-cone bearing arrangement. Two sets of cups and cones, one between the fork and head tube and one on top of the head tube, work together to hold the fork and allow it to turn in relation to the frame. The upper cone and lower cup are attached to the head tube of the frame. The lower cone and upper cup are attached to the steering column of the fork. A set of bearings—either loose or in a retainer—

separates each cup and cone, allowing the steering column to twist within the head tube. (Each set of cup, cone, and bearings is referred to as a "stack.") This is the conventional headset, the type most commonly encountered.

In recent years, a number of sealed-bearing headsets have appeared, both as standard equipment on new bikes and as replacement units for older bikes. Also, there have been a number of exotic designs on the market that tried a variety of concepts, such as interlocking Teflon sleeves or single-axis

Integrated headsets function just like threadless headsets with one difference: Instead of separate bearing cups that are pressed into the head tube, integrated headsets use cartridge bearings that fit directly into a specially designed head tube.

roller bearings, in an attempt to improve a headset's ability to do its job.

Because there are forks with threaded and threadless steerers (the column at the top of the fork that the headset attaches to), there are also threaded and threadless headsets. Today, threadless headsets are found on nearly all mountain bikes, most higher-quality road bikes, and even many midpriced hybrid and comfort bikes.

A threadless headset is adjusted differently than a threaded one. All that's needed is a hex key or two. In fact, a threadless headset is quite simple to adjust, disassemble, and overhaul compared to a threaded one. One big difference, though, is that it requires a different stem, and this stem is integral to the adjustment of the headset. A threadless stem locks the adjustment of the headset by tightening to the outside of the fork.

A variation on the threadless headset is the integrated headset. Integrated headsets forego the separate bearing cups that are pressed into the frame on a standard headset. Instead, sealed cartridge bearings are fitted directly into an enlarged headtube. The rest of the components of an integrated headset remain the same as most other threadless headset designs.

WHAT MAKES A HEADSET

Like the crankset and the wheel hubs, the headset on a bicycle is not simply one component but a series of separate parts that function together as one system. Despite variations in design, all headset systems employ a similar combination of parts. Working from the top down, the typical threaded headset is made up of the following parts, which are shown in the exploded-view illustration found at the beginning of this chapter.

1. locknut (this is tightened to secure the adjustment)
2. lockwasher (this keeps the headset from loosening)
3. adjustable cup (this is turned to adjust the headset)
4. bearing retainer (the balls are in a metal or plastic holder)
5. top head race
6. lower head cup
7. bearing retainer
8. fork crown race

Some threaded headsets also have a reflector bracket or a centerpull brake cable hanger that fits between the locknut and the lockwasher.

Threadless headsets typically are made up of the following parts (from the top down):

1. adjusting bolt (this is for adjusting the headset after the stem is loosened)
2. top cap
3. recessed seated nut (this is inserted inside the fork column)
4. stem (this is clamped to the fork to lock the bearing adjustment)
5. spacers (these can be placed on top of or beneath the stem, or even removed)
6. washer
7. beveled lock washer
8. cup
9. bearing retainer
10. top head race
11. lower head race
12. bearing retainer
13. fork crown race

Integrated headsets vary slightly in dimension— so slightly that the differences often cannot be detected by the naked eye. Check specifications with the manufacturer of your frame and of your headset before beginning installation or the results could be disastrous.

BUYING A HEADSET

Generally, if you're shopping for a new headset, the conventional cup-and-cone models are a good choice because they're affordable, simple in design, easy to maintain, and easy to service.

Some headsets are called sealed-bearing models. On cheaper ones, the bearings are shielded by the addition of a plastic seal or rubber O-ring in the openings between the cups and cones. Sometimes, interlocking pieces form a labyrinth as a shield: The dirt must work its way around the barriers before it can get into the bearings. Both shielding techniques work quite well and have no detrimental effects on a headset's performance, nor do they make servicing any more difficult.

Then there are the most expensive and most impressively designed headsets, which employ true sealed-cartridge bearings, such as Chris King headsets. Servicing a King headset is as simple as popping off a couple of seals and squirting in some fresh grease on occasion. We've even seen a few neglected King headsets that still perform flawlessly after nearly 20 years. Someone once said, "You rent a headset; you buy a King," and it's possible that truer words were never spoken.

If a true sealed-bearing headset does develop problems, it's usually easy to get replacement bearing cartridges, depending on the model. Check the owner's manual, the manufacturer's Web site, or a shop for advice.

A few cup-and-cone headsets use tapered roller bearings rather than ball bearings. If you dismantle your headset and find that the retainers contain what appear to be small cylinders rather than balls, these are tapered roller bearings. The load-bearing points of contact are larger on roller bearings than on ball bearings, and this can extend the life of the roller bearing units by spreading the load over a wider area. The only problem with this system can be trying to find replacement bearings when the time comes. If you can't find them, you'll need to replace the headset.

If you're considering replacing your current headset and are thinking of changing to a different brand or model, choose one of the many conventional ball-bearing headsets. The reliability of these units is hard to beat, and they're affordable. If you aren't interested in upgrading to a "better" headset, try to get the same brand and model that your bike originally had. This way, you won't have to worry about whether it will fit your bike.

Headsets come in a variety of price ranges. They can run from less than $20 to more than $125. More expensive headsets generally perform better and last longer than cheaper ones. Before you drop a small fortune on a new headset, give some thought to the overall worth of the bike. After all, why pay big bucks for a top-quality headset if it's going on a second-rate beater bike that you may junk in a couple of years anyway?

There are a variety of headset sizes, and it's important to match a new one to the old to ensure that things will fit. A good source of information on dimensions is *Sutherland's Handbook for Bicycle Mechanics*, which most shops use. You can also take the frame, fork, and headset to the shop for comparison.

Before installing a professional-grade headset in your bike, it's a great idea to take the bike to a shop to have the frame's head tube and fork prepared with headset reaming and cutting tools. This will ensure proper headset fit and alignment, excellent performance, and long life.

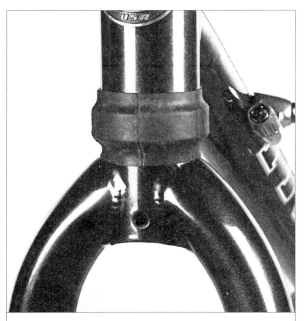

Fit short sections of an inner tube over the ends of the head tube during a headset overhaul, then pull them over the cups later to shield the bearings from wind and road grime.

MAKING HEADSET SEALS

If you wish to shield your nonsealed headset, you can do so by covering the opening between the cup and race of the upper and lower stack with a piece of rubber. Cut a section of inner tube, about 1 to 1½ inches long, to form the shield. It's usually necessary to disassemble the headset before you can install this rubber doughnut over the lower stack. Only the stem needs to be removed to install such a shield over the upper stack. Usually, people cover only the lower part of the headset (the part between the fork and the frame) because it receives the most dirt and crud from the road.

If you frequently transport your bicycle on the roof of your car, you may be blowing the grease out of your headset bearings. The 65-mph wind can get through the openings between cups and races and blow the grease out onto the frame. This not only makes a mess, but also you lose the corrosion protection and lubrication from your bearings. Using a headset shield will stop this from happening. If you don't have the facility to install such a shield, at least wrap a piece of plastic around the head tube when transporting the bike on your car.

ADJUSTMENT

If your headset seems either loose (you hear a clunking sound and feel a looseness from the front end when riding over rough roads or trails) or tight (the steering binds and sounds crunchy, and it's difficult to ride no-handed), you can usually remedy the problem with a simple adjustment. It may take several tries to get the adjustment right, so don't get discouraged if it's not perfect after the first attempt.

If your headset is a threadless type, adjustment couldn't be simpler. All it takes is a hex key or two. The headset parts slide onto the fork (instead of being threaded on, as on threaded designs), so you only need to loosen the bolts that are clamping the stem, tighten the adjusting bolt on top of the stem (or loosen it if the adjustment is too tight), and retighten the stem bolts to lock the adjustment in place.

Threaded headsets are more difficult to adjust. The only tools needed are wrenches that are large enough to fit the flats on the locknut and the adjustable cup. Headset wrenches make the job easy, but they're not absolutely essential. A large adjustable wrench works fine for the locknut. Use a

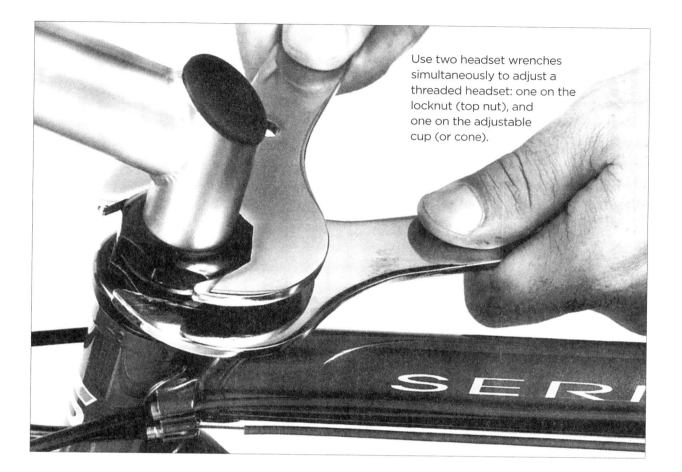

Use two headset wrenches simultaneously to adjust a threaded headset: one on the locknut (top nut), and one on the adjustable cup (or cone).

pair of adjustable pliers to hold the adjustable cup if it's steel, but wrap a rag around the cup to protect its finish. Some adjustable cups have serrated edges to make it easy to turn them by hand.

If the exposed headset parts are made of aluminum, purchase the proper wrenches to fit the wrench flats on the locknut and adjustable cup. Otherwise, you'll probably damage these parts when you attempt to tighten and loosen them.

When making a headset adjustment, leave the stem in place. Many people also like to leave the front wheel on the bike to act as a handle to hold the forks still while the locknut is being turned. However, leaving the wheel in place makes it more difficult to tell if the headset is too tight. An alternative is to remove the wheel and slide the handle of a hammer or some similar tool between the fork legs to hold the fork steady while you apply force to the locknut.

Adjust a threaded headset by turning the locknut counterclockwise to loosen it. If the headset

was too tight, loosen the adjustable cup by turning it counterclockwise a fraction of a turn. If the headset seemed too loose, tighten the adjustable cup by turning it clockwise. Turn the adjustable cup down until it contacts the bearings, then back off the adjustment one-eighth to one-quarter turn. Now, while holding the adjustable cup in position, tighten the locknut by turning it clockwise.

To see if your headset needs adjusting, or to check an adjustment you've made, grasp the front fork with one hand and the frame with the other. Alternately push and pull the two toward and away from each other. Do the push-pull check with the fork turned to several different positions. For threadless headsets, if you feel any looseness at any position of the fork, once again loosen the stem and snug the top bolt to remove play. For threaded headsets, loosen the locknut and turn the adjustable cup clockwise, then tighten the locknut.

When done, repeat the push-pull test. You can also check the headset by picking up the front of the bike and dropping the front wheel onto the ground while gently holding the stem. If you hear or feel anything rattle, the headset is still loose. Another method is to apply the front brake and push and pull the bike back and forth, checking for a knocking sensation that would indicate play in the headset.

Make a second check of the headset by lifting the front of the bike and slowly turning the handlebar to see if the bearings bind, causing resistance, at any point in the rotation. If the headset binds, loosen the adjustment a bit by turning the adjustable cup counterclockwise on threaded headsets, or loosening the stem bolts and backing off the top nut slightly on threadless systems.

Again, don't be discouraged if it takes a couple of tries to get the adjustment where there is neither binding nor play in the headset. If you cannot get it adjusted so it's just right—that is, not tight and not loose—adjust it so that it is slightly tight.

Double locknut (on threaded headsets only). Some headsets have two locknuts. The extra locknut helps in the initial assembly of the bike but does not provide any substantial benefit to the rider. The second locknut usually resembles a threaded washer with two or three notches in it, and it sits beneath the top locknut. If you work on a headset with two locknuts, you must loosen both before attempting to adjust your headset. To loosen the second locknut (the lower one), it is often necessary to use a hammer and punch. Retighten the top locknut when all the other steps are completed.

If you wish to eliminate this second locknut, thus simplifying any future adjustments, you can do so by replacing it with extra headset lockwashers to take up the space it occupies. You can get these extra washers from your bike shop.

OVERHAUL

As part of a regular maintenance program, road bike headsets should be overhauled every year, and mountain bike models every 6 months if they're used off-road. There's no quick way to overhaul a headset; but after you've done it a couple of times, you'll find that it's not that difficult. For this job, you'll need the same tools you used in the headset adjustment. The only additional tools necessary will be those required to loosen the stem (usually, a 5 or 6 mm hex key will do the job) and a wrench of the proper size to loosen the brake.

You'll also need some medium-weight grease and new bearings. Your shop mechanic may know what bearings fit in your headset, or you can just take in the old ones to match up the new ones.

Why buy new bearings? Because with use, ball bearings cease to be completely round, making proper adjustments difficult to impossible. If yours are nice and shiny, in like-new condition, reuse them. If they're tarnished, rusty, or pitted, replace them with new ones of the same type.

Before you begin the process of rebuilding your headset, spread an old sheet below your bike to catch any stray bearings that might fall on the floor. Put the bike in a repair stand or hang it so the front wheel is suspended.

Remove the front wheel. For road bikes, remove the front sidepull brake by unscrewing the nut that holds it to the fork. For mountain bikes, unhook the link wire (on a cantilever) or lift the noodle out of its holder (on a direct-pull) to release the brake. Unscrew the bolt from the side of the brake that's attached to the cable to remove it from the fork (keep the parts together with a rubber band or tape).

Threadless headsets. For threadless headsets, disassembly is usually simple. Remove the adjusting bolt on top of the stem, and extract the top cap. If the top cap is stuck (as plastic ones sometimes are), carefully pry it off the top of the fork with a screwdriver. You may also run into a complicated top cap that's made up of several pieces. Usually, loosening the top bolt will allow removal. You may need to tap the top of the cap to loosen the unit. If it won't come out, don't force things; check the instructions in the owner's manual or the headset instruction manual, or check with a shop mechanic for help.

Once the top bolt and cap are off, hold the fork so that it can't fall out, loosen the bolt or bolts securing the stem, and slide the stem off the top of the fork. You'll now be able to lift the parts off the fork and extract the fork from the frame.

Sometimes the fork won't come out after removing the stem because the headset parts are stuck. If this happens, try tapping the top of the fork with a plastic mallet to knock the fork out. If tapping doesn't move it, hit harder until it comes out, but be careful not to damage the fork (and make sure you don't miss and hit the frame).

Threaded headsets. For threaded headsets, loosen the stem by turning the expander bolt (on top of the stem) counterclockwise. Turn the bolt two or three full turns, and then hit it on the head with a hammer. This knocks loose the expander wedge at the base of the stem (inside the fork), which is holding the stem tight.

If the stem hasn't been loosened in a long time, it may take more than one blow to make the stem binder wedge inside the steerer tube drop free. However, it's best not to strike the binder bolt directly unless you use a plastic mallet. Otherwise, place a small block of wood over the bolt before hitting it. (Put on goggles first because the wood may shatter.)

Dealing with a frozen stem. If the stem bolt is loose but the stem won't come out, it's probably corroded inside the fork. If you're lucky, you'll be able to muscle it out. Put the front wheel in the fork, clamp it between your knees, and turn the bar from side to side to loosen and extract the stem. If it's really stuck, remove the wheel, carefully clamp the fork crown in a vise, and wrestle the stem out with the bar.

If these measures don't work, turn the bike upside down and spray Liquid Wrench or a similar penetrating solvent down the fork steerer so it can pool on top of the stem wedge and penetrate. Let it sit for a day, then try again; repeat until it's possible to remove the stem. Tapping on the stem will help the Liquid Wrench penetrate the corrosion. You can also try heating the stem with a propane torch, but do this carefully and only in a well-ventilated area because the fumes can be hazardous to breathe. If you're patient enough, the Liquid Wrench will eventually break the bond and allow the stem to be removed. It may take some time, though—even days!

Once they're loose, lift the handlebar and stem unit out of the steering tube. Hang it on the top tube because the rear brake cable and shifting cables will still be attached. If you wish to remove the handlebar completely, you'll have to detach all cables.

Remove the headset locknut by turning it counterclockwise. If you have a headset with two locknuts, remove the second locknut as well. Slip off the lockwasher, the reflector bracket, the brake cable hanger, and anything else you find positioned above the adjustable cup.

While holding the front fork from underneath, spin the adjustable cup off by turning it counter-

clockwise. Be careful. If the bearings are loose (not held in a retainer), they might momentarily stick to the adjustable cup as it spins away from the top headrace and then fall on the floor. If the bearings are loose, you may want to take the frame off the stand and tip it over on its side near the floor before removing the adjustable cup. When you remove the race, the bearings can fall the short distance onto the cloth and be controlled. Even though you'll be replacing them, you need to know how many and what size were used in each race.

If possible, turn the frame upside down (or at least on its side) before sliding the fork out of the head tube. If the bike is upside down, the remaining bearings will be less likely to drop on the floor since they'll be held in the cup-shaped race of the lower head cup. Retrieve and save all the bearings. Try to keep the two sets of bearings separated if they are loose—some headsets use different numbers of bearings in the upper and lower races. Clean and count the bearings before taking them to a bike shop to purchase the proper size and number of replacements. If you discover any damaged bearings, look for corresponding damage inside the bearing races.

Most conventional headsets use $\frac{5}{32}$-inch ball bearings, but some use $\frac{3}{16}$- and $\frac{1}{8}$-inch bearings. The only way to know for sure is to measure them. Take a couple to the bicycle shop to be sure that you get exact replacements. Even though the difference between the sizes may seem insignificant, it's enough to make the headset not work. If you're purchasing loose ball bearings, buy a few extra because they're very easy to lose.

Clean the adjustable cup, top headrace, lower head cup, and fork crown race. Inspect them for pits and cracks. If they have any pits or cracks, all or part of the headset may have to be replaced. We will say more about headset replacement later.

Reassembling threaded and threadless headsets. Once you have new bearings and all the headset components are clean and in good shape, you're ready to reassemble the headset. Apply a heavy coat of grease to the fork crown race, lower head cup, top headrace, and the adjustable cup. Never be afraid of using too much grease: Any extra will just move out of the way once the headset is reassembled.

Lightly grease the steerer tube from the fork crown race all the way up to and including the threads. (For threadless headsets, leave the stem clamping area clean.) This will help prevent any corrosion of the tube and its threads as well as make it easy to thread on the adjustable cup or slide on threadless components. If you're using caged bearings, apply a coat of grease to them as well.

If you're going to use a headset shield, slide the first shield over the lower head cup. Curl the shield up as high on the frame as possible so that it won't interfere with the adjustment of the headset.

Arrange the appropriate ball bearings inside the lower head cup of the inverted frame. Usually, the bearings are in a retainer. Be sure that the bearing retainer faces the correct direction. To determine this, take a close look at the retainer. There are two types: One has a round profile, and the other has a flat profile. On both, metal fingers curl around between balls in a kind of C formation. What we call the "closed" side of the retainer is the backside of the circle of little C shapes. For round-profile bearings, this side of the retainer should always be set against the cup-shaped bearing surface. This means that the open side of the retainer faces the cone, and vice-versa for flat-profile bearings.

If your headset uses loose bearings, put the same number in as were removed. If you're not sure how many were in there, put in as many as will fit while still leaving a small gap. The grease should hold loose bearings in place while you replace the fork. If you do drop a bearing, clean it off before replacing it so that dirt doesn't get packed into the headset.

When the bearings are in place, slide the fork carefully all the way into the frame so that the bearings make full contact with the lower head cup. Hold the fork in place while you turn the frame right side up and install the bearings on the top headrace. Again, if the bearings are loose, use the same number as were removed and use enough grease to hold them in place.

For threaded headsets, spin the adjustable cup down on the steerer tube until it presses firmly against the upper bearings. If you have loose bearings, hold the threaded cup and spin the fork clockwise. This will draw the cup onto the bearings without disturbing their position. For threadless headsets, simply slide on the top cup and press on the lockwasher. Then add any spacers.

For threaded headsets, slide the lockwasher, the reflector bracket, the brake cable hanger, and any-

thing else that came off the steerer tube back on in the same order they were removed. After these are in place, thread on the locknut, but don't tighten it yet. Also put the upper shield in place now, if you plan to use one. Slide it over the locknut and down as far as possible so that it won't interfere with the adjustment.

For threadless headsets, you're ready to complete the assembly and adjustment. Slide on the stem, press in the top cap, and screw in the bolt on top. (If you have a multipart top cap, see below.) Screw in the bolt until the fork turns smoothly and there is no play when you push and pull on the fork. Then secure the adjustment by tightening the stem bolts (making sure the stem is centered over the wheel first), and you're ready to roll.

For threaded headsets, install and tighten the stem because it can affect threaded headset adjustment. Then, while holding the adjustable cup in position, tighten the locknut by turning it clockwise.

Dealing with complicated top caps. During removal we mentioned complicated top caps on threadless headsets. These caps are made up of several parts and are designed to jam inside the fork steerer with a wedge action. This differs from the traditional recessed nut (sometimes called a star-fangled nut) found on most threadless headsets, which is pressed into the fork with a special tool and remains in place thanks to sprung tabs around the nut that dig into the walls of the fork.

Complicated top caps are often used on forks with carbon steerer tubes (the tube that's inside the frame when the fork is installed) because the sprung-tab model, which is harmless on a metal fork, can cut into the carbon tube, causing a weakness that can lead to failure. The complicated ones, on the other hand, use a gentler mechanical principle. Another reason they're used is because they're reusable. (The sprung-tab models, once installed, cannot be easily removed so they're usually left inside the fork and you must purchase a new unit for the new fork.)

There are several types of these complicated top caps, but they're usually installed by assembling them first and then sliding them as a unit into the fork before the stem is installed. Tightening the bolt should jam the base of the mechanism inside the fork. Then, unscrew the bolt, remove the top cap, and install the stem. Finish the adjustment/installation by putting the top cap on top of the stem, installing the bolt, and tightening until play is removed from the headset bearings. Center the stem and snug its bolts.

If the top cap doesn't jam inside the steerer, it will be impossible to make a good bearing adjustment. Usually the problem is that the parts of the cap have been assembled in the wrong order. Study them and determine what order will cause the lower parts to jam inside the fork when the bolt is tightened. You can usually figure it out with a little inspection because it's logical and you're smart. Or, experiment to find the arrangement that looks right. In most cases, the top bolt pulls a piece that causes another piece to expand inside the fork, which causes the base to jam in place.

If you can't figure it out, you might find directions in your owner's manual or the directions that came with the headset. If necessary, take the top cap or your bike to a shop and ask for help. For your safety, it's important to make a proper headset adjustment.

Fine-tuning the adjustment. Grab hold of the front wheel and the handlebar and alternately push and pull them in relation to each other. Do the push-pull check with the fork turned to several different positions. You can also by pick up the front of the bike and drop the front wheel onto the ground while holding the stem, and listen for a rattle that indicates looseness. If you discover any play in the headset through either method, loosen the stem, snug the adjusting bolt, and retighten the stem (for a threadless headset). For a threaded headset, loosen the locknut, turn the adjustable cup clockwise a little, and retighten the locknut. Then check the adjustment again.

When all looseness has disappeared from your headset, check to make sure it's not too tight. Lift the front of the bike and turn the bar slowly to feel if the bearings bind, causing resistance, at any point in the rotation. If the headset binds, it'll cause excessive wear on the headset and slow your steering. Loosen a threadless headset by loosening the stem bolts and backing off the adjusting bolt (counterclockwise), and retighten the stem. Turn the adjustable cup counterclockwise a little to loosen a threaded headset. Recheck the adjustment. Keep tuning until the adjustment feels smooth with no play.

Once the headset is properly adjusted, install the front wheel and fully tighten the stem. Be sure that the stem is aligned with the front wheel. Reattach the brake and cable, and center the brake over the wheel. If you installed them, unfold the headset shields so that they fully cover the openings in the upper and lower headset assemblies.

ADJUSTMENT TIPS

Let's say that you're very careful, yet you cannot get the headset to adjust properly. Here are some possible sources of the problem and what to do about them, plus other important adjustments to check.

1. If the bearing adjustment is always loose or tight and you have a headset with loose ball bearings in it, check to make sure that you have the correct number of bearings in the upper and lower races. You may have left some out.

2. If the headset feels tight no matter how you adjust it and the bearings are in retainers, be sure that the retainer is properly oriented. If it's upside down, it will cause the headset to bind.

3. Make certain that the stem is installed properly. Sometimes, the bolt will feel tight but the stem won't be. Try turning it by twisting the bar, and make sure that the stem is tight enough that it doesn't move.

4. If the headset binds and you recently crashed, take the bike to a shop see if it's bent. If it is, it'll have to be straightened or replaced. Check with your local bike shop about the best method to remedy this problem. Also, check to see if the steerer tube is bent. If it is, either the steerer or the entire fork may have to be replaced.

5. Be sure that all the washers, reflector brackets, and other parts originally on your steerer tube are back in place. If they're left out, you'll have to replace them or the headset adjustment may not work correctly.

FITTING A NEW HEADSET

If you decide to replace your current headset, it's best—and usually easiest—to replace it with the same model you removed. If you're going to install a different model, have your bike shop consult *Sutherland's Handbook for Bicycle Mechanics* to be sure that the new headset will fit your frame. Your frame and fork may have to be modified by a professional mechanic to accept the new headset.

You'll need the bicycle shop's help in several other areas as well. Special tools are required to remove the old fork crown race, the lower head cup, or the top headrace without damaging the frame or fork, as well as to install the new headset parts. It may be necessary to have the head tube and the fork crown race cut to fit the new headset components. Tools for this task are very expensive and require special care and skill to use.

Have a bicycle shop remove and fit the fork crown, lower head cup, and the top headrace. Attempting to fit a headset without having the frame properly prepared can damage not only the headset but the frame as well. Once the fork crown, lower head cup, and top headrace are installed, you can then reassemble your headset by following our instructions for a headset overhaul.

HEADSET QUICK FIX

If your fork seems to fall into notches as it twists from side to side, it's because the bearings have made pits in the races. This is known as brinelling. The only permanent way to fix this is to overhaul the headset and replace the pitted parts. However, if you don't have the necessary new parts to replace the pitted ones, you can still make a temporary repair that will help for a little while.

Remove the front wheel, the front brake, the handlebar, and the stem. Spin the fork around three times and reinstall the parts that you removed. This spinning should cause the ball bearings to realign themselves at slightly different points on the races. Such realignment will reduce the effect of the pits. Keep in mind that this is only a temporary repair and that you should not delay too long before you go to a bicycle shop to get the proper parts for a complete repair.

The headset is a wonderful invention created to fulfill some very vital functions. It makes it possible for you to steer your bike rapidly in different directions, turn sharply, or ride in circles. It also enables you to make the ongoing steering adjustments needed to keep you upright on two wheels. While enabling the two sections of your bike frame to function together while moving in relation to each other, the headset must also be able to withstand the weight of your body and a considerable amount of shock. When properly lubricated and adjusted, it's

able to carry out its assignment so well that you may be tempted to take it for granted.

Don't give in to the temptation. Check the adjustment of your headset frequently, shield its bearings from the wind when you carry it on top of your car, and give it a complete and thorough overhaul at least once a year. Smooth and safe handling will be your reward. It's worth the effort.

TROUBLESHOOTING

PROBLEM: On a threaded headset, you've loosened the stem bolt several turns but the stem isn't loose.

SOLUTION: Tap the top of the stem bolt with a mallet. That'll knock free the wedge at the base of the stem (inside the fork) that's holding the stem tight in the fork. That should loosen the stem.

PROBLEM: Your threaded headset will not stay in adjustment even though you keep tightening the locknut.

A common type of wear and tear found on headset cups and cones is brinelling, which is when the bearings wear a series of dents in the parts and cause a notched feeling in the steering. When it's really bad, it almost locks the steering, making it impossible to ride no-handed.

SOLUTION: Make sure there's a notched lockwasher between the locknut and the adjustable cone, and hold the adjustable cone as you tighten the locknut.

PROBLEM: When you disassemble the fork for overhaul, the fork crown race is loose on the base of the fork (it should be tight enough that you cannot remove it by hand).

SOLUTION: Replace it with a tight-fitting crown race, or try securing the one you have by applying a bit of thread adhesive to the fork crown and re-seating the race. Or ask a shop to enlarge the crown race seat on the fork.

PROBLEM: Your threaded headset will not stay tight, even though you keep tightening the locknut.

SOLUTION: The fork may be too long. Remove the stem and check to see that there's a small gap between the top of the locknut and the top of the fork. If not, remove the locknut and install a spacer, then readjust the headset. (Too long a fork will mean that the locknut tightens against the fork instead of against the cone.)

PROBLEM: You've removed the bolt on the top of your threadless headset but you can't get the top cap out.

SOLUTION: You may not need to remove it. Try loosening and removing the stem—the cap should come off with it. Just keep track of the cap (if it falls off the fork) and any cap parts that are inside the fork.

PROBLEM: You want to install a fork, but the fork's steerer tube is the wrong diameter for the headset and frame.

SOLUTION: It may be best to get the correct fork for the frame. If you absolutely insist on using a fork with a steerer too small for your frame, Chris King manufactures special headsets that can adapt a 1-inch fork to a 1⅛-inch frame, or a 1⅛-inch fork to a 1¼-inch frame. Because of the limited availability of 1½-inch forks, there are several companies manufacturing adapters to reduce a 1½-inch frame to the current standard of 1⅛ inches.

PROBLEM: While trying to disassemble a threaded headset, the adjustable cup turns and turns but will not come off.

SOLUTION: Unfortunately, this usually means that the adjustable cone and the fork have developed stripped threads. You may need to replace both.

PROBLEM: You loosen the stem bolts but the stem won't budge.

SOLUTION: The stem may be corroded in place. Try carefully and securely clamping the fork crown in a vise and twisting the bar to break the stem free and wiggle it off. That didn't work? Apply Liquid Wrench, wait overnight, and try again. Still stuck? Keep applying the penetrant and waiting, even if it takes weeks. Or try carefully heating the stem with a propane torch.

PROBLEM: On a threaded headset, you've loosened the stem bolt and knocked it with a mallet. The stem feels loose but it won't come out.

SOLUTION: The stem wedge is probably stuck inside the frame. Unscrew the stem bolt all the way. Remove the stem. Take the bolt and screw it back into the wedge, which you should now be able to see inside the fork. Use the bolt as a handle to wiggle and remove the wedge. Reassemble the stem, being sure to grease the parts.

233

Threaded Headset Adjustment

1 When a headset is either too loose or too tight, it should be readjusted because either problem can negatively affect the steering of the bike and cause unnecessary damage to headset parts. Severe looseness or tightness in the headset bearings will probably be obvious to you while riding. However, there are some simple tests to make while off the bike to determine whether a headset needs adjustment.

To check for looseness in the headset, stand beside your bike. Hold the handlebar with one hand and the front wheel with the other hand. Alternately pull the two together and push them apart (see photo).

2 If you feel any play in the bearings, the adjustment is too loose. To be really thorough, repeat this test with the front fork turned to several different positions. If you discover looseness when the fork is turned to one position, but not another, that is a sign of possible pitting in one of your bearing races. In that case, your headset needs to be overhauled rather than simply adjusted.

Another method to check for a loose headset adjustment is to lift the front wheel a few inches off the ground, then let the bike drop (see photo). If you hear rattles in the headset area, it's a sign that your bearings are too loose.

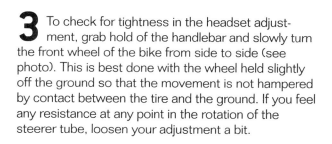

3 To check for tightness in the headset adjustment, grab hold of the handlebar and slowly turn the front wheel of the bike from side to side (see photo). This is best done with the wheel held slightly off the ground so that the movement is not hampered by contact between the tire and the ground. If you feel any resistance at any point in the rotation of the steerer tube, loosen your adjustment a bit.

4 Adjusting a headset is not particularly difficult, though it may take you several tries to get it just right. Begin by loosening the locknut, which is positioned at the upper end of the steering column. If you have a special spanner made to fit your locknut, use it. Otherwise, you can get by with a large adjustable wrench (see photo) if you are careful not to round the edges of the locknut's wrench flats. Turn the locknut counterclockwise to loosen it.

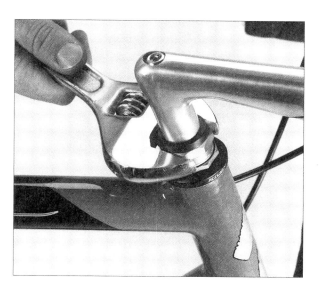

5 If the headset feels loose, turn the adjustable cup clockwise until you feel it make contact with the bearings, then back it off one-eighth to one-quarter turn and check it again. You should be able to adjust the cup by hand, but you can use a suitable tool if you'd like (see photo). If a reflector bracket or brake hanger is in your way, move it up the stem, along with the lockwasher and locknut, while you adjust the cup.

If you feel any binding in the headset, turn the adjustable cup counterclockwise to loosen it slightly. Start with an eighth- to a quarter-turn, then check it again. After each adjustment of the cone, snug the locknut and recheck the adjustment.

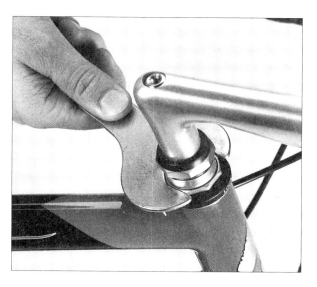

6 Continue to work in small increments, adjusting and checking until you feel neither binding nor looseness in the headset. Be patient and try to get the adjustment just right. If you simply cannot find the precise point between tightness and looseness, leave the adjustment slightly on the tight side.

Once you have the adjustment right, secure it by holding the adjustable cup in position while tightening the locknut.

Threaded Headset Overhaul

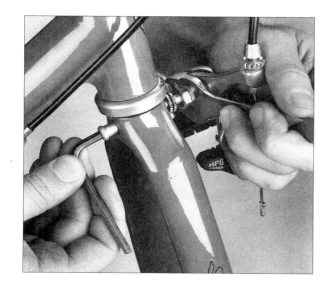

1 On most bikes, headsets should be overhauled yearly. This involves disassembly, cleaning and inspecting, installing new bearings, and repacking with fresh grease.

Put the bike in a repair stand and lay an old sheet under it. If the bearings are loose and fall, they'll land on the sheet instead of disappearing. Count them and keep track of their number for replacement purposes. Also, take some of them to the bike shop to get new ones of the same size.

To take a headset apart, you'll need to remove the handlebar and stem from the head tube, which is complicated by the brake levers and cables. It may be necessary in many cases to remove the brake caliper from the fork.

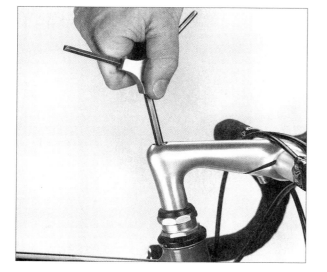

2 Loosen the handlebar stem by turning the expander bolt counterclockwise two or three turns. Don't turn it too far—you don't want the threads on the end of the bolt to lose contact with the wedge at the bottom of the stem.

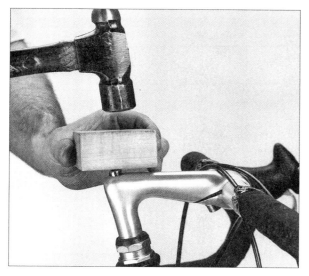

3 Set a small block of wood on top of the bolt (see photo), and give it a sharp blow to dislodge the expander wedge inside the steerer tube. A wedge that has not been loosened in a while may take more than one blow to free.

Lift the handlebar and stem out of the steerer tube and hang them on the top tube of the bike. If you prefer, you can disconnect the cable to the rear brake and shifter cables, if you have them, and set the bar aside while you work. Remove the front wheel.

4 Loosen the headset locknut by turning it counterclockwise (see photo). If it's tight, slide the handle of a hammer between the fork legs and use it to hold the fork while turning the wrench. Thread it completely off the steerer tube and set it aside. If there's a second locknut, take it off as well.

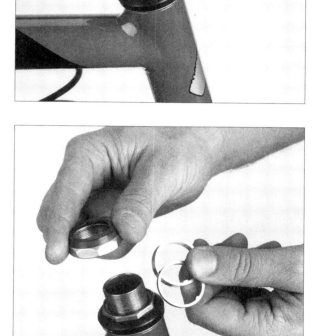

5 Lift off the lockwasher, the reflector bracket, the brake hanger, and anything else between the locknut and the adjustable cup (see photo). Remember the order in which each item comes off so you can replace them in the same way.

You're now ready to remove the adjustable cup. Support the fork with one hand to hold the lower set of bearings inside the lower head cup until you're ready to remove them (see photo 6).

6 Be cautious as you remove the adjustable cup. Any bearings clinging to it may drop and roll away. Once the bearings are visible, you may discover that they are in a metal retainer. If so, you no longer have to worry about any errant balls getting away from you. However, do not assume that just because the upper set of bearings are in a retainer the lower set will be also. Be wary of loose balls until you're sure they are all enclosed in retainers.

If you find that the bearings beneath the adjustable cup are loose, you may want to momentarily thread the cup back down and lay the bike on its side on the floor. Then when you take the adjustable cup off, the bearings can fall out onto the sheet or rags you've spread on the floor.

7 Remove the bearings from the top head race and save them for inspection.

8 If you can, turn the bike upside down to prevent the bearings from falling out of the lower head cup while you lift the fork out of the head tube. Set the fork aside while you extract the bearings (see photo).

Keep the two sets of bearings separate in case they're not identical in size and number. Clean and count each set, then take a sample to the bike shop to buy replacements to match.

Clean all the parts and inspect them for pits and cracks in the bearing areas. Replace any damaged parts. If the fork crown race, the lower head cup, or the top headrace must be removed for replacement, have the work done at a bike shop, which will have the tools and skills needed.

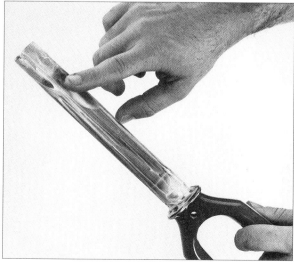

9 When you're ready to reassemble the headset, lightly grease the steerer from the fork crown race up to and including the threads at the upper end (see photo). This will help prevent corrosion and protect working parts from damage and excessive wear.

10 Pack grease into the lower head cup, the adjustable cup, and the top headrace. If you wish, fit a rubber shield over the lower cup and fold it back out of the way until the headset is back together. Install a set of bearings in the lower cup.

11 Place the fork steerer tube back through the head tube, pushing the fork crown race against the bearings. Install the bearings in the upper race. Then thread on the adjustable cup and turn it down until it makes contact with the bearings (see photo).

Don't fine-tune the adjustment until after the stem is locked back in place. Replace the reflector bracket, brake hanger, lockwasher, locknut, and whatever else was taken off. Be sure that everything goes back on in the right order, but don't tighten down the locknut yet.

12 Drop the stem into the steerer tube. When it's at the right height and the bars are straight, turn the expander bolt clockwise to tighten the expander wedge (see photo).

Check the headset adjustment by performing the various tests described on pages 227 and 228. When you have the cup adjusted so you can feel neither binding nor play between the cup and bearings, hold the cup in place and tighten down the locknut.

Reconnect the brake. Replace the front wheel, and your bicycle should be ready to ride again.

Threadless Headset Adjustment and Overhaul

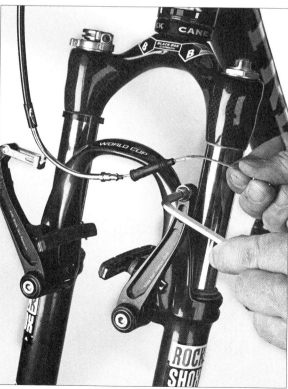

1 Threadless headsets, by design, require adjustment less frequently than their cone-and-locknut predecessors. The parts of a threadless headset simply slide onto the fork's steerer tube, making assembly and disassembly easy. Clamp bolts on the side of the stem lock the system in place. On rare occasions when it is necessary, adjustment is easily accomplished with only a hex key or two.

Feel for headset play by pushing and pulling on the fork with one hand while holding the down tube of the frame with your other hand. You can also lift the front end of the bike, drop it, and listen for a rattle. Another method is to apply the front brake and push and pull the bike back and forth, checking for a knocking sensation that would indicate play in the headset.

To check if the headset is too tight, pick up the front end of the bike and turn the wheel from side to side very slowly to see if you feel any binding in the bearing. It should turn smoothly, and if it doesn't, it may be too tight.

To adjust the headset, loosen the stem bolt(s), tighten the adjusting bolt (see photo) on top of the stem (or loosen it if the adjustment is too tight), and retighten the stem bolts to lock the adjustment in place. Then recheck the adjustment and fine-tune it as needed.

2 If you can't get a good adjustment or the headset feels crunchy and full of dirt while turning, you will need to overhaul the headset or replace the cartridge bearings. Place the bike in a repair stand and start by disconnecting the front brake cable or by removing the brake caliper entirely and removing the front wheel, which will make it easier to remove the fork (see photo).

3 Now unscrew and remove the top bolt and extract the top cap (place the parts on a table in order of removal). Loosen the bolt(s) holding the stem and lift the stem off the fork while holding the fork with one hand so that it can't fall out of the frame. Use a rag to protect the paint and secure the stem to the frame with rope or an elastic or bungee cord (see photo).

You can now slide the headset pieces off the fork and pull the fork out of the frame. Pay attention to how each piece fits, so you'll know how to properly reassemble them. You're ready to remove the fork.

If you find that the fork is stuck and won't come out, carefully strike it with a mallet to knock it free (you may have to hit it hard, but be careful).

If your headset is a cup and cone type with either loose ball bearings or bearings in retainers, clean and inspect all the parts for pits and cracks in the bearing areas. Replace any damaged parts. If the fork crown race, the lower head cup, or the upper head race must be removed for replacement, have the work done at a bike shop, which will have the special tools needed.

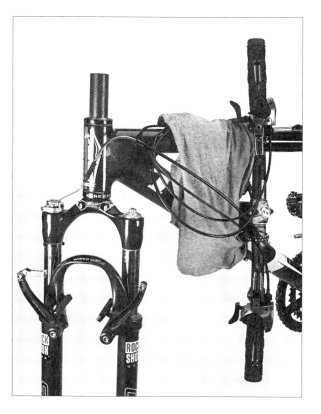

4 Most threadless headsets now use sealed cartridge bearings. The cartridges are sealed to keep the elements out and designed to be replaced when the bearing surfaces wear out, rather than being rebuilt. Still, moisture can find its way inside and cause premature wear. To increase the life span of your cartridge bearings, regrease them as part of your normal maintenance schedule.

Carefully pry out the rubber seal that covers the bearings. Flush the bearings with a light solvent such as WD-40 or White Lightning Clean Streak, and let them dry. Inject fresh grease and snap the seal back in place.

When you're ready to reassemble the headset, coat most of the steerer tube with grease to prevent corrosion, but don't coat the top section that the stem clamps to. On ball bearing type headsets, now is the time to pack grease in both cups, coat the bearings with grease, and place them in the cups. Be sure to install them in the correct direction (See photos on pages 238 and 239).

You can now put the fork back in the frame and install the parts, stem, top cap, and adjusting bolt. Tighten the bolt until the fork turns smoothly without play. Then to finish the job, center the stem and tighten the stem bolt(s) to lock the adjustment. Reattach the front brake and cable, install the front wheel, and you're ready to roll again.

13 BRAKES

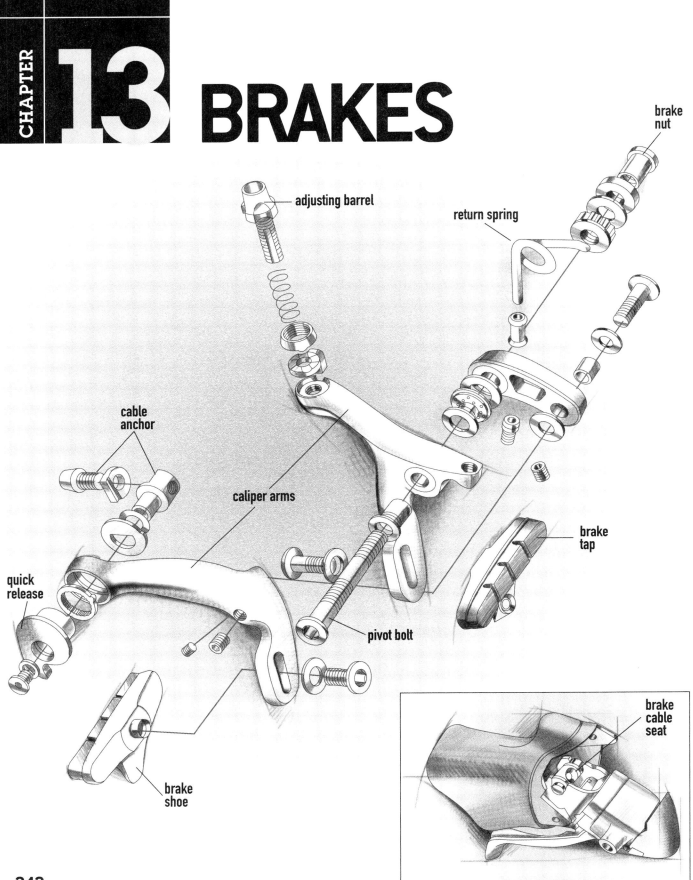

brake
nut

adjusting barrel

return spring

cable
anchor

caliper arms

quick
release

brake
tap

pivot bolt

brake
shoe

brake
cable
seat

Wheels may be what make a bicycle a bicycle, but without brakes, many of us might never get to enjoy riding that bicycle more than once. Early bicycles had no separate braking system, and riders relied on resisting the motion of their cranks with leg power to gradually slow down. Modern track-racing bikes are still made with fixed drivetrains like those early bikes had. The common thread between the two is that neither has ever had to deal with busy intersections or rush-hour traffic on their brakeless cycles.

Thanks to smooth roads and multispeed drivetrains, bicycles move so quickly that they can often outpace city traffic. With the ability to go fast comes the need to slow down and stop, sometimes in a hurry. So a reliable set of stoppers has become of critical importance. Even as we get out of town and into the country—or into the woods, for that matter—controlling speed with a good set of brakes can mean the difference between making a corner and launching into a ravine.

MAJOR TYPES OF BRAKES

Today, there are two major classifications of bicycle brakes: hub brakes and rim brakes. Hub brakes work through pressure applied at the wheel's hub; rim brakes work by applying pressure on both sides of the wheel rim.

Included in the general category of hub brakes are three types: coaster brakes, drum brakes, and disc brakes. Coaster brakes are commonly found on children's bikes, where small hands and young, undeveloped coordination would make other types of brakes more hazard than help. Since this type of brake is quite durable, we will not describe it further. If yours needs service, have it repaired by a shop mechanic.

Drum brakes are generally found on tandems and bikes intended for short, urban commutes. For tandems, increased weight and speed potential are the primary concerns. It's not unheard of for two skilled tandem riders to reach speeds near 60 mph on long mountain pass descents. With 300 to 400 pounds of bike and riders at these speeds, friction from rim brakes alone could heat the rims enough to melt the tubes inside. The potential for a horrific crash is obvious. A drum brake applied at the hub can generate tremendous friction to slow the bike down, yet the heat poses no greater threat than a blister on your finger if you are unfortunate enough to touch it at the bottom of your descent.

Commuters seek simplicity and reliability. Drum brakes have both of these in spades. While not as large as those used on tandems, drum brakes on city bikes have plenty of stopping power and thick brake pads that can yield years of service for the average bicycle commuter. What's more, minor wobbles and dents in the rim that might give a rim brake fits go almost unnoticed when a hub drum brake is in use. This isn't license to let your wheels go to pot, but it is comforting to know that you could break a spoke on that nasty pothole you hit and still make it to work on time.

Disc brakes have come a long way from the heavy, inconsistent nightmares of just a handful of years ago. Today's bicycle disc brakes are light and sophisticated, with an impressive balance of power and modulation (the ability to control and feel the application of power).

Hub brakes put stress on a wheel more evenly than rim brakes, which is one mark in their favor. Any hub brake system requires a specifically designed hub and a frame equipped to handle the stresses applied to the stays. Thanks to the advent of a widely accepted standard for fitting brake rotors and calipers, most mountain bikes today are designed with disc brakes in mind. Even models already equipped with rim brakes include specially designed dropouts to which a disc brake caliper can be installed should the rider wish to upgrade in the future. Some even have disc-ready hubs to make the switch that much easier and more cost-effective.

Possible disadvantages of discs may include a rubbing noise due to disc drag, specialty equipment needed for servicing, and high cost. Drum brakes are just plain heavy and can lack modulation.

HYDRAULIC DISC BRAKES

If you have hydraulic discs on your bike, get a copy of the owner's manual for your brakes and rely on it for service information. Beyond replacing brake pads and aligning the caliper, it's best to leave service of a hydraulic disc brake to the experts. Each system, though similar in principle, has subtle differences in procedure and handling to which you must strictly adhere. For the adventurous, here are a few tips common to all hydraulic systems.

THE BASICS OF HYDRAULICS

There are, no doubt, many millions of pages in texts dedicated to the principles of hydraulics. For the purpose of bicycle brakes, though, the idea is pretty simple.

The system starts at the brake lever, which actuates a piston in the master cylinder. When the brake lever is pulled, a volume of fluid in the master cylinder is pushed out by the piston and into the brake line. Fluid flowing through the brake line eventually reaches the caliper, which contains the slave cylinder(s). The slave cylinders fill with fluid and force their pistons out, clamping the brake pads onto the brake disc. This system of hydraulics can achieve pressures of up to 3,000 psi, generating tremendous braking power despite the diminutive appearance of the caliper and disc.

CARE AND FEEDING

Disc brakes require a minimum of regular maintenance once they have been set up and adjusted properly. Of course, nothing is 100 percent carefree, and your disc brake set is no exception. Beyond the obvious necessity of replacing brake pads when you've worn a set out, there are a handful of things you can do to keep those powerful and consistent speed controllers functioning their best.

Keep it clean. Disc brake pads are extremely susceptible to oil contamination. It's possible for these pads to become permanently ruined as a result

The Six-Bolt International Standard is the most commonly found pattern for attaching brake discs. Shimano's new CenterLock design allows the use of a steel brake disc mounted on an alloy carrier to reduce weight and aid in heat dissipation.

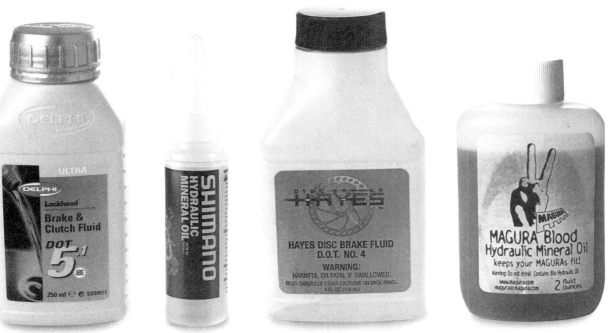

Some manufacturers use environmentally benign mineral oil as brake fluid, while others use high-performance but caustic automotive and motorcycle DOT fluids (such as DOT 4 or DOT 5.1) for heat resistance. Never use fluid that is not specified by the brake manufacturer. DOT fluids will attack the seals of a brake designed for mineral oil, and vice versa. Even all DOT fluids are not created equal, so if you're not sure what was used in a DOT system last time, flush the entire system and rebleed it rather than just topping off.

of even the tiny amounts of oil from your own skin. Whenever handling disc brake pads or rotors, minimize contact of the braking surfaces with your bare skin. If you do touch the braking surfaces, or if you're unsure, clean the pads and disc with rubbing alcohol or with a product approved for cleaning disc brake parts, such as Disc Doctor or White Lightning Clean Streak. If your brake pads become soaked with oil, throw them out and replace them. Once oil has soaked into the pad it cannot be flushed out, and the heat of braking friction will cause the oil to degrade the pad material, diminishing braking power and causing it to wear prematurely.

Keep it dirty. Believe it or not, it's best to *not* clean your discs on a regular basis. Oil contamination is one thing, but everyday dirt and mud will not harm—and they can even help—braking performance. Tiny particles of dirt embedded into the surfaces of brake pads and discs increase the amount of friction the brake can generate. In fact, after cleaning or changing pads, there is a brief period of dimin-

ished braking power. By riding the bike for a few minutes while dragging the brakes—called "bedding" the brakes—particles of the brake pad material are ground into the disc's surface, restoring power.

The fluid controversy. There are two basic types of hydraulic fluid currently used in bicycle brakes— mineral oil and automotive-type DOT (Department of Transportation) brake fluid. Each has a specific benefit and drawback. Mineral oil is environmentally friendly and easy to work with, but it is not as heat-resistant as DOT-type fluids and may expand under prolonged, heavy braking. DOT fluids are engineered to resist heat expansion and in some cases have boiling points of over 500°F. DOT fluids, however, are extremely caustic. Great care must be taken to avoid contact with the skin and painted surfaces.

DOS AND DON'TS

Keep in mind that you should use only the fluid recommended by your specific brake's manufacturer. Mineral oils and DOT fluids are not interchangeable, and serious damage can be caused by not using the correct fluid. There is no evidence of long-term damage from using different brands of mineral oil than the brake manufacturer's own blend. Even so, it's best to stick with Shimano fluid for Shimano brakes, Magura fluid for Magura brakes, and so on, since that is what they used in the development of their system. DOT fluids are a little trickier. Gener-

ally speaking, DOT-3 and DOT-4 are interchangeable. DOT-4 and DOT-5.1 are interchangeable, as well. But DOT-3 and DOT-5.1 are not. Moreover, it's important never to mix fluids of different types. In some rare cases, it's best not to even mix fluids of the same designation but from different manufacturers. Wait, it gets even more confusing. There is also a DOT-5 fluid that should not be confused with DOT-5.1, as DOT-5 is silicone-based and will not work in any bicycle brake system currently on the market. So, while DOT fluids are widely available at auto and motorcycle part stores, your best bet is to get yours from the local bike shop. They will carry only those fluids approved for bicycle brake use.

Hands off. One of the most common errors in the handling of disc brakes is also, unfortunately, sometimes the most difficult to correct. Whenever a wheel is removed from the frame or fork, don't squeeze the brake lever! Doing so on today's self-adjusting systems can cause the brake pads to clamp tightly together. Separating pads after this has happened can require the skill and patience of a surgeon at best, and a complete brake bleed at worst. After-market disc brake sets include a spacer that can be stuck in the caliper while the wheel is out to prevent this embarrassing and frustrating problem, but most disc-equipped bikes don't include them. If you don't have one, fold a piece of cardboard or a few business cards in half and stuff these between the brake pads.

Read the fine print. Before servicing a hydraulic disc, it's important to understand the steps, which are similar but slightly different for each model.

Fortunately, most discs, once set up, require little maintenance. In fact, on a good system, about the only thing needed is occasional brake pad replacement—usually a simple matter—and an even less occasional brake-bleed. Because there is no single method for bleeding we can describe in this book that could be applied to every hydraulic disc brake, we must defer to the manufacturers themselves. Before attempting to service your own hydraulic brake, carefully study that specific brake system's manual and be sure you have all the tools, supplies, and skills necessary.

Forces generated by disc brakes can be so great that disc brakes with discs larger than 165 mm should be used only on forks approved by the manufacturer for large discs.

MECHANICAL (CABLE-ACTUATED) DISC BRAKES

Though not quite as powerful as their hydraulic cousins, mechanical disc brakes take the greatest

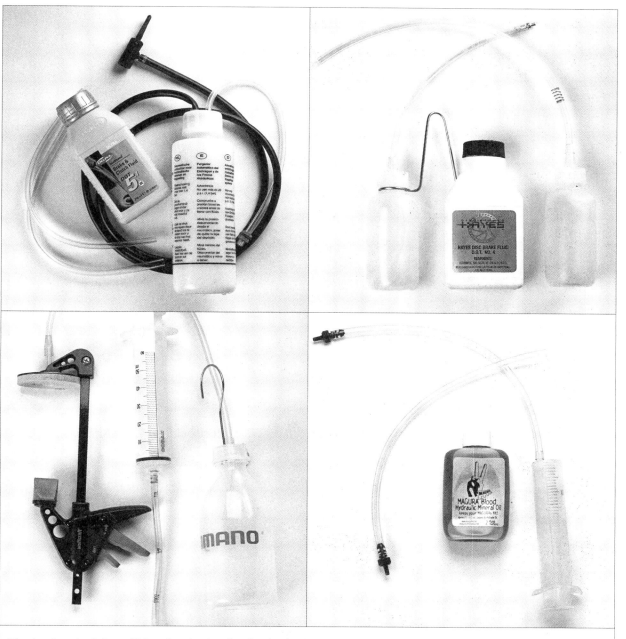

The basic principles of bleeding hydraulic disc brakes apply to all examples. Each manufacturer, however, has devised a system that it believes works best with that particular brake design. If you want to bleed your own brakes, it is highly recommended that you purchase a factory bleed kit tailored to your brake set and carefully follow the manufacturer's instructions.

benefit of the disc—consistency in all weather—and match it with the simplicity and user-friendliness of rim brakes. A standard brake lever pulls a cable leading to the caliper, just like a rim brake. The caliper, rather than a pair of arms, consists of one fixed brake pad and one that rides on a large screw. The cable pulls on a lever arm, turning the screw, which pushes the mobile pad against the disc and, in turn, the disc against the fixed pad. Though some performance is lost in the force it takes to deflect the disc before both pads make contact, it's hardly noticeable from the rider's standpoint. Plenty of riders feel that the benefit of a mechanical system's ease of adjustment outweighs its very slight lack in power as compared to a hydraulic system.

Mounting the disc. In the beginning, every disc brake manufacturer had a unique system for mounting their brake disc to the hub. Naturally, consumers didn't like the idea that a certain brand of disc brake would only work with a certain brand of hub; thus, disc brake sales grew very slowly. When Hayes decided to enter the scene in the mid-1990s, the first thing they did was work with other manufacturers to arrive at a standard for mounting calipers and discs. The Six-Bolt International Standard (I.S.) was born and disc brake sales took off like Saturn V. Shimano has recently mixed things up by introducing a spline-mount interface for discs and hubs. It's a good system that allows for lighter-weight discs and hubs, but it had a lot of people up in arms for a short time after its introduction. Luckily for us, Shimano's Spline-Lock discs come in a couple of common diameters that allow use of Shimano hub and disc with another brand of caliper, or vice-versa. There are also now adapters that allow fitment of a Six-Bolt I.S. disc to a Spline-Lock hub. We're still much better off now than we were then.

Aligning disc brake calipers. There are a few different systems used by disc brake manufacturers for aligning the caliper to the disc. The two most common are the shim-mount caliper and the floating-mount caliper, the latter of which has two distinct designs in current use.

Hayes brake calipers incorporate a floating-mount design. The Hayes caliper is mounted to the frame or fork using an adapter. On this adapter, the caliper has a small amount of free side-to-side movement before it is tightened in place, centered over the disc. The only two exceptions are Manitou forks, which are designed to allow Hayes calipers to be directly mounted, and mountain bike frames from the late 1990s that used a Hayes-specific mount on the left chainstay. In either of those cases, the procedures described here still apply, though the adapter is not present.

To begin, it's important to first be sure that the two bolts holding the adapter to the frame's or fork's mounting tabs are tight. Use a 5 mm hex key to loosen the two bolts holding the caliper to the adapter. About one full turn should allow the caliper to freely float side to side on the adapter, yet have a minimum of free up-and-down movement. If the caliper wants to pull to one side, remove any guides or zip-ties holding the hydraulic line to the frame so the line doesn't tug at the caliper.

Wrap an elastic band over the handlebar and brake lever to clamp the caliper to the rotor while keeping both your hands free to work with the caliper. Assuming that both pistons of the caliper are moving an equal distance, the caliper should center itself on the disc.

As with Hayes' floating mount, the bolts holding the caliper to the adapter should be tightened little by little. Turn one bolt about one-eighth turn, then the other, and repeat until both are tight.

Remove the elastic that holds the brake lever, and check the caliper alignment. Hold a sheet of white paper on the other side of the caliper as you look through from behind. Daylight should be visible between both pads and the disc. If one pad is touching or if the disc scrapes as the wheel spins, slightly loosen the bolts holding the caliper to the adapter and move the caliper by hand to fine-adjust the pad clearance.

Avid disc brake calipers also have a floating-type mount, but with a series of hemispherical washers that allow the caliper to be aligned in all directions, compensating for inconsistencies in a frame's or a fork's brake mounting tabs.

Calipers from Avid come out of the box with adapters already mounted. Don't disassemble these until you've taken note of the exact sequence of all of the washers—the sequence of the washers is critical to the function of Avid's Tri-Align system. Mount the caliper and adapter into place on the frame or fork using the supplied bolts. If you're readjusting an existing system, remove the brake cable from the caliper.

Loosen the bolts holding the caliper to the adapter about one full turn. With this done, the caliper should slide and rotate smoothly in the hemispherical washers. The red dials on either side of the caliper adjust the position of the brake pads. Turning these clockwise moves the pads closer to the disc; counterclockwise retracts the pads back into the caliper. Using these dials, clamp the disc with the pads roughly in the center of the caliper body.

Snug the bolts holding the caliper to the adapter

little by little. The best technique is to turn one bolt about one-eighth turn, then the other, and repeat until the caliper is tight. This will help prevent the caliper "walking" side to side from friction with the bolt.

Back the outside pad out as far as it will go by turning the outside dial adjuster counterclockwise. Turn the inside dial adjuster just a few clicks counterclockwise. Push the caliper's lever arm by hand to ensure that the pad is fully retracted, and give the wheel a spin. If there is any rubbing, turn the inside adjuster one click counterclockwise and repeat until there is no more contact. Ideally, there will be a gap of less than 0.5 mm between the fixed pad and the disc with no scraping.

Adjust the position of the outside pad by turning the outside dial adjuster clockwise. Do this a few clicks at a time and then push the lever arm up by hand. When it stops at a point about halfway through its travel to the cable stop, the adjustment is correct.

Now you're ready to anchor the cable. Run the cable from the lever to the caliper as described previously in this chapter. Using your fourth hand tool, pull the free end of the cable through the anchor and set the lever arm about one-quarter of the way through its travel and give the lever a few good, strong squeezes to make sure everything is settled into place. It's best to make fine adjustments to lever feel at the cable anchor, rather than using the adjusting barrel on the lever. The barrel adjuster is there primarily to quickly adjust for pad wear while out on the road or trail.

To finish, trim the free end of the cable no more than 20 mm (¾ inch) from the anchor bolt to prevent it getting caught in the disc. Crimp the cable end and you're all square.

Magura, Hope, and Shimano disc brakes, among others, use shims between the caliper and mounting tabs on the frame or fork. Shims are essentially just thin washers made in specific thicknesses. On these brake systems, the shims are used in stacks between the caliper and frame or fork to position the caliper perfectly over the brake disc. The process is relatively easy but requires a steady hand and a little bit of technique to perform quickly. On the up side, shimming usually has to be done only once.

Start by setting the caliper in place by turning the bolts in just a few threads so the caliper can float from side to side. The hydraulic line will try to pull the caliper to one side or the other, making precise adjustment more difficult. Remove any clips or zip ties holding the line to the frame or fork to minimize this tendency.

Wrap an elastic band over the handlebar and brake lever to apply constant pressure to the brake pads. Both pistons of the caliper should move an equal distance, and the caliper will clamp itself, centered on the disc.

Determining the correct number of shims for each mounting bolt is a simple process of trial and error. The correct number of shims is as many will fit snugly between the mounting tabs of the frame/fork and caliper. It's possible—even likely—that each mounting bolt will require a different number of shims. Magura and Hope shims are circular washers that require the removal and reinstallation of the mounting bolts to be put in place, while Shimano shims are Y-shaped and can be installed and removed easily using a pair of needlenose pliers. Tighten the mounting bolts and you're ready to check your work.

Check the brake pad clearance in the caliper by first removing the elastic band squeezing the brake lever. Ideally, there will be small gaps between both brake pads and the disc through which you can see daylight. To make this easier to see, hold a sheet of white paper on the other side of the caliper.

RIM BRAKES

There are two types of rim brakes in common use today: sidepulls and cantilevers. A third type, the centerpull, can be found on road bikes dating back to the 1960s and 1970s and on mountain bikes from the 1980s.

Sidepulls were popular in the early and mid-1950s mainly because that was all that was available. Then in the late 1950s and early 1960s, quality centerpull brakes were introduced by Universal, Mafac, and Weinmann, and they quickly gained favor. Though seldom found on new bikes sold in the United States today, centerpull brakes are still available. One of their attractions is that after the initial installation and adjustment are complete, these brakes are basically self-centering, whereas early sidepull brakes were always dragging one shoe on the rim (a problem that's been solved on modern designs).

249

A second attractive feature of centerpull brakes that popularized them when they came out is the greater mechanical advantage they offered over most sidepulls made at the time. This was because the pivot points for centerpull caliper arms are closer to the rim. Sidepulls pivot on a single mounting bolt, which is directly above the tire. Centerpulls, by contrast, are provided with a pivot on each side of the brake body, decreasing the distance from the pivot to the brake shoe and thus increasing the mechanical power of the brake.

When it first occurred, this design innovation made possible the use of levers that were smaller and had shallower contours than those previously required for sidepull brakes. This was a distinct advantage for cyclists with small hands, such as younger children and smaller-framed women.

Despite the mechanical advantage of centerpull brakes, by the mid-1970s the trend had reversed and the sidepull was again becoming the brake most favored by riders. Starting with the Campagnolo Record model, greatly improved and refined sidepulls began to appear on the market. Many of the attractive features of the popular centerpull systems were now incorporated into the newer sidepulls. Quick-releases, cable adjusters, and better finishes were the order of the day. Now there are even dual-pivot sidepull brakes that rely on pivots closer to the brake pads, which creates more braking power and easier brake centering. In fact, the design is so good, it's doubtful that centerpulls will ever become popular again.

A cantilever brake works much like a centerpull brake but has shorter, stiffer arms that bolt to pivots built into the fork and stays. Because the posts are very close to the rim and each short arm has its own mount, cantilevers have a great mechanical advantage. This is why they're commonly used on tandems and loaded tourers, which carry much greater loads than ordinary lightweight bikes. Cantilevers are also the brakes on many mountain bikes because fat tires create reach problems for ordinary caliper brakes.

As off-road riders ventured farther into the woods and tested their skills on dangerous descents, two new mountain bike brake designs evolved in the late 1980s: the U-brake and the rollercam. Both have more power than conventional cantilevers and were standard equipment on many mountain bikes for several years. U-brakes are heavy-duty centerpulls with arms that attach to the frame like cantilevers. Rollercams use a cam-and-pulley system to amplify pressure on the rims. One advantage of both types is that they do not protrude from the side of the frame like cantilevers. Consequently, they provide more heel clearance on small frames and are less likely to cut you in a crash. These brakes are quite rare today—unfortunately, they are difficult to adjust and maintain, so they went out of favor fairly quickly, while cantilevers were continuously refined.

The refinement of the cantilever brake eventually led to the direct-pull cantilever—sometimes called the V-brake because of Shimano's popular V-Brake model. Direct-pull cantilevers are awesome grippers, great for mountain bikes, tandems, and tourers. Interestingly, they share the best designs of cantilever and sidepull brakes. The arms mount to posts attached to the fork and stays, but the cable runs directly to the brake arm instead of to a hanger as on regular cantilevers. This makes the cable action much more efficient and greatly simplifies adjustment. Two other things make the direct-pull an outstanding stopper. The brake pads are mounted in the stiffest possible location so all the force reaches the rim, and the brake arms are quite long, increasing the leverage applied at the rim. Direct-pulls are great new brakes, and they have quickly become the gotta-have item for mountain bikers who push the limits of speed and control.

BRAKE CABLE HOUSINGS

These days, nearly all brake manufacturers have switched over to flat-wound cable housing, first used by Campagnolo. The flat-wound housing gives a more solid feel because, when the faces of the coil wires lie flat against each other rather than being round as in the older housings, there's less compression and slippage between the coils.

Cable housings lined with nylon, now a common practice, also helps produce a brake system that gives a more responsive feel. A further improvement is the practice of coating the cables with Teflon. When these various innovations are combined into one system, most of the friction formerly incurred in the cable portion of a brake system is reduced or eliminated.

There are even supercable systems today such as Avid Flak Jacket cable sets and others. These sets include the inner wires, housing sections, and ferrules (the caps for the ends of the housing sections). What's unique about these supercables is that, when assembled, the cables are sealed so no dirt can get in to contaminate things, and they're designed with slippery materials so that the cables move with hardly any friction. At about $50 for a pair of brake or shift cables, they're much more expensive than ordinary cables and housings. However, if you need to improve braking or shifting and minimize your cable maintenance, or if you're looking for a way to get the cables working smoothly on a bike with an unusually twisty cable path, these supercables are a great upgrade.

BUYING THE RIGHT BRAKES

Before purchasing new brakes, make sure they'll fit your bike. For sidepulls, first determine the dimension from the brake mounting hole to the center of the rim. Measure the distance with a caliper. There are two general "sizes" in which most brakes are available—short-reach 47 mm, and long-reach 52 mm. Both have a range of adjustment of approximately 5 to 10 mm in each direction. There are other sizes on the market, but these two make up 90 percent of those used on lightweight bikes. Make sure that the brakes you want will fit your frame. You can always take your bike to the shop for a trial fit.

For cantilever and direct-pull cantilevers, it's a little simpler. They'll fit on almost any bike with braze-on brake posts, such as most mountain bikes, hybrids, many touring bikes, and tandems. Today, there's a standard position for these braze-on brake posts, and almost all cantilever brakes and direct-pull cantilevers will fit well.

The exception is if you happen to have an older bike that is equipped with a U-brake or rollercam. These use posts that are mounted in a different location. With these, it's probably best to stick with the brakes you have. If you must replace them, it's possible to have a frame builder remove the old posts and braze on new ones that will accept modern cantilevers or direct-pulls. It won't cost too much (no more than about $50), but because the brazing will damage the paint, you'll need to have the frame, or part of it, repainted.

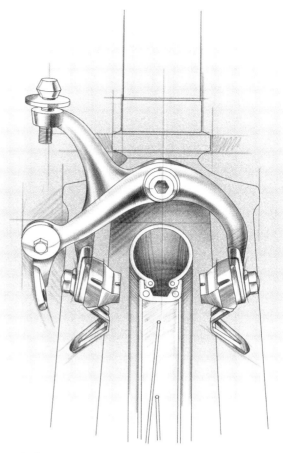

Before buying a new set of brakes, make sure the calipers can be adjusted to fit the distance between the brake-mounting hole on the frame or fork and the center of the rim.

INSTALLING BRAKE LEVERS

There are two types of road brake levers—conventional and aero—commonly used on drop handlebars, and they are installed differently. With aero levers, which are common today, the cable housing starts inside the lever and runs under the bar tape. This streamlines the front of the bike, protects the cable and housing better than conventional levers, and offers a more comfortable hand position. It also makes it possible to work on your bike upside down because there are no cables in the way. Conventional levers are still found on many older road and touring bikes and are distinguished from aero levers by cables and housing that exit from the top. Today, they are commonly referred to as non-aero levers, since aero-type levers are now the norm.

The first step in installing a new set of brakes with nonaero levers is to fasten the levers to the bar of your bike. However, it's best to mount aero levers to the bar after installing the cable and housing because the brake spring tension will ensure that the housing is properly seated in the lever.

Many brake sets come with rubber hood covers that fit around the lever bodies. These covers increase the comfort of riding with the hands resting on the lever hoods. If you are reusing a set of levers that lack these covers or if you need new ones, consider buying a pair. Fit them over the levers before sliding the levers on the handlebar. Spray a little rubbing alcohol inside the new hoods to ease installation. They'll slide into place with less effort and won't slip once the alcohol has evaporated.

Of course, before you can attach new levers, you must remove the old ones, and that means stripping off your handlebar tape. Old bar tape is seldom reusable, so buy new tape to go along with your new brake system. Even if you are not installing new levers but only repositioning the old ones, you may need to remove the old tape before the lever clamp can be moved. (If the levers are being moved a tiny amount, you can sometimes wiggle them into place without removing the tape.)

Once the tape is out of the way, loosen the brake cable anchor nut and pull the cable free from the brake caliper. Unhook the fitting on the upper end of the cable from the lever and remove both the cable and the cable housing from the bike. Squeeze the lever in so that it touches the handlebar. Look inside the lever body and you'll see a clamp bolt or nut that's holding the lever to the bar. Find the tool you need to loosen that nut. It will probably be either a flat-head screwdriver, a thin-wall 8 mm socket, or an Allen wrench. Loosen the nut, then slide the lever off the handlebar. On Shimano STI and Campagnolo Ergopower brake levers, the clamping screw is on the side of the lever body and is loosened with an Allen wrench.

The positioning of brake levers varies with the personal riding style of each rider, but a standard used by many veteran riders is to position the lower end of the lever even with the extension of the lower part of the handlebar. Move them up or down a bit to suit your taste.

If you are installing non-aero levers, find the tool that fits the nut on the clamp bolt and fasten the levers to your bar. Take care in doing this: Some models of levers have mounting bolts that bear on the lever pivot pin. If you have this type of lever and you overtighten the bolt, it may cause some binding in the lever movement. In this case, tighten the mounting bolt just enough to keep the lever assembly from twisting on the handlebar when you tug on it.

Mountain levers. Removing and installing mountain bike brake levers means dealing with the handlebar grips. If you're replacing a worn pair, simply cut off the old ones with a utility knife. Be careful—it's easy to slip when cutting against the round handlebar beneath.

If you want to save the old grips, slide a small screwdriver beneath an edge and drip in a little alcohol. Twist the grip a bit and add a little more alcohol until the grip slides off the bar. Loosen the lever clamping bolt with an Allen wrench and slide the lever off the handlebar.

When installing new levers, consider the order of assembly of the shift levers first. Sometimes the shifter goes on first (thumb levers), sometimes the brake lever does (twist grips). Before tightening the lever, place it so that its end does not protrude past the end of the bar. That will ensure that if you crash, the bar will hit before the lever, so the lever will be less likely to be damaged.

Even more important, adjust the lever so that it's in line with the natural bend in your wrist when you sit on the seat and rest your hands on the grips. You don't want to squeeze the brake lever with bent wrists. When the lever is positioned correctly for you, tighten the clamping bolt. Then install the shifters, if necessary, and the grips. Lubricate them with alcohol if needed. They'll be slippery at first, but the alcohol will evaporate quickly and the grips will stick.

INSTALLING BRAKES

To remove an old pair of sidepull brake calipers, loosen the nut on the tail end of the mounting bolt and take the calipers off the bike. To install a new set of calipers, first differentiate the front calipers from the rear by comparing the length of their respective mounting bolts. The caliper with the longer bolt

Use a third-hand tool to hold brake pads against the rim while the cable is being tightened.

goes on the front, and the one with the shorter bolt goes on the rear. Once you've determined which is which, insert the mounting bolt through the mounting hole in the frame, thread on the mounting nut, and snug it down. Don't worry about getting it really tight until later, after you have centered the calipers on the wheel.

Cantilever and direct-pull cantis are attached to the frame with two Allen bolts that screw into the frame posts. Once the cable is detached, removing the brakes requires only removing the Allen bolts and wiggling the brakes off the posts. It's important, though, to keep track of the small parts that are inside each brake arm, so take off one side at a time. That way, if you drop something, you can always refer to the other side to see how the parts should fit together. If you tie or tape the brake arm parts together during removal, they'll stay put.

When installing cantilever or direct-pull cantis, grease the outside of the brake post and slide the brake arm in place, first making sure that any springs

or washers are in the right place and seated. Then install the Allen bolt (there's usually a washer that goes beneath it), screwing it fully into the post. Sometimes new brakes come with a drop of factory-applied thread adhesive on the brake bolts. If yours did not, apply a drop now, before installation. It'll help the bolt stay put. Be very careful not to over-tighten this bolt—it needs to be just snug. If you overtighten it, you can damage the brake post, bulging it and binding the brake.

When the brake is in place on the frame, adjust the brake shoes. The pads should strike the rim squarely. Too high and they may rub the tire; too low and they may dive beneath the rim. If the shoes are on a post, ensure that it's adjusted evenly on both sides.

CABLES AND CABLE HOUSING

The next step is to install the cables. Many cyclists try to reduce friction in their cables by making the cable runs as short as possible, often trimming several inches off the housing that comes with their bikes. While there is certainly no need for enormous cable loops over or in front of your handlebar, don't go overboard in the other direction, either. Unnecessarily long cables are a source of excessive friction, but so are cable runs that are too short—they produce bends that bind the cable in the housing and may even prevent you from turning the bar far enough to the side. When you install new cables and housing, cut away the excess, but leave sufficient length for loops that are large enough to prevent any kinking in the housing or joints when the handlebar is turned sharply to one side or the other. Kinks will cause premature wear and fraying of your cables.

On mountain bikes, copy the old housing path. Usually, the only tricky section is where the rear brake cable exits the lever. It can pass on either side of the stem. Try it on both sides and use the position that provides the least amount of resistance when the bar is turned from side to side. Usually, this means that the housing will run from the brake lever, around the left side of the stem, and onto the housing stop on the top tube.

If you're working with aero levers, size your housing carefully before cutting it. The rear housing passes in front of the head tube and through the top tube cable guides to the back brake. Be sure to make it long enough so that the handlebars turn freely. Both the front and rear brake housings should be long enough to follow the shape of the handlebar, run beneath the tape, and exit near the stem. Before cutting, grease the brake cables, install them in the aero levers, and thread them through the housing

and into the anchor bolts on the calipers. Pull each cable end so that the housing seats inside each lever. Then, while pulling on the cable, squeeze the caliper and tighten the anchor bolt. It helps to use a third-hand tool (a special tool that hooks over both brake shoes and presses them toward each other) or a toe strap to hold the caliper together.

Fasten the aero lever to the handlebar so that the lower end of the lever is even with the extension of the lower part of the bar. Tape the housing to the handlebar in two places on each side. Check that there is enough housing to allow the bar to turn freely without binding the cable.

SIZING CABLE HOUSING

Once you've laid out the cable runs and determined the lengths, trim the housing. The tools that are needed to cut the housing cleanly are a pair of purpose-built cable cutters like the Felco C-7 cable cutter or a sharp pair of diagonal cutters, a small file, and an awl or similar pointed tool.

With aero levers, because you've already installed the cables, you must first pull the cable out of the housing a little. Do this by loosening the cable anchor bolt and squeezing the brake lever. When the lever is open, reach inside and pull out the head of the cable with needlenose pliers. You will cut the housing near the caliper, so don't pull the cable out very far.

Cut the housing at the proper length with the cutters. Look closely at the end of the housing to see if a burr has been created. You want a clean cut. If

Cut cable housing using a sharp pair of cable- or diagonal-cutters. If a burr forms at the end, snip it away. File the end of the housing flat so it doesn't try to bite-in under pressure and bind the cable.

there's a burr, cut the end again or file the end square. Usually, it's also necessary to reopen the liner inside the housing. That's what the awl is for. Work it into the liner to round it out.

If you're installing a new set of brakes, the cable housing may have small metal ferrules mounted on each end or supplied loose in the package. If they're loose, save them to put on the ends of your housing after you cut it to length. These ferrules provide protection for the ends of the housing and help support the housing where it seats in the lever and the calipers. If you leave them off, the cable will have a tendency to cock to one side and not line up with the lever housing or caliper housing stop, giving a spongy feel, and wearing the cable prematurely. Some brakes do not use ferrules, though. If you're trying to install ferrules to a brakeset but they just won't fit, the brake probably wasn't designed for them.

ATTACHING CABLES TO BRAKES

If you are working with road aero levers, reattach the cables to the calipers. To do this, push the cable back into the lever until it comes out of the housing, then pull on the cable end until the head of the cable seats in the lever. Thread the cable into the anchor, squeeze the caliper, and fasten the anchor bolt.

With non-aero levers, before running the cable through the housing, grease the cable and install the housing ferrules (if your brakes came with them). Thread the cable through the hole in the upper part of the brake lever. Catch the head of the cable in the anchor provided for it inside the lever, making certain the anchor is turned so that the cable head will properly seat itself when the cable is pulled taut.

On mountain bike levers, you usually must rotate the adjusting barrel to line the slots up so the cable can be fit into place. With the cable and housing in place, turn the adjuster back to its starting position seated against the lever (fully clockwise).

Once the cable has been routed through the housing, fasten it to the calipers and trim away any excess. For this, you need some means of holding the calipers against the wheel rim while tightening the cable. There is a tool called the third hand that is made for this purpose. It hooks over both brake shoes and presses them toward each other. If you don't want to invest in this handy tool, ask a friend to help you, or create your own third hand by using a shoestring or a toe strap from your bicycle. Still

another approach is to slightly tighten the anchor nut on the cable, then hold the calipers together with one hand while pulling the cable taut, then tighten the anchor nut with the other hand. Experiment to find the method that works best for you.

Before tightening the cable, check to make sure the brake quick-release (the lever or button on road brakes that is used for opening the brake for wheel removal) is shut. Screw the cable adjusting barrel all the way down, then back it off a couple of turns. Check to make sure that the cable end is seated properly in the brake lever and the housing ends are seated in the frame stops. If all is in order, pull the cable taut and tighten the anchor nut.

Release the calipers and squeeze the brake lever several times to stretch the cable. If the cable seats and stretches so much that the lever hits the handlebar when you squeeze it hard, squeeze the brake pads against the rim again and pull the cable tighter. Anchor the cable at a point that will provide ⅛ to 3/16 inch of clearance between each brake shoe and the rim before you squeeze the lever, and ½ to 1 inch of space between the lever and the bars when you squeeze it hard. (You may opt for a different setting later, but this is a good starting point.) Once you have the cable in that position, tighten the anchor bolt enough to prevent any cable slippage when braking hard. Leave 1 to 2 inches of cable protruding from the anchor bolt and use sharp cable cutters to trim away the rest.

Once you have trimmed the end of the cable, you need to do something to prevent it from fraying. The sharp strands of a frayed bike cable are not kind to human hands. One way to prevent cable fraying is to use premanufactured end protectors. They're available in aluminum or plastic. The aluminum type are slipped over the cable end and then crimped with your cutters. The plastic ones are installed similarly, except that they don't have to be crimped. They're easier to install, but less permanent.

If you don't have one of the little end caps, you can solder the cable end. To do this, a soldering gun (a cigarette lighter will work, too), solder, and flux are needed. Use alcohol to wipe off any dirt and lubricant from the end of the cable. Stick the portion of the cable that is to be soldered into the flux. Apply the hot tip of the soldering gun to the cable, and the heated flux will begin to smoke and sizzle as the heat rises. Test the cable with the solder, and as soon as the solder starts to melt, work it up and down the cable end. While the solder is still fluid, wipe it with a damp rag to give it a clean finish.

A word of caution: Solder *just the tip* of the cable. Don't solder anywhere near where the anchor nut holds the cable. Soldering makes the cable very stiff, and the cable must be flexible for the brake to work properly. Also, depending on the nature of your anchor, stiffening the anchor point itself may encourage the anchor to cut through the cable.

CENTERPULL, CANTILEVER, AND U-BRAKES

Centerpull, cantilever, and U-brakes resemble sidepulls in some ways. The method of attaching levers to handlebars is the same, but the way brake cables are connected to the calipers is different. The main cable on a centerpull, cantilever, or U-brake attaches to a metal yoke or "pick-up," which in turn is attached to a short transverse cable, also known as a linking, stirrup, crossover, or straddle cable. The ends of the stirrup cable are attached to the caliper arms. When you squeeze the lever, the main cable lifts the stirrup cable, which then pulls the caliper arms and brake pads against the rim.

The body of a centerpull brake is fastened to the bike frame the same way that a sidepull is. A mounting bolt and nut lock it to the frame. Cantilevers, by contrast, do not have one body to which two arms are attached. Instead, each side of the brake is independently attached to the frame. Each half of a cantilever brake is bolted to a braze-on boss that is equipped with a steel spring that pushes the brake shoe away from the rim after the lever is released.

U-brakes are attached to the frame like cantilevers but look like heavy-duty centerpulls. Additionally, in the rear, they are usually attached to the chainstays (near the bottom bracket) instead of to the seatstays.

On a centerpull brake, you'll find a cable stop mounted on a hanger that is suspended above the calipers, usually on the top of the headset or the seat tube, depending on whether it is the front or rear brake. Some hangers are integrated into the stem or are brazed to the seatstays.

The rear U-brake housing stop is located under the down tube. The cable housing will end at the stop, while the brake cable will continue to the stirrup cable pick-up. Rear U-brake cables run through a guide under the bottom bracket and then to the stirrup.

For all three types of brakes, if the hanger has a quick-release, be sure it is closed before adjusting the cable length. The stirrup cable pick-up will have an anchor with a hole in it. Thread the cable through the bolt. Once the brake cable is threaded through the bolt and the stirrup cable is in place in the channel provided for it on the yoke or pick-up, pull the cable taut and tighten the nut on the cable anchor bolt.

Hold the brake pads against the wheel rim with a third-hand tool or some other means while finishing this cable attachment. As with sidepull brakes, adjust the cable length so that there is ⅛ to 3/16 inch of clearance between each brake shoe and the rim when the levers are released. After you initially tighten the anchor bolt on the cable, squeeze the levers several times to stretch the cable and seat the housing. If necessary, take up the slack at the anchor. Once you've accommodated the initial cable stretch and have anchored the cable in a position where it should remain for a while, trim away the excess cable. Leave only an inch or two sticking through so the loose end of the cable will not foul up the operation of the calipers. Protect the cut cable end from fraying by installing a cable cap or by coating it with solder, as described earlier.

DIRECT-PULL CANTILEVERS

The first factor in setting up direct-pull cantilever brakes is making sure that you have the right parts. Direct-pulls won't work with just any brake lever. If you combine a direct-pull canti with a brake lever that is designed for conventional brakes, you won't get proper performance. Usually, it's best to purchase the brakes and levers as a set. In some instances, however, this may not be possible. One example is using direct-pulls on a tandem with drop handlebar brake levers. These levers are certainly not designed to be used with direct-pulls. Fortunately, there's a good solution now because a few companies offer adapters that fit on the cable or lever and adapt the pull of the lever to work with direct-pulls.

Once you're sure that the levers are compatible,

direct-pull canti adjustment is pretty easy. The arms should be close to parallel in the final setup. To achieve this with different rim widths, each brake pad usually has a thick and thin washer. Place the appropriate washers for your rims between the pads and arms (keep one inside and one outside). Tighten the pads so that they strike the rim squarely and flat (it's not necessary to toe-in pads on direct-pull brakes). One way to make pad adjustment easy is to release the spring on the side that you're working on. This will hold the pad against the rim, making it easy to find the best position and tighten the pad. Then adjust the cable at the anchor bolt until the arms are close to parallel, which should provide good clearance and brake function. If you squeeze and release the lever and one side of the brake remains closer to the rim, center the brake by turning the centering Phillips screws on either side. Tightening pulls the pads away, and loosening pushes them closer.

It's possible to set the pads slightly wide on direct-pulls because the stopping power is so great. Because you have more mechanical advantage in your hands as the levers get closer to the bar, experiment with this setting. It's a favorite of racers who also want to ensure that the pads don't rub the rims.

ROLLERCAM BRAKES

Rollercam brakes are somewhat similar to cantilevers and U-brakes but are much more difficult to adjust. If you have trouble adjusting rollercams, have the job done by a professional mechanic.

It's important to grease the frame posts that the rollercam arms attach to. Do not get grease in the threads of the posts—this will cause the brake-mounting bolts to loosen. While the brakes are off the posts, grease the springs and spring caps.

Mount the brake arms by threading the bolts into the posts, but do not tighten them or add tension to the brake springs yet. At this point, you should be able to easily pivot the arms on the posts toward and away from the rim.

Check the rollers (also called pulleys) at the tops of the arms. Each should spin freely. If one is tight, loosen it so that it turns. Lubricate both.

Rollercam brakes come with a triangular cam instead of a cable stirrup. Place the cam between the two rollers at the top of the arms (don't install the cable yet). Squeeze the arms against the cam. The rollers should automatically move to the deepest point of the cam. The cable will be attached to the cam in this position. Adjust your brake shoes so they are ⅛ to 3⁄16 inch away from the rim with the cam held between the rollers. It may help to wrap an elastic band around the top of the brake arms to keep the rollers in the "sweet spot" of the cam. Be sure to toe-in the shoes slightly. (You want the front of the brake shoe to hit the rim before the back.) Rollercams are very powerful brakes, so be sure to fasten the brake shoes tightly once you find the right position. Otherwise, they may change position when the brakes are applied.

It's easier to attach the cable to the cam if you remove the cam from the rollers first. With the cam free, attach the cable and tighten the anchor bolt enough that the cam won't slide on the cable. Put the cam between the rollers again, and pull the cable while you lift the cam. This should be easy because there is no tension on the brake springs yet. Tighten the cam on the cable in this position.

To finish the adjustment, add spring tension to the brake arms. Use a wrench to turn the spring holder, and lock it in place by tightening the pivot bolt with an Allen wrench. You need to put the right amount of tension on the arms to make them release and center properly. If one side has too much tension, its brake shoe will drag on the rim. Tighten one side at a time, and check progress by repeatedly applying the brake. It may take several attempts to achieve the correct tension.

The last step is to test the cable anchor. Squeeze the brake lever hard to ensure that the cable won't slip when you brake hard out on a ride, and to stretch the cable. If the anchor slips or the cable stretches excessively, loosen the anchor bolt and readjust cable tension.

If you've carefully followed the adjustment procedure and the end result is less than satisfactory, you may have a frame problem. If the frame posts are not exactly parallel, the brake arms will not line up with each other, the two pulleys will be misaligned, and the cam won't move freely when you operate the brake. If the post(s) has been brazed to the frame in the wrong position, your only options are to experiment with the adjustment to try to improve it, or have the post moved by a frame builder.

(The frame will need to be repainted at the point of repair.) If the posts are bent, however, it is possible, though difficult, to fix them.

To bend slightly crooked posts, place the jaws of an 8-inch adjustable wrench tightly over the post and bend it slowly and gently. Check your progress by installing the brake arms and observing the new position. When done, the two pulleys should be aligned.

BRAKE CENTERING

Before beginning the brake-centering process, spin the wheel to see if it's true, that it's centered, and that it's fully inserted in the frame/fork. If it's not, true the wheel or center it before proceeding. Otherwise, either the wheel will end up dragging on the brake pads, or the adjustment will have to be on the loose side and may result in a pulsating or jerky braking action. If you have as much as ¼ inch of clearance between either brake pad and the rim at any point during the revolution of the wheel, and contact between rim and pad at any other point, your wheel definitely needs truing.

Once the wheel is running true, it's time to check the distance of the brake pads from the rim. The clearance should be equal on both sides. To check whether sidepull calipers are centered, loosen the rear mounting nut just enough to allow the calipers to move from side to side, but not so much that the calipers become floppy. Squeeze the brake lever to bring the shoes into firm contact with the rim. Keeping the pressure on, snug up the mounting nut enough to keep the calipers from pivoting on the fork crown or brake bridge.

Release the lever and check to see if the calipers are, in fact, centered. If the arms don't contact the rim evenly or one brake shoe leans against the rim after you release the brake lever, you'll have to align the calipers. How this is done depends on the type of brakes.

There are several ways to center a sidepull. First, try loosening the mounting bolt, twisting the caliper, and retightening the mounting nut. That should do it for Shimano and Campagnolo dual-pivot designs. If they need a little fine-tuning to get the centering perfect, there are centering Allen screws for this purpose on the top of the Shimano brake and on the sides of the Campy. These should

be used for minor adjustments only; make major ones by repositioning the caliper as we described.

Lesser-quality sidepulls don't have centering screws. If yours is off-center and repositioning it doesn't do the trick, try using the two nuts that hold the caliper arms on the front of the brake. First, lock the two nuts tightly together by turning the inner one counterclockwise and the outer one clockwise. Move one wrench to the rear mounting nut, leaving the other at the front. Twist both wrenches in the same direction to rotate the brake body.

If you need to rotate the brake body in a clockwise direction to center the calipers, keep your wrench on the outer of the two front nuts. If you need to rotate the brake body counterclockwise, keep your wrench on the inner of the two. This way you will not loosen these nuts in relation to each other while making the adjustment.

Some sidepull brakes have a nut with centering flats located behind the calipers, between the calipers and the frame. Placing a cone wrench on this nut allows you to turn the brake to the right or the left and hold it there until you have tightened the nut on the end of the mounting bolt. Once it's tight, hold the wrenches on these two nuts and turn them together to rock the brake body into the desired position.

Centering a centerpull brake is similar, though simpler, than centering a sidepull because there is only one place to put your wrench. Loosen the nut that is found on the tail end of the mounting bolt, twist the body of the calipers (the part the caliper arms attach to) until it is centered, then hold it there while you retighten the nut. (In a pinch, gently tap on one side of the brake with a mallet to center the brake.)

The pads on a cantilever brake should be set equidistant from the rim for even braking action. If the arms do not move against the rim at the same rate, slide the cable pick-up along the stirrup toward the brake pad that is slowest to reach the rim. Squeeze and release the brake lever a few times to see if the pads stay centered. If not, disconnect the stirrup cable from one side of the brake, and add spring tension to the arm that's sticking. To do this, rotate the brake away from the rim. The brake will rotate freely up to a point and then resist. Turn the brake another quarter-turn past this point. This unwinds the spring and increases spring tension. You may have to rotate the brake against the spring several times to add enough tension.

Many brakes have provisions for unequal spring tension. Look for multiple spring holes on the frame posts. If there are several holes, you can adjust spring tension by removing the brake and moving the spring tab to another hole.

Another nifty feature found on direct-pulls, U-brakes, and cantilevers is tension-setting screws (centering screws). Some brakes have screws on both sides, while others use them on only one side. The screws may be Phillips types (direct-pulls) or a single Allen turned with a tiny Allen wrench (U-brakes). Turning a screw clockwise increases spring tension and moves the shoe away from the rim. Turning it counterclockwise reduces tension and effectively moves the other pad away from the rim.

If a U-brake is too far off center, the screw adjustment may not suffice. To make larger changes, release the stirrup cable and loosen the pivot bolt of the weak arm. Rotate the arm (the brake pad end) away from the rim, and retighten the bolt. This resets the spring tension. The farther you move the brake shoe away from the rim, the greater the spring tension will be. Some cantilevers are adjusted this way, too.

One last point about brake centering: A sticking brake pad can make you think the brake is not centered, when the brake pad is actually the culprit. When the brake pad is positioned wrong, it wears unevenly. The part of the pad that strikes the rim wears down, but a thin lip develops at the edge of the pad that is not hitting the rim. When this lip catches on the rim when the brake is applied, it causes one side of the brake to stick. To fix this problem, cut off the lip with a sharp knife, and sand the pad so it's the same depth throughout. Readjust the pad so it strikes the rim properly.

Once your brakes are centered, check the cable slack a final time. If the brake pads are within ⅛ inch of the rim, leave the initial adjustment. If not, loosen the cable, take up more of the slack, then reanchor the cable. Use the cable adjusting barrel to fine-tune the brake so that the pads end up being between ⅛ and ³⁄₃₂ inch from the wheel rim.

As you use the brakes, you will discover some gradual stretching of the cable. Take this up with the adjusting barrel. If the stretch becomes so great that you use up all the fine-tuning that is available

through the cable adjusting barrel, simply screw the barrel down as you did when you installed the cable, hold the calipers against the rim, and take up the slack at the cable anchor.

SOLUTIONS TO COMMON PROBLEMS

A common problem with new brake installations or newly installed brake pads is the nerve-wracking squeal caused by pad misalignment. If brake pads hit rims perfectly flat or with the rearmost edge first, they can vibrate and squeal. There are several ways to fix this, and most involve changing the way the brake pads meet the rim. With the exception of direct-pull cantilever brakes, brakes should be adjusted so that the leading (front) edge of the brake pad hits slightly before the trailing edge. This adjustment is called toe-in.

On sidepull brakes, the pads either include a holder that allows for angling the pads, or the pads are toed-in by gently bending the brake arms. To do this, remove the brake shoes and use two adjustable wrenches simultaneously. Put one on the flat surface of each arm and gently bend. When you reattach the brake shoes, you'll notice that they are now positioned differently. The gap shouldn't be too large at the rear of the brake shoe—³⁄₁₆ inch is about right. If you bent the arms too far, remove the shoes and reverse the toe-in procedure.

Most cantilevers, U-brakes, and rollercams have special spacers on the pad holder that allow you to make pad angle adjustments. You can toe-in the pads by loosening their mounting nuts and moving the pad or shaped spacers by hand. When the pad is in the correct position, tighten the nut.

If you reposition the brake pads and your bike still squeals, try sanding the rims with medium emery cloth. They can develop a glaze that creates excess friction when the brake pads hit them.

Hardened brake pads can also cause squealing. This occurs with age. Try scratching the rubber with your fingernail. It should be resilient, not hard. If it doesn't give, replace the pads.

One common problem on mountain bikes today is direct-pull brakes that squeal no matter what you do. If you run into this, try installing a brake booster. This aluminum or carbon horseshoe-shaped device attaches to the bolts that hold the direct-pull brakes on the frame. The booster acts as a brace, tying together the sides of the frame, and preventing the flex and vibration that causes the squealing.

The booster also adds braking power because it prevents the seat stays from flexing outward when the brake is applied. Although it may be unsightly, you'll probably grow to appreciate having it.

Cables also may suffer the ravages of the elements. Covered cables and those coated with a protective layer of Teflon fare pretty well, but exposed sections of cable need special care and protection. Periodically, wipe the cables clean with a rag, then coat them with a thin layer of oil or grease. On any bike with split housing stops, pop the housings out of the stops after creating some cable slack. To get the slack, open the brake quick-releases, and pull the housing out of the stops. Then slide the housing down and lube the cable. This is an easy, quick way to clean and oil the brake cables, which will keep them operating smoothly and make them last longer.

Depending on how often you ride and the conditions that you ride in, you may choose to replace the cables at least once a year. If you have supercables or don't ride much, it isn't necessary. If you ride your bike a lot over demanding terrain, though, it's a smart thing to do because it will ensure that you will always have cables in reliable condition.

Because brakes slow a bike through the friction that's created between the brake pads and wheel rim, don't go crazy lubing the calipers. Use a spray or drip lube, applying it on the pivot points—the mounting bolt shank, the mating surfaces of the caliper arms (if there are any), and the return spring anchor points. Then wipe off the excess.

REGULAR MAINTENANCE PROCEDURES

To keep the brake system working at optimum level, get into the habit of cleaning the system after each ride. Wipe down the rims with a damp rag (or alcohol if there are rubber deposits on the rims) to keep the brake surface clean. A good once-over with a clean rag will remove surface dirt from the calipers. After completing these wipe-downs, use a clean medium-bristle paintbrush to remove the dirt from the cracks and crevices that are too small to get into

with a rag or your fingers. If it was a particularly dirty ride, wash the brake system with brushes, rags, liquid detergent, and warm water. Use a minimal amount of lubricant because too much lube causes dirt to stick to the calipers.

Finally, open the quick-releases and inspect the brake pads for anything that may be imbedded in the soft material. If you spot anything, carefully pick it out with a small screwdriver, being careful not to slip and damage the tire or rim.

HOW TO COPE WITH BRAKE BREAKDOWNS

Regardless of how much care you take, the law of averages says that one day your brakes may fail. The most common and devastating occurrence on a ride, short of a broken lever or caliper, is when one of your cables snaps. For that reason, we recommend that when you go out on multiday rides, you carry a spare brake cable along with a spare derailleur cable.

What if you're caught without a spare cable? You may have to ride temporarily with only one brake. In such a circumstance, your first inclination may be to favor the rear brake. However, the front brake on a bicycle is actually more valuable than the rear brake. When both brakes are applied, the front brake does 65 to 70 percent of the work. Therefore, if the cable breaks on the front caliper, remove the cable from the rear brake and install it on the front. This will give you maximum braking power, under the circumstances, until you get to someplace you can replace both cables. Keep in mind that the use of just the front brake will tend to pitch you forward more than the use of both brakes, so control your speed so that it won't override your braking capabilities. If you must brake rather quickly, slide your body as far back on the saddle as possible to compensate for the tendency of your bike to pitch you headfirst over the handlebar.

The brake system is extremely important and should be treated with care and respect. When other parts stop working, it usually means some inconvenience—the bike goes slower or makes noise. If your brakes stop working, it may mean you'll go careening into the next intersection and become a hood ornament. Don't play games with your brakes. Keep them in top shape all the time.

TROUBLESHOOTING DISC BRAKES

PROBLEM: The pads constantly rub on the discs.

SOLUTION: For a constant rubbing of the disc on one brake pad, there are two possible solutions. Check the disc where it enters and exits the casting of the caliper. If the caliper body is centered over the disc, then you have a sticky piston. Remove the wheel and brake pads. Hold a broad, flat tool like a bladed screwdriver between the pistons, and give the brake lever a few pumps to expose about $\frac{3}{16}$ inch of both pistons. This allows oil from inside the caliper to lubricate the O-rings. Spray the exposed parts of the pistons with rubbing alcohol to clean them and let them dry. Use the screwdriver to carefully push the pistons back into the caliper. Do not notch the pistons—especially on their sides—use firm, even pressure and don't pry or twist.

If the caliper body is not centered over the disc or if the technique described above didn't cure the problem, you'll need to repeat the alignment steps detailed in this chapter.

If your rubbing is an intermittent tick, your disc may be bent. Though it's nearly impossible to get a bent disc perfectly straight again, you can get it pretty close with a few common items. Remove the caliper (and adapter, if one is used) from the frame or fork. Zip a plastic cable-tie around the fork leg or stay, and snip it short. Now you have a makeshift caliper to gauge where the disc is bent. Slide it into place so there is a small gap between the end of the tie and the disc, and slowly turn the wheel. Using an adjustable wrench, gently bend the disc wherever it deviates from true. The process is time-consuming and tedious, but it saves the cost of replacing an expensive brake disc.

PROBLEM: Your brakes honk.

SOLUTION: Some disc brakes just make noise and it can't be avoided; it's the unfortunate truth. There are a few things you can do to mitigate the annoyance.

Remove your brake pads, and lightly scuff them on a piece of sandpaper laid out on a flat surface. You don't need to really dig into the pads; just a few light strokes will remove glaze from the pads' surface.

Experiment with different types of brake pads.

Different brake pad compounds and even different manufacturers' interpretations of the same compound can make a big difference in how much vibration is created. Be aware that different pads will also perform differently. Weigh the costs and benefits of ideal performance and low noise when making your final decision.

Try a self-cleaning "wave" disc. A wave-shaped disc like those developed by Galfer will gently scrape the brake pads clean with each pass. Some also speculate that the wave shape pumps cool air through the pads, keeping the system from overheating during prolonged braking.

PROBLEM: The brake line is kinked.

SOLUTION: There's no quick fix for a kinked brake line, but it shouldn't be left unattended. A kink in the line can restrict the flow of fluid to the caliper, or worse, can develop into a leak. Get this fixed immediately. If the kink is near the fitting at either end and there is sufficient extra hose to do so, it's possible to trim off the kink and reconnect the line. This will require some new fittings and a brake bleed. If the kink is farther down the line or the hose is too short to trim, replace the whole line.

PROBLEM: The brakes feel vague or mushy.

SOLUTION: If the brake lever pulls all or most of the way back to the grip, there are a few possible causes.

Check your brake pads. If they're worn down to less than 0.5 mm thick at any point, it's time to replace them. With new pads in place, the slave pistons will be pushed back into their cylinders, returning fluid to the master and renewing brake feel.

Top off the reservoir. If your brakes have an external reservoir like those used by Shimano, Magura, Hope, and others, remove the cap and add fluid to the reservoir without performing a full bleed. Wrap a clean rag around the lever body, leaving the cap exposed so it can be removed. With the cap off, fill the reservoir about halfway. Give the brake lever a few slow, steady pumps to evacuate any air and draw fluid down into the system. Lightly tap the lever body to help air escape. When there's no more evidence of air, top off the reservoir and replace the cap.

TROUBLESHOOTING RIM BRAKES

PROBLEM: When you squeeze the brakes, a pad drags on the rim or stays closer than the other pad.

SOLUTION: Check that the wheel is properly centered in the frame. Check that the wheel is true. Does the brake still stick? Center the brake. Still sticking? Check the pads. If they're worn unevenly, they may be catching on the rim. If so, carve or sand the pads flat.

PROBLEM: The brakes squeak.

SOLUTION: Make sure the pads are aligned correctly and angle them so that when the brake is applied, the front tips touch before the backs (this is called toeing-in the pads). Still squeak? Try sanding the rims with medium emery cloth to remove buildup and roughen the surface. Still squeak? On mountain bikes, it's often possible to add a brake booster, which may stop the squeak. This device attaches to the brake posts, tying them together.

PROBLEM: The brake feels mushy, and the levers must be squeezed too far.

SOLUTION: Check the pads for wear, and replace them if necessary. Make sure that the cable anchor bolt is tight—the cable may have stretched. Tighten the adjustment by turning the brake adjustment barrel on the lever or caliper counterclockwise.

PROBLEM: The brake is binding. You squeeze the lever, but the brake doesn't feel right. It's harder to pull the lever, and the brake doesn't snap back after you use it.

SOLUTION: Inspect the cables (be sure to look inside the levers at the head of the cable) and housing sections (look for cracking and rust), and replace them if they're worn. If the cables are okay, try lubricating them with oil or grease. Also lubricate the pivot points on the brake.

PROBLEM: The bike is braking poorly.

SOLUTION: Check for oil on the rims and pads. Inspect the pads for wear and replace them. Replace pads that are old, as they can harden with age and stop gripping the rim. Make sure the cables are in excellent shape; replace them if needed.

PROBLEM: You brake and get a grabby, jerky feel from the bike as it slows down.

SOLUTION: You may have a ding or dent in your rim. This will hit the brake on each revolution of the wheel, causing an unnerving jerky sensation. Remove the dent and get the rim as straight as possible. Replace the rim if it can't be fixed.

PROBLEM: The brake feels too tight. Squeezing and releasing the lever barely moves the brake.

SOLUTION: The cable adjustment is too tight. Look for a housing section that's twisted somehow or a housing end that's not seated in its frame stop. Housing okay? Try loosening the adjustment barrel at the lever or caliper (turn clockwise). Make sure there's at least ⅛ inch clearance between the pads and rims, more on cantilever and direct-pull brakes.

PROBLEM: You installed cantilevers and now one is tight on its post and it won't pivot freely.

SOLUTION: You may have overtightened the bolt, which bulges the frame post it's screwed into, causing binding. Remove the bolt and brake arm, and sand the post until the brake fits on easily again. Don't overtighten the bolt.

PROBLEM: You've removed the cable for maintenance and discovered that the brake action is jammed. It seems stiff and barely moves when you try to squeeze it by hand.

SOLUTION: Corrosion has seized the brake. Dismantle it and sand the corrosion from the brake and brake mount(s) with sandpaper. Then lubricate all moving parts (keep lube away from the pads) and reassemble.

PROBLEM: You crashed and bent the brake or lever.

SOLUTION: If you can still ride, pedal home. If the part is seriously bent, replace it—it will break when you try to straighten it, or worse, when you're riding sometime in the future. If it's a minor bend, you may be able to carefully straighten the part by hand or with a pair of pliers.

PROBLEM: One cantilever brake pad sticks to the rim.

SOLUTION: If there is a triangular cable carrier at the end of the main brake cable, try pushing it sideways on the transverse cable. When the carrier is out of position, it can cause one pad to hug the rim.

PROBLEM: You crashed and broke the cantilever brake. Now one side isn't attached to the frame.

SOLUTION: Usually this can be repaired with a cantilever repair kit, which includes everything needed to repair the frame post and reattach the cantilever. Shops may carry these kits, or contact Loose Screws.

PROBLEM: On long descents, you hear a disconcerting grating sound when braking steadily. It sounds like metal on metal, and the braking action is poor.

SOLUTION: Check the pads. They may have worn out. You might also have bad pads (even some new pads are inferior); replace them. The pads may have gotten contaminated by aluminum from the rim or have road grit embedded in their surface. Pick out the debris with an awl or replace the pads.

PROBLEM: Turning the handlebar sideways causes the rear brake to grab the rim.

SOLUTION: The cable housing may be too short, or it may have gotten twisted somehow. Fix the housing so that you can turn the handlebar as needed without causing the brake to be applied.

Nonaero Lever Replacement

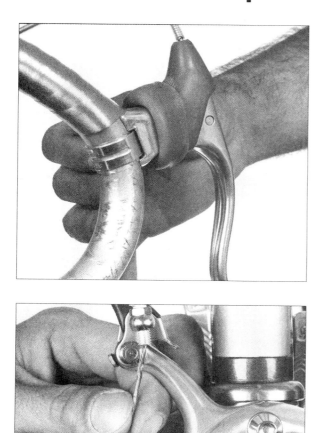

1 It is unlikely that a pair of brake levers will wear out or break, but there may be occasions when you'll need to remove them. Perhaps you wish to keep your old set of brakes, but you want to replace the handlebar and have to remove the levers for that reason. Or you may decide to upgrade your old bicycle by fitting it with a whole new set of brakes. New levers will be part of the package, so the old levers will need to be removed.

On a typical drop-handlebar bike, the levers cannot be removed or relocated without the handlebar tape first being unwound from the lever clamp (see photo). You may as well completely remove the old handlebar tape at this time and replace it with new tape after the levers are back in place.

2 To completely remove a lever, first release the cable that is attached to it. Loosen the small bolt that anchors the cable to the brake calipers and pull the cable free.

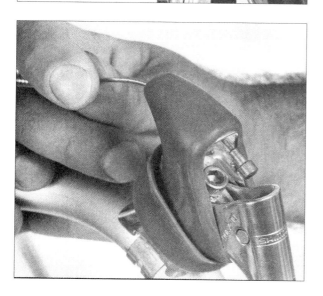

3 Unhook the fitting on the upper end of the cable from its seat in the lever (see photo). Pull the cable all the way out of the lever body and cable housing.

If you wish only to relocate a lever on the handlebar rather than remove it, you may be able to leave the cable inside the lever body. Unhook it from the lever, and pull it out of the way while you loosen the clamp.

4 When you're ready to loosen the lever clamp, squeeze the lever against the handlebar and look inside the lever body. You'll see a bolt or screw that's used to fasten the clamp to the bar. Find the appropriate tool to remove this fastener (see photo). You'll probably need a flathead screwdriver, an Allen wrench, or a thin-walled socket.

Loosen the lever clamp bolt enough to allow you to reposition the lever or to slide it around the bend and off the end of the bar. If you like, when both levers are off, clean the bar of any residue left behind by the old tape.

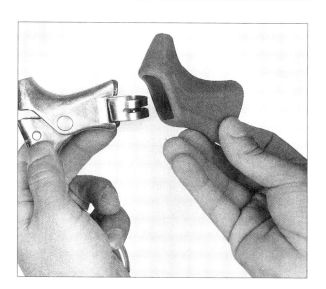

5 Many brake sets come with rubber hood covers that fit around the lever bodies. These covers increase the comfort of riding with the hands resting on the lever hoods. If you are reusing a set of levers that lack these covers or if you need new ones, buy a pair and fit them over the levers before sliding the levers on the handlebar.

After putting the levers on the bar, position them both horizontally and vertically. Set the levers in locations that feel comfortable and also allow you to get a good grip for solid braking action. The best location is almost certainly directly in front of the bar, rather than off at an angle.

6 The vertical position for levers is more open to individual preferences. However, a standard used by many experienced cyclists is to set the levers at a height where their tips line up with the lowest part of the bar. A straightedge held beneath the bar will show you exactly where that is (see photo).

When you have the levers where you want them, tighten the clamp bolts. Check to see if the tightened bolts interfere with the lever action. If they do, try loosening them slightly to see if that eliminates the problem. Make certain that the clamps are tight enough to prevent the levers from twisting on the bar when squeezed hard. Once the levers are properly secured, retape the bar, then install and adjust the brake cables.

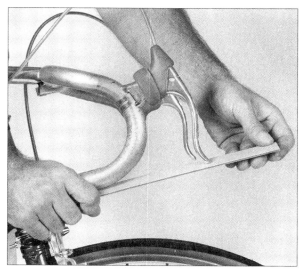

Nonaero Lever Cable Installation

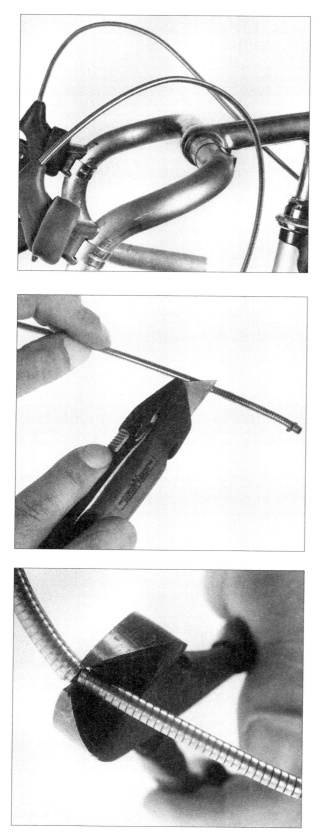

1 Simple as it may appear, replacing a brake cable is a task not to be taken lightly. There are several considerations to be made before the job even begins.

For starters, decide which lever to connect to which brake. The recommended rule in North America is to connect the right lever to the rear brake, and the left to the front. This is typically done because the prescribed method for signaling movements in traffic on a bicycle is with the left hand, as it is more visible to passing traffic. With the left hand off the handlebar, the right controls braking. In a panic situation, grabbing a fistful of front brake could send the rider over the handlebar. Logically, if you live in a place where traffic moves on the left side of the road, like the UK or Japan, brakes will typically be connected left-to-rear and right-to-front. Some riders prefer having their dominant hand in control of the rear brake, which gets the most use. For left-handers, this would mean operating the rear brake with the left lever. Feel free to experiment, but always be cognizant of which brake is connected to which lever.

2 Once you've reached a decision about the lever-to-brake connection, determine how long the cable housing should be. Many new bikes come fitted with excessively long housing, which means large cable loops that can be a nuisance to the rider. Cable that is longer than necessary also creates unneeded friction in the braking system. Ideally, the brake cables should arch as low as possible under the bicycle handlebar.

Avoid going to an extreme when you cut back on the length of brake cable housing. If you make the housing too short, it will bend sharply and kink the cable. Short housing can also obstruct the proper movement of the handlebar. Pick a length that will allow your handlebars to move from side to side through its full range of motion without creating cable kinks. Trim the housing to that length.

Mark the position on the housing where you wish to trim it, and cut through the vinyl covering with a sharp knife.

3 Use a sharp pair of cable cutters (or diagonal cutters) and work one jaw between coils so that you can make a clean cut through a coil without smashing the housing.

4 After trimming the housing, file the cut end smooth to prevent the possibility of it snagging and damaging the cable (see photo). Use an awl to reopen the plastic liner inside the housing.

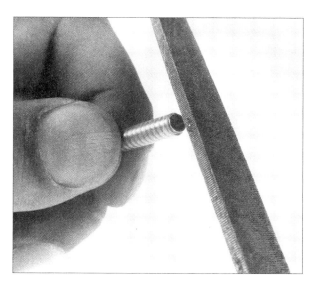

5 Get out one of your new cables. Unless these cables were made specifically for your brake system, they may be universal cables, which have a different fitting attached to each end. Determine which fitting you need by looking inside the lever at the rotating barrel into which it must fit. Trim away the fitting that you do not need.

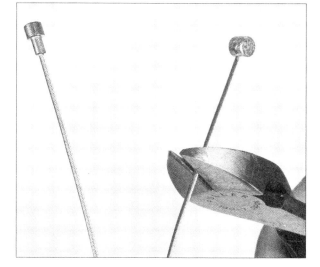

6 Lubricate the cable before running it through the housing. The medium-weight grease you use elsewhere on the bike will work fine, as will some oil. Just put a little on your fingertips and pull the cable through to coat it lightly. Squeeze the lever open, and thread the cable through the lever body and into the cable housing.

Push the cable on through the housing, but do not fasten it to the brake yet. Leave yourself some slack at the upper end so you can hook the cable fitting onto the lever. Rotate the cylinder as needed, and tug on the loose end of the cable to make sure the fitting is properly seated in the lever (see photo).

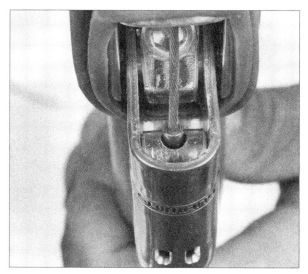

Nonaero Lever Cable Installation *continued*

7 Thread the loose end of the cable through the housing stop, and pull on it to seat the housing against the stop (in this case, the housing stop is the adjustment barrel on the front brake).

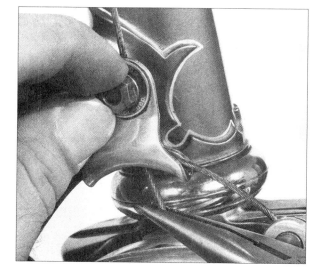

8 If you have sidepull brakes, run the end of the cable through the anchor bolt. If you have centerpull brakes, make sure the fittings at each end of the short stirrup cable are properly seated in the slots provided for them in the upper ends of the caliper arms. Run the end of the main cable through the anchor on the yoke used to lift up the stirrup cable. You may wish to tighten the nut with your finger to prevent the cable from pulling free until you are ready to firmly anchor it.

9 Before you securely anchor the cable, check back over the entire braking system. First, find the cable adjusting barrel. On sidepulls, this barrel may be located either at the lever end or the caliper end of the cable housing. A few systems have adjusting barrels in both places. On centerpulls, the adjusting barrel will probably be on the cable housing hanger.

Thread the barrel all the way down, then back it off a couple of turns (see photo). This will leave you plenty of room to take up slack in the cable as it stretches with later use.

10 If your brake system is equipped with a quick-release lever, make sure it is closed so the calipers can be adjusted to their operating position.

Check again to make certain that the fitting at the upper end of the cable is properly seated in the lever (see photo).

Use a toe strap or a third-hand tool to hold the calipers shut against the rim while you pull up the slack in the cable and anchor it firmly (see photo 11).

11 Release the calipers and squeeze the lever firmly a few times to stretch the new cable. If this immediately produces a good deal of slack in the system, fasten the calipers back against the rim, loosen the anchor bolt, pull the cable tight, and reanchor it.

After prestretching the cable, you should be able to handle some slack by turning the adjusting barrel so that it moves away from the brake calipers, thus tightening the cable.

When you reach the point where there is very little room left for fine-tuning the cable length by means of the adjusting barrel, it usually indicates worn-out brake pads.

12 A new brake cable will almost certainly be longer than necessary. After the installation process is complete, allow an inch or two of cable to extend beyond the anchor bolt and trim away the rest (see photo).

The cut end of a new cable is likely to fray if left unprotected. To prevent fraying, cover it with a little aluminum or plastic cap made for this purpose.

Another possibility is to coat the tip of the cable with solder. To solder the cable end, use alcohol to clean away all grease and dirt. Stick the cable tip into flux, then heat it with a soldering gun. When it starts to sizzle, hold solder against it. As the solder begins to melt, rub it up and down to coat the area, then wipe it smooth with a damp rag.

Mountain Bike Lever and Cable Installation

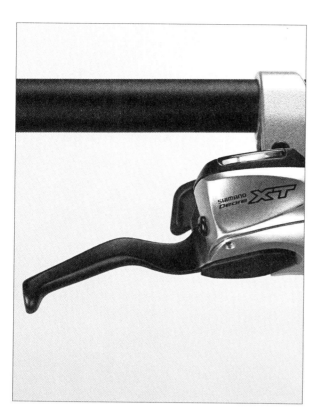

1 Removing and installing mountain bike brake levers means dealing with the handlebar grips. If you're replacing a worn pair of grips, simply cut off the old ones with a utility knife. Be careful: It's easy for the knife to slip when cutting against the round handlebar underneath.

If you want to save the old grips, slide a small screwdriver beneath an edge and drip in a little alcohol. Twist the grip a bit and add a little more alcohol until the grip slides off the bar. Loosen the lever clamping bolt with an Allen wrench and slide the levers off the handlebar.

When installing new levers, consider the order of assembly of the shift levers first. Sometimes the shifter goes on first (thumb levers), sometimes the brake lever does (twist grips). Before tightening the lever, place it so that the end of the lever does not protrude past the end of the bar (see photo). That will ensure that if you crash, the bar will likely hit before the lever, so the lever is less likely to be damaged.

2 Even more important, adjust the lever so that it's in line with the natural bend in your wrist when you sit on the seat and rest your hands on the grips (see photo). You don't want to be squeezing the brake lever with bent wrists. When the lever is positioned correctly for you, tighten the clamping bolt. Install the shifters, if necessary, and the grips. Lubricate them with alcohol if needed. They'll be slippery at first, but the alcohol will evaporate quickly, and the grips will stick.

3 To install the cable in the levers, turn the adjusting barrels to line up the slots inside. Squeeze the lever to find the cable holder, and insert the cable end (grease it first) in the holder (see photo). Place the cable in the slot in the adjusting barrel and brake lever, and turn the adjuster clockwise to keep the cable in place. Now squeeze the lever while pulling on the cable to make sure it works smoothly. If not, look closely to find problems and reinstall the cable if necessary.

When running the cables, copy the old housing path. Usually, the only tricky section is where the rear brake exits the lever. It can pass on either side of the stem. Try it on both sides, and use the position that provides the least amount of resistance when the bar is turned from side to side. Usually, this means that the housing runs around the left side of the stem.

Aero Lever and Cable Installation

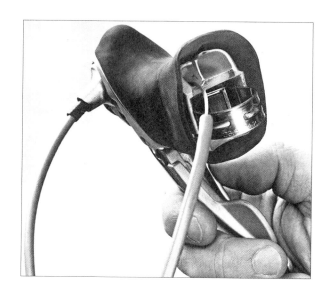

1 When installing aero levers, it's important to seat the housing and ferrule (if there is one) carefully inside the lever. If either is not secure, the cable can bind and reduce the brake's effectiveness. With the brake lever off the handlebar, grease the cable lightly and thread it through the lever, the ferrule, and the housing (see photo). The cable end should be cut cleanly and travel smoothly through the housing. If it does not, recut the cable end with cutters made for the purpose. Make sure the ends of the housing should be free of burrs; recut the ends if necessary.

2 Thread the brake cable through the brake caliper's adjustment barrel and anchor bolt. Use a third-hand tool or toe strap, or squeeze the caliper with your hand and pull on the brake cable until the head of the cable and the housing seat inside the lever. Tighten the anchor bolt (see photo). Remove the third-hand tool so the brake spring tension will hold the housing and ferrule in place inside the lever.

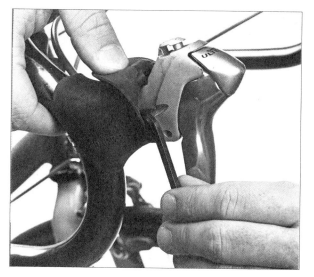

3 Move the housing to the slot for it inside the lever, and wiggle the lever onto the handlebar. To ease lever installation, roll back the rubber hood. Tighten the lever in place (see photo). The most common way to position levers is to hold a straight-edge against the underside of the handlebar and slide the lever so its tip rests on the straightedge. The lever should also face directly forward rather than point off at an angle. Secure the levers by tightening the bolt inside the lever body with an Allen wrench.

4 Aero lever cable housing works best when the rear section travels in front of the stem before returning to the top tube cable stop. This loop will provide enough slack for you to turn the handlebar without binding. The front brake housing should go through this loop to the front brake (see photo). The cable routing should always follow smooth, gradual bends for optimal braking action.

5 Use electrical tape to affix the housing to the underside of the handlebar. Trim excess housing so the brake is as responsive as possible. To do this, loosen the cable anchor bolt to release the brake cable, grasp the head of the cable inside the brake lever with needlenose pliers, and pull the cable out of the housing enough so you can cut off a section (see photo). Again, make sure there are no burrs on the end of the housing. Use cable cutters or a file to fix this if necessary. Be careful not to cut off too much housing, which would cause the brakes or handlebar to bind.

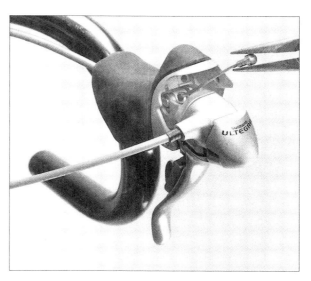

6 Push the cable back through the housing and the brake anchor bolt. Use the third-hand tool to compress the brake caliper and pull on the end of the cable while you tighten the anchor bolt. Wrap the bar with handlebar tape. It's easier to wrap it around the brake levers if you roll the rubber hoods back.

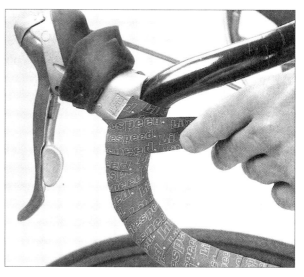

Sidepull Installation

1 To remove the caliper of a sidepull brake, loosen the cable anchor bolt and free the end of the cable. Loosen and remove the nut on the rear end of the mounting bolt that runs through the brake body.

Thread the nut off the end of the bolt, then pull the brake body away from the frame (see photo 2). If you have removed the brake to service it rather than replace it, clean it thoroughly. Use a rag dipped in solvent and a brush to loosen the grease and dirt that's on the surface of the calipers and hiding inside all nooks and crannies.

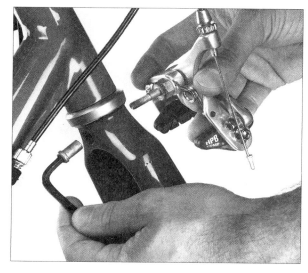

2 Unless you're using something mild like alcohol, keep the solvent away from the rubber brake pads. Better yet, remove the brake shoes to clean the pads separately.

Since oil and grease have a tendency to attract dirt, use them only where needed. On sidepull brakes, that means only at the pivot points and the spring anchors on the back of the calipers.

To minimize the possibility of getting lubricant on your brake pads, use grease rather than oil on the spring where it rubs against its anchors. Because it is difficult to work grease into the pivot area without dismantling the brake, spray those points with a small amount of lubricant containing Teflon.

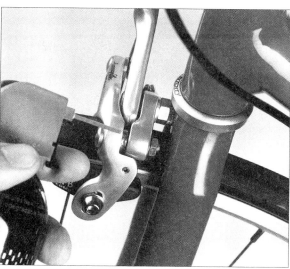

3 To install a brake, insert the mounting bolt through the hole in the frame and thread on the mounting nut. Tighten the nut fairly tight, but leave it loose enough for the brake to be centered over the wheel by hand. Reconnect the brake cable to the brake calipers and adjust the cable length by following the instructions starting on page 255. Check the caliper alignment.

Before you can properly align the calipers, ensure that the wheel is true and centered in the frame. If the wheel is out of true, no amount of brake adjustment will give you good performance.

Before attempting to center the brakes, check the relationship of the caliper arms to each other. If they're too tight, they will not spring back after you release the lever.

4 If the caliper arms are too loose, they will vibrate excessively when you press them against the rim of the moving wheel. They should be as tight as they can be and still operate freely.

The tightness of lesser-quality calipers is controlled by a nut or pair of nuts on the front end of the mounting bolt. Because this part of the bolt functions as the pivot for the calipers, it is often referred to as the pivot bolt. If there are two nuts, the outer nut must be loosened and the pressure on the calipers must be adjusted with the inner one. Stop tightening the inner nut just before the calipers start to show resistance to pivoting, then lock the two nuts against one another to maintain the adjustment (see photo).

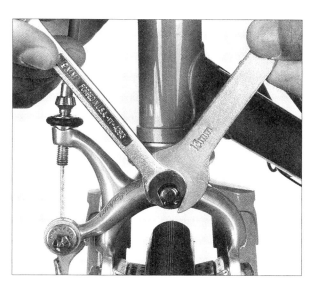

5 If your brakes have only a single nut or bolt head in front, turn that to adjust the caliper tension.

Rotate the brake to center the pads. Hold the brake in that position while you snug up the mounting nut (see photo).

Squeeze the brake lever a few times to see if the brake pads are striking the rim at the same time and whether the brake remains centered after being used. If the brake needs minor centering and it's a modern dual-pivot model, look for a centering screw on top of or on each side of the caliper. Turning these small Allen screws will move the brake slightly, centering it over the wheel.

6 On older sidepulls, hold the brake steady again while you snug up the mounting nut a bit more. Then turn both wrenches together to rock the entire brake body in the direction needed to center it.

Basics of Disc Brake Maintenance

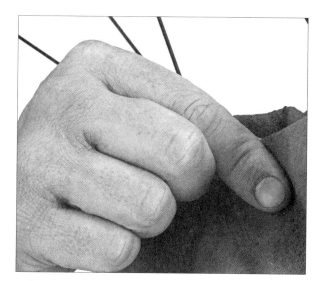

1 Disc brakes work best when tiny particles of brake pad material are embedded in the surface of the disc, so in general it's best to not clean the discs too often. Keep in mind that disc brake pads are extremely sensitive to oil contamination: Even trace amounts of oil from your fingertips can be enough to affect your brakes performance.

The best solution is to simply not touch the discs and prevent oil splatter from reaching them. But this is not a perfect world. To clean your discs in the event of possible contamination, use a solvent that specifically states on the label that it is safe for cleaning brake discs. Suitable products include Wrench Force Metal Prep, White Lightning Clean Streak, and Disc Doctor, among others. In the absence of these products, plain old rubbing alcohol that you can buy at any pharmacy works great. Soak a corner of a clean rag with your chosen solvent and wipe the entire disc. Then, with a clean, dry corner of the rag, wipe the disc again.

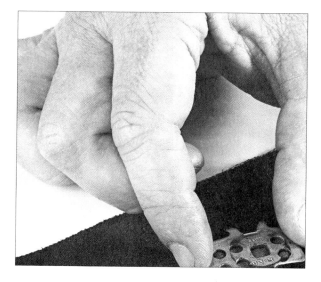

2 If oil gets on your disc brake pads, you may be able to salvage them by rubbing them lightly across a piece of sandpaper or emery cloth laid out on a flat surface. If the pads have gotten soaked with oil or if heat is applied after the pads became contaminated (such as applying the brakes while riding), you'll likely have to replace them.

3 Proper alignment of disc brake calipers is critical to their performance. If standard aligning techniques still leave your brakes feeling vague and mushy, you may need to have your brake bosses milled.

Milling is the process of shaving material from the disc brake tabs on your frame to make their mounting surfaces perfectly parallel to the brake disc. The tools to perform this task are expensive for how infrequently a home mechanic might use them, so it's advisable to leave this job to your local bike shop.

4 A kinked hydraulic line is more than an eyesore. The inner lining can also be compromised, making a brake failure likely.

If the line is kinked near a fitting and there is sufficient extra line to do so, trim away the affected portion of the line and bleed the system. If the kink is too far from a fitting to do this, there is no choice but to replace the line.

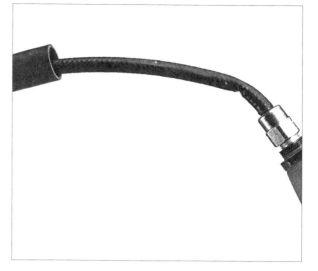

5 Exposure to rocks and logs means that brake discs will get bent. It's just the way it is. If yours is tweaked, all is not lost. Remove the caliper, zip a plastic cable tie around the fork leg or seatstay, and snip the end short to create a makeshift truing caliper.

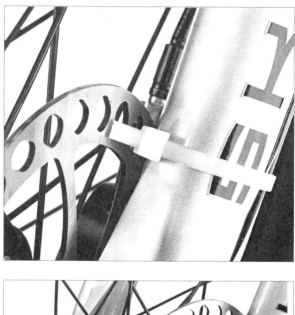

6 With your caliper in place, you can now gauge where and how far the disc is bent. Use a set of Morningstar disc truing tools or an adjustable wrench to straighten the disc. It may never be perfect again, but it can be made passable.

Mechanical (Cable-Actuated) Disc Brake
Installation and Setup (Avid and Similar)

1 Avid disc brake calipers are mounted using a set of hemispherical washers. This ingenious mounting system allows the caliper to be aligned in all directions, compensating for inconsistencies in a frame's or a fork's brake mounting tabs.

Avid calipers come out of the box with their adapters already mounted to the caliper. The sequence of the washers is critical to the function of the Tri-Align system, so don't remove the caliper from the adapter unless you have taken note of the proper orientation of the hemispherical washers. Bolt the caliper and adapter into place on the frame or fork. If you're readjusting an existing system, remove the brake cable from the caliper.

Loosen the bolts holding the caliper to the adapter about one turn. The caliper should slide freely from side to side and should rotate freely in the hemispherical washers.

2 Each brake pad has a red dial adjuster. Turning it clockwise moves the pad closer to the disc; counterclockwise moves it away from the disc. Use these adjusting dials to clamp the disc between the pads, roughly in the center of the caliper body.

In small increments—one, then the other—tighten the bolts holding the caliper to the adapter. Watch the caliper closely as you're doing this, making certain that it doesn't try to "walk" side to side from friction with the bolt.

Turn the outside dial adjuster counterclockwise, moving the mobile brake pad as far from the disc as it will go. Turn the inside dial adjuster just a few clicks counterclockwise. Push the caliper's lever arm by hand to ensure that the pad is pushed back, and give the wheel a spin. If there is any rubbing, turn the inside adjuster one click counterclockwise and repeat until there is no more contact. There should be a gap of less than 0.5 mm between the fixed pad and the disc.

Turn the outside dial adjuster clockwise, a few clicks at a time, and push the lever arm by hand until it stops at a point about halfway through its travel to the cable stop.

3 Anchor the cable in place using a 5 mm hex key. Use a fourth hand tool to simultaneously pull the cable and push the caliper's lever arm about one-quarter of the way through its travel. Give the brake lever a few firm squeezes to settle the housing and pads into place, and then repeat your cable adjustment. In your shop, you'll find it's best to make fine adjustments to lever feel at the cable anchor, rather than using the adjusting barrel on the lever. The barrel adjuster is there primarily to quickly adjust for pad wear while out on the road or trail.

4 Cut the free end of the cable no more than 20 mm or ¾ inch from the cable anchor. Too long and the end of the cable could swing into the disc, locking up your wheel and sending you flying. Crimp the cable end to prevent fraying, and you're good to go.

Hydraulic Disc Brake Installation and Setup
(Hayes and Similar)

1 Hayes brake calipers incorporate a two-part system with the caliper mounted to the frame or fork using an adapter. The only two exceptions are Manitou forks, which are designed to allow Hayes calipers to be directly mounted, and mountain bike frames from the mid- to late 1990s that used a Hayes-specific mount on the left chainstay. In either of those cases, the procedures described here still apply, though the adapter is not present.

Use a 5 mm hex key to ensure that the two bolts holding the adapter to the frame's or fork's mounting tabs are tight. Use a 5 mm hex key to loosen the two bolts holding the caliper to the adapter by about ½ turn. The caliper should float freely from side to side. Disengage the hydraulic line from its guide on the chainstay to help the caliper move more freely.

2 Wrap an elastic band over the handlebar and brake lever. This will apply constant pressure to the brake pads, clamping them on the disc. Assuming that both pistons of the caliper are moving an equal distance, the caliper should center itself on the disc.

3 In small increments—one, then the other—
tighten the bolts holding the caliper to the
adapter. Watch the caliper closely as you're doing
this, making certain that it doesn't try to "walk" side
to side from friction with the bolt.

4 Remove the elastic holding the brake lever.
Looking through the caliper from behind, you
should be able to see daylight between both pads
and the disc. Hold a sheet of white paper on the
other side of the caliper to make this easier to see.

Hydraulic Disc Brake Installation and Setup
(Shimano, Hope, Magura, and Similar)

1 Magura, Hope, and Shimano disc brakes, among others, are aligned using very thin washers called shims between the frame's or fork's mounting tabs and the caliper. Shimming a caliper sounds simple enough to do—and it can be if you're patient. Fumbling around with small parts in tight spaces can be frustrating, though, so take a few deep breaths and rest assured that when it's done right, you may well never need to touch it again.

Set the caliper in place by turning the bolts in just 2 or 3 threads. The caliper should be able to float from side to side. Disengage the hydraulic line from its guide on the chainstay to help the caliper move more freely.

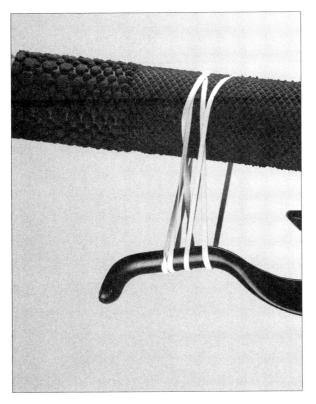

2 Wrap an elastic band over the handlebar and brake lever. This will apply constant pressure to the brake pads, clamping them on the disc. Assuming that both pistons of the caliper are moving an equal distance, the caliper should center itself on the disc.

3 Determine the correct number of shims for each mounting bolt. This is a trial-and-error process, and it is likely that each mounting bolt will require a different number of shims. The correct number is however many will fit snugly between the mounting tabs of the frame/fork and caliper. Magura and Hope supply washers that require the removal and reinstallation of the mounting bolts to be put in place. Shimano supplies their brakes with Y shims that can be installed easily using a pair of needlenose pliers. Tighten the mounting bolts using a 5 mm hex key.

4 Remove the elastic band from the brake lever, and check for brake pad clearance in the caliper. You should be able to see daylight between both brake pads and the disc. Hold a sheet of white paper on the other side of the caliper to make this easier to see.

Centerpull Installation

1 A centerpull brake system makes use of two cables: a long main cable similar to that used in a sidepull system, and a short transverse (also called "linking," "crossover," or "stirrup") cable. The two connect with each other by means of a triangular metal yoke. The main cable is bolted to the yoke, which supports the center of the shorter cable (see photo).

Each end of the stirrup cable hooks onto one of the caliper arms. When you squeeze the lever, the main cable lifts the yoke, pulling up the center of the stirrup cable, and thus pulling the calipers against the wheel rim.

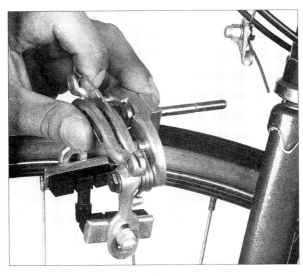

2 To remove a centerpull brake for cleaning or replacement, unhook the yoke from the stirrup cable. Loosen the nut on the rear end of the brake mounting bolt, and remove the brake from the bicycle.

If you intend to reuse the old brake, clean it thoroughly. Use a rag dipped in solvent and a small brush to remove the grease and grime from the caliper arms and the areas where the arms pivot on the mounting bolt. Avoid getting any strong solvent on the brake pads. Clean them with alcohol and, to increase grip, buff the surfaces with fine-grit sandpaper.

3 To mount a centerpull brake, insert its mounting bolt through the hole in the frame, and thread on the mounting nut. Before tightening the nut, center the brake on the wheel, making sure the wheel is true and centered in the fork.

Rock the brake by hand until the pads appear to be equidistant from the sides of the wheel rim (see photo). Tighten the mounting nut on the mounting bolt to hold the brake in that position.

4 Make sure the fittings on the ends of the stirrup cable are properly seated in the slots in the caliper arms (see photo). Hook the yoke under the center of the short cable.

5 Turn the cable adjusting barrel down almost all the way to give yourself room for later fine-tuning. Hold the brake shoes against the wheel with the help of a toe strap or third-hand tool. Pull the end of the main cable taut, and hold it with a pair of pliers while you tighten the anchor nut with a wrench (see photo).

Release the calipers and test the brake by squeezing the lever a few times. If you have installed a new cable, it may stretch enough that you need to take up the slack at the anchor nut. Otherwise, fine-tune the length of the cable with the adjusting barrel. Leave only ⅛ to 3/16 inch of space between each brake pad and the wheel rim.

6 As you squeeze the lever, check to see that the brake pads contact the rim at the same time. If they do not, shift the position of the yoke on the stirrup cable in the direction of the slower arm. If that does not solve the problem, try bending the spring to increase the tension on that arm.

Lightly lubricate the moving parts of the caliper. Work a small dab of grease or some spray lube into the area where contact is made between the two arms and into each arm's pivot points.

Brake Pad Maintenance

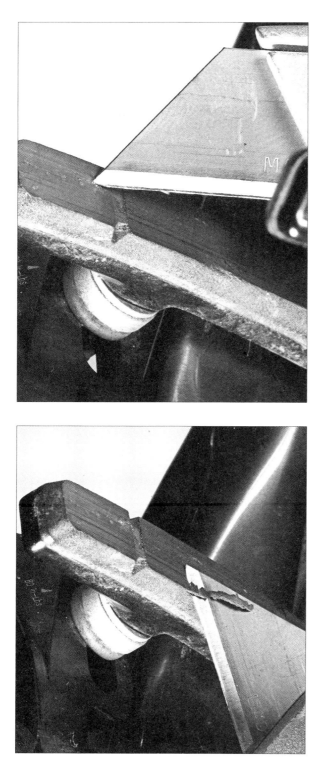

1 The brake pads are small, but they're vital to braking. Keep them close to and lined up right with the rim so they don't hit the tire when you brake (which can cause a flat) or dive into the spokes (which might cause a crash). Bad pad alignment also causes poor braking, as well as squeaking and chattering when braking. As the pads wear and age, they'll stop working properly, so it's important to maintain, inspect, and replace the pads regularly.

Different types of brakes use different pad designs, but they all need the same basic care. Besides keeping them tight and aligned correctly with the rims, it's important to keep them clean. Gravel travels up the rims, and small bits get pressed into the pads during braking. When enough grit gets in there, the pads become terribly abrasive, so that you actually wear out your rims if you keep braking with them. You might think that only mountain bike brake pads get this way, but it will happen to any brake given the right conditions. To keep the pads clean, closely inspect them regularly, and use an awl or sharp tool to pick out any debris stuck in them (see photo). To make it easier to work on the pads, first remove the wheels.

2 Watch for uneven wear, too. Sometimes a pad will develop a lip if it's aligned slightly too low or too high. This may cause the brake to stick when it's applied because the overlapping bit of pad gets stuck beneath the rim. Refurbish the pad by trimming it flat with a utility knife (see photo). If it's a small defect, smooth it away with sandpaper.

Pad wear varies greatly. It's actually possible to wear out a set in a single off-road ride if it's muddy enough! They may last several years on a minimally used road bike, however.

3 Most pads have grooves on them to help gauge wear (see photo). When the grooves begin to disappear, replace the pads. Also replace the pads any time they are worn to the point that the metal pad holders are close to touching the rim—if the holders strike the rims, they'll damage the braking surface. When this happens, you'll lose most of your braking power and hear a gritty scraping sound.

4 There are two basic pad types: one-piece pads that must be unscrewed, and cartridge pads, on which the rubber pieces can be pulled or pried out of their holders so that you can slide in new ones.

The second type makes pad replacement much faster and simpler because popping in new ones doesn't require realigning the holders (repositioning the holders means resetting the alignment to the rim).

If your bike came with nonreplaceable pads, do yourself a favor when they wear out and upgrade to replaceable pads. This is an especially good idea if you ride a mountain bike with direct-pull or regular cantilevers, because these pads can wear incredibly quickly.

To install a new one-piece pad, do one side at a time so you can compare the alignment and the arrangement of the fastening pieces with the other side. Release the spring if you can, which will make alignment easier. Align the new pad so it strikes the rim squarely. On all brakes except direct-pull cantilevers, toe-in the pads very slightly. This means angling the pads so the front ends strike the rim first, which prevents squeaking.

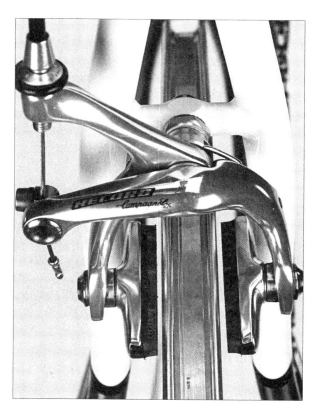

Brake Pad Maintenance *continued*

5 Tighten each pad securely when it's set up right, and move on to the next. If you have a brake on which the pads cannot be angled by adjustment (usually basic sidepulls or centerpulls), upgrade to adjustable pads or achieve toe-in by gently bending the brake arms with an adjustable wrench. Sometimes, to get enough leverage you need to use two adjustable wrenches, one on each arm. Use one to hold the brake steady while you bend with the other.

6 To install a cartridge-style pad, look for a set screw or small press-in pin holding it in place. If there isn't one, pry the old pad out by pressing a thin-blade screwdriver behind it and working the pad free. Then slide in a new pad. If it goes in supertight, press it in with water-pump pliers.

7 If the pad has a retaining screw or pin, remove it, extract the pad, slide the new one in, and reinsert the pin. You may have to press on the end of the pad to get the pin to seat fully. When seated, the tip of the pin should be visible on the bottom of the pad holder.

Cantilever Installation and Adjustment

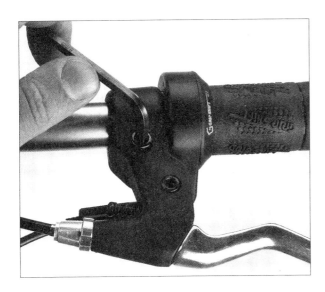

1 Mountain bikes are often equipped with flat handlebars, regular brake levers, and cantilever brakes. Since mountain bike handlebars are not wrapped with tape, brake levers can be relocated or replaced fairly quickly. To reposition a lever, locate and loosen the clamp bolt (see photo). Move the lever to the desired place and retighten the clamp.

2 The cantilever brakes used on mountain bikes, tandem bikes, and most loaded touring bikes are mounted differently than sidepull and conventional centerpull brakes. Each front cantilever is fastened by a bolt to a metal post that is brazed to the front side of one of the fork legs (see photo). Cantilevers on the rear are attached to posts brazed on the back sides of the seatstays.

There are brake pads on cantilevers are slightly different from those on caliper brakes. The posts that extend from the backs of the shoes on cantilevers are fairly long and are used to adjust the distance of the shoes from the rim.

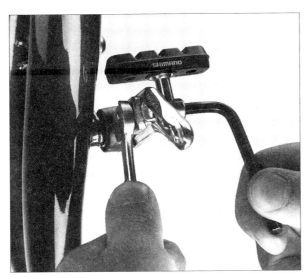

3 When installing a new set of cantilevers or readjusting an old set, make sure that the wheel is true and centered in the frame. Set all the brake pads equidistant from the rim. You'll probably need an Allen wrench for the head of the pad mounting bolt and a combination wrench for the nut at its end (see photo).

There are two factors to take into account in determining the proper setting of the pad. First, the pad should be turned so that it is parallel with the rim. Second, it should be set so it solidly contacts the rim when the arm is pushed toward the wheel. Too high, and it may strike the tire; too low, and it may dive into the spokes.

4 Cantilever brakes, like centerpull calipers, make use of a short cable—known as the linking, transverse, stirrup, or straddle cable—to connect the two braking arms. This cable may have a permanent fitting on only one end. If so, the other end is anchored by a bolt and the cable length is adjustable.

Hook the end with the fitting into the cantilever arm that has a slot to receive it (see photo). Thread the other end through the anchor bolt found on the other arm. Where you anchor it depends in part on the frame. As a general rule, set the stirrup cable length such that when you pull up on its center, the angle formed there is less than 90 degrees.

5 Give the main cable a light coating of grease, then push it through the housing and seat the fitting on its upper end into the groove provided for it on the lever. Hook the yoke around the center of the stirrup cable and run the loose end of the main cable through its anchor bolt. If it's a Shimano cantilever, the cable may not end at the yoke—it may pass through it and end at the anchor on one brake arm.

Before anchoring the main cable at the yoke or at the arm, thread the adjusting barrel at the lever end down almost against the lever to provide plenty of adjustment space as the cable stretches.

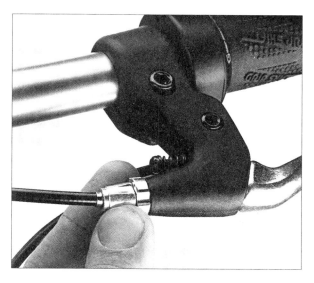

6 Hold the cantilever arms against the wheel rim, pull the main cable taut, and tighten the bolt to anchor it (see photo). If the cable passed through the yoke on its way to the anchor on the brake arm, tighten the nut at the yoke, too, after making sure that both sides of the cable are the same length.

Squeeze the brake a few times with the lever. Make further adjustments in pad position and cable adjustment if needed. If the brakes do not contact the rim at the same time, try shifting the position of the yoke along the stirrup cable toward the slower side. If that doesn't solve the problem, look for centering screws in the sides of the arms. Or release the straddle wire to open the brake, and rock the sticky arm away from the rim to increase spring tension. Hook it back up.

Direct-Pull Cantilever (V-Brake) Adjustment

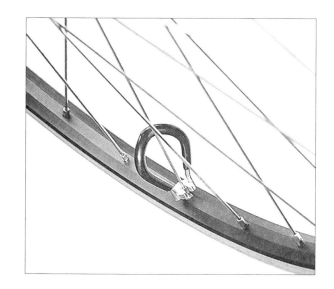

1 Direct-pull cantilevers are pretty easy to adjust. One caution though: They require a special, direct-pull-compatible lever that pulls more cable than old-style levers. You won't get good performance without one. However, there are adapters available that convert non-direct-pull levers. Get some if you plan to use incompatible levers.

Wheel problems will cause poor brake adjustment. Make sure your hoops are true and centered in the frame before adjusting the brakes (see photo).

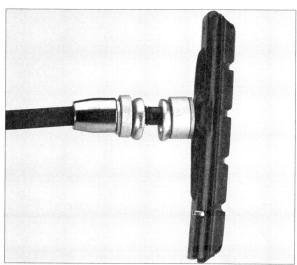

2 When adjusted correctly, direct-pull cantilever brake arms should be close to parallel to each other. To achieve this with different rim widths, each brake pad has a thick and a thin washer (see photo). Place the appropriate washers for your rims between the pads and arms (keep one inside and one outside the brake arm). Then adjust the cable at the anchor bolt until the arms are close to parallel.

3 When working on the pads, it helps to release the spring on the side you're working on so the other side will pull the pad into the rim. Sight along the pad. Unlike all other types, which are normally toed-in slightly, you should adjust direct-pull pads so that they strike the rim flat and are in line with the center of the rim (see photo). If not, loosen the 5 mm fixing nut, adjust the pad, tighten it securely, and then reattach the spring.

4 If one pad stays closer to the rim when you squeeze and release the brake, use the small Phillips screws at the base of the arm to center the arms. Clockwise turns increase spring tension, moving the pad on that side away from the rim, and counterclockwise turns loosen tension.

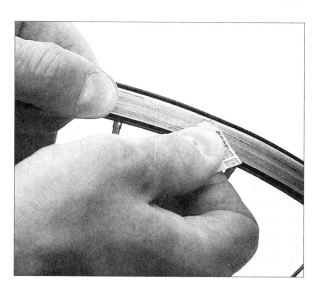

5 It can be challenging to quiet squeaky direct-pull brakes. Try these tricks: Check the mounting bolts to ensure that the arms are tight in the frame. If that's not the problem, scuff the rim sidewalls with emery cloth or the sandpaper in your patch kit to break the glaze. Still noisy? Take the bike for a ride and take along a 5 mm Allen wrench. Under these circumstances, you can experiment with different brake pad toe-in angles to see if you can shut them up. (The front of the pads should strike the rim before the rear.) No? Try a different brand of brake shoe. Howling anyway? Purchase and install a "brake booster," an add-on piece that joins the two brake bosses and stiffens things up.

U-Brake Adjustment

BRAKES

1 U-brakes are obsolete now, but you might still run into some. They're a powerful type of center-pull designed specifically for mountain bike applications. Like cantilevers, they're bolted to frame posts, and this secure mounting is one reason that they're so powerful. U-brakes are often mounted under the chainstays. Turn the bike upside down to make it easy to work on the brake. Grease the cable where it passes through the guide on the bottom bracket and slide the yoke onto the cable.

2 Tighten the yoke on the cable, but not so much that you can't slide it. Slide it up the cable against the bottom bracket guide and pull the rear brake lever to the handlebar. This will cause the yoke to move to the correct position on the brake cable. Use small locking pliers and a combination wrench to tighten it securely (see photo). Don't overtighten it: These small bolts are prone to breaking. You'll have an opportunity to check tension later.

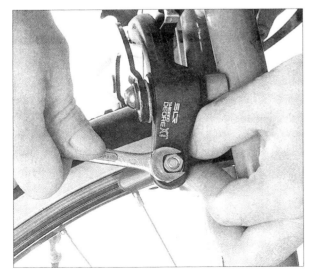

3 Loosen the nut on each brake shoe, one at a time, and adjust the shoes so they strike the rim squarely. It's important to consider what will happen to brake shoe travel as the pads wear. Positioning them squarely now will prevent later problems, such as having the shoes go under the rim and into the spokes, or over the rim and into the tire. Toe-in the shoes so the front edge hits the rim before the back edge. Use your fingers to hold the shoe while you tighten it with a combination wrench. The shoes must be tight or they may change adjustment when you brake hard.

4 Loosen the stirrup cable anchor bolt on the brake, and thread the stirrup cable through the yoke and the bolt (see photo). Pull the stirrup cable tight while you hold the brake shoes against the rim and tighten the anchor bolt. Squeeze the lever several times to stretch the cable and test the tightness of the anchor bolts. If the cable slips in the anchor bolts, loosen them, readjust the cable, and tighten the anchor again. Always use two wrenches to tighten the anchor bolts securely.

5 Add spring tension to the brake arms by discon- necting the stirrup cable, moving each arm away from the rim, and tightening the pivot bolt with an Allen wrench (see photo). The farther away from the rim the brake shoe is when you tighten the pivot bolt, the greater the spring tension will be. If one arm over- powers the other, causing the shoe to drag on the rim, increase the tension in the weak arm or decrease the tension in the strong one. The goal is to have each shoe an equal distance from the rim once the lever is released.

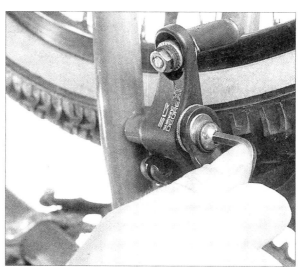

6 Some U-brakes have small adjustment screws on one arm that can be used for minor spring- tension adjustments. Turning the screw with an Allen wrench will increase or decrease the tension of one spring (but will affect both arms). Counterclockwise turns lessen the spring tension of that arm, which allows the other arm to move away from the rim.

Rollercam Adjustment

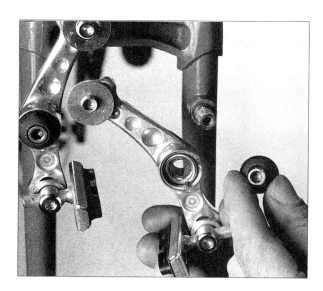

1 Rollercams are a powerful type of centerpull brake that use a special cam-and-roller system to amplify braking power. Although pretty rare today, they're somewhat similar to cantilevers and U-brakes, but they are more difficult to adjust. You may need to have a professional mechanic do the work.

Start rollercam brake adjustment by removing the brake arms and lubricating the frame posts. Use a 5 mm Allen wrench to unscrew the pivot bolt and detach the arm (see photo). Lightly lubricate the post, and reassemble the brake. Do not lubricate the pivot bolt or the inside of the frame post, and do not tighten the pivot bolt yet.

2 Spin the rollers on the tops of the brake arms. If they resist, loosen them with Allen and combination wrenches.

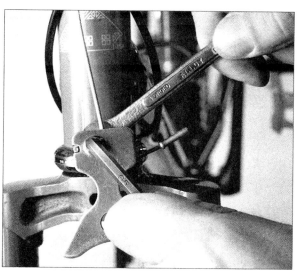

3 Rollercam brakes come with a triangular cam instead of a cable stirrup. Grease the brake cable lightly where it passes through housing or a cable guide. Loosen the cam anchor bolt and slide the cam onto the cable. Tighten the cam anchor bolt, but not so much that you can't slide the cam (see photo). Place the cam between the rollers by squeezing the brake shoes to the rim.

4 The rollers should rest near the narrowest portion of the cam. This gives you the greatest mechanical advantage when the brakes are applied. To make the rollers move together against the cam, adjust the brake shoes so there is ⅛ to ³⁄₁₆ inch rim clearance on each side. It may help to wrap an elastic band around the top of the brake arms to keep the rollers in the sweet spot of the cam. Be sure that the shoes contact the rim squarely and that there is some toe-in. (The front edge of the shoe should hit before the rear.) Tighten the brake shoe locking nut securely with a wrench while grasping the shoe holder with an Allen wrench so the shoe cannot twist.

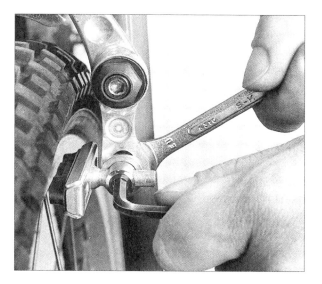

5 Hold the end of the brake cable with pliers and slide the cam (which is between the rollers) up the cable (see photo). If the brake shoes are the correct distance from the rim, the rollers should rest on the narrow spot of the cam. If not, move the shoes closer to the rim and readjust the cable. Once this is set, use an Allen wrench and combination wrench to tighten the cam on the cable.

6 To adjust the tension on the brake arm springs, turn the large nut on the outside of the brake arm with a combination wrench and lock it in place with an Allen wrench (see photo). This winds the brake springs, creating tension. Turn the right-side nut clockwise to add tension; turn the left counterclockwise to add tension. Don't wind the springs too far. Usually, a quarter-turn provides enough spring tension. If you twist the spring too far, you will make the brake difficult to apply, and you may damage the spring.

Squeeze the brake repeatedly to check centering. If one pad is closer to the rim, lessen the tension on that side or increase tension on the other side. It may take several attempts to achieve the right tension. It's important to have the pads equidistant from the rim so the wheel can travel freely. Squeeze the lever hard to check the cable anchor tension. Readjust the brake.

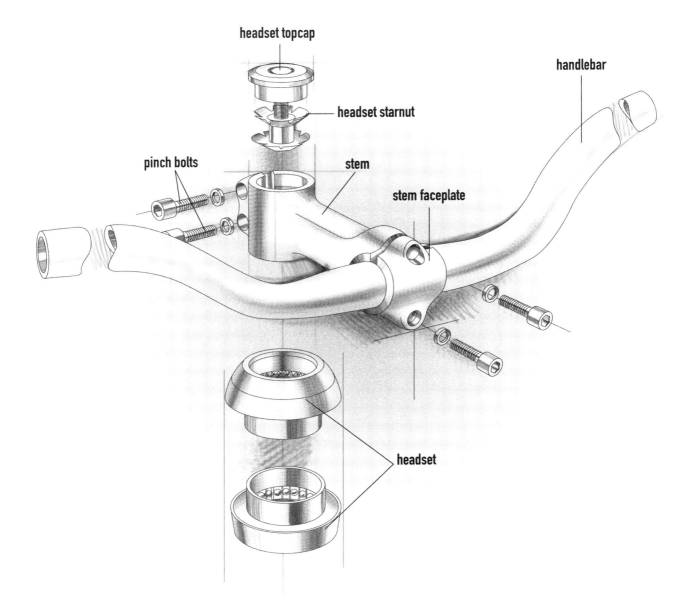

headset topcap

headset starnut

pinch bolts

stem

stem faceplate

handlebar

headset

The frame is the foundation; the wheels make it a bicycle. Derailleurs and drivetrain make it go, and brakes make it stop. But the handlebar and stem make it fit—and if the bike doesn't fit, you're getting only half the experience.

With the right choice of stem and handlebar, even a frame that's a little too big or a little too small can be made to ride like it was custom-tailored to you. Or, you can start with a bike that was well fitted for one purpose and create something different of it. We often see older lightweight racing bikes that have been retired from competition and become stylish commuting bikes or coffee-go-getters simply by switching to a more relaxed handlebar and stem combination.

THE RIGHT STEM

Before purchasing a new stem, you have to figure out what type fits on your bike. There are two main types: quill-style, and threadless-style.

QUILL-STYLE

A quill-style stem is L-shaped and was commonly found on all types of bikes until the 1990s when threadless stems gained popularity. Now quill stems are most commonly found on casual-type bikes like hybrids and children's models. One part of the stem fits inside the fork, with an expander wedge on the bottom. When the expander bolt running through the center of the stem is tightened, the wedge pulls up inside or alongside the stem, jamming the stem inside the fork. You can identify this stem by a 6 mm hex bolt, or a 12 or 13 mm common bolt on top of the stem directly over the fork. (Don't be confused by the 5 mm hex bolt in the cap that is found on threadless stems.)

The diameter of your stem must match your fork. For quill stems, first determine whether you have a fork that requires a French-dimensioned 22.0 mm,

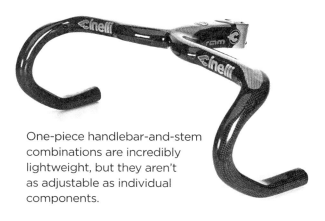

One-piece handlebar-and-stem combinations are incredibly lightweight, but they aren't as adjustable as individual components.

the fairly universal 22.2 mm (commonly called 1-inch), the 1990s standard for mountain bikes 25.4 mm (commonly called 1⅛-inch), or short-lived oversize diameters like 28.6 (1¼-inch) or 32 mm (1⅜-inch) quill. If these numbers don't seem to correspond, that's because the quill dimensions given here in millimeters fit inside fork steerers with the given inch dimensions. Confusing? Yes. But if you ask your local shop for a 1⅛-inch quill stem, they'll know exactly what you're talking about.

If you don't have an inside micrometer or inside calipers, simply borrow a stem of each diameter and try them out, or take your bike along to the bike shop to get the proper fit. Unless yours is an older French road bike, it's unlikely you'll have 22.0.

There is a third size, .833-inch, that is found mostly on U.S. department store brands. However, in the vast majority of cases, lightweight bikes use 22.2 mm or 25.4 mm quills.

THREADLESS STYLE

Threadless stems have eclipsed quill stems in recent years as the standard design. Stems of this type can be found on almost all bikes in all price ranges, but are most common on mid- to high-priced road and mountain bikes. A threadless stem clamps to the outside of an extended fork steerer tube, rather than gripping the inside the way a quill stem does. The easiest way to identify a threadless stem is by locating a pinch-bolt or a pair of pinch-bolts on either side of the stem where it grips the fork.

Threadless stems also come in a variety of sizes, though 1⅛ inches is by far the most common. In fact, 1-inch threadless was used for such a brief time that most manufacturers of stems simply supply a shim to fill the void between a 1-inch threadless steerer and a 1⅛-inch stem, rather than supplying specific models anymore.

For mountain bikes there is a new, oversize option called OnePointFive (1½-inch) that takes advantage of a very large diameter steerer tube to enhance strength and minimize flex for long-travel suspension forks.

The threadless system takes better advantage of materials properties than threaded-type steerers and quill stems, creating a connection between stem and

Handlebars and stems are available with various clamp-surface diameters. Be certain of the size of your handlebar and stem before changing one or the other.

fork that is at the same time lighter and stronger than a traditional quill-type connection. Most mid- to high-priced bikes now come equipped with threadless front ends.

There is a drawback, though, to the threadless design. Once a stem height is decided upon, the steerer is cut to length, making it impossible to ever raise the handlebar without changing the stem entirely. As a result, it is common practice to "stovepipe" the steerer (cut the steerer long and take up the excess with spacers on top of the stem) so that the stem height can be played with until the ideal level is found. Remember, you can cut the steerer all you want, but you can never make it longer.

BAR AND STEM COMPATIBILITY

After determining what stem fits your fork, you'll need to figure out whether that stem fits your handlebar or vice versa. There were once several different diameters of road handlebar: 25.4 mm was the Japanese standard; 25.8 mm the standard for the manufacturer TTT; and 26.4 mm was the standard for bars manufactured by Cinelli. While Nitto still holds true to the 25.4 mm diameter, it's not as great a problem as it could be since this is also the original standard for mountain bike handlebars and stems. All others had just settled on 26.0 mm as a common standard when a new oversize standard was introduced: 31.8 mm.

At present, both 31.8 mm and 26.0 mm can commonly be found on new road bikes, with 31.8 mm bars and stems generally specified on higher-priced models.

Mountain bike handlebars and stems all had 25.4 mm handlebar clamps until very recently. About the same time that the 31.8 mm standard was introduced for road bikes, it was also introduced for mountain bikes.

Both styles of bikes are able to take advantage of different aspects of the oversize handlebar diameter. Road handlebars can shave weight while maintaining strength and rigidity. Mountain handlebars can maximize strength with little or no weight penalty. It's like looking at both sides of a golden coin.

There is another benefit of common dimensions for both steerers and handlebars on road and mountain bikes. The variety of stems available essentially doubles for consumers without increasing inventory for suppliers and retailers. So a cross-country mountain bike racer looking for a lightweight stem and a low riding position can use a road stem, while a casual road rider interested in a strong, upright stem for some light touring can install a mountain stem.

Once you know what stem will fit your fork and handlebar, it's time to determine the length and angle of extension that's correct for your body. Unfortunately, there's no simple or foolproof method for doing this. The correct stem length is predicated on several variables that don't always correlate in the same way. The variables include torso length, lower- and upper-arm length, saddle position, top tube length, choice of handlebars, and intended purpose for the bike.

Getting a good fit between rider and bike begins with the selection of a frame (see page 28 for a discussion of matching a body to a frame). Once that choice is made, fine-tune your bike fit by adjusting the saddle up and down and, to a limited degree, fore and aft. These adjustments affect leg and pedal position.

Once the saddle position is set, the proper handlebar position can be determined in relationship to it. One traditional technique for road bikes is to place the back of the elbow against the nose of the saddle, and extend the forearm and hand toward the stem and handlebar. As a general rule, the top of the handlebar should lie about 1 inch beyond the tips of the fingers. This is a fairly good place to start.

You might want the bar a little closer to allow for easier breathing and a more upright riding position. This is particularly the case for cyclists touring on loaded-to-the-hilt rigs or simply those riding for long periods of time. Racers and some sport riders like to have their bars a bit farther out because they prefer a more stretched-out riding position.

For mountain bikes, this guideline may be partially applicable to cross-country riders, but downhillers and freeriders will want a much shorter cockpit for increased control in technical situations.

If you're having trouble finding a comfortable position, one trick is to install an adjustable stem and ride with it for a while to determine what position works best. This works as long as the special stem is used on the same frame and with the components the new stem will be used with—or at least with a frame of the same geometry and similar components. Also, when working with an adjustable stem, make changes in small increments so your body has a chance to get accustomed to each change in order to properly evaluate it. Don't forget to measure the length you like when you find it, so you can match up the new stem.

SELECTING A HANDLEBAR

The size of the handlebar, like the stem, should be based on the physical characteristics of the rider. Road cyclists and casual riders will want a handlebar about as wide as the distance between their shoulders to provide a position on the levers that permits unrestricted breathing. Mountain bikers will want a bar width suited to the terrain and type of riding that they do. Generally speaking, cross-country riders will want a handlebar 1 to 3 inches wider than their shoulders, and downhillers and freeriders often like their bars 27 or more inches wide for stability.

In any case, it's important that the reach and height of the bar allows you to grasp the brake levers without stretching, and the hooks on a drop bar should offer a position that maximizes the pulling power of your arms and back.

ROAD HANDLEBARS

Road handlebars once came in a few specific styles that bore easily recognizable differences between them. Nowadays, there are seemingly limitless, subtly different styles of road handlebars. Ranging from ultra-lightweight, one-piece molded bar-and-stem combinations made from carbon fiber to ergonomically shaped road-comfort and touring models, there is a handlebar made by someone, somewhere to suit nearly every rider's needs.

Handlebars designed for road racing, sport, and touring riders all share a few common characteristics. The flat top part of the bar allows an "upright" position with the hands placed not quite shoulder-width apart—far enough to allow relaxed breathing while powering the flats or working up steady, moderate climbs. A more prone position of the upper body results when the hands are placed on the brake hoods or just above the hoods on the upper curved portion of the bars. This position is good for a faster effort because the body generates less wind resistance. It also leaves the chest cavity open for easy breathing. This position puts the hands at quite a

ROAD HANDLEBARS

MOUNTAIN HANDLEBARS

The three most common types of road handlebars are anatomic road, track, and time trial/triathlon. The two basic types of mountain handlebars are flat and riser.

different angle than the bar-top position. Switching between the two thus varies the pressure on the hands.

As the hands move to the "drops" or bottom of the bar, the upper torso is forced down into a prone or nearly prone position, depending on how the bike is set up. This position exposes the least amount of body area to head wind and also maximizes the use of the back muscles for all-out efforts, such as sprints. The drawback in riding for too long in this position is that most of the upper-body weight is supported by the palms. This puts pressure on the ulnar nerves and can lead to numb hands, which in some cases may take hours to regain their sensitivity.

Regardless of what type of road handlebar you end up with, it's important that it fits. Most drop handlebars come in different widths and drops. The width (usually measured center to center across the bottom portion of the bar) should come close to matching the width of your shoulders. An easy way to check is to have a friend hold the handlebar against your back and see if the bar lines up with the centers of your shoulders. If so, it'll allow you to breathe more normally than would a narrow bar. A wide bar is also good for those who climb frequently because it adds leverage. Tandem captains like wide bars because the leverage adds control. Narrower bars are more comfortable for smaller riders.

The drop of the handlebar is how deep the hook sections are. Usually, riders with larger hands prefer a deeper drop, and vice versa.

MOUNTAIN BIKE HANDLEBARS

There are two basic types of handlebars for off-road riding: flat bars and riser bars.

Flat bars are not perfectly straight; they have a slight bend ranging from 3 to 9 degrees on each side of the clamping area for the stem. They are favored by cross-country racers for their balance of light weight and rigidity.

While it's arguable that a stronger, lighter handlebar can be made—and the same position achieved—with a flat bar and a slightly taller stem, the more popular of the two handlebar types among off-road riders is by far the riser bar. Riser bars have a slight upward sweep, ranging from 1 to 2½ inches, and angle back toward the rider from 6 to 11 degrees on each side.

UPRIGHT HANDLEBARS

The tourist bar is available for those riders who desire a permanent upright position. This bar is almost flat or slightly rising, with ends that turn back toward the rider, and it is very similar to the handlebars used on the three-speed English racers of years past. This bar essentially offers only one hand position: on the grips at the ends of the bar. Also, this bar must be equipped with straight brake levers similar to those used on mountain bikes.

These three basic types are little more than a sampling of the many styles of handlebars available. What we have tried to do in this text is cover the handlebar types of most common interest to cycling enthusiasts. Rest assured that whatever it is you seek in a handlebar—whether it is a casual, upright riding position or a vintage look for a treasured, old bike—it's out there somewhere.

INSTALLING HANDLEBARS AND STEMS

Installing a stem and handlebar is pretty simple. Many stems today come apart, which makes removing and replacing the bar supersimple. Unscrew the bolts, separate half of the bar clamp, and remove and replace the bar.

On stems that don't come apart, it's often helpful to work the handlebar onto the stem before mounting the stem onto the bike. This way, you can twist the handlebar in various directions (and drop bars can take some twisting to install) without being in danger of hanging them up on the front of the bike.

Flat mountain bike handlebars are usually easy to install. Loosen the stem binder bolt, and push the bar into the clamp until the bulged middle portion of the stem is centered in the clamp. Some designs rely on shims between the bar and stem, which make the job a little trickier: It just gives you one more thing to center. If the bar is a tight fit, try *gently* wedging the clamp open slightly with a screwdriver as you insert the bar. (You don't want to bend the clamp.) If your clamp has a bolt that threads in to tighten the bar, try the coin trick: Remove the bolt, insert a dime in the binder slot, then screw the bolt into the threaded part of the clamp so it presses on the dime. Snugging the bolt will spread the clamp, making installation of the bar easy.

303

It's also crucial to position a mountain bike handlebar correctly. The ends are angled slightly to correspond with the way your wrists are angled on your arms. To find the best position for the handlebar, sit on the bike and rotate the handlebar in the stem until it feels natural to your wrists. Usually, there's only one position that feels right, and if you use another you'll pay for it with sore wrists.

The most frustrating part of mounting a drop handlebar is getting the bar stuck inside the stem. There's a trick that'll eliminate this problem. Look at the clamp—its width narrows at the bottom near the binder bolt. As you insert the bar, take your time and keep turning the bar so the tighter inside radius of the bar is always next to the narrow part of the clamp as you push the bar through and center it. When the bar is centered, snug the binder bolt just enough to keep the bar from moving.

Once the bar and stem are together, you'll probably find it easier to mount them on the bike before attempting to install the levers and grips or tape the bar. If you're working with a quill-style stem, exercise some caution here. Before installing the bar and stem on the bike, determine the length of threading on the steerer tube to see what the minimum insertion depth will be. The expander portion of the stem (at its base) must extend beyond this depth, or the chance of deforming or even splitting the steerer tube will greatly increase because of the thinner wall thickness at the threads. However, in no case should there be less than 2 inches of the stem inside the fork—that's what's needed for sufficient strength. Most quill-style stem makers are now marking the minimum-insertion point on their stems so you'll know when it's inserted enough.

Before inserting a quill-style stem into the steerer tube, smear a generous coat of grease over the inserted portion to keep the dissimilar metals from corroding together and to provide a grease seal against moisture. Lower the stem to where you think you'll want it (keeping in mind the safe limit), and tighten the bolt.

If you perspire heavily while riding or if you frequently ride in the rain, moisture may work its way down inside your head tube. One way to cope with the problem is to replace the locknut on your headset with a locknut that has an O-ring seal built into it. This will minimize the possibility of corrosion developing, which, if left unchecked, will

actually weld the stem to the steering tube.

You're less likely to have problems with threadless-style stems. They can get stuck on the fork, but usually they come off with a little twisting and tugging. They're easy to put on, too, because they just slip over the top of the fork, and then you tighten the clamping bolts. The only tricky part is that threadless-style stems are part of the headset (the steering bearings) system, so when installing and removing them, you must deal with headset adjustment.

This means working with the top cap, the cap that sits on top of the stem. Seat the stem on the fork, then put on the top cap and screw in the top bolt. Tightening the top bolt is how you adjust the headset. Snug the bolt until the headset has no play. Then you can center the stem and tighten the clamping bolts to fix it in place.

Bar-ends. Some people like to add bar-ends to flat and riser handlebars. These add-ons provide another hand position, which can help eliminate some of the discomfort on jarring rides. They're handy on technical climbs, too, because they allow a rider to shift body positions to increase traction.

It's important to install bar-ends correctly, however. Use care not to scratch or pinch the end of the handlebar when installing the bar-ends because this can lead to a broken handlebar. Tighten them just enough so that they support your weight and cannot move. Position the bar-ends so they feel like natural extensions of your wrists when you're comfortably sitting on the seat. If you feel any discomfort or pressure on your wrists while riding, the bar-ends are probably set at the wrong angle; readjust them. Carry along a wrench on the first few rides and you can easily dial them in.

Finally, when you're riding on a bike with bar-ends, don't make the mistake of using them all the time. It takes more time to get to the brakes when you're on your bar-ends. Reserve them for safe stretches, and stay off them on treacherous descents.

PADDING THE BARS

Many people find that after riding bicycles for long periods of time, they begin to experience numbness in their hands. This is a problem that should not be ignored because it can develop into a serious and chronic condition. One easy way to minimize the problem is to wear padded gloves. Another way is to place some kind of padding on the handlebar itself. Check to see if the adjustment of your seat, stem, and/or bar is contributing to the problem by either allowing an excessive amount of your weight to rest on the bar or placing your wrists in a strained position.

For adding cushion to a flat bar, experiment with different grip types and shapes.

For drop handlebars, there are a number of shock-absorbing handlebar wraps and pads on the market today. One of the most popular, Specialized Bar Phat, includes silicon-gel-filled packets in different thicknesses. The packets adhere to the top section and to the drops of road handlebars and are then wrapped over. Another favorite is Cinelli Gel wrap. By splicing a layer of gel material to a layer of Cinelli's natural cork wrap, they've been able to create a more comfortable wrap that doesn't increase the overall diameter of the grip. This is welcome news to riders with small hands as well as racers who want increased comfort but can't risk using a thick grip that could rob power in the sprint.

INSTALLING BRAKE LEVERS

When installing a new drop handlebar and/or stem on your bike, it's a good idea to set the brake levers before wrapping the bar. This way you can make subtle adjustments to the position of the lever hoods until you find a spot that's most comfortable.

Slip the levers onto the bars, partially tighten the clamps, then position the clamps. A good place to start is to install them with the tips of the levers even with (or up to ½ inch higher than) the bottom section of the drop bar. Hold a straightedge along the underside of this part of the bar to help you align the levers. Snug up the levers a bit and try them out for fit. No good? Move them to where they're more comfortable. For more detailed instructions on installing road brake levers, see page 272.

If you wish to use padding below your drop bar brake levers, add it now. Then proceed to tape your bar.

To position mountain bike levers, sit on the bike and rest your hands on the levers. Move the levers until you don't have to bend your wrists for your hands to fall naturally onto the levers. It's that simple.

TAPING DROP HANDLEBARS

There are two ways that handlebar tape can be wrapped: from the top down, or from the bottom up. Each method has its advantages and disadvantages. The advantage in wrapping from the top down is that the end where you begin can be neatly wrapped over itself, and the other end can be tucked into the end of the bar and sealed with a plug. Thus there are no loose ends to unravel. The disadvantage is that the overlaps face upward on the bends. With time and use, pressure from the hands has a tendency to peel or roll the tape back.

This problem can be avoided by wrapping the tape from the bottom up. A little tape is left at the beginning to tuck into the bar-end, then that end is secured with a plug. However, the finishing end at the stem sleeve has to be secured in some way to prevent unraveling. The accepted technique is to wrap a piece of electrician's tape or colored plastic stretch tape around that end. Electrician's tape has a good deal of elasticity in it, so as you wrap it around the bar, pull it taut. When you let go, it will shrink back into a tight bond around the handlebar tape.

Whichever taping method you choose, before beginning to actually wind tape around the bar, cut a short piece of tape from each roll, just long enough to cover one of the brake lever clamp bands on the side of the bar that you are about to wrap. Don't cut off more than you need so you don't run short of tape. Also, check the package; the manufacturer may have included the short pieces.

As you wrap, try to overlap about one-half the width of the tape, if possible. When you reach curved sections of the bar, you will have to use more overlap on the inside curves and less on the outside. How much you can overlap depends on the length of tape provided. Unfortunately, you can determine the proper overlap only by trial and error. If you get to the end of the tape before you've wrapped the whole bar, just unwind the tape and try again. Also, don't forget to maintain some tension on the tape to stretch it a bit as you wrap. This will make for a smooth, snug fit and will help you get enough length out of the tape to cover the bar.

When you reach a lever, hold a cut-off piece of tape over the clamp band while you make a figure-eight loop around the lever hood and the bar, along with an additional loop around the lever hood, as shown in the illustration. This will secure the short

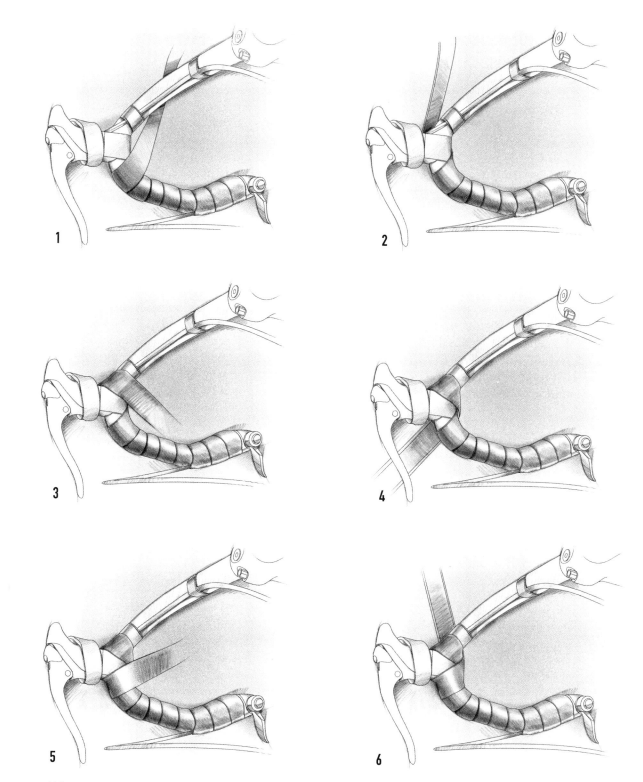

When wrapping tape around brake levers, hold a short strip over the lever clamp, then cover it with a figure-eight loop of the main tape around the lever hood and handlebar.

piece of tape and completely hide the clamp band. When the tape wrapping is complete, don't forget to plug the ends of the bar. Even if you don't need plugs to secure the tape, push them in place because if you crash and fall on open bar-ends, you can get badly hurt.

INSTALLING MOUNTAIN BIKE GRIPS

While they look simple, mountain bike grips can be challenging. They're designed not to slip around because that would make it difficult to hang on to the handlebar. Unfortunately, this can make them tough to remove and install. If the grips are worn out, the easiest way to remove them is to carefully cut them off with a utility knife. If you plan to reuse the grips, try lifting them by sliding a thin-blade screwdriver underneath and squirting in alcohol. If you get enough under the grips, you'll be able to work them off. Don't use oil, which will make the grips permanently slippery.

To install new grips, make sure the handlebar is clean of any oil or grease, which may make the grips slip. Coat the inside of the grips with rubbing alcohol and slide them in place, making sure they're all the way on. The alcohol will evaporate quickly, so work fast. Some mechanics recommend hair spray, which works in a similar fashion by lubricating the grips initially and then evaporating so that the grips will stick.

A trick that we've found helpful, especially in very wet conditions, is wiring on the grips. Mountain bike racers often encounter muddy conditions that can cause the grips to loosen on the handlebar. When a grip comes loose, the rider can have trouble controlling the bike. Wrap a small-gauge wire around the grip in two places, then wind the ends to constrict the wire and secure the grips in place. To finish the job, cut the wire and press the end into the grip so it can't scratch you. This treatment ensures that the grip won't come loose no matter how much muck you ride in.

ADJUSTING THE BAR AND STEM

The height of your stem and handlebar cannot be properly set until the saddle has been adjusted to its appropriate height and angle. Once that's taken care of, check the height of the bar in relation to the saddle. For general-purpose riding, the bar should ideally be about 1 inch lower than the saddle. Another way of checking both the bar height and the stem length is to sit in the saddle and place your hands just behind the brake lever hoods (on a road bike) or grab the grips (on a mountain bike). When you straighten both your arms and your back, your back should be at a 45-degree angle in relation to the ground.

Here again, the rule may vary somewhat for specialized riding needs. Cyclists who expect to ride primarily in an upright position may wish to set the bar at approximately the same height as or even slightly higher than the saddle; those who wish to do a lot of fast riding in a low, aerodynamic position may wish to drop the bars a couple of inches below the saddle. The 1-inch rule should be taken as a starting place from which to find the height that suits your particular needs. To experiment with different bar and stem heights, try each one for a week or two and make changes in increments of no more than ¼ inch each time. This will make it easier for your body to adjust and thus give each setting a fair try.

Keep in mind that threadless-style stems don't usually have a lot of height adjustment. Sometimes there are spacers that can be flip-flopped from beneath the stem to above it, or vice versa, to dial in position. If not, you can get a higher-rise stem or a new bar that corrects your position.

After the stem height has been set, the last adjustment to be made is the handlebar position. For drop road bars, many riders like the flat portion at the ends of the bars to be parallel to the top tube. Others like it with the hooks pushed forward a bit so the ends slope slightly downward. One suggested rule is to set the bar so that the slope of its ends follows an imaginary line that bisects the seatstays. The argument is that this position places the wrists in the most natural and comfortable position when the hands are on the drops.

For a flat mountain bike handlebar, adjust the angle so that you can hold the bar comfortably without any wrist strain.

Because the bar angle is easily adjustable, experiment with various settings if you'd like. If you want to change your position, do it a little at a time. Let

Here's an example of the difference a handlebar makes. Notice the lower, flatter back of the rider using the dropped handlebar (*top*), and the more upright position of the rider with the flat bar (*bottom*). Both positions are ideally suited for their types of riding.

your body get used to each increment of change before moving the position again. Otherwise, you may struggle to adapt to the change.

Since your hands provide approximately one-third of the contact that occurs between your body and your bicycle and perform about 90 percent of the control work, it's worth spending some time and effort in finding the most comfortable and efficient handlebar position. An unsuitable riding position irritates the nerves in the hands and arms and strains the back. That, in turn, leads to numb hands and sore neck, shoulder, and back muscles. Nothing is more likely to take the pleasure out of riding a bike. A little time spent finding the right equipment and adjusting it to the optimum position will be more than repaid in riding enjoyment.

TROUBLESHOOTING

PROBLEM: You hear constant clicking when you stand to climb.

SOLUTION: Loosen the handlebar binder bolt, move the bar over enough to grease the center section of the bar, grease it, push the bar back in place, and tighten the bolt.

PROBLEM: You've loosened the quill-style stem and tapped the bolt. The bolt is now slightly loose and the stem turns, but when you pull on the bar, the stem will not come out of the frame.

SOLUTION: The wedge at the base of the stem (inside the fork) has probably gotten stuck inside. Unscrew the bolt completely and lift the stem out of the fork. Then carefully thread the bolt back into the wedge, which you'll be able to see down in the fork. Wiggle the stem bolt to work the wedge out and reassemble the stem.

PROBLEM: Your hands get numb while riding.

SOLUTION: Try thicker, softer, or differently shaped grips. On a dropped bar, add padding to the bar tape. Wear padded gloves. Move your hands every few minutes while riding. Make sure the stem and bar position doesn't put too much of your weight on the handlebar.

PROBLEM: You've tightened the quill-style stem bolt a lot, but the stem isn't tight enough. It turns when you twist the handlebar.

SOLUTION: Remove the stem and make sure that the wedge in its base is seated correctly. Sometimes the wedge gets cocked off to one side during installation, and tightening it won't secure the stem. Reposition the wedge so it'll jam the stem in place, and retighten the bolt. Still not tight? Make sure that there is only a trace of grease on the stem.

PROBLEM: The stem has corroded inside the fork and will not come out.

SOLUTION: Apply some penetrating solvent. Clamp the fork crown in a vise (use wood blocks to protect the crown), and twist the bar from side to side to break the bond. No? Heat the stem with a propane torch—but work in a well-ventilated area and be careful not to touch the heated zones.

PROBLEM: You tighten the handlebar-clamping bolt but the drop bar won't get tight in the stem, and when you hit the brakes hard, they change position.

SOLUTION: The bar diameter and the handlebar-clamping diameter of the stem must match. If they do not, get parts that fit. If they do, slide the bar out of the clamp, sand the bar center section just enough to rough it up, reinstall it, and tighten the bolt.

Handlebar and Stem Adjustment

1 In a bike crash, the handlebar often gets twisted out of line. This may even occur as the result of a strong tug on the bar after hitting a rut. Whatever the cause, correct any misalignment of the bar as soon as possible, and then tighten the stem sufficiently to minimize the possibility of it occurring again.

Before you can make a lateral adjustment in the handlebar, loosen the stem. On quill-type stems, turn the stem expander bolt counterclockwise a turn or two. On threadless stems, loosen the clamping bolt(s) on the side. Hold the front wheel of the bike between your knees, and twist the bar sideways until the stem is properly aligned with the wheel. Retighten the bolt(s) (see photo).

When tightening a quill-style stem expander bolt that has an Allen fitting, make it as tight as you can get it with the leverage provided by the small wrench. If the bolt head can be turned by a large adjustable wrench, do not try to tighten it as far as possible because you might end up cracking the steerer tube.

2 One way to test the stem for adequate tightness is to hold the front wheel between your knees and give the bar a vigorous twist. You should not be able to easily move it back out of line. For general riding purposes, the handlebar should be set about 1 inch below the level of the saddle. To adjust the height, loosen the stem expander bolt. If the stem has not been moved for some time, you may find the expander wedge (quill-style stem only) does not drop down with the loosening of the bolt. In this case, give the head of the bolt a sharp rap with a plastic mallet. Lacking that tool, hold a small block of wood on top of the bolt to cushion the shock, and hit it with a hammer (see photo).

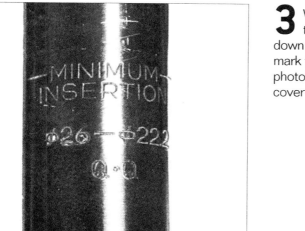

3 When setting the handlebar height, make certain that at least 2 inches of a quill-style stem extend down into the steerer tube. Many manufacturers mark their stems with a minimum insertion line (see photo). Make sure that the stem is in far enough to cover this line.

4 Some people like to set their handlebar with the lower part of the drops parallel to the top tube. Others prefer to set them along an imaginary line that runs from the bar back to the midpoint between the saddle and the rear axle. You should set them at least somewhere within this range. To adjust the angle of the bar, loosen the binder bolt on the clamp (see photo). Rotate the bar into the desired position, and retighten the bolt.

5 Before you can remove a handlebar from the stem, you must strip off the handlebar tape and unclamp and slide off the brake levers. Then you can loosen the binder bolt and work the bar out of the stem.

When installing or removing bars, when you reach a bend, the bar will become difficult to move (see photo). To make it easier, rotate the bar so that its inside radius stays next to the narrowest part of the clamp. You may find you have more room to maneuver if you mount the bar on the stem with the stem off the bike.

6 Before installing a new stem or reinstalling an old one, give the part of the stem that will be inserted into the steerer tube a good coating of grease. That will make it easier to get the stem out later and will prevent moisture from seeping down inside.

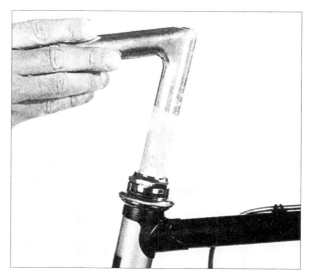

Removing and Installing Road Stem and Bar for Threadless Headset

1 To remove the stem, loosen the Allen bolt in the cap on top of the stem by turning it counter-clockwise (see photo), then remove the bolt. Lift off the top cap (if it's stuck, it will come off when you remove the stem).

2 Use an Allen wrench to loosen the Allen bolt(s) in the stem's side.

3 Remove the stem, being sure to hold the fork from below because the stem was what was holding it in the frame (see photo). If the stem is stuck, tap the bolt(s), apply a little lube on top, clamp the wheel between your knees, grab the bar, and twist to free and remove the stem.

4 To get a bar through the clamp easily, try this trick: Remove the stem bolt and place a dime between the "ears" that the bolt goes into. Place the bolt in the lower hole and thread it until it strikes the dime (see photo). By tightening the bolt, you'll gradually open the clamp, making bar installation much easier. Don't overdo it, though: If you tighten too much, you'll permanently deform the clamp, and you won't be able to put the bolt back in.

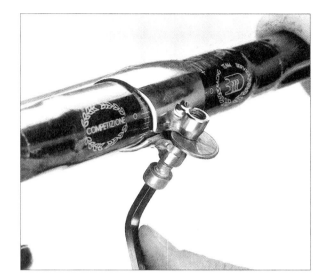

5 Remember to work the bar through the clamp in the correct direction so that it doesn't end up upside down.

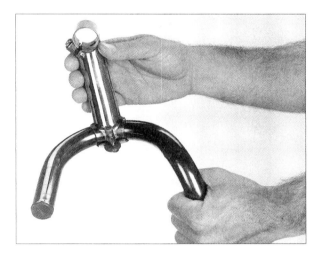

6 Reinstall the binder bolt and turn it clockwise to securely tighten the bar (see photo). Check the bar's tightness by pulling on the drops. Did they move? If so, loosen the bolt, reset the bar in the correct position, and retighten until it can't move.

Reinstall the stem and top cap and the Allen bolt. Turn the Allen clockwise to seat it in the cap. This also adjusts the headset bearings. Hold the fork with one hand and the frame with the other, and push and pull to feel for play. Keep tightening the top bolt until there's no play in the headset and the fork turns smoothly from side to side. When the adjustment feels right, center the stem and tighten the Allen bolt(s) on the stem's side.

Taping a Handlebar

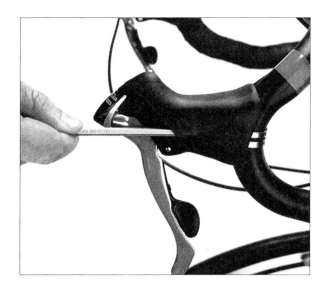

1 Handlebar tape is both practical and decorative. It enables a handlebar to be gripped more firmly and more comfortably than if it remained bare metal. At the same time, brightly colored and nicely wrapped tape on a handlebar adds a lot to the visual beauty of a bike.

Even if the handlebar is never removed, from time to time it can use retaping. After a while, any tape will become worn and dirty. New tape is inexpensive and is a nice way to recondition a bike.

Before applying new tape, clean off any remaining residue from the old tape. Also, use this opportunity to check the location and tightness of the brake levers. The bolt for loosening and tightening these clamps is located either inside the body of the lever or beneath the rubber hood.

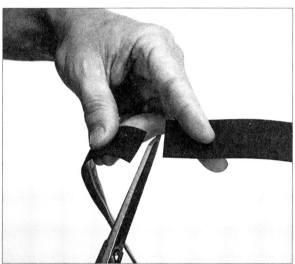

2 If the new tape didn't come with precut pieces, cut a piece of tape off the end of each roll that's just long enough to fit over the visible part of the brake lever clamp (see photo 5). Set it aside until your wrapping reaches that point. You can wrap two ways: top to bottom, or bottom to top. We recommend the latter because the tape is less likely to unravel.

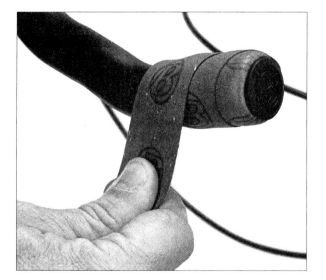

3 Start wrapping the handlebar at the end and work your way up to the stem area. Tape the end of the tape onto the end of the bar so that about two-thirds of the width of the first tape wrap overlaps the bar-end. Tuck the tape in, and push in the handlebar plug to keep the tape in place (see photo).

Overlap the beginning end completely, then continue along the straight section of the bar, overlapping between one-third and one-half the width of the tape. Keep tension on the tape as you wrap to make it stretch a little bit.

4 When wrapping the curved parts of the bar, use slightly more tape overlap on the inside of the curves and less on the outside.

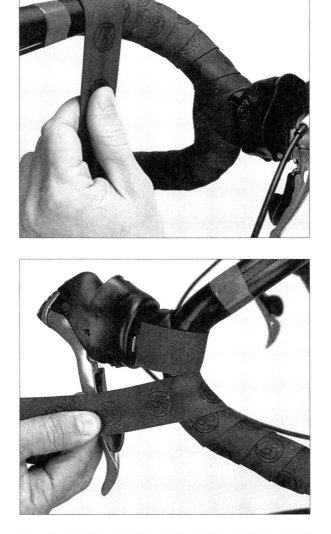

5 For a neat job at the lever clamp, wrap the short piece of tape around it and hold the piece there while covering it with a figure-eight pattern of the tape (see photo).

At the ends of the figure eight, continue the regular taping pattern along the bar.

6 When you reach the top of the bar, there should be enough tape left to go around the bar once. If you have a lot left over, cut it off after checking that you didn't leave any gaps in your wrap job (if you did, unwrap and try again). Finish the job by wrapping electrical tape around the bar tape to keep it in place. Use a contrasting color to add a touch of class (see photo).

If you wrapped from top to bottom, fold over the final loop of tape, and push it into the end of the bar along with any tape remaining on the roll. Secure the tape by pressing the plugs into the ends of the bar.

If you did not have enough tape to complete the job, you overlapped more than you should have. Unwrap most or all of the tape, winding it back into a roll as you go, and try again. Stretch the tape more this time so it'll go farther.

Installing Mountain Bike Stem and Grips

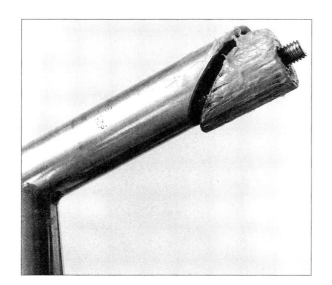

1 There are two types of mountain bike stems. The most common is the threadless style, but there are also quill-style stems that are similar in design to most road stems. The latter type attaches by inserting it into the fork and tightening the Allen bolt, which pulls up a wedge that tightens the base of the stem inside the fork. Before installing a new quill-style stem, coat the lower portion with grease to prevent corrosion.

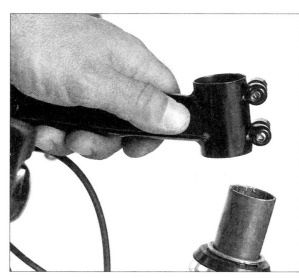

2 To either remove or adjust the stem, you usually have to loosen the Allen bolt and strike the bolt with a plastic mallet to knock down the wedge inside, which will free the stem.

3 The threadless-style stem slides over a fork with a threadless steerer and clamps in place. On this system, the stem is an integral part of the steering's bearing mechanism, acting as the main locking mechanism. To install a threadless-style stem, slide it over the fork (see photo) and install the top cap of the headset. Thread in the Allen bolt and tighten it—this adjusts the headset—and tighten the clamping bolts of the stem. If you've done it right, there will be no play in the steering bearings, and the stem will be tight and centered.

4 Usually, it's easy to install a mountain bike handlebar because there are no curves in the bar to deal with. If yours is a tight fit, however, try this: Remove the binder bolt and use a screwdriver to wedge the clamp open slightly while inserting the bar (see photo). Don't overdo it, or you'll bend the clamp, which can make it difficult to get the bolt back in.

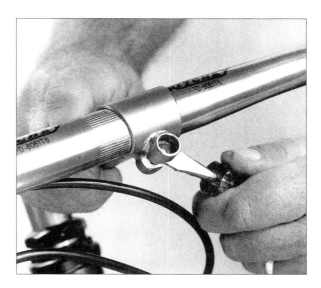

5 Another way to make it easier to insert the bar in the clamp is to try the coin trick: Remove the binder bolt and insert a dime between the two holes that the bolt goes through. Place the bolt in the lower hole, and screw it until it presses on the dime. Snugging the bolt will spread the clamp, making bar installation easy (see photo).

6 When the handlebar and the shift and brake levers are in place, finish the job by installing the grips. Clean the bar with a solvent such as alcohol because any residual oil or grease can make the grips slip around dangerously on the bar. New grips do fit snugly, so to make things easier, pour a small amount of alcohol into each before sliding it onto the bar. The alcohol will make the grips slippery at first but will then evaporate, so the grips will hold fast.

To remove old grips, carefully cut them off with a utility knife. If you wish to reuse them, lift the edges with a thin-bladed screwdriver and drip some alcohol underneath the grips (see photo). If you get enough between the grips and handlebar, you should be able to slide the grips off fairly easily.

15 SADDLES & SEATPOSTS

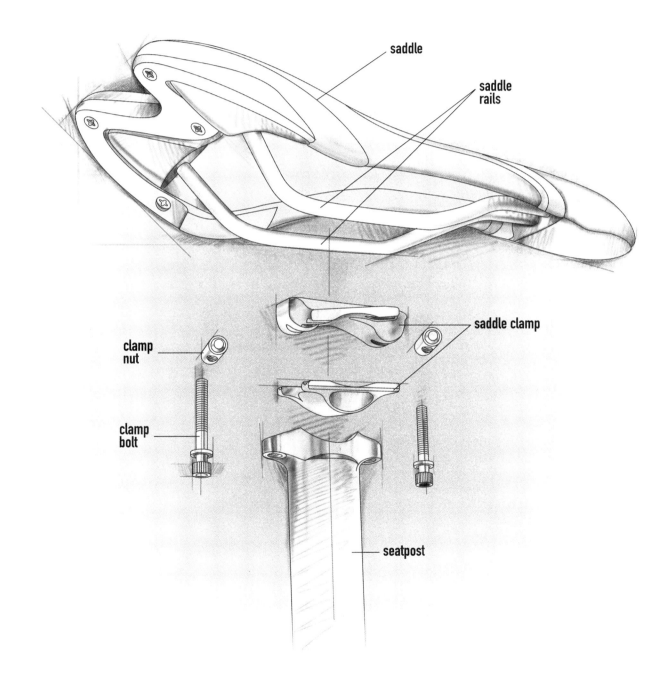

saddle

saddle rails

saddle clamp

clamp nut

clamp bolt

seatpost

There are three places on every bike where the rider and bicycle meet. Feet on pedals provide drive, hands on handlebar lend guidance, and your backside on the seat . . . well, this is probably a bit more involved than you have always believed.

The seat on a bicycle is more properly called a saddle. Though it sounds like a simple argument of semantics, it's not. A saddle serves multiple purposes. Most obviously, it supports the greatest portion of your body weight while you are seated on the bike, but it also positions you correctly over the pedals for greatest efficiency and acts as an important control surface that lets you use your entire body weight in steering. A seat is little more than a place to park your buttocks. That thing in front of your TV is a seat. Atop your bicycle is a saddle.

As a cyclist, the most intimate relationship that forms between you and any part of your bicycle is with your saddle. That is probably the principal reason that it's the prime source of complaints about pain on a bike. Often the reason that a saddle is uncomfortable is because it's improperly adjusted or simply not well matched to the cyclist's anatomy. Bicycle saddles are not all alike; there's an amazing diversity to be found both in design and construction materials. Somewhere in all this diversity should be a saddle that's right for you.

And if you can't find a traditional saddle that's comfy, there are even bikes called recumbents that are completely designed around an entirely different seating position, one where riders recline in lawn chair-like seats (complete with backs) and pedal with their legs out in front. It may seem an extreme solution, but recumbents are not just comfortable, they're a blast to ride. Many cyclists who make the switch find that they ride more than ever and enjoy it more, too.

The most important rule to remember about conventional saddles is that everybody's posterior is different, and what is comfortable for one person

If you've tried and tried but can't get comfortable on any conventional saddle, consider giving a recumbent a go. Named for their reclined riding position, these bikes are incredibly comfortable because your weight is fully supported in a hammocklike seat.

may be torture for another. Not only that, but a saddle that is well suited to short, fast racing events may be ill-suited to long-distance touring. Proper saddle selection must take into account both bodily structure and riding needs. In short, saddles are a very personal thing, so no matter what anyone else says about a particular model, you have to make the final decision.

BASIC SADDLE CONSTRUCTION

The bicycle saddle consists of a shell, which is the part you sit on, and a carriage or frame, the part that supports the shell.

The shell can be made of steel, leather, or plastic. Steel shells are sometimes found on inexpensive adult and juvenile bicycles. The steel shell is

319

covered with a piece of low-density foam covered in vinyl. Though these saddles may feel soft, they aren't very comfortable. The foam compresses easily, and you end up sitting on a plate of steel that doesn't conform to your body.

Saddles that feature a piece of thick leather mounted over a metal frame are probably the oldest style still available. Given adequate time for a proper break-in, the leather top will become soft and resilient and will conform to the particular anatomy of the person using it. At one time, leather saddles of this type came in all price ranges but these days are found only in the upper price ranges.

This type of leather saddle requires special care. Carry along a plastic bag to protect it from the rain in case you get caught in a storm. Leather saddles like this also need some breaking in before they're really comfortable and conform well to your hind side. You can help this process along by applying some type of saddle dressing. Some people use saddle soap; others use products like Lexal, Proofhide, or Hydropane, all of which are available from leather goods stores.

Padded saddles with vinyl bases and vinyl, leather, and artificial-leather tops are probably the most popular today. Some consist of nothing more than a top shaped much like the basic leather saddle. More exotic models have shells that vary in thickness to allow for different levels of softness or hardness at different points. These saddles use special high-density foams for padding and feature "bumps" that put a little extra padding under the pelvic contact points. Saddles with these bumps are generally called anatomic saddles, and the tops are usually vinyl or leather.

The rails and frame are the structures that support the shell and connect it to the seatpost. Normally, the rails are made of steel, although aluminum and titanium are used as well. Generally, steel is the best choice for bigger riders or for hard use. Titanium rails can flex slightly, offering a little shock relief, and they're usually found on the lightest saddles.

The saddle's nose is supported by one end of the frame, and the tail of the saddle is supported by the other. Connecting the two are the saddle rails. These two rails also link the saddle to the seatpost.

SADDLES

Generally, there are three basic kinds of saddles: cruiser, comfort, and racing. The cruiser saddle is quite wide, sometimes includes springs, and is heavily padded. Like the cruiser saddle, comfort saddles are designed with comfort in mind, as the name implies, but also are intended to allow easy pedaling. There are many variations. Racing saddles consider comfort from a slightly different perspective. Firm support and a trim exterior minimize chafing and excessive movement while pedaling at high cadence for long periods of time.

Cruiser saddles. Cruiser saddles are designed to provide lots of cushioning for cyclists who sit in the bolt-upright cruiser position, which puts a lot of weight on the saddle. They're wider, so they're not as practical if you're trying to pedal quickly, but for spinning casually around the neighborhood, they're quite adequate.

Comfort saddles. Comfort saddles range widely in design to suit cyclists from those looking for a cushy ride around the block to long-distance tourists covering great distances, spending hours on end in the saddle. Most have extra padding to help cushion the shock of rough country roads and unpaved trails. The extra padding is usually placed under the ischia, the pelvic bones that press into the saddle when you're sitting down. The ischia, sometimes called the sit bones, bear the weight of your upper body. You can see this extra padding on the saddle in the form of bumps. Some saddles don't appear to have bumps, but the extra padding is there; it's just that the bumps go down instead of up. The extra padding weighs a bit more, so many racers forgo it.

Oddly enough, what have proven through the years to be the favored saddles of long-distance tourists and cycling purists appear at first glance to be the most uncomfortable saddle you could imagine. Hard leather saddles like those made by Brooks can take many hundreds of miles to break in properly, but in that time they take on a molded shape that closely matches the rider's hindquarters. Though those first 500 miles might be torturous, the result is a saddle formed to your shape that, properly cared for, can carry you in comfort for decades.

Racing saddles. Racing saddles are built to allow full movement of the legs with a minimal amount of chafing. These design goals lead to some interesting and unusual-looking shapes. Thanks to careful development over the years, it is now possible to find a racing saddle that provides an efficient platform for pedaling while at the same time reduces

Cutaway saddles such as these are intended to reduce pressure in a sensitive area and eliminate postride numbness and other longer-term health risks.

the fatigue and numbness once equated with slender saddles.

Because women have wider hips than men, they also have wider ischial bones. This means that when they sit on a men's saddle, the ischial bones are not supported by the saddle. This can be quite uncomfortable. Women's saddles are designed with slightly wider tails to ensure proper pelvic support. The anatomic women's saddle also has material relieved or entirely cut away just behind the nose for increased riding comfort. Keep in mind that not all women find women's saddles comfortable. Some women feel best on other types.

The most recent development in saddle design goes by many names. Comfort groove, cutaway, soft center, and channeled saddles are all essentially the same thing. By creating a void or soft spot in the center portion of the saddle, pressure is relieved from the area of soft tissue associated with reproduction.

Supporting evidence connecting long-term health concerns with saddle time has been shown in recent years to have some gaps. If Eddy Merckx could sire a son . . . well, you get the picture. Still, "better safe than sorry" would seem to apply here, so millions of cutaway saddles have been sold since their introduction just a few short years ago.

For people who can't seem to get comfortable even on cutaway saddles, the inventors of the world have been busy dreaming up some bizarre interpretations of the bicycle saddle—using the term "saddle" very loosely. There are inflatable saddles, ones with independent cushions (one for each cheek), and saddles so bizarrely shaped that you might wonder if you could actually sit on them.

If you're basically satisfied with the shape of your bicycle saddle but would appreciate a little additional padding, you might wish to try a saddle cover, such as the Trico Saddle Pad or other models available at shops. Covers are usually designed with foam or gel materials to make your ride more comfortable. There are also covers on the market that employ air or water to create a cushion between you and your saddle. Many people even use sheepskin saddle covers. These help prevent saddle chafing, but they don't add much padding.

SELECTING A SADDLE

Bicycle saddles, like most other products, are available in so many different models that it's helpful to solicit opinions from friends and acquaintances. Talk to other riders who have physical builds and riding habits similar to your own. They can give you information on saddles that they've tried, and that may help you narrow down your choices. Also, don't neglect to discuss the matter with your bicycle dealer. He'll know what saddles are most popular and should know better than most people the quality and materials that go into each model.

If you like your saddle but want to try something new, don't make the mistake of tossing your old one before you're sure you like the new one. When you decide to purchase a new saddle, be sure you're buying what works for you. Don't worry about what everybody else is riding. You have to find something that agrees with your anatomy and riding style. For example, if you're a man with wide hips, don't pick a skinny racing saddle just to be in style. If a wider saddle, such as one designed for a woman, fits your body, don't hesitate to give it a try.

Most important, don't stubbornly keep riding on a saddle if it is numbing your crotch or causing other pain. If you've just started riding, you may be getting used to sitting on a saddle, and the break-in period can take a few rides, but the pain should go away as you get used to the saddle. If not, try different saddles. It's best to ride in padded cycling shorts, too, or at least in shorts that don't have seams in the crotch, because these can also cause numbness and pain.

SEATPOSTS

The seatpost attaches your saddle to the bicycle. It also allows you to adjust the height and the fore and aft position of the saddle on the bike.

A bicycle seatpost consists of a pillar and a clamp. Sometimes these parts are integrated into one unit, in which case they are referred to as a one-piece seatpost. The two-part seatpost consists of a tube with a clamp attached around its upper end. The clamp simultaneously holds the rails of the saddle in the chosen position and fastens the saddle to the top of the seatpost. On this type of seatpost, the clamp is usually made of steel and has serrations that allow the saddle to be tilted up or down and set at various angles. These serrations are rather coarse in order to support a cyclist's weight, and they don't allow fine adjustments. The pillar part of the seatpost on which this clamp fastens may be made of either steel or aluminum.

A one-piece seatpost is more rigid than a two-piece model because the clamp is integrated into the upper end of the post. This gives the rider a better base to push against and thus is more efficient. On the most basic level, the clamp assembly on this type of post is the same as that in a two-piece system, in that it controls tilt as well as fore-and-aft position of the saddle.

The cheapest one-piece seatposts are also similar to the two-piece models in that they employ a clamp with serrations, which allows only finite adjustments, and a bolt running through the side of the clamp. This type of one-bolt system is easy to use and quite reliable. You can fine-tune the adjustment on these seatposts more than on one-piece seatposts without bolts.

As you move up in quality, you can find one-piece seatposts that employ a single bolt that runs vertically through the clamp. Shimano manufactures several posts of this type, which make use of a set screw instead of serrations to set the tilt. These posts are thus infinitely, or "micro," adjustable.

The double-bolt micro-adjusting seatpost has the best adjustment system available. Two bolts pull in opposition to each other, which allows you to make very small changes to the angle of the seatpost. This system prevents the angle of the saddle from changing unless a bolt breaks or the saddle rails bend.

SADDLE TILT

Often the discomfort that people feel when riding is not the fault of the saddle design, simply a matter of improper adjustment. If, for example, the nose of the saddle is tilted down, the cyclist's body weight is thrown forward, creating extra strain on the arms and shoulders. On the other hand, if the nose of the saddle is tilted up, the cyclist may feel discomfort in the genital area. This is particularly true for the male cyclist, and it is especially likely to occur when he rides with his hands on the dropped parts of the handlebar.

As a general rule, your bicycle saddle should be set parallel to the ground. If the top of your saddle is sloped or curved, simply lay a straightedge (a ruler will work) along the top of your saddle, from the nose to the back, and use that as your line of reference.

If your seatpost has a standard clamp or is a single-bolt one-piece design, loosen the clamp, move the saddle so that it's parallel to the ground, then retighten the clamp. On two-bolt designs, loosen the bolt on the end that you want to go up, and tighten the bolt on the end that you want to go down.

Some bikes, usually less-expensive models, have saddles that are attached by a clamp to a basic tube-style seatpost (there's no built-in hardware for holding the saddle). These clamps are prone to slipping, which causes the saddle to change angles when you're riding. If a saddle has been rocking like this and changing angles for a while, the clamp is probably worn out and should be replaced. Take the saddle or bike to a shop so they can find the correct clamp. There are two sizes, ⅝ and ⅞ inch, the latter being more common.

When you work on the clamp, you'll notice the serrations that allow the clamp to hold its position when it's tightened. When these grooves wear, however, the saddle can slip. It's important when installing a clamp-style saddle to level it and then tighten the clamp securely. First loosen the nut(s) and apply oil to the threads on the bolt that passes through the clamp. Make sure that the seatpost is all the way through the clamp and protruding from the top of the clamp (otherwise the clamp won't tighten adequately). Tighten the clamp when you're sure you have the saddle at the angle you want. If the clamp has two nuts, tighten them evenly until the saddle can't be turned sideways or rocked.

SADDLE HEIGHT

Proper saddle height is very important. If the saddle is too low, riding becomes very difficult. If it's too high, you can't get the leverage that you need on the cranks for efficient pedaling. Improper height in either direction can lead to injury: When the saddle is too low, excessive stress is placed on the knees; when it's too high, your hips tend to rock, causing you to rub excessively against the saddle and possibly creating saddle sores.

The correct saddle height makes riding comfortable and efficient. To find the correct height, sit on the bicycle with both feet on the pedals. Hold yourself up by hanging onto a wall, asking a friend to help, or putting your bike on a trainer (make sure that the bike is parallel to the ground). Pedal backward until one pedal is in the 6-o'clock position and the other pedal is in the 12-o'clock position.

Place your heel on the lower pedal. In this position, your leg should be fully extended. If your knee is bent, raise the saddle. If your hips must rock to allow you to reach the pedal or if your leg won't reach it, lower the saddle. When you spin the cranks and your foot is properly positioned on the pedal, your leg will be almost, but not completely, extended.

To adjust the height of the saddle, loosen the seatpost binder bolt on the seat tube, move the saddle up or down to the desired position, then retighten. Most bicycles require an Allen wrench or some other type of wrench to loosen the seatpost binder bolt. However, some bicycles, primarily mountain bikes, use quick-release seatpost bolts. Such bolts allow you to adjust the saddle height without tools. This is useful for mountain bikers who like to lower their saddles when descending steep terrain. For road use, they aren't very useful because the terrain is fairly constant. They also make your saddle an easy target for thieves.

After using the recommended technique to set your saddle height, try it out. If your feet are long and you tend to point your toes down while pedaling, you may find that your saddle now feels too low. Don't raise it right away—your body may simply need to readjust to the correct pedaling position. Try it for a few rides and see if your riding comfort and efficiency improve.

Once you have your saddle at the proper height, reassess the saddle angle. Normally, parallel to the ground is best. But ride your bike for a while to see how it feels. Then move the nose up or down a little, if necessary, to get it to the position that's most comfortable for you.

SADDLE POSITION

The correct fore-and-aft saddle position allows you to get the maximum leverage from your muscles. Too far forward and you sacrifice leverage; too far back and you experience back strain. As with height and tilt, this is an adjustment worth getting right.

To find the correct position, you will once again have to sit on the bike with both feet on the pedals and have someone or something hold you up. This time, backpedal until the pedals are at the 3- and 9-o'clock positions.

Tie a weight (a large nut or a small wrench will work fine) to the end of a string, and hang it next to your knee on your forward leg. Hold the string against the notch in the side of your knee-cap. The string should pass through the center of the pedal axle. If the string is behind the pedal, loosen the clamp and move the saddle forward. If it's in front of the pedal axle, move the saddle back. After completing this fore-and-aft adjustment, check again to make sure that the saddle has the right tilt.

If you've put a lot of miles on your bike after making all the proper adjustments but you still find your saddle uncomfortable, try a new one. Many riders find that a change of saddle drastically changes their outlooks on cycling. With such a wide range of saddle designs from which to choose, there's really no reason for any cyclist to experience persistent discomfort while riding a bike.

Wearing cycling shorts can make a major difference in comfort, too. Regular gym shorts and exercise clothing have seams in the crotch area, which cause chafing and can pinch blood vessels leading to numbness and discomfort. Cycling shorts, which come in all manner of styles these days (not just skintight nylon), have a padded and seamless crotch. Riding in a good pair is surprisingly comfortable.

SUSPENSION SEATPOSTS

Although it's no cure for a bad saddle, one way to improve comfort is a suspension seatpost. There are many models, from telescoping-post to linkage designs, from short travel to long travel, from posts with springs inside to those that rely on rubber shocks.

These posts are awesome for turning a hardtail mountain bike into a better, more comfortable machine for riding on harsh or technical trails. They're also great for taking the bite out of rough pavement, and many century riders and commuters swear by the posts.

Suspension posts add a little weight compared to ordinary models, and they usually can't be set as low in the frame due to interference by the mecha-

nism that's often built into the top of the post. They sure are nice if you'd like to sweeten the ride of your bike a bit, though.

When you buy a shock post, be sure to read the owner's manual for tips on adjusting it to your weight. There's usually a way to set the preload, either by adjusting part of the post or by changing the rubber bumpers in the post, and the owner's manual will explain this.

Setting the saddle height is a little different with a suspension post. Because it will sink slightly when your weight is on it, it must be set slightly high. The best way to find the right height is to ride a bit. Take along an Allen wrench, if necessary, and adjust the post until it feels right when you're spinning along. You want it to absorb the hits, but you also want it to support your body in the right position. If it's too high or too low, you risk injuring your knees the same way that you would by riding a wrongly positioned rigid post. Spend some time getting it right.

TROUBLESHOOTING

PROBLEM: You try to raise or lower the seatpost but discover that it won't budge, no matter how you yank, twist, and tug.

SOLUTION: Completely loosen the seatpost binder bolt in the frame. Apply penetrating oil to the top of the seatpost and tap the post with a plastic mallet to vibrate it, which will help the oil penetrate into the frame. Do this every day for a week or so and keep trying—the seatpost will free if you wait long enough. If you're in a hurry, try this: Remove the saddle, flip the bike upside down, and clamp the top of the seatpost in a sturdy vise. Then grab the bike and rock it from side to side to break the post free. You can also try heating the post with a propane torch, but do it in a well-ventilated area, don't scorch the paint, and don't touch the hot post by mistake.

PROBLEM: The saddle won't hold its position. Every time you hit a bump it changes, tilting up or down.

SOLUTION: The clamp is worn. Replace it. If it's a one-piece post, replace the parts that hold the saddle. Usually, clamps wear out because the saddle loosens and you keep riding. Keep it tight and it should last.

Suspension seatposts have gained in popularity by leaps and bounds in recent years. What was once a tool of mountain bikers looking to soften the ride of their racing hardtails has been discovered by road riders, tourists, and casual cyclists as a great way to smooth out rough roads.

PROBLEM: You can't level the saddle. It's tipped slightly either up or down.

SOLUTION: You might be okay riding on it in the slightly tipped position. If not, set it so that it angles slightly up, then whack the saddle a few times with a plastic mallet or your hand to slightly bend the rails (don't overdo it) and get the saddle where you want it.

PROBLEM: The seatpost is the right size and the bolt in the frame works, but as you ride, the seatpost slides down in the frame.

SOLUTION: Remove the seatpost and lightly sand it to rough up the surface. You need to sand only the section of the post that's inside the frame. Usually, this will increase the frame's purchase on the post and keep it from slipping.

PROBLEM: When you're lowering the seatpost, you loosen the bolt, and the post goes partway down then stops.

SOLUTION: You may have bent the post. Remove it and lay it on a flat surface to check it. Replace it if it's bent. Not bent? Check to see that something inside the frame isn't preventing the seatpost from going lower, like the water bottle screw or perhaps part of the frame. If the seatpost must be lowered permanently, you can create the space to lower it by cutting a section off the end of the seatpost.

PROBLEM: The saddle creaks when you're riding.

SOLUTION: Drip a tiny amount of oil around the saddle rails where they enter the saddle and into the saddle clamp where it grips the rails. Leather saddles sometimes creak the same way that fine leather shoes can. There's not much that you can do about this.

PROBLEM: When you tighten the seatpost binder bolt on the frame, the seatpost doesn't tighten in the frame.

SOLUTION: If you have a two-piece bolt that passes through the frame ears, it's likely that the bolt is bottomed against itself and can't tighten the seatpost. Fix this by adding a washer under one end of the bolt, which will add length to the bolt and allow you to tighten it a little bit more. This should then clamp the post in the frame.

PROBLEM: You've tried padded shorts and every saddle angle but you still get a numb bum from riding.

SOLUTION: Try different saddles until you find one that's comfortable. Don't rule out unconventional ones, such as those that have strange shapes or cutouts. You might also consider a different bike, such as a recumbent.

PROBLEM: You loosened the seatpost binder bolt and the seatpost slid down inside the frame.

SOLUTION: Turn the bike upside down and tap on the frame with a mallet to knock the post loose. With luck it'll slide right out. No? Try spraying some lube down the frame and try again (put newspaper on the floor to catch the dripping lube). Still stuck? Fish it out with a long piece of coat hanger after bending a hook into the hanger's end.

Saddle Installation and Adjustment

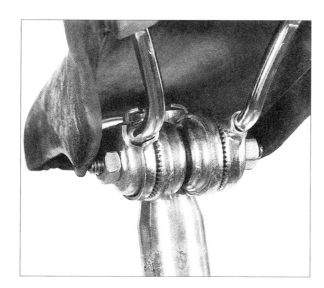

1 If a saddle feels uncomfortable, careful adjustment of its position may make a big difference. It certainly is critical to providing an overall proper fit between rider and bike. If adjusting the saddle does not help, there simply may be a poor match between the saddle and your anatomy. The only remedy for that problem is to try a different saddle.

Saddle height is determined by how deep the seatpost is set within the seat tube of the bicycle frame. The tilt and fore-and-aft positions of the saddle are controlled by the clamp that holds the saddle onto the seatpost.

Old-fashioned saddle clamps have a nut on either side that must be loosened before the saddle can be removed or have its angle or fore-and-aft position changed (see photo). The serrations on this type are rather coarse and do not allow for fine adjustments.

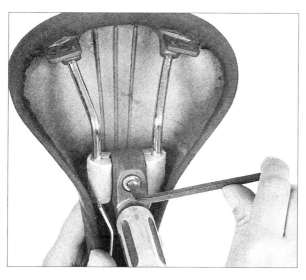

2 Another common type of seatpost is one that is fitted with a one-bolt clamping system, which does allow for very fine adjustments. When this single bolt is loosened, the rails of the saddle can slide forward or backward within the jaws of the clamp, and the tilt of the clamp can be changed. The bolt is then retightened to hold the saddle in the new position.

3 Another seatpost is truly micro-adjusting. This type has two bolts working in opposition to one another (see photo). Changing the tilt of the saddle involves loosening one bolt and tightening the other. This system not only allows very minute changes to be made in saddle tilt but also holds the adjustment very securely.

4 To completely remove a saddle from a seatpost, you must loosen the clamp bolt(s) enough for the saddle rails to slip out of the jaws of the clamp (see photo). The clamp does not need to be this loose for adjusting saddle position.

5 To set the tilt of the saddle, loosen the seatpost clamp just enough to allow the nose of the saddle to be easily moved up or down. Place a straightedge along the top of the saddle and adjust the saddle angle until the straightedge is parallel with the top tube of the bike (assuming that the top tube is level with the ground). Then retighten the clamp bolt.

The fore-and-aft position of the saddle should be set according to how your knees relate to the pedals at a particular point in the revolution of the crankset. Since the saddle height will also influence this, set it first.

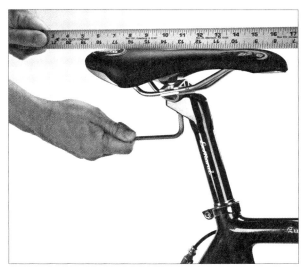

6 To determine your appropriate saddle height, sit on the bike while wearing riding clothes. It's helpful to have a friend hold you and the bike upright while you do this. Otherwise, place your bike in a doorway, near a wall, or in a stationary trainer that holds the bike level with the ground.

Rotate the crankset to the 12-o'clock and 6-o'clock positions. Then set your heel on the lower pedal. In this position, you should be able to place your heel comfortably on the pedal and your leg should be fully extended (see photo).

If there's a noticeable bend in your knee, your saddle is too low. When pedaling backward, if you have to rock your hips to reach the pedals, the saddle is too high. In either case, adjust and retest the height.

Saddle Installation and Adjustment *continued*

7 To raise or lower the saddle, loosen the binder bolt that is located at the top of the seat tube (see photo). Move the seatpost up or down as needed. Check to make sure that the saddle is aligned with the top tube of the bike, then retighten the binder bolt.

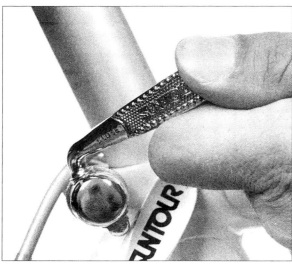

8 Some city bikes and certain models of mountain bike are equipped with quick-release binder bolts for rapid and frequent changes of saddle height (see photo). These work quite well and are certainly convenient if you need to adjust the height of the seatpost. However, this system makes it easy for thieves to make off with your saddle and seatpost (the best bet is to remove it and take it with you when you leave the bike). For most types of riding, once you've determined the ideal height for your saddle, it should be set there and left alone.

9 One important thing to watch for when raising your saddle is the manufacturer's line indicating maximum recommended height (see photo). Riding with the seatpost raised above that point is dangerous because there may not be enough post within the seat tube to support your weight. If you can't set your saddle to the proper height without moving above that line, then you probably need a bike with a larger frame. A less-expensive solution is to purchase a longer seatpost.

10 Any time you pull the seatpost out of the frame, clean it off and apply a fresh coat of grease before sliding it back in (see photo). This helps protect it from corrosion and makes it easier to raise and lower the saddle. This type of maintenance should be done periodically. You don't want your seatpost permanently rusted into the frame.

11 After setting your saddle to the proper height, adjust the fore-and-aft position. Sit on the bike as you did before, and rotate the crankset to the 3-o'-clock and 9-o'clock positions. Hold a plumb line (or a string with a weight tied on the end) next to the knee of your forward leg. Place the top of the string in the groove next to your kneecap and observe where the weight falls. It should touch your foot at a point in line with the pedal axle (see photo).

If the weight falls in front of the pedal axle, the saddle needs to be moved back a bit. If it falls behind the axle, the saddle needs to go forward. Loosen the seatpost clamp and move the saddle in the direction needed. Before retightening the clamp, check to make sure the tilt of the saddle is still right.

12 Once you've properly set the saddle height, tilt, and horizontal position, check the position of the handlebar and stem. For general riding purposes, the top of the bar should be set about 1 inch below the level of the top of the saddle.

As a rough guideline, check the distance between the bar and the saddle by placing your elbow against the nose of the saddle and extending your forearm toward the handlebar. The tips of your fingers should fall about 1 inch short of touching the bar (see photo).

Racers may want the bars a little lower and farther away from the saddle; tourists may want them a little higher and closer to the saddle. If the distance from the saddle to the bar doesn't fall within a suitable range for your type of riding, replace the stem to dial in your position.

 PEDALS

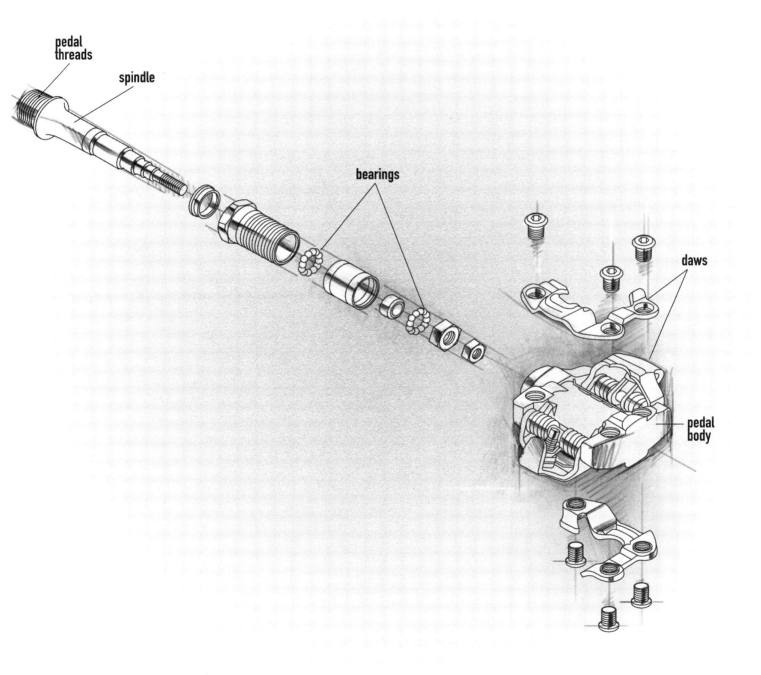

pedal
threads

spindle

bearings

daws

pedal
body

P edals are not only the means of applying your muscle power to the drivetrain of your bicycle. They also serve an important function as a control surface. By moving the pedals to different positions and shifting your weight on them, it is possible to steer your bike more quickly and more accurately, to increase the rear tire's traction on climbs, and to stabilize the bike on descents and technical trails.

All of these abilities come with their own specific demands. Pedals must be strong, have smooth bearings, and complement your footwear. No, this isn't vanity. Simply put, if your choice of shoes can't maintain contact with your pedals, the rest becomes difficult, if not impossible.

Bicycle pedals come in many different types and levels of quality. Some types, the ones most serious cyclists use, are made to work with special shoes that have cleats screwed onto the bottoms. These attach to the pedal, improving your pedaling efficiency immensely. Other pedals cannot be used with cleats, such as nylon models found on entry-level bikes, and wide-platform BMX pedals used for stunt riding. There are also pedals designed for both cleats and noncleated shoes.

Although pedals come in many different shapes, almost all pedals share several common characteristics. At the heart of a pedal is a spindle that threads into the end of a crankarm. The inner races of two sets of bearings are located on this spindle: one at the inside end of the spindle next to the crankarm, and the other at the spindle's outer end. A separate body holds the outer races of the two bearing sets. Attached to this pedal body is a pair of "rattraps," a quill cage, or some sort of platform, which acts as the pushing surface for your foot.

Most of the apparent differences between pedals are just that, cosmetic differences; their internal parts are usually strikingly similar. As you'll see later, that also means that servicing is usually the same

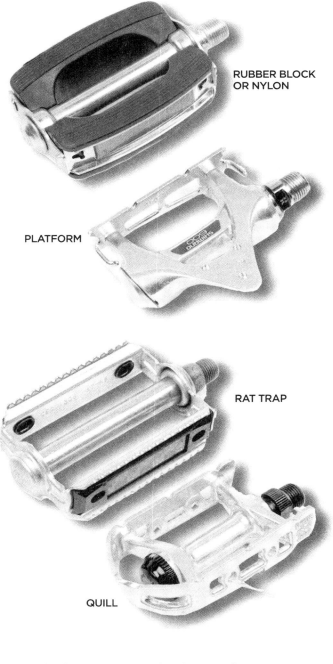

RUBBER BLOCK OR NYLON

PLATFORM

RAT TRAP

QUILL

Standard pedals come in four basic styles.

331

procedure for different types and even different brands of pedals.

PEDAL TYPES

When shopping for pedals, it helps to have a good idea of how you ride your bike. For instance, if you're a road rider who seldom stops, you probably aren't concerned with a pedal system that includes a shoe geared to "walkability." A tourist or mountain biker finds walking quite important, so a shoe that has a sole with decent tread and a little flexibility is desirable, and your choice of pedal will need to take that into account.

Most bicycles are equipped with pedals belonging to one of five basic types: rubber block or nylon, rattrap, quill, platform, and clipless. There are many variations within these basic types, as well as new pedals that come along every year. In terms of the century-long history of the bicycle, the clipless pedal is a relatively new design. It utilizes a clamping mechanism that grips special hardware attached to cycling shoes. It renders toeclips and straps unnecessary. Clipless pedals are easier to use and are more comfortable than pedals using clips and straps. Once you get used to them, the best ones almost instantaneously release your foot in a crash or emergency. Clipless pedals are now widely used by all types of cyclists because of the many advantages they offer.

RUBBER BLOCK OR NYLON

If you see these on a bike, you know right away that it's not intended for serious use. These pedals shine in commuter situations where the cyclist will most likely be wearing dress shoes. If you've ever tried the slippery combination of leather soles on metal pedals, you can appreciate the sticky advantage of leather on rubber pedals. On the down side, rubber pedals are usually heavy and nonserviceable, and they don't hold your foot in the right position when you're pedaling.

Lots of lower-priced mountain bikes and hybrids come equipped with nylon pedals. These are okay for starting out. They don't weigh much, and they can take a fair bit of abuse. Sometimes it can be difficult to attach toeclips and straps, which is a drawback. Most riders use the nylon pedals for a while and then upgrade to a better system such as clipless.

RATTRAP

You'll find rattrap pedals on less-expensive road bikes. Their thin cage plates allow the use of cleated shoes and also provide a location for bicycle touring shoes with ridged soles. Unfortunately, the thin cage plates also mean that shoes without some sort of re-inforcement in the soles, like your garden-variety sneakers, will transmit pressure unevenly to the soles of your feet, and you may develop tender spots on rides longer than 5 to 10 miles. If that happens and you don't want to switch to a flatter-topped plat-form-type pedal, buy touring-style cycling shoes. They have stiffer soles than most athletic shoes but are still flexible enough for walking.

On many rattrap models, the dustcap at the outer end of the pedal has no provision for a wrench or other tool to remove it. Normally, this would mean that the pedal is unserviceable; that's often the case with inexpensive rattraps. Sometimes, the cap can be pried off with a small screwdriver to get to the bearings beneath it. If that doesn't work, it's often possible to drip oil into the bearings from the crankarm end of the pedal if you remove the pedal.

There are racers who prefer the rattrap design to clipless pedals, so rattraps are not limited just to cheap pedals. One example is the track (velodrome) rider. A rattrap designed for track use has the twin-cage-plate rattrap design because of the extra ground, or banking, clearance it provides at the end of the pedal, which is all-important for racers who are jamming around a banked oval track. Some track riders produce explosive sprinting power, and it's possible for their feet to come out of clipless pedals. So instead, they'll use a rattrap pedal with toeclips and straps (often they use two straps for each foot), which essentially locks their feet in place.

QUILL

The only real difference between quill pedals and rattraps is that a quill pedal has a curved section of metal that connects the front and rear cage plates, making the two of them one part. This creates a stronger structure and also provides a little more shoe contact area. The latter point is especially im-portant for people with large, wide feet. For years, this was the only "acceptable" design for road racing pedals, and Campagnolo Record pedals were the model for a legion of imitators.

Quill pedals are almost always serviceable.

However, you cannot disassemble a pedal without first removing its dustcap, and you may have to purchase a special dustcap wrench in order to remove that part.

PLATFORM

As you might guess from the name, platform pedals offer a flatter, larger area for foot contact than do other types of pedals. These pedals are adaptable to different types of shoes, although some models are designed to accommodate cleats. People with large feet, downhill racers, tourists, and commuters are all riders who like wider pedals.

Platform pedals don't necessarily have a completely flat body, although some designs approach it. Even pedals that at first glance might appear to be rattrap or quill can be classified as platform pedals if some parts of the pedal other than the cage plates are raised high enough to provide additional shoe contact. This is usually accomplished with the cross members that connect the barrel of the pedal body to the cage plates. There are even platform clipless pedals, such as the Shimano models that many downhillers race on.

Most modern platform pedals are some variation of a single rear cage plate attached to the wide end of a V- or U-shaped body. This hybrid design works well with cleats, and it also provides a fair amount of contact surface for touring shoes. In addition, the internal parts are sometimes identical to those of rattrap or quill designs from the same manufacturer.

Toeclips for these designs usually mount on the horizontal surface of the pedal body instead of on the vertical surface of the missing front cage plate. Because in most cases this means that the toeclip can move forward and backward as well as side to side, small adjustments can be made to accommodate shoes of different sizes. If your toeclips don't fit your feet, try adjusting them to provide more room before shopping for larger-size toeclips.

Pedals for mountain bikes are either platform style or the less-common "bear trap" style, which used to be quite popular before clipless pedals took off. The former looks like a square doughnut with a spindle running through it, and the latter looks like a quill pedal with a round or rounded cage. The bear trap cage invariably has a notched or "tooth" profile for a secure grip on your shoes. Extra gripping power on the platform type is often provided by small flat-top pins that are far less damaging to your shins than notches or teeth.

Happily, the insides of mountain bike pedals are virtually identical to those of their road cousins, with one difference: Seals and sealed mechanisms are the rule here rather than the exception.

CLIPLESS

Among both mountain and road enthusiasts, there's been a long-standing movement away from the traditional pedal, toeclip, and toe strap trio toward a system that invariably involves a pedal/cleat combination, which locks the rider's foot onto the pedal. This integrated locking feature makes clips and straps, and their adjustment, obsolete. It's fast and easy to lock and unlock cleats into and out of these pedals, which makes them safer and more convenient than other contemporary pedals. The Look pedal, produced by the makers of Look ski bindings in 1983, was the first successful clipless pedal.

Currently, there are more than a dozen different clipless pedal systems. Some of the more popular ones include Look, Shimano, Time, and Speedplay. The primary difference between systems is in the way that the pedal grips the cleat. It's always important to purchase shoes that are compatible with the cleat system used by the clipless pedals that you plan to purchase.

COMMON PEDAL FEATURES

These days, although most top-quality bikes come with clipless pedals, you'll find toeclips and straps on older models and entry- to medium-level bikes. There is a misconception that the purpose of toeclips is to prevent your feet from slipping forward on the pedals; in reality their primary function is to hold up the toe strap loops so you can easily place your feet through them. The strap's function is to prevent your feet from slipping off the pedals, particularly if you wear cleated shoes that permit you to pull up slightly on the back side of your pedaling circle. Even under racing conditions, toe straps are not normally cinched down tightly. This is done only at the start of particularly steep hills and just before finish-line sprints.

Under normal conditions, most people don't

CAMPAGNOLO

CRANK BROTHERS EGGBEATERS

Clipless pedals are available to handle many riding styles for road and off-road cyclists. Here are just a handful of possibilities.

CRANK BROTHERS CANDY

TIME ATAC Z

keep their straps tight, just without much slack. That way, the straps provide a measure of security without preventing you from being able to quickly remove your feet from the pedals. With a little practice, the technique of lifting your foot up before you pull it back out of the strap becomes automatic.

Toeclips should be just long enough to give a little clearance for your toes when the balls of your feet are centered over the pedal spindle. The right-length clip will have a little clearance for your toes. Your toes should never be jammed against the clip. Toeclips come in different sizes. If you have really large feet, you may need to add spacers between the toeclips and pedals, which can give you the needed clearance.

Many quill pedals feature replaceable cages. This makes it fairly easy (provided you can find replacement parts) to repair the pedals when the cage gets worn from use. That's important for your knees because worn cage plates can allow your shoes, especially cleated ones, to cock themselves to one side or the other. That can result in knee damage such as tendinitis. Keep an eye on the top edges of the cage plates. If either plate appears to have a curve in it, check it by fitting the shoe onto the pedal by hand. Slide the shoe sideways and back and forth. See if it rocks from side to side. If it does, replace the cage plate, if possible, or the entire pedal.

Pedals with replaceable cage plates use Phillips or flathead hex screws to hold the cage plates on the pedal bodies. Pedals with irreplaceable cage plates use rivets. Put a small drop of low-strength Loctite on the screws as a worthwhile precaution when assembling new cages onto old pedals. This will discourage the screws from loosening and dropping out while the pedals are in use.

Sealed bearings are just as popular a feature in pedals as they are in other components. Some models require special tools to remove the bearings for service, and it is often best to leave the work to someone at a well-equipped shop.

In line with today's emphasis on serviceability, most recent "sealed" designs can be disassembled with regular tools. The seals in question are actually shields that are incorporated around regular pedal bearing construction. These pedals can be serviced in the same manner as any "nonsealed" type.

KEEPING CLIPLESS PEDALS WORKING

A clipless pedal must hold the cleat tightly to keep the rider's foot secure and to prevent accidental release. Reduce cleat wear by not walking in them. Except for walkable cleat designs, which are recessed, most clipless cleats wear faster than regular types because they are thicker and protrude more from the shoe sole. It's better to remove your shoes and ruin your socks if you have to walk any distance.

You can tell that the cleats are worn if you have excessive foot movement on the pedals. Some clipless models allow your foot to swivel, but when a cleat becomes worn, the shoe begins to move in several directions and can rattle around on the pedal. When a Shimano SPD cleat wears enough, it becomes difficult to get your feet out of the pedals. You can also identify a worn cleat by comparing it to a new one. Worn cleats should be replaced before they get so bad that they release prematurely or, in the case of SPDs, stick.

The other part of the release mechanism is the cleat-gripping pedal hardware. Look, Shimano, and Time pedals use plastic, carbon, and steel parts, and constant use can grind them down. The parts may also become loose and vibrate. If the mechanism loosens, the fit between the cleat and pedal is not secure enough, and engagement and release suffer. Additionally, you may develop an annoying squeak that's most noticeable when climbing. The noise is made by two pieces of plastic or steel—the cleat and the pedal backplate—rubbing against each other. You can temporarily quiet plastic parts by applying oil or Armorall to the pedal and cleat, but if the noise is chronic, a more lasting solution is to replace the hardware. Oiling SPDs is considered regular maintenance, and the cleats shouldn't need replacing until you experience difficulty releasing them.

In wet and cold conditions, the small cleats and retention mechanisms common on mountain biking shoes and pedals can become clogged with mud and snow, and they then resist engaging. Manufacturers have recognized this and improved cleat and pedal shapes, but some riders still experience difficulty in extreme conditions. A trick to alleviate clogging is to spray your cleats and pedals with Pam cooking spray or some similar product. Just as it can help keep your eggs from sticking to the frying pan in the morning, it can keep mud and ice off of your cleats and pedals during your sloppy rides.

TENSION AND FLOAT ADJUSTMENTS

On most clipless pedals, there's a provision for adjusting how hard it is to get out of the pedal. Mountain bikers need to get in easily, but even more important is getting out in a hurry when the trail turns dangerous. Look for a small bolt on each end of the pedal or inside the pedal body. These are usually marked in some way, but they're almost always turned counterclockwise to loosen the tension setting and turned clockwise to tighten the tension.

Another consideration is float, a feature that allows your foot to swivel slightly to protect your knee. Certain pedal designs rely on the cleat to provide the float, so it's possible to simply switch to these other cleats to make the pedals fixed or floating. Some pedals have set screws that are adjusted to reduce or increase the amount of float on the pedals.

With new clipless pedal systems coming out all the time, the best bet is to study your owner's manual to understand all the adjustments that are offered by your type of clipless pedals and how to dial them in.

CLEAT ADJUSTMENT

While cleat adjustment is not really bicycle maintenance, it's an important consideration when setting up cleated shoes. Cleats hold your feet on the pedals in a certain position. The problem is, it's possible to get the cleat in the wrong position. Everyone has a natural gait or position where his or her foot sits on a pedal. When the cleat is adjusted incorrectly, it forces you to pedal with your foot in an unnatural position, which puts stress on the knee and often leads to injury. Additionally, for clipless pedals, if the cleat is not adjusted properly, it's more difficult to click into the pedals.

These days, many pedal systems include a float feature, meaning that the cleats move slightly on the pedals, allowing the feet to pivot laterally. This float is designed to allow the feet to find their natural position throughout the pedal circle. It's a mistake to assume that because there's some float in the cleat, it's okay to set the cleat position any which way. The proper cleat position will be at the center of the cleat float. That way, your feet can move either way, as necessary, while you're riding.

The best way to adjust cleats is to have it done by a shop that uses the Fit Kit. You may have to call a few shops to locate one with this service. This bicycle-sizing system includes Rotational Adjustment Devices, which are actually two special pedals that gauge cleat position. They are installed on your crankset and your bike is mounted on an indoor trainer. As you ride, the mechanic can determine how to adjust your cleats for best performance by observing special wands that are attached to the pedals. The final position will be biomechanically correct for your knees. This greatly reduces the chance of knee injuries and ensures easy entry into the pedals.

WHEN TO SERVICE PEDALS

There are four general pedal conditions that indicate that it's time for service. The first is simply the passage of time. In the absence of any other condition, mountain bike pedals ought to be serviced every 6 months, and road models should be serviced yearly as preventive maintenance. Open up the pedal and make sure that you don't have water or other contaminants trapped inside. (Those seals can work both ways.) These problems are difficult to detect from the outside.

The second condition is when you hear or feel a maddening click with every complete revolution of the pedal or crank. This could result from a loose bottom bracket cup, crankarm, or toeclip bolt, so check those easily fixed problems first. If those parts are all tight and the click continues, it's probably something within the pedal bearings. If you've recently overhauled your pedals, try to isolate the offending side and service only that one. If it's been a while since their last servicing, you may as well do both of your pedals now. Ironically, you'll most likely never find the small bit of dirt that causes the problem, which almost always goes away after cleaning and regreasing.

The last two conditions are easily detected with a simple inspection that you should perform regularly, either before or after every few rides. Hold each pedal body with your fingertips while you rotate it around the crankarm. A slight roughness to the touch suggests that there may be dirt in the pedal bearings or that they may be slightly out of adjustment. If the pedal binds, you have a very dirty or a badly adjusted set of bearings. If the pedal works okay to this point, try to rock it back and forth. An adjustment is called for if you discover any play in the bearings.

Keep in mind that it's not worth the effort to overhaul cheap pedals. Parts are rarely available, so it's best to upgrade to a better model.

REMOVING PEDALS

Pedal removal is something you don't do frequently. You might need to remove pedals to fit your bike into a shipping box so you can take it on vacation with you or to an event. Removing the pedals makes servicing them easier. And you'll definitely have to remove them to upgrade to better or different models.

Many people have difficulty removing pedals. It's usually because they don't know one fact: The left pedal is reverse-threaded. This means that you must turn it clockwise to loosen it. The right pedal is regular-thread. It's turned counterclockwise to loosen. The left is the opposite because if it were regular-thread, the action of pedaling would cause the pedal to loosen on the crankarm. Since it is reverse-threaded, the pedaling action turns it in the direction that will tighten it.

It can take considerable force to loosen a pedal that's been adequately tightened or one that's been on a bike for some time. There are some sharp things down there, too, such as the chainrings, which can cause injury. When you're removing the right pedal, it's a good idea to shift onto the largest chainring. The chain will prevent you from slipping and getting jabbed by the chainring teeth.

Sometimes pedals seem stuck. If you're sure that you're turning them the right way but they won't budge, one of these methods should get the pedal off: Add a cheater bar to your pedal wrench, heat the crankarm slightly with a propane torch, or remove the entire crankarm and place it in a vise, then use the wrench and cheater bar.

CLEANING AND GREASING

You can perform certain adjustments on some pedals while they're still screwed onto the crankarm, but don't try to disassemble a pedal without first removing it from the bike. You'll probably need a thin 15 mm wrench like that found at the small end of the fixed cup wrench in most bottom bracket tool sets. Remember that the direction in which each pedal is threaded is the same as the side of the bike that it's on. That means that as you straddle the bike, the pedal on your right side unscrews counterclockwise, while the pedal on your left side unscrews clockwise. In each case, to remove the pedals, turn the wrench toward the rear of the bike.

To disassemble the pedal after taking it off the crankarm, hold its threaded end down in a vise with soft jaws or between two pieces of wood. Remove the dustcap with the appropriate tool. Underneath the dustcap, you'll find the locknut and cone for the outboard bearings.

At this point, determine whether the pedal you are working on is one you can easily disassemble or whether you might prefer to take it to a shop. Some pedals, including most clipless models, have precision sealed-cartridge bearings that require special tools for service. Sealed bearings require less maintenance than loose bearings because it's more difficult for dirt and water to enter. However, they can wear and develop play. When they need to be replaced or serviced, you might prefer to have shop personnel do the job. All that's visible of cartridge bearings is the seal (the bearings are underneath it), which is a black plastic ring that often has writing on it. Regular bearings, however, are easy to spot when you remove the dustcap. They are small shiny steel balls.

If the pedal has regular bearings, hold the cone in place with one wrench while you loosen the locknut with another. In an emergency, if you don't have a wrench for the cone, you can sometimes hold it steady by wedging a screwdriver between it and the inside of the pedal body. Unscrew the locknut and cone.

Pick the ball bearings out of their race with a pair of tweezers or, holding the spindle firmly within the pedal body, turn the pedal upside down and dump the bearings into a container. Before you go any further, count the ball bearings—if you drop any during disassembly and the inside bearing has a different number of balls, you may not know if you found all of the ones you dropped. Don't lift the pedal body off the spindle, or all the inboard bearings may drop on the floor. Turn the pedal upside

down if it isn't already, and lift the spindle out of the pedal body. If the pedal has a rubber seal, gently pry it out of the body to make it easy to remove the inboard ball bearings. Count them before any get lost.

Replace your ball bearings with new ones. The old ones are invariably slightly out of round, which will make adjusting them difficult when they're reassembled into the pedal. Most loose-ball pedals use ⅛-inch bearings, but take a sample to the bike shop to make sure you get a good match.

Use a rag to clean everything well. Clean all metal parts with solvent, but keep the solvent away from plastic parts and rubber seals. Use something mild, such as alcohol, to clean those parts. Make sure that you remove all the old grease from the inside of the pedal body. If the inner end of the pedal body has a rubber seal that you didn't remove and you can't get the area behind it clean, gently pry it out of the body.

If any of the bearing races have pitted areas or more than a slight groove, check into replacement parts. Availability varies considerably among manufacturers.

Apply a layer of medium-weight grease to the races in the pedal body. Hold the inside end up and place the required number of ball bearings in the layer of grease. Repeat for the outer end. Carefully place the spindle halfway back into the body, then apply additional grease to the ball bearings either directly or by loading up the area next to the inside cone. Seat the spindle and turn it to make sure it isn't binding. Grease that oozes out of the inboard bearings indicates that the bearings are fully packed and will resist contamination.

Holding the spindle tightly in the pedal body, turn the assembly over, and turn the cone onto the spindle just a couple of turns. Hold the cone still, and turn the spindle. This will draw the cone onto the bearings without scrambling them. Add the lockwasher and locknut. Now you're ready to do a pedal adjustment.

PEDAL ADJUSTMENT

The spindle should turn smoothly with no play in the bearing adjustment. Snug the locknut and feel the adjustment. If it's tight (binding), loosen the locknut, back off the cone, tighten the locknut, and recheck the adjustment. For play, back off the locknut and tighten the cone, then tighten the locknut. Continue the process until the pedal turns smoothly on the spindle without any rough feel.

Replace the dustcap and you're done. Take it easy when you tighten it; most dustcaps are made of plastic.

Pedals may seem like an insignificant part of a bicycle, something you should be able to take for granted. While it is true that proper pedal adjustment is less critical to the safe operation of a bike than proper adjustment of its brakes and headset, there is still no point in neglecting this process. Smooth-turning pedals add a lot to the joy and efficiency of cycling. All it takes is a little time and proper maintenance.

TROUBLESHOOTING

PROBLEM: The pedal makes squeaking sounds when you're pedaling.

SOLUTION: Spray the cleats with Armorall or lube (just don't walk in the house in your now-oily shoes).

PROBLEM: The cleats won't engage when mountain biking in wet or cold weather.

SOLUTION: Spray Pam cooking spray on the cleats and pedals before a ride so mud and ice won't stick.

PROBLEM: You're having trouble getting out of your SPD-style clipless pedals.

SOLUTION: The cleats have probably worn enough that they can no longer spread the pedal jaws to release. Install new cleats.

PROBLEM: You have huge feet and can't find any toeclips to fit.

SOLUTION: Put washers between the pedals and toeclips for additional clearance, or try different pedals with wider cages.

PROBLEM: With each pedal stroke, you hear a click coming from one side.

SOLUTION: The pedal may have loosened. Tighten it.

PROBLEM: You're having trouble getting into clipless pedals.

SOLUTION: Make sure that the cleat is installed correctly on the shoe. Reread the directions or ask a shop for help. If they're Look-type plastic road cleats and you have small feet, you may have curved the cleat too much when tightening it to your shoes. The cleats must be fairly flat to engage correctly. Shim the edges with leather to flatten the cleat.

PROBLEM: Even though you're using a good pedal wrench, you can't get the pedal off.

SOLUTION: Make sure that you're turning the pedal the right way. The right pedal is turned counterclockwise to loosen it, but the left pedal is turned clockwise. It's still not coming off? Add a cheater bar to the pedal wrench. Still stuck? Heat the crankarm with a propane torch slightly. Or remove the crankarm, put it in a vise, and use a long cheater bar on your wrench to remove the pedal.

PROBLEM: It's hard to get in and out of your clipless pedals.

SOLUTION: The parts that make up the jaws on top of the pedals may have come loose. Tighten the screws. No problem with the pedals? Check the cleats on the bottom of your shoes. If they have broken, replace them.

PROBLEM: You need to replace your clipless pedal cleats but the bolt heads are full of crud or damaged.

SOLUTION: Clean them out with an awl, and then force a hex key in by tapping on it with a hammer. If you can get the hex key to reform the hole in the bolt, you should be able to loosen the screws.

PROBLEM: You installed the pedals in the wrong sides before you realized it. Now the left pedal is in the right crankarm and the right is in the left.

SOLUTION: Next time, look at the pedals right at the threaded portion of the spindle. Usually, pedals are marked with an R or an L designating right and left. (The R pedal is for the right crankarm and the L is for the left.) All you can do to fix pedals threaded into the wrong sides is to remove the pedals and hope for the best. Usually, threading them into the wrong sides destroys the threads in the crankarms. If that's the case, you'll need to replace the crankarms. You can try to have a shop repair the crankarms with something called a helicoil kit, though this doesn't always work. The good news is that the pedals should be reusable, as the crankarm threads are soft and shouldn't damage the pedal threads.

PROBLEM: Your clipless pedal cleats will not come off because the bolts are damaged or frozen.

SOLUTION: Apply a penetrating lubricant, then use a punch and hammer to loosen the screws. Use a pointed punch and strike the bolt to make a small divot. Put the point of the punch into the divot and strike the punch so that the force pushes the screw counterclockwise and loosens it.

PROBLEM: You stripped the threaded plate inside your shoe.

SOLUTION: In some shoes, it's possible to lift up the liner inside the shoe and replace the threaded insert. If not, it's usually possible to cut a hole in the shoe that's just large enough to allow you to perform surgery and replace the threaded insert. Then you can glue or tape the liner back in place.

PROBLEM: You need to remove the pedal but can't find a place to fit your pedal wrench.

SOLUTION: The pedal may be a type that's installed and removed with a hex key only. Look at the back of the crankarm to see if there is a hex-shaped hole in the pedal spindle. If so, get the appropriate hex key and use it to loosen and remove the pedals.

PROBLEM: You crashed and now it feels like the pedal wobbles when you're riding.

SOLUTION: You probably bent the pedal spindle when you crashed, which will cause a wobbly feeling when you're pedaling. This can also lead to ankle problems if you ride on it a lot. You might be able to get a replacement spindle, or replace the pedal or set of pedals.

PROBLEM: You're trying to thread a toe strap through the pedal cage, but it's too thick to fit.

SOLUTION: Trim the end of the strap so that it's pointed, then poke it into the side of the cage as far as you can get it. Clamp a small vise grip on the end and pull with the vise grip to get the strap through the pedal.

Mountain Bike Clipless Pedal Maintenance

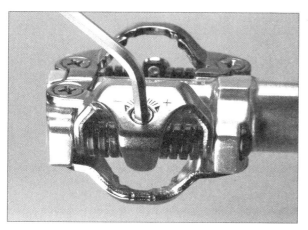

1 Unless they're abused, conventional pedals require little maintenance. In fact, superior models often perform flawlessly without service for 3 to 5 years. Once you've tried clipless pedals, however, it's hard to tolerate clips and straps. Unfortunately, click-in convenience comes at the cost of more upkeep, primarily because cleat engagement mechanisms complicate the pedal designs. Here are adjustment and repair tips for many common mountain bike clipless pedals.

If you're having trouble getting in or out of a new pair of clipless pedals, make sure that the cleat engages the pedal completely and properly. On certain shoe/pedal combinations, the shoe's sole may interfere and prevent proper engagement. Trim it with a sharp knife to get the clearance needed. Still problematic? Most pedals have a spring tension adjustment. Look for a single bolt on the front and back of the pedal (or just a rear one on single-sided pedals). Turn these screws counterclockwise (see photo) to ease entry and release. Lightly lube the cleat and jaws.

2 Snug the screws that secure the jaws atop the pedals because they can loosen. Many models also have screws to check on the pedal ends facing the crankarms.

With enough use, cleats wear and it begins to get difficult to escape the pedals. At the first signs of unreliable release, for safety's sake, replace the cleats. Mark the position by scratching indicator lines in the soles.

If the cleat bolts won't budge, use a hammer and punch to drive the screws counterclockwise (see photo), or use a propane torch to slightly heat them (wrap wet rags around the sole to prevent it from melting). Grease the bolts and the nuts inside the shoes. Align and install the new cleats.

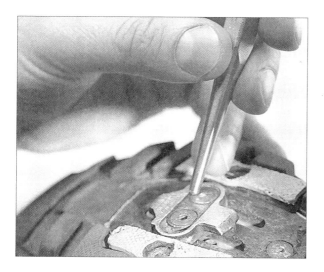

3 To remove the pedals, shift onto the large chainring, place the pedal in the 3-o'clock (right side) and 9-o'clock (left) positions, attach the pedal wrench so that it's nearly in line with the crankarm, and push down to loosen and remove the pedals (see photo). If they won't turn, ask a strong friend to help, use a cheater bar on the wrench, or remove the crankarm, put it in a vise, and try again (remember that the left pedal turns clockwise to loosen). When the pedals are off, spin the spindles between your fingers. If they turn without resistance or feel dry, tight, loose, or rough, regrease the bearings. If there's a hydraulic resistance while turning the spindle, the grease is still fine.

4 Most of Shimano's pedals, as well as some other brands, come apart by unscrewing and removing the spindle and bearings as a unit. Use the pedal spindle tool (see photo) or appropriate wrench to unscrew the spindle/bearing assembly. Hold the right pedal in the vise with the spindle upright, and turn the tool clockwise to unscrew the spindle. To unscrew the left pedal spindle, turn the tool counterclockwise.

5 Some clipless pedals have a dust cap that you must remove to access the bearings. Some, like Shimano's PD-M535, use a simple plastic cap that can be pried out (see photo). Others require the use of a hex key or a flat screwdriver. In most cases, it's relatively obvious how the cap is removed. With the number of different designs in current use, it's best to consult the owner's manual before delving too deep.

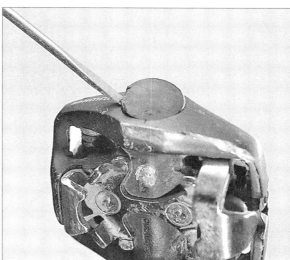

6 If you add grease every few months, the pedals may never need new parts. For most Shimano models and similar pedals with cartridge spindle/bearings, put about ½ ounce of grease inside the pedal body and reinstall the spindle assembly, which will re-grease all the bearings (see photo). Lube Speedplay pedals by removing the tiny bolts in the ends and pumping grease in with a needlenose grease gun. For Shimano pedals with a plastic dust cap, remove the cap and push grease into the exposed bearings. Pull back the rubber seal on the spindle, and push fresh grease into the inside bearings.

Shimano SPD Pedal Bearing Overhaul

1 Shimano SPD pedals are nicely sealed and should resist penetration by water and dirt under most conditions. Check the pedals by removing them from the crankarm, turning the spindles slowly in your fingers, and pushing sideways to feel for play. If the spindles turn with a hydraulic smoothness and there is no play when you push and pull the spindles, the pedals are in fine shape and don't need service. If the spindles turn roughly or you feel play, take the following steps to refurbish them.

You'll need a Shimano spindle removal tool and a wrench that fits on it to separate the spindle from the pedal body (see photo). You can use an adjustable wrench. (It's also possible to place the spindle removal tool in a vise and turn the pedal to remove the spindle.)

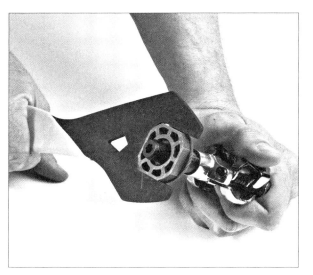

2 Place the tool on the splined portion of the spindle, attach the wrench to the tool, and turn the tool to unscrew and remove the spindle (see photo). If you look closely at the face of the tool, you'll see that it's marked to show which way to turn the tool for both the right and left pedals. Turn the tool clockwise to loosen the right spindle and counterclockwise to remove the left.

3 Don't force the tool. If it doesn't turn with a little pressure, you may be turning it the wrong way. If it doesn't turn, apply pressure in the other direction. After a few turns, you should be able to pull the spindle out of the pedal.

4 Clean off any dirt that's on the end of the spindle, which is where one of the bearing cartridges resides. Clean off any contaminated grease or dirt that you find on the rest of the spindle. Use a swab to wipe any dirt, contaminated grease, or water from inside the pedal body.

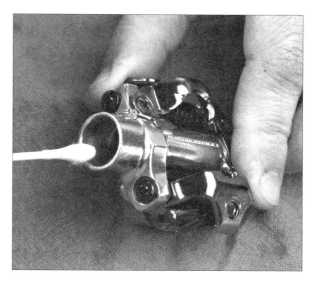

5 Place a dollop of grease on the end of the spindle assembly (see photo). Place a small dollop (about the size of a marble) inside the pedal body. Turning it by hand only, screw the spindle into the pedal a few turns. Extract it and repeat. This will push the fresh grease into the spindle body and work it along the spindle.

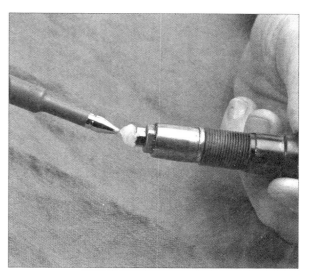

6 To finish the job, install the tool on the spindle, and thread the spindle back into the pedal body fully by hand (see photo). Sometimes the new grease will cause a hydraulic resistance that can damage plastic parts inside the pedal if you force the spindle. If the spindle resists at any point, extract it and start again. When you have hand-turned the spindle all the way into the pedal, use the wrench to hold the tool and tighten the spindle. Don't overtighten—it needs little effort to remain tight. The pedal spindle should now turn smoothly and without play.

Conventional Pedal Repair and Maintenance

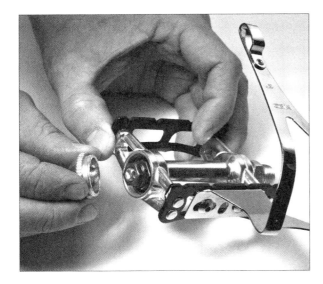

1 Pedals are always easiest to maintain when they are removed from the crankarms. Keep in mind that a left-hand pedal threads in the opposite direction from a right-hand pedal.

To loosen a pedal for removal, rotate its crankarm forward (toward the front of the bike), put the pedal wrench on the pedal, then push the wrench down toward the ground. This procedure will work for both pedals.

To disassemble a pedal, remove the dustcap from the end of the spindle opposite the threaded end. On many models, you pry off the dustcap with a flat-blade screwdriver or similar tool (see photo).

If you have a bench vise, use it to hold the pedal in an upright position while you disassemble it. If you don't have a vise, hold the pedal with locking pliers or by hand. It won't make the job that much more difficult.

2 Once the dustcap is off, you'll see a locknut on the end of the spindle. It holds the spindle and the bearings inside the body of the pedal.

Hold the spindle with a 15 mm wrench while you use an appropriately sized wrench to loosen the locknut inside the pedal body. A keyed washer usually separates the cone and locknut, making it possible to loosen the locknut without holding the cone directly.

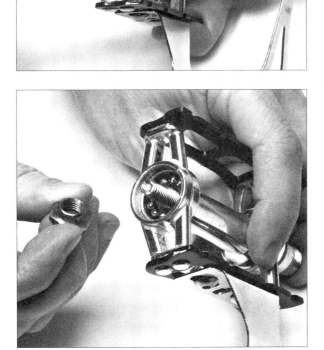

3 Remove the locknut and the lockwasher behind it. Thread off the cone. Be careful as you remove the cone because there are bearings behind it that can easily fall out and become lost.

To remove the bearings, either turn the pedal upside down and shake the bearings into a container, or use a pair of tweezers to pick them out one by one. Make sure that the spindle remains inside the pedal body while the first set of bearings is being removed. As soon as the outer bearings are out, record the number so you'll know how many replacements to put back in.

4 Turn the pedal over and pull the spindle out. If the spindle has a rubber seal, this may take some effort. Once it's out, remove the second set of bearings and count them. Take a sample with you to buy replacements of the same size. Clean all metal parts with solvent. For plastic parts and rubber seals, use something mild, such as alcohol. Get all of the old grease out of the inside of the pedal body. Inspect the bearing races. If they are pitted, check with a bike shop to see if replacement parts are available.

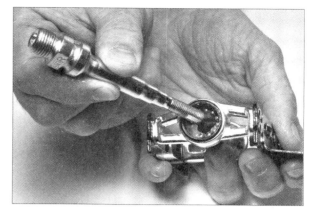

5 When you have clean and usable parts, re-assemble the pedal. Pack medium-weight grease into the bearing race, and install new sets of bearings.

As you insert the spindle, it's important that you don't turn it because that can dislodge the bearings.

Turn the pedal over. If you just screw on the cone, you'll scramble the bearings in the top race, forcing you to reposition them and try again. Hold the bottom of the pedal spindle and push up to keep the spindle fully inserted in the pedal. Holding the pedal spindle like this, screw the cone only a couple of turns. To seat the cone on the bearings, turn the bottom of the spindle while you hold the cone. Don't turn the cone

or the pedal, just the spindle. This will draw the cone onto the bearings without unseating them in their race. Put the lockwasher back in place, and thread the locknut back on the end of the spindle.

Make sure that the locknut is loose enough to give you some working room, then back the cone off until you know it's too loose. Slowly turn the cone down. Once you reach the point where most of the play is out of the adjustment, hold the spindle with a 15 mm wrench, and use a second wrench to tighten the locknut.

Spin the pedal. If you feel any binding, your adjustment is too tight. If binding is no problem but you feel play in the bearings when you wiggle the spindle up and down, loosen the locknut and turn the cone down a little more. Tighten the locknut and check the adjustment again.

Work in small increments in this way until you reach the point where there is neither binding nor looseness in the adjustment. Then make sure that the locknut is firmly fastened, and replace the dustcap.

6 When installing a leather toe strap, put a single twist in it as you run it between the two sides of the pedal. This prevents it from shifting position. Lace the strap through the upper end of the toeclip, then press the buckle open and run the end of the strap straight through both the inner and outer plates of the buckle (see photo). When you release the buckle, the end of the strap should be caught between the cylinder of the inner plate and the teeth in the outer plate of the buckle.

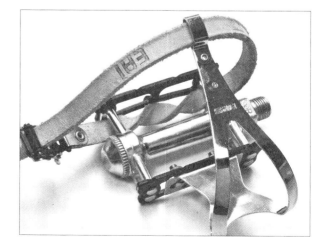

Look Pedal Bearing Overhaul

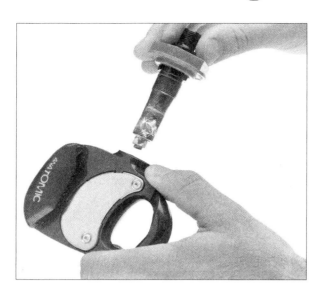

1 Look pedals were one of the first clipless types and are perhaps the most widely used ones today. The backing plates on newer models rarely wear out and do not need service. If you have problems in this area, the best remedy is to install new cleats on your shoes. (Also, avoid walking on your cleats, which wears them.) The pedal spindles employ cassette-type cartridge bearings. While these are quite resistant to dirt and water, they still require service occasionally. To service Look pedal bearings, remove the spindle cap with a 15 mm open-end wrench or pin tool. The cap also serves as the outer bearing retainer. Therefore, a loose cap will allow the pedal to rattle on the spindle. Keep the cap tight when in use.

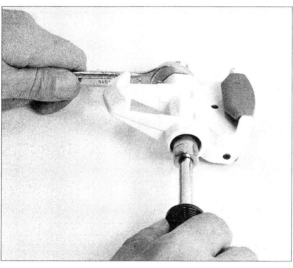

2 While holding the pedal spindle near its threads with the 15 mm wrench, loosen the spindle end nut with an 11 mm socket wrench (see photo 1). (Note: The left spindle nut is left-hand threaded, while the right one is right-hand threaded.) You'll feel resistance most of the way because the nut has a nylon bushing. (The left and right nut bushings are different colors for identification.) Stop when the nut protrudes from the pedal body but still has three or four threads engaged.

Tap the nut against your workbench, or free the spindle with a wooden or plastic mallet (see photo). Unscrew the nut completely, and pull the spindle out of the pedal. Wipe off the grease and inspect the spindle's bearing surface for roughness or discoloration. If you find any, replace the spindle.

3 The outer bearing slip-fits into the pedal and can be removed by gently poking it from behind with a driftpin or screwdriver (see photo). Soak the outer bearing and pedal body/inner bearing in solvent to loosen the dirt and old grease.

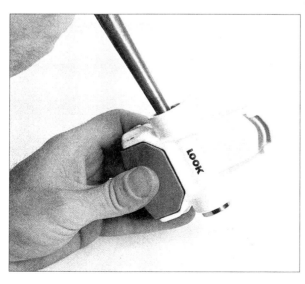

4 Use a bottle brush to gently clean the inside of the inner bearing (don't dislodge any of the needle bearings) and the outer bearing (see photo).

If you have access to compressed air, blow the bearings dry. If not, rinse them with clean solvent and let them air-dry on a rag or paper towel.

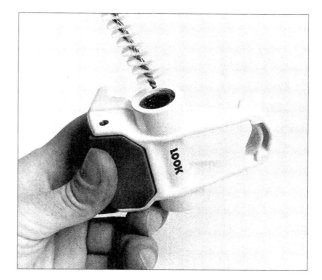

5 Work some grease into the dry bearings. Lightly grease the entire inner portion of the spindle and insert it into the pedal (see photo). Slide the outer bearing into the pedal body so the spindle threads protrude through the center. Thread on the correct spindle nut, hold the spindle with the 15 mm wrench, and tighten the nut with the 11 mm wrench. Don't overtighten! The spindle should barely protrude from the nut when tight and should rotate freely within the pedal body until the spindle cap is attached.

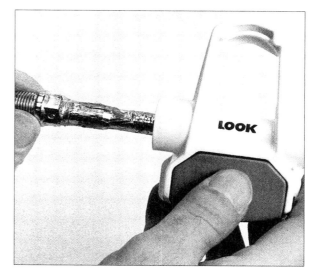

6 Screw on the spindle cap, and gently tighten it with the 15 mm wrench or pin tool. Spin the pedal to make sure it rotates easily (see photo).

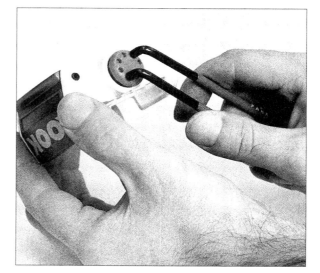

17 GEARS

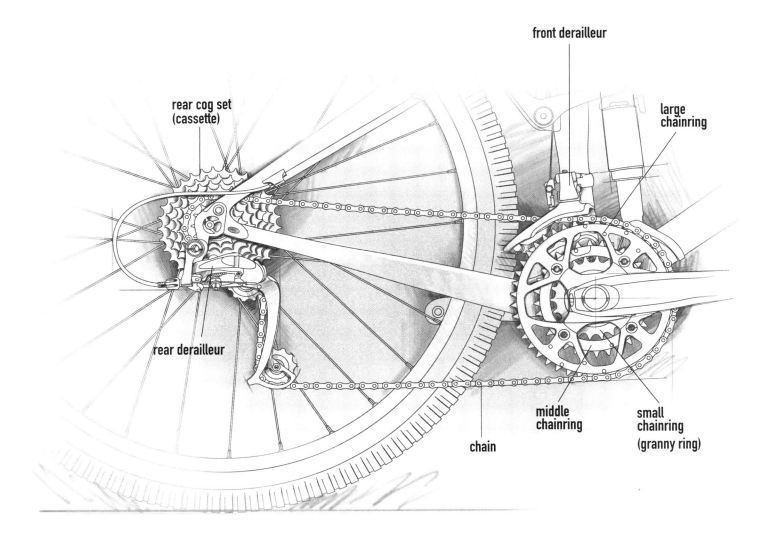

front derailleur

rear cog set
(cassette)

large
chainring

rear derailleur

middle
chainring

small
chainring
(granny ring)

chain

ith a limited range of motion and gross power output, the human body is not well equipped to move very fast, very far, for very long. There are, of course, super-athletes who run double marathons, but what of the rest of us: the mere mortals?

The bicycle is a way that even the most average of us can move quickly over distances with much less effort than would be possible on foot. This is all thanks to gearing.

Add the convenience of variable gearing provided by a derailleur drivetrain or internally geared hub, and our range extends for miles. Low gears allow you to climb steep grades, and high gears can propel you as fast as your nerves will allow coming back down. Of course, we mustn't forget those perfectly comfortable medium gears that are ideal for a casual ride to the corner store or a relaxing cruise to the ice cream shop by the beach.

But what is the right medium gear? What makes a good high gear or low gear? Gearing is often misunderstood. So here, we take some time to explain the basics of gearing.

THE LINGO

In the United States, designated gear sizes date back to the days of highwheelers, those antique bikes you sometimes see in Memorial Day parades. With a highwheeler, each complete revolution of the pedals resulted in a single wheel revolution. The diameter of the front wheel was a gauge of how fast you could go. A highwheeler with a 56-inch-diameter front wheel was faster than one with a 48-inch-diameter front wheel but was harder to ride up hills.

Today, we still refer to gears by the equivalent highwheeler size that would give you the same distance traveled per pedal revolution as the distance you would cover with one pedal revolution on your 26- or 27-inch wheel. For example, when you ride

on a 52-tooth chainring and a 14-tooth cassette cog, your gear ratio is $^{52}/_{14}$, or 3.714. If you multiply that ratio by the wheel diameter of a standard derailleur road bike—27 inches—you have a 100-inch gear. (See the tables on pages 354 and 355 for the gear-inch equivalents of most bicycle gear combinations.)

Notice that the gear ratio is determined by dividing the number of teeth on the chainring by the number of teeth on the rear cog—54 divided by 14 equals 3.714. A 52-tooth chainring and a 14-tooth cog are in a ratio of 3.714 to 1. If the chainring is reduced in size to 30 teeth and the size of the rear cog increased to 30 teeth, it would be a 1-to-1 ratio. Multiplying this ratio by the wheel diameter, we find that this combination of chainring and cassette gives us a gear of only 27 inches. The difference in the size of these numbers reflects the different levels of effort needed to propel a bicycle using the two gears. A 100-inch gear will move you 3.714 times as far down the road with each revolution of the pedals as will a 27-inch gear. However, the smaller gear will

Sample Road Gearing

CASSETTE COG	INNER CHAINRING	OUTER CHAINRING
	39*	53*
12	88	119
13	81	110
14	75	102
15	70	95
16	66	89
17	62	84
19	55	75
21	50	68
23	46	62
26	41	55

* IN GEAR INCHES

allow you to pedal up a steep grade with a heavy load, while the larger gear is useful only on fast descents or, if you are quite strong, on flat terrain.

Later in this chapter, charts display common road and mountain bike gear ranges, giving some different chainring and cassette cog combinations. For now, we want to make clear the logic of how these numbers are derived and what they mean in relation to one another. The higher the number, the greater the size of the chainring in relation to the cassette cog, and the greater the effort needed to use the gear (in other words, the bigger the chainring, the harder it is to pedal). Conversely, the lower the number, the smaller the size of the chainring in relation to the cassette cog, and the less effort needed to propel the bike (in other words, the smaller the chainring, the easier it is to pedal).

From this, you can see that there are two ways you can move to a gear that is larger (harder to pedal) or smaller (easier to pedal) than the one you are in. To move to a larger gear (harder), you can either shift the chain onto either a larger chainring or a smaller rear cog. Either move will increase the gear ratio and thus the size of the gear. Conversely, you can move to a smaller gear (easier) by shifting onto either a larger rear cog or a smaller chainring.

The manner in which bicycle gearing systems are set up makes the distinction between larger and smaller gears easy to remember. The smaller the chainring or the larger the rear cog, the closer it is to the bicycle frame; the larger the chainring or the smaller the cog, the farther it is from the bicycle frame. Thus, the lowest gear—the easiest to pedal—is formed with the chain all the way to the inside on both front and rear. You're in the highest gear—the hardest to pedal—when the chain is shifted as far to the outside as it can be, both front and rear.

To simplify references to different gear combinations when you're planning or analyzing a gear pattern, it's helpful to assign numbers to the cassette cogs and letters to the chainrings. Mentally number the cogs consecutively from inside to outside in order to reflect their relative effects on gear size. Thus, the innermost cog is referred to as 1, and the outermost is referred to as 6, 7, 8, 9, or 10 (depending on the total number). In a similar way, use an L to refer to the inner chainring (the one that produces lower gears) and H to refer to the outer chainring (the one that produces higher gears). In

Sample Mountain Bike Gearing

CASSETTE COG	INNER CHAINRING	MIDDLE CHAINRING	OUTER CHAINRING
	22*	32*	42*
11	52	76	99
12	48	69	91
14	41	59	78
16	36	52	68
18	32	46	61
20	29	42	55
23	25	36	47
28	20	30	39
34	17	24	32

* IN GEAR INCHES

the case of triple-chainring cranksets, add the letter M to designate the gears formed on the middle chainring.

Using this code, the gear formed on the inner chainring and the inside cog is L-1, and the gear formed on the outer chainring and outside cog is H-8 (or H-9 or H-10, depending on whether there are 8, 9, or 10 cassette cogs). This works for either a double- or triple-chainring system, as the gears formed on the middle ring of a triple will be identified as M-1, M-2, and so on.

The most common method used for charting a gearing system is to write the chainring sizes across the top and the cog sizes down the side of vertical columns, calculate all combinations of the two (or use a gear chart to find them), and list the results in gear inches within the columns. In this chapter, we've provided charts of this type for two common gear arrangements.

The primary value of creating gear charts of this sort is that they let you make a quick numerical comparison so you can figure out how many usable gears you have and how large or small the jumps are between gears. Once you know this, you may decide to modify the gearing to better suit the terrain or your strengths as a rider.

The ease of altering your gearing, however, depends on your drivetrain components. Some cassettes and chainrings are easy to modify, and others are more difficult. It's almost always easy to install lower or higher gears, however, which satisfies most riders' requirements.

When analyzing your gears, keep in mind that two combinations are usually not used: the small chainring/small cassette cog combination and the large chainring/large cassette cog combination. These "crossover" gears put the chain at an extreme angle, and it's best to avoid them because they wear the chain and cassette cogs rapidly. Because of this, they're generally considered unusable gears and are not shown in gear charts.

GEARING SIMPLIFIED

Only a few years ago, it was necessary for tourists, mountain bikers, and even commuters to customize gearing to get the gear ratios they needed. Gearing was limited because freewheels were available only in five- and six-cog models, which required some compromise in gear choice to get the low and high gears you needed, a reasonable range in between, and a smooth shift sequence.

These days, with index drivetrains (ones where the shift levers click into position with each shift) that shift beautifully under the most adverse conditions and 9- and even 10-cog cassettes that provide a wide gear range, there's far less need to customize drivetrains. Perhaps predictably, options have been reduced as well. Index shifting relies on precisely spaced cassette cogs and chainrings, so most manufacturers make a limited range of replacements. This makes it difficult to change the gearing too much. Fortunately, the options that are offered satisfy most needs and work best with the index system for which they're designed.

To give you an idea of modern gearing, here are examples of common road and mountain bike drivetrains. The road bike may be equipped with 39- and 53-tooth chainrings and a 12-, 13-, 14-, 15-, 16-, 17-, 19-, 21-, 23-, and 26-tooth 10-speed cassette. The mountain bike may have 22-, 32-, and 42-tooth chainrings and a 11-, 12-, 14-, 16-, 18-, 20-, 23-, 28-, and 34-tooth 9-speed cassette.

The road bike gearing is an example of what you'd find on many racing bicycles. A $^{39}/_{26}$ lowest gear combination results in a 41-inch gear, which is low enough for a fit rider to use to tackle most paved hills at a reasonable pace. A $^{53}/_{12}$ highest gear produces a 119-inch top end, which is a "tall" enough

gear for all-out sprinting and pushing the pace down hills. In between, there are one-tooth jumps on the low end of the cassette, which allow a very gradual change in effort that's ideal for a racing or training rider to fine-tune the gear while jamming on the flats or descending. On the upper end of the cassette, the jumps are two- and three-tooth because these gears are used for climbing, when you are moving more slowly and need greater changes with each shift.

Normally, road riders fine-tune gear selection by shifting the rear derailleur—each rear shift here makes a small difference in pedal effort. For a major change, they shift the front derailleur to move between chainrings.

The mountain bike has a wider range that is better suited to the demands of dirt riding, including gravity-defying ascents and bone-jarring trails. One of the main differences between the two drivetrains is the third chainring, which is known as a "granny" gear (presumably low enough for Granny to get over hills). You'll also notice that the high end is not nearly as high as on the road bike—because of the tire size and shape and the terrain covered, the speeds achieved off road are rarely equal to road speeds. Furthermore, the cassette cog spacing is wider than that of the road bike, so one shift usually results in at least a two-tooth jump, whether you're shifting between chainrings or between cogs. This is important because on a mountain bike you're generally not moving as quickly as on a road bike, and it's best to have a reasonable gear change with each shift.

Just as road bikers do, mountain bikers usually shift the rear derailleur for small changes in pedal effort and shift between chainrings for major changes. Because there are three chainrings, and because off-road terrain can change more abruptly than pavement, front shifts are more frequent in mountain biking than in road riding.

MODIFYING YOUR GEARING

To fit a gearing system to your particular needs, you need to determine five things:

1. An optimum high gear
2. An optimum low gear
3. An appropriate shift pattern (jumps between gears)

4. Chainring and cassette cogs that will combine these high-low choices with the chosen shift pattern

5. The appropriate derailleurs, shifters, and chain to make your selections work.

If you want to modify your current bike without completely replacing your drivetrain, determine the optimum high and low gears, decide on a shift pattern, and pick replacement cogs and chainrings that are compatible with your derailleurs. Use the tables on pages 354 and 355 to quickly determine which combinations will give you gears in the desired range.

On paper, it's possible to invent just about any gear range and shift sequence. In reality, options are limited. Before getting too carried away crunching numbers, check with shops to see what replacement cassette cogs and chainrings are available for your drivetrain, then plan your gearing modifications accordingly.

HOW HIGH?

The 90- to 120-inch high gear found on most bikes represents a kind of gear ceiling that is based on human limitations. Even the strongest road racers use only slightly larger gears (maybe 125 or so). In fact, average riders can't maintain a brisk cadence in a 119-inch gear even on a level road; that gear exists for downhills and tailwinds.

If you're not concerned about the bit of extra speed you'll lose by coasting downhill instead of pedaling, you can use a slightly smaller high gear—something in the mid- to upper 90s—and shift down your whole gear pattern to emphasize the middle and low ranges. It's a trade-off that is commonly made by mountain bike riders and by touring cyclists who carry a lot of equipment.

HOW LOW?

Deciding on the optimum lowest gear is a lot more difficult than choosing the highest. Some factors to consider are your strength, the steepness and length of the worst hills you usually encounter, and the amount of extra weight (if any) you may carry. You should also take into account the size of gaps between gears and how much extra difficulty in shifting you'd be willing to put up with in order to get extra-low gears.

Obviously, lots of personal factors influence your decision of how low your lowest gear needs to

be. Nonetheless, in the table we make some rough recommendations for those who don't have a good idea, based on personal experience, of what the low should be. The recommended gears range from those suitable for an average to a strong rider within each category. Thinking in terms of categories is important because an average racer planning some loaded touring can use a larger low gear than that recommended for a strong cyclist who's touring with a heavy load.

HOW MANY GEARS?

The number of gears in your drivetrain won't affect your choice of high or low gears, but it will affect how many intermediate gears you have. The 22 or 14 gears provided by a well-chosen eight-speed cassette and triple or double crankset will satisfy most riders. (These would actually provide 24 and 16 gears, but remember that you don't use your two extreme "crossover" gears.)

Competition road and mountain riders may prefer nine-speed cassettes, which provide one extra cog. The extra gears can be used on the high or low end or to bridge a too-large jump between gears. With older five- and six-speed drivetrains (and sometimes even with seven-speeds), racers occasionally find themselves wishing for a gear they didn't have. If they shift up a gear, it's too easy to pedal; if they shift down, it's too difficult. With nine cogs, this almost never occurs. Consequently, nine-speed cassettes have become very popular with competitive cyclists both on and off road.

In fact, many century riders find nine-speed drivetrains—such as a $^{12}\!/_{26}$ cassette combined with a $^{39}\!/_{53}$ chainring combination—ideal because they provide closely spaced gears and an adequate high and low.

Likewise, mountain bikers as well as tourists and commuters carrying loads benefit from the added convenience of a third chainring. Being able to drop down into a granny gear when the trail steepens or when you're tackling a tough climb at the end of a long day's ride can make a significant difference.

PUTTING IT TOGETHER

At this point, we should mention that if you need to change most of the drivetrain components on your bike to get the kind of gearing you want, it might be more economical to sell your bike and buy one that

Recommended Low Gears

TYPE OF RIDING	TERRAIN	GEAR INCHES
Mountain biking	steep hills	17–20
	technical trails	17–20
	dirt roads	20–27
Loaded touring	steep hills	20–27
	medium hills	32–42
Casual road riding	steep hills	27–37
	medium hills	32–42
	flat	37–47
Road racing	steep hills	47–60
	flat to rolling	57–66

has gearing closer to what you desire. On the other hand, if you're considering starting with a bare frame and custom-equipping it, the sky's the limit as to what you can do with the gearing.

Most people's needs can be satisfied with some cassette cog changes and maybe a new chainring. Those are the cheapest options. When you start changing cranksets or even adding a third chainring and making the required bottom bracket axle change, the costs mount rapidly. Substantial changes in the range of your bike's gearing may also require new derailleurs. Be sure to check their gearing capacities before you start.

In general, if you have to buy a new inner chainring or a new crankset, it's wise to get a smaller chainring than you think you'll need. You can always match it with smaller cassette cogs to get big enough gears. If you need smaller gears, it's a lot easier and cheaper to make further modifications at the cassette end of your drivetrain than it is to reorder smaller chainrings.

Your local shop should be able to tell you what size cogs are available to match your equipment.

Make sure that you order the right type of cog for its particular position on the cassette. Remember, it may be less expensive and easier to buy a new cassette with the cogs you want already on it than to replace more than two cogs on the cassette you already own.

The gearing system on a bicycle makes it possible for humans to transcend their boundaries of speed and distance by several quantum leaps. In a nutshell, you are the motor that drives the bike. In the same way an automobile's motor is most efficient running at a certain rate (rpm, or revolutions per minute), your body is most efficient running at a certain rate, called cadence (for the revolutions per minute you're pedaling). When you have gearing that's appropriate for your ability as a cyclist and the terrain you ride in, and you know how to use the gears, you become incredibly efficient as a pedaler.

The key is shifting often and correctly, an easy skill to master. Don't worry about what gear you're in and whether it's the right or wrong gear. Instead, shift according to feel. You should have a comfortable cadence you like to pedal, a certain rpm that's most efficient for you. Most cyclists pedal about 60 rpm when they're just learning to ride and speed up to 90 as they gain experience. Top racers can fan the pedals upward of 150 rpm.

To use the gears most efficiently, all you have to do is monitor your pedal speed, something that becomes second nature in time. When it drops below your comfortable rate, shift into an easier-to-pedal gear. When you have to pedal too fast, shift into a harder gear. Your goal is always to be in a gear that allows you to pedal at a comfortable cadence. With practice, shifts will become reflexive—you won't even realize you're doing it. Your shifting skill will make easy work of long and hilly rides.

To not utilize the full potential of today's easy-shifting, wide-range gearing systems is to ignore the most significant advance that has been made in the design and equipment of the modern bicycle. So even if you're not planning to revamp your drivetrain, take the time to get to know its strengths and weaknesses.

Gear Chart for 27-Inch Wheels

FORMULA: $\dfrac{\text{Number of teeth on chainring}}{\text{Number of teeth on cog}} \times \text{Wheel diameter} = \text{Gear inches}$

NUMBER OF TEETH ON CHAINRING

	34	33	32	31	30	29	28	27	26	25	24	23	22	21	20	19	18	17	16	15	14	13	12	11
56	44.5	45.8	47.3	48.8	50.4	52.1	54	56	58.2	60.5	63	65.7	68.7	72	75.6	79.6	84	88.9	94.5	101	108	116	126	137
55	43.7	45	46.4	47.9	49.5	51.2	53	55	57.1	59.4	61.9	64.6	67.5	70.7	74.3	78.2	82.5	87.4	92.8	99	106	114	124	135
54	42.9	44.2	45.6	47	48.6	50.3	52.1	54	56.1	58.3	60.8	63.4	66.3	69.4	72.9	76.7	81	85.8	91.1	97.2	104	112	122	133
53	42.1	43.4	44.7	46.2	47.7	49.3	51.1	53	55	57.2	59.6	62.2	65	68.1	71.6	75.3	79.5	84.2	89.4	95.4	102	110	119	130
52	41.3	42.5	43.9	45.3	46.8	48.4	50.1	52	54	56.2	58.5	61	63.8	66.9	70.2	73.9	78	82.6	87.8	93.6	100	108	117	128
51	40.5	41.7	43	44.4	45.9	47.5	49.2	51	53	55.1	57.4	59.9	62.6	65.6	68.9	72.5	76.5	81	86.1	91.8	98.4	106	115	125
50	39.7	40.9	42.2	43.5	45	46.6	48.2	50	51.9	54	56.3	58.7	61.4	64.3	67.5	71.1	75	79.4	84.4	90	96.4	104	113	123
49	38.9	40.1	41.3	42.7	44.1	45.6	47.3	49	50.9	52.9	55.1	57.5	60.1	63	66.2	69.6	73.5	77.8	82.7	88.2	94.5	102	110	120
48	38.1	39.3	40.5	41.8	43.2	44.7	46.3	48	49.8	51.8	54	56.3	58.9	61.7	64.8	68.2	72	76.2	81	86.4	92.6	99.7	108	118
47	37.3	38.5	39.7	40.9	42.3	43.8	45.3	47	48.8	50.8	52.9	55.2	57.7	60.4	63.5	66.8	70.5	74.6	79.3	84.6	90.6	97.6	106	115
46	36.5	37.6	38.8	40.1	41.4	42.8	44.4	46	47.8	49.7	51.8	54	56.5	59.1	62.1	65.4	69	73.1	77.6	82.8	88.7	95.5	104	113
45	35.7	36.8	38	39.2	40.5	41.9	43.4	45	46.7	48.6	50.6	52.8	55.2	57.9	60.8	63.9	67.5	71.5	75.9	81	86.8	93.5	101	110
44	34.9	36	37.1	38.3	39.6	41	42.4	44	45.7	47.5	49.5	51.7	54	56.6	59.4	62.5	66	69.9	74.3	79.2	84.9	91.4	99	108
43	34.1	35.2	36.3	37.5	38.7	40	41.5	43	44.7	46.4	48.4	50.5	52.8	55.3	58.1	61.1	64.5	68.3	72.6	77.4	82.9	89.3	96.8	106
42	33.4	34.4	35.4	36.6	37.8	39.1	40.5	42	43.6	45.4	47.3	49.3	51.5	54	56.7	59.7	63	66.7	70.9	75.6	81	87.2	94.5	103
41	32.6	33.5	34.6	35.7	36.9	38.2	39.5	41	42.6	44.3	46.1	48.1	50.3	52.7	55.4	58.3	61.5	65.1	69.2	73.8	79.1	85.2	92.3	101
40	31.8	32.7	33.8	34.8	36	37.2	38.6	40	41.5	43.2	45	47	49.1	51.4	54	56.8	60	63.5	67.5	72	77.1	83.1	90	98.2
39	31	31.9	32.9	34	35.1	36.3	37.6	39	40.5	42.1	43.9	45.8	47.9	50.1	52.7	55.4	58.5	61.9	65.8	70.2	75.2	81	87.8	95.7
38	30.2	31.1	32.1	33.1	34.2	35.4	36.6	38	39.5	41	42.8	44.6	46.6	48.9	51.3	54	57	60.4	64.1	68.4	73.3	78.9	85.5	93.3
37	29.4	30.3	31.2	32.2	33.3	34.4	35.7	37	38.4	40	41.6	43.4	45.4	47.6	50	52.6	55.5	58.8	62.4	66.6	71.4	76.8	83.3	90.8
36	28.6	29.5	30.4	31.4	32.4	33.5	34.7	36	37.4	38.9	40.5	42.3	44.2	46.3	48.6	51.2	54	57.2	60.8	64.8	69.4	74.8	81	88.4
35	27.8	28.6	29.5	30.5	31.5	32.6	33.8	35	36.3	37.8	39.4	41.1	43	45	47.3	49.7	52.5	55.6	59.1	63	67.5	72.7	78.8	85.9
34	27	27.8	28.7	29.6	30.6	31.7	32.8	34	35.3	36.7	38.3	39.9	41.7	43.7	45.9	48.3	51	54	57.4	61.2	65.6	70.6	76.5	83.5
33	26.2	27	27.8	28.7	29.7	30.7	31.8	33	34.3	35.6	37.1	38.7	40.5	42.4	44.6	46.9	49.5	52.4	55.7	59.4	63.6	68.5	74.3	81
32	25.4	26.2	27	27.9	28.8	29.8	30.9	32	33.2	34.6	36	37.6	39.3	41.1	43.2	45.5	48	50.8	54	57.6	61.7	66.5	72	78.5
31	24.6	25.4	26.2	27	27.9	28.9	29.9	31	32.2	33.5	34.9	36.4	38	39.9	41.9	44.1	46.5	49.2	52.3	55.8	59.8	64.4	69.8	76.1
30	23.8	24.5	25.3	26.1	27	27.9	28.9	30	31.2	32.4	33.8	35.2	36.8	38.6	40.5	42.6	45	47.6	50.6	54	57.9	62.3	67.5	73.6
29	23	23.7	24.5	25.3	26.1	27	28	29	30.1	31.3	32.6	34	35.6	37.3	39.2	41.2	43.5	46.1	48.9	52.2	55.9	60.2	65.3	71.2
28	22.2	22.9	23.6	24.4	25.2	26.1	27	28	29.1	30.2	31.5	32.9	34.4	36	37.8	39.8	42	44.5	47.3	50.4	54	58.2	63	68.7
27	21.4	22.1	22.8	23.5	24.3	25.1	26	27	28	29.2	30.4	31.7	33.1	34.7	36.5	38.4	40.5	42.9	45.6	48.6	52.1	56.1	60.8	66.3
26	20.6	21.3	21.9	22.6	23.4	24.2	25.1	26	27	28.1	29.3	30.5	31.9	33.4	35.1	36.9	39	41.3	43.9	46.8	50.1	54	58.5	63.8
25	19.9	20.5	21.1	21.8	22.5	23.3	24.1	25	26	27	28.1	29.3	30.7	32.1	33.8	35.5	37.5	39.7	42.2	45	48.2	51.9	56.3	61.4
24	19.1	19.6	20.3	20.9	21.6	22.3	23.1	24	24.9	25.9	27	28.2	29.5	30.9	32.4	34.1	36	38.1	40.5	43.2	46.3	49.8	54	58.9
23	18.3	18.8	19.4	20	20.7	21.4	22.2	23	23.9	24.8	25.9	27	28.2	29.6	31.1	32.7	34.5	36.5	38.8	41.4	44.4	47.8	51.8	56.5
22	17.5	18	18.6	19.2	19.8	20.5	21.2	22	22.8	23.8	24.8	25.8	27	28.3	29.7	31.3	33	34.9	37.1	39.6	42.4	45.7	49.5	54
	34	33	32	31	30	29	28	27	26	25	24	23	22	21	20	19	18	17	16	15	14	13	12	11

NUMBER OF TEETH ON COG

These numbers represent "gear inches," which can be used to compare the various combinations of cogs and chainrings. The lower the number, the easier the gear is to pedal, and vice versa.

Gear Chart for 26-Inch Wheels

FORMULA: $\dfrac{\text{Number of teeth on chainring}}{\text{Number of teeth on cog}}$ X Wheel diameter = Gear inches

NUMBER OF TEETH ON CHAINRING

Chainring	34	33	32	31	30	29	28	27	26	25	24	23	22	21	20	19	18	17	16	15	14	13	12	11
56	42.8	44.1	45.5	47	48.5	50.2	52	53.9	56	58.2	60.7	63.3	66.2	69.3	72.8	76.6	80.9	85.6	91	97.1	104	112	121	132
55	42.1	43.3	44.7	46.1	47.7	49.3	51.1	53	55	57.2	59.6	62.2	65	68.1	71.5	75.3	79.4	84.1	89.4	95.3	102	110	119	130
54	41.3	42.5	43.9	45.3	46.8	48.4	50.1	52	54	56.2	58.5	61	63.8	66.9	70.2	73.9	78	82.6	87.8	93.6	100	108	117	128
53	40.5	41.8	43.1	44.5	45.9	47.5	49.2	51	53	55.1	57.4	59.7	62.6	65.6	68.9	72.5	76.6	81.1	86.1	91.9	98.4	106	115	125
52	39.8	41	42.3	43.6	45.1	46.6	48.3	50.1	52	54.1	56.3	58.8	61.5	64.4	67.6	71.2	75.1	79.5	84.5	90.1	96.6	104	113	123
51	39	40.2	41.4	42.8	44.2	45.7	47.4	49.1	51	53	55.3	57.7	60.3	63.1	66.3	69.8	73.7	78	82.9	88.4	94.7	102	111	121
50	38.2	39.4	40.6	41.9	43.3	44.8	46.4	48.1	50	52	54.2	56.5	59.1	61.9	65	68.4	72.2	76.5	81.3	86.7	92.9	100	108	118
49	37.5	38.6	39.8	41.1	42.5	43.9	45.5	47.2	49	51	53.1	55.4	57.9	60.7	63.7	67.1	70.8	74.9	79.6	84.9	91	98	106	116
48	36.7	37.8	39	40.3	41.6	43	44.6	46.2	48	49.9	52	54.3	56.7	59.4	62.4	65.7	69.3	73.4	78	83.2	89.1	96	104	113
47	35.9	37	38.2	39.4	40.7	42.1	43.6	45.3	47	48.9	50.9	53.1	55.5	58.2	61.1	64.3	67.9	71.9	76.4	81.5	87.3	94	102	111
46	35.2	36.2	37.4	38.6	39.9	41.2	42.7	44.3	46	47.8	49.8	52	54.4	57	59.8	62.9	66.4	70.4	74.8	79.7	85.4	92	99.7	109
45	34.4	35.5	36.6	37.7	39	40.3	41.8	43.3	45	46.8	48.8	50.9	53.2	55.7	58.5	61.6	65	68.8	73.1	78	83.6	90	97.5	106
44	33.6	34.7	35.8	36.9	38.1	39.4	40.9	42.4	44	45.8	47.7	49.7	52	54.5	57.2	60.2	63.6	67.3	71.5	76.3	81.7	88	95.3	104
43	32.9	33.9	34.9	36.1	37.3	38.6	39.9	41.4	43	44.7	46.6	48.6	50.8	53.2	55.9	58.8	62.1	65.8	69.9	74.5	79.9	86	93.2	102
42	32.1	33.1	34.1	35.2	36.4	37.7	39	40.4	42	43.7	45.5	47.5	49.6	52	54.6	57.5	60.7	64.2	68.3	72.8	78	84	91	99.3
41	31.4	32.3	33.3	34.4	35.5	36.8	38.1	39.5	41	42.6	44.4	46.3	48.5	50.8	53.3	56.1	59.2	62.7	66.6	71.1	76.1	82	88.8	96.9
40	30.6	31.5	32.5	33.5	34.7	35.9	37.1	38.5	40	41.6	43.3	45.2	47.3	49.5	52	54.7	57.8	61.2	65	69.3	74.3	80	86.7	94.5
39	29.8	30.7	31.7	32.7	33.8	35	36.2	37.6	39	40.6	42.3	44.1	46.1	48.3	50.7	53.4	56.3	59.6	63.4	67.6	72.4	78	84.5	92.2
38	29.1	29.9	30.9	31.9	32.9	34.1	35.3	36.6	38	39.5	41.2	43	44.9	47	49.4	52	54.9	58.1	61.8	65.9	70.6	76	82.3	89.8
37	28.3	29.2	30.1	31	32.1	33.2	34.4	35.6	37	38.5	40.1	41.8	43.7	45.8	48.1	50.6	53.4	56.6	60.1	64.1	68.7	74	80.2	87.5
36	27.5	28.4	29.3	30.2	31.2	32.3	33.4	34.7	36	37.4	39	40.7	42.5	44.6	46.8	49.3	52	55.1	58.5	62.4	66.9	72	78	85.1
35	26.8	27.6	28.4	29.4	30.3	31.4	32.5	33.7	35	36.4	37.9	39.6	41.4	43.3	45.5	47.9	50.6	53.5	56.9	60.7	65	70	75.8	82.7
34	26	26.8	27.6	28.5	29.5	30.5	31.6	32.7	34	35.4	36.8	38.4	40.2	42.1	44.2	46.5	49.1	52	55.3	58.9	63.1	68	73.7	80.4
33	25.2	26	26.8	27.7	28.6	29.6	30.6	31.8	33	34.3	35.8	37.3	39	40.9	42.9	45.2	47.7	50.5	53.6	57.2	61.3	66	71.5	78
32	24.5	25.2	26	26.8	27.7	28.7	29.7	30.8	32	33.3	34.7	36.2	37.8	39.6	41.6	43.8	46.2	48.9	52	55.5	59.4	64	69.3	75.6
31	23.7	24.4	25.2	26	26.9	27.8	28.8	29.9	31	32.2	33.6	35	36.6	38.4	40.3	42.4	44.8	47.4	50.4	53.7	57.6	62	67.2	73.3
30	22.9	23.6	24.4	25.2	26	26.9	27.9	28.9	30	31.2	32.5	33.9	35.5	37.1	39	41.1	43.3	45.9	48.8	52	55.7	60	65	70.9
29	22.2	22.8	23.6	24.3	25.1	26	26.9	27.9	29	30.2	31.4	32.8	34.3	35.9	37.7	39.7	41.9	44.4	47.1	50.3	53.9	58	62.8	68.5
28	21.4	22.1	22.8	23.5	24.3	25.1	26	27	28	29.1	30.3	31.7	33.1	34.7	36.4	38.3	40.4	42.8	45.5	48.5	52	56	60.7	66.2
27	20.6	21.3	21.9	22.6	23.4	24.2	25.1	26	27	28.1	29.3	30.5	31.9	33.4	35.1	36.9	39	41.3	43.9	46.8	50.1	54	58.5	63.8
26	19.9	20.5	21.1	21.8	22.5	23.3	24.1	25	26	27	28.2	29.4	30.7	32.2	33.8	35.6	37.6	39.8	42.3	45.1	48.3	52	56.3	61.5
25	19.1	19.7	20.3	21	21.7	22.4	23.2	24.1	25	26	27.1	28.3	29.5	31	32.5	34.2	36.1	38.2	40.6	43.3	46.4	50	54.2	59.1
24	18.4	18.9	19.5	20.1	20.8	21.5	22.3	23.1	24	25	26	27.1	28.4	29.7	31.2	32.8	34.7	36.7	39	41.6	44.6	48	52	56.7
23	17.6	18.1	18.7	19.3	19.9	20.6	21.4	22.1	23	23.9	24.9	26	27.2	28.5	29.9	31.5	33.2	35.2	37.4	39.9	42.7	46	49.8	54.4
22	16.8	17.3	17.9	18.5	19.1	19.7	20.4	21.2	22	22.9	23.8	24.9	26	27.2	28.6	30.1	31.8	33.6	35.8	38.1	40.9	44	47.7	52
	34	33	32	31	30	29	28	27	26	25	24	23	22	21	20	19	18	17	16	15	14	13	12	11

NUMBER OF TEETH ON COG

Glossary

A

Adjustable cup: the left-hand cup in a nonsealed bottom bracket, used in adjusting the bottom bracket bearings, and removed during bottom bracket overhaul

Aero levers: road bike brake levers employing hidden cables that travel out the back of the level body and under the handlebar tape

AheadSet: a type of headset made by Dia-Compe that fits on a fork that has a nonthreaded steerer

Allen wrench: a specific brand of hex key

All-mountain bike: a mountain bike designed to balance climbing and descending abilities with slightly more emphasis on descending prowess; features dual-suspension with 4 to 6 inches of travel

All-terrain bike (ATB): a term sometimes used for mountain bike

B

Bar-ends: mini handlebar add-ons that fit on the ends of mountain bike bars to add another riding position

B/b: common shorthand for bottom bracket

Beach cruiser: a bike that is designed for casual and comfortable road riding and that features a relaxed frame, fat 26-inch tires, a wide saddle, a wide handlebar, and rubber pedals

Bicycle Moto Cross (BMX): a type of racing done on a closed dirt track over obstacles, usually on 20- or 24-inch-wheel bikes with one gear

Binder bolt: the bolt used to fasten a stem inside a steerer tube, a seatpost inside a seat tube, or a handlebar inside a stem

BMX: *see* Bicycle Moto Cross

Bottom bracket: the cylindrical part of a bicycle frame that holds the crankset axle, two sets of ball bearings, a fixed cup, and an adjustable cup

Brake pad: (1) a block of rubberlike material fastened to the end of a rim-brake caliper; it presses against the wheel rim when the brakes are applied, also known as a brake block; (2) a thin block of resin, organic, or metallic-compound material that is clamped onto the disc (of a disc brake system) by the caliper

Brake shoe: the metal part that holds a brake pad and is bolted to the end of a brake caliper

Braze-ons: parts for mounting shift levers, derailleurs, water bottle cages, and racks, which are fastened to a bicycle frame through a type of soldering process known as brazing

Brinelled: a type of wear in bearing components that is a series of dents in the races or cups

Bushing: a sleeve that fits between two parts to act as a bearing, often found in suspension systems

Butted tubing: tubing with an outside diameter that remains constant but with a thinner-walled midsection where less strength is needed

C

Cable end: a small aluminum or plastic cap installed on the ends of brake and shift cables to keep them from fraying; also known as a cable crimp

Cage: on a front derailleur, a pair of parallel plates that push the chain from side to side; on a rear derailleur, a set of plates in which pulleys are mounted to hold and guide the chain from cog to cog

Calipers: (1) brake arms that reach around the sides of a wheel to press brake pads against the wheel rim; (2) the fixed portion of a disc brake system that houses the pistons and brake pads

Cam: the triangular piece of metal that fits between the rollers on rollercam brakes and moves the brake arms when the brake lever is squeezed

Cantilever brakes: rim brakes with pivoting arms mounted on fork blades or seatstays

Cassette hub: a type of rear hub that has a built-in freewheel mechanism

Chain: the series of links pinned together that extends from the chainring to the cogs on the back wheel and allows you to propel the bike by pedaling

Chainring: a sprocket attached to the right crankarm to drive the chain

Chainring nut spanner: a special tool used to loosen the slotted chainring bolts (the ones behind the inner ring) that fasten a chainring to a crankarm

Chainstays: the two tubes of a bicycle frame that run from the bottom bracket back to the rear dropouts

Chainwheel: *see* Chainring

Chain whip: a tool consisting of a metal bar and two sections of chain, used in changing cogs on a cassette; also known as a chain wrench

Chrome-moly: a type of high-quality steel tubing; also known as chrome molybdenum or cro-mo

Clincher tire: a tire with edges that hook under the curved-in edge of a rim

Clipless pedals: pedals that use a releasable mechanism like that of a ski binding to lock onto cleated shoes and do not use toeclips or toe straps

Coaster brake: a foot-operated brake built into the rear hub; normally found on one-speed kids' bikes and cruisers

Cog: a sprocket that is attached directly to the rear hub on a single-speed bike and mounted on a cassette on a multispeed bike

Cone: a bearing race that curves to the inside of a circle of ball bearings and works in conjunction with a cup

Corncob: a term used to describe a cluster of cogs on a racing cassette because of the small variation in number of teeth on adjacent cogs

Cottered crankset: a crankset in which the crankarms are fastened to the axle by means of threaded cotters and nuts

Cotterless crankset: a crankset in which the crankarms are fastened to the axle by means of a taper and nuts or bolts (instead of cotters)

Crankarm: a part, one end of which is attached to the bottom bracket axle and the other of which holds a pedal, that, through its forward rotation, provides the leverage needed to power the bicycle

Crankarm bolt: the bolt that holds a crankarm onto the end of the axle in a cotterless crankset

Crankset: the bottom bracket, two crankarms, and one or more chainrings of a bike

Cross-country bike: a mountain bike suited to racing on varied terrain; features include wide-range gearing with super lows, sometimes with short travel (3 inches or less) dual-suspension, great brakes, and a light performance-oriented frame

Crossover cable: *see* Stirrup cable

Cruiser: *see* Beach cruiser

C-spanner: a wrench with a C-shaped end that is used to loosen the lockring on certain bottom brackets and headsets

Cyclo-cross bike: a bicycle designed specifically for cyclo-cross racing, an event where lightweight bicycles that resemble road bikes are raced on an off-road course that includes sections where the rider must dismount and run with the bike; features include specific geometry, drop handlebars, knobby tires, and cantilever brakes

D

Damping: the process of controlling suspension action, without which a suspended fork would bounce like a pogo stick

Derailleur: a lever-activated mechanism that pushes the chain off one sprocket and onto another, thus changing the gear ratio

Derailleur hanger: a threaded metal piece that extends below the right rear dropout and is used as a mount for the rear derailleur

Diamond frame: the traditional men's bicycle frame, the principal parts of which form a diamond shape

Direct-pull brake: a type of very powerful centerpull brake used mostly on mountain bikes from the 1980s and early 1990s

Disc brake: a braking system that uses a small caliper mounted near a front or rear dropout (usually on the left side) that clamps onto a stainless steel disc attached to the hub to generate braking force

Dish: on a multispeed bike with a cassette or freewheel, the rear wheel's hub is located off center (to provide room for the cogs); to ensure that the rim aligns in the frame, the rim is centered over the axle instead of the hub, which means that right-side spokes are more tightly tensioned and more steeply angled than left-side spokes, a condition known as "dish"

Downhill bike: a bike designed for racing down mountains; features include long-travel (6 inches or more) dual-suspension frame, great brakes, single chainring, long saddle, and a riser handlebar

Down tube: the frame tube running from the headset to the bottom bracket; one part of the main triangle on a bicycle frame

Down-tube shift levers: shift levers that are mounted to the down tube of the bike

Drafting: tucking in closely behind another rider so he'll break the wind, saving you energy

D-ring: a D-shaped ring that is found on some models of shift levers and is used to adjust the level of tension on the inner parts of the lever

Drivetrain: the derailleurs, chain, freewheel, and crankset of a bike

Drop: the vertical distance from the horizontal line connecting the two wheel axles and the bottom bracket; one way of determining the location of the bottom bracket in relation to the rest of the bicycle frame; sometimes referred to as b/b drop or bottom bracket drop

Dropout: slots in the frame and fork into which the rear and front wheel axles fit

Drops: the lower straight portions of a turned-down-type handlebar

Dual-crown fork: a type of suspension fork that resembles a motorcycle fork due to crowns above and below the head tube, which increase stiffness

Dual-suspension bike: a bike with front and rear suspension; also known as a "dualie"

Dustcap: a metal or plastic cap that fits into a hub shell to keep contaminants out of hub bearings; or a metal or plastic end cover for an axle in a pedal or a cotterless crankset

E

Elastomer: a material, usually urethane, that is used in suspensions to provide shock absorption and damping, and that is favored due to its low cost and simple maintenance requirements

End plugs: the caps that fit onto or into the ends of the handlebars

Enduro bike: a mountain bike for cross-country endurance races; generally lightweight, mid-travel (3 to 4 inches) dual-suspension designs to balance performance and long-ride comfort

Epic: a remarkable mountain bike ride for either length, elevation gain, or spectacular views

Ergopower levers: the name for Campagnolo's shifting brake levers

F

Face: to shave the outer edges of a bottom bracket shell or the upper and lower ends of a head tube to make them parallel with one another and square to the tube's centerline so that, when the bottom bracket or headset is installed, the bearings will run as smoothly as possible

Ferrules: removable cylindrical metal or plastic caps used to reinforce the ends of cable housing

Fixed cup: the right-hand cup in a bottom bracket

Fixed gear (wheel): as found on track-racing road bikes, a hub-and-cog combination that's designed in such a way that one must always pedal; it's impossible to coast

Fixing bolt: a bolt used to hold a crankarm on an axle in a cotterless crankset

Flange: the part of a hub shell to which spokes are attached

Fork: the part of the frame that fits inside the head tube and holds the front wheel; a term also sometimes applied to the part of the frame where chainstays and seatstays join to hold the rear axle

Fork blades: the parallel, usually curved tubes that hold the front wheel

Fork crown: the horizontal piece on the upper part of the front fork to which the fork blades attach

Fork rake: the shortest distance between the front axle and an imaginary line extending through the head tube down toward the ground

Fork tips: the slotted tips of the fork blades into which the front wheel axle fits; also called dropouts

Freeride bike: a type of mountain bike designed to ride the most technical and punishing of downhill trails; features include long-travel (6 to 8 inches) dual-suspension and components manufactured for ultimate strength

Freewheel: a removable component on the rear hub that carries gear cogs on the outside and contains a ratcheting mechanism inside that provides the connection to the wheel for pedaling while also allowing coasting; sometimes used to refer to the ratcheting mechanism inside a cassette

Friction shifters: conventional (nonindex) levers that retain their position through the use of friction washers

Front fork: *see* Fork

Front triangle: a quadrilateral with one short side, it is the section of a bicycle frame that consists of the head tube, top tube, seat tube, and down tube

G

Gear: one position on a drivetrain; for example, being on the largest chainring and smallest rear cog is the largest gear

Gooseneck: slang for stem

Granny: slang for the tiny inner chainring on a triple-chainring crankset

Grips: the rubber or foam sleeves that fit on the ends of upright handlebars; you grip them when riding

Guide pulley: *see* Jockey pulley

H

Half-step gearing: a gearing system in which a shift between chainrings in a double-chainring set is equivalent to half a gear step on the freewheel

Headset: the combination of cups, cones, and ball bearings that creates the bearing mechanism that allows the fork column to rotate inside the head tube so you can steer

Head tube: the shortest tube in the main triangle, it is the one in which the fork column rotates

Hex key: a small L-shaped hexagonal wrench that fits inside the head of a bolt or screw; sometimes referred to as an Allen key or an Allen wrench

Housing: the plastic-covered tubing inside which the cables run

Hub: the center of a wheel, consisting of a shell to which spokes attach and containing an axle along with two sets of bearings, bearing cones, lock-washers, locknuts, and parts for attaching the wheel to the frame

Hub brake: any type of brake (disc, drum, or coaster) that operates through the wheel hub rather than the rim

Hydraulic brake: a brake relying on a sealed fluid system instead of a cable for operation

Hysteresis: the damping provided by elastomer springs

I

Idler pulley: the pulley in a rear derailleur that stays farthest from the cassette cogs and keeps tension on the chain

IMBA: *see* International Mountain Bicycling Association

Index shifters: levers that "click" into distinct positions that correspond to certain cassette cogs and don't require fine-tuning after each shift

International Mountain Bicycling Association (IMBA): an organization that protects mountain bike trails

J

Jockey pulley: the pulley in a rear derailleur that stays closest to the cogs and guides the chain from cog to cog during a gear shift; sometimes called the guide pulley

K

Knobby tires: heavy-duty tires with large rubber knobs spaced relatively far apart to provide traction in off-road terrain

L

Ladies' frame: the type of frame in which the top tube is replaced by a second down tube to make mounting and dismounting the bike easier

Left-hand threading: threading that's the opposite of regular threading, meaning you must turn left to tighten and right to loosen; always found on the left pedal; also known as reverse threading

Linking cable: *see* Stirrup cable

Loaded tourer: a bicycle with structural strength, geometry, and equipment that is designed to allow a cyclist to travel with a full load of gear

Locknut: a nut used along with a washer or a second nut to lock a mechanism in place, such as the nut at the upper end of a headset or the nut in front of the calipers on some caliper brakes

Lockring: the notched ring that fits on the left side of some bottom brackets and prevents the adjustable cup from turning

Lockwasher: a washer with a small metal tab to prevent it from turning, such as the washer beneath the locknut on a headset or between the locknut and cone on a hub

Loose ball bearings: bearings inside a component that are not held in a metal or plastic retainer

Lug: an external metal sleeve that holds two or more tubes together at the joints of a frame

M

Main triangle: *see* Front triangle

Master link: a special link on a bicycle chain that can be opened by flexing a plate, removing a screw, or some other means besides driving out a pin

Mixte frame: a frame that replaces the top tube with twin lateral tubes that run all the way from the head tube back to the rear dropouts

Mountain bike: a bicycle with a straight handlebar, sturdy fat tires, and wide-range gearing designed for off-road use

Mounting bolt: *see* Pivot bolt

N

National Off-Road Bicycle Association (NORBA): the United States' governing body of off-road racing

Nexus: a type of Shimano hub that has four or seven internal gears and an internal brake

Nipple: a small metal piece that fits through a wheel rim and is threaded inside to receive the end of a spoke

Noodle: the L-shaped tubing piece found on the side of Shimano V-Brakes and some other direct-pull cantilevers

NORBA: *see* National Off-Road Bicycle Association

P

Panniers: luggage bags used in pairs and fastened alongside one or both wheels of a bike

Pickup: *see* Yoke

Pin spanner: a wrench with pins on forked ends that is used to turn certain adjustable cups on some bottom brackets

Pivot bolt: a bolt on which the arms of caliper brakes pivot and which also serves as the means for mounting the brakes on the bike frame

Plain gauge tubing: tubing of a thickness that remains constant over its entire length

Potato chipped wheel: *see* Taco'd wheel

Preload: an important suspension adjustment that usually involves modifying pressure or adjusting the elastomers to ensure that the suspension responds appropriately to the rider's weight

Presta valve: a bicycle tube valve with a stem that has a small nut on top that must be loosened during inflation, instead of a spring such as is found on a Schrader valve

Q

Quick link: a special connecting link that allows derailleur-type chains to be disassembled and reassembled without the use of tools

Quick-release: a cam-lever mechanism used to rapidly tighten or loosen a wheel on a bike frame, a seatpost in a seat tube, or a brake cable within cable housing

Quick-release skewer: a thin rod that runs through the center of a wheel axle; a cam lever is attached to one end, and the other end is threaded to receive a nut

Quill: similar to the rattrap type of pedal except that the two sides of the pedal frame are joined by a piece of metal that loops around the dustcap

R

Races: curved metal surfaces of cups and cones that ball bearings contact as they roll

Rake: *see* Fork rake

Rattrap: a type of pedal that has thin metal plates with jagged edges running parallel on each side of the pedal spindle

Rear triangle: a frame triangle formed by the chainstays, seatstays, and seat tube

Recumbent: bikes that place the rider in a reclining feet-first position

Regular threading: the threading that's found on almost all bike parts; turn to the right to tighten and to the left to loosen

Reverse threading: *see* Left-hand threading

Replaceable derailleur hanger: a type of derailleur hanger that can be easily replaced using hand tools if it gets damaged

Retainer: a metal or plastic ring that holds the bearings in place in a headset, bottom bracket, or sometimes a hub

Rim: the metal hoop of a wheel that holds the tire, the tube, and the outer ends of the spokes

Rim brake: any type of brake that slows or stops a wheel by pressing its pads against the sides of the wheel rim

Riser handlebar: a mountain bike handlebar that bends up on the ends; found on downhill, freeride, and some cross-country bikes

Rollercam brakes: mountain bike brakes that affix to frame posts and employ a cam-and-pulley system to modify pressure on the rims

Rollers: a stationary training device with a boxlike frame and three rotating cylinders (one for the front wheel and two for the rear wheel) on which the bicycle is balanced and ridden

S

Saddle: the seat on a bicycle

Schrader valve: a tire valve similar to the type found on automobile tires

Sealed bearings: bearings fastened in sealed containers to keep out contaminants

Sealed pulley: a type of derailleur pulley that has sealed bearings

Seamed tubing: tubing made from steel strip stock that is curved until its edges meet, then welded together

Seamless tubing: tubing made from blocks of steel that are pierced and drawn into tube shape

Seat cluster: the conjunction of top tube, seat tube, and seatstays near the top of the seat tube

Seatpost: the part to which the saddle clamps and which runs down inside the seat tube

Seatstays: parallel tubes that run from the top of the seat tube back to the rear axle

Seat tube: the tube that runs from just below the saddle down to the bottom bracket

Semislick tire: a type of mountain bike tire with limited tread; popular for not-too-technical courses because it rolls faster than a knobby tire

Sew-up: *see* Tubular

Shallow angles: angles that position frame tubes farther from vertical and closer to horizontal; also known as slack angles

Skipping: a popping feeling in the drivetrain when you pedal hard; it occurs when a cog is worn out and when you install a new chain on worn cogs

Slack angles: *see* Shallow angles

Solvent: a liquid used to cut grease and grime, such as when cleaning components or chains

Spanner: another name for a wrench; applied to many bicycle tools

Spider: the multiarmed piece to which the chainwheels are bolted; usually welded to or part of the right crankarm

Spindle: another term for an axle (such as a pedal axle or a bottom bracket axle)

Spoke: one of several wires used to hold the hub in the center of a wheel rim and to transfer the load from the perimeter of the wheel to the hub and onto the frame

Sports tourer: a bicycle with structural strength, geometry, and components designed to make it a compromise between a bike suitable for racing and one suitable for loaded touring; good for general pleasure riding

Sprocket: a disc bearing teeth for driving a chain; a general term that applies both to chainrings and to cassette cogs

Stainless steel: a type of steel that will not rust; ideal for spokes

Stationary trainer: device you attach your bike to so you can ride in place

Steep angles: angles that position frame tubes nearer to vertical than do shallow angles

Steerer tube: the tube that forms the top of the fork and rotates inside the head tube

Stem: the part that fits into or on the fork and holds the handlebar

STI: Shimano's name for its shifting brake levers

Stirrup cable: on centerpull-type brakes, a short cable, each end of which attaches to a brake arm and which is pulled up at the center to activate the brakes; also known as straddle cable, transverse cable, linking cable, or crossover cable

Suspension: as found on all cars, most mountain bikes, and some road- and casual- bike models, a component featuring forks and frames that absorb road and trail shocks to improve comfort and control

Swingarm: the movable rear end of a suspended bicycle

T

Taco'd wheel: a wheel that's been bent so severely that it curls back on itself and resembles a hard taco

Tandem: a bicycle that has seats, bars, and pedals for two or more riders, one behind the other

Tap: to cut threads inside a tube or opening; also the name of the tool that does the cutting

Threadless headset: a type of headset that fits on a fork with a threadless steerer; often found on mountain bikes

Thread locking compound: a liquid applied to threads to ensure that the part stays tight after it's attached

Three-cross: a spoking pattern in which a spoke passes over two and under a third spoke before being attached to the rim

Thumb shifter: a shifter designed to be operated with the thumbs, such as Shimano Rapid Fire models or Sturmey Archer three-speed models

Toeclips and toe straps: a cagelike kit attached to pedals to keep your feet in the correct position (unnecessary on clipless pedals)

Top tube: the horizontal tube that connects the seat tube with the head tube

Tourist: a cyclist who takes excursions by bicycle, often carrying several panniers containing clothing and camping equipment

Track bike: a type of bike used for racing on a bicycle track (velodrome); looks a lot like a road bike but features only one gear and has no brakes

Transverse cable: *see* Stirrup cable

Trials: a type of mountain bike competition that tests riders' abilities to negotiate large obstacles such as boulders, logs, and parked cars; these competitions are judged on technical ability rather than speed

Triple crank: a triple-chainring crankset designed to provide a wide range of gears

Tubular: a type of tire that has a tube sewn inside the casing; also known as a sew-up

Twist shifter: a type of shift lever that's twisted to shift the gears, such as GripShift models

U

U-brakes: heavy-duty centerpull mountain bike brakes that affix to frame posts

UCI (Union Cycliste Internationale): international governing body of professional and amateur bicycle racing

U-lock: a U-shaped lock; called D-locks in Britain

Unicrown fork: a fork (usually on mountain bikes) on which the blades curve in at the top and are welded to the steerer instead of fitting into a fork crown (there is no fork crown on a unicrown fork)

Universal cable: a shift or brake cable that's designed to fit all types of levers; on each end is a different lead end, and you cut off the one you don't need

USA Cycling (USAC): the United States' governing body of professional and amateur bicycle racing

V

V-Brake: Shimano's brand name for their model of direct-pull brake

W

Wheelbase: the distance between the front and rear axles

Wind trainer: a training device consisting of a frame in which a bicycle is fastened for stationary riding and a fan that creates wind resistance to simulate actual road riding

Y

Yoke: a triangular metal piece used to connect the main brake cable with the stirrup cable in a centerpull brake system; also known as a pickup

Z

Zip-tie: a plastic strap that, when threaded through its end and pulled, tightens and stays tight to affix cables or number plates to a bicycle

Resources

Answer-Manitou
www.answerproducts.com

Avid
(800) 346-2928 (IL)
www.avidbike.com

Bacchetta Bicycles
(727) 341-1881 (FL)
www.bacchettabikes.com

Barnett Bicycle Institute
(719) 632-5173 (CO)
www.bbinstitute.com

Bell Sports
(800) 776-5677 (CA)
www.bellbikehelmets.com

Bianchi
(510) 264-1001 (CA)
www.bianchiusa.com

Bike E
(800) 231-3136 (OR)
www.bikee.com

Bike Friday
(800) 777-0258 (OR)
www.greengear.com

Bilenky Cycle Works
(800) 213-6388 (PA)
www.bilenky.com

Bontrager
(800) 879-8735 (WI)
www.bontrager.com

Brompton
(800) 783-3447 (CA)
www.bromptonbike.com

Burley
(800) 311-5294 (OR)
www.burley.com

CamelBak
(800) 767-8725 (TX)
www.camelbak.com

Campagnolo
www.campagnolo.com

Cane Creek
(828) 684-3551 (NC)
www.canecreek.com

Cannondale
(800) BIKE-USA (CT)
www.cannondale.com

Cars-R-Coffins
www.carsrcoffins.com

Chris King Components
(503) 972-4050
www.chrisking.com

Continental
www.conti-online.com

Crank Brothers
(949) 464-9916 (CA)
www.crankbrothers.com

da Vinci Designs
(800) 873-3214 (CO)
www.teamspirit.net

Diamondback
www.diamondback.com

Dirt Designs
(800) 269-6641 (CO)

DT/Hugi
www.dtswiss.com

Easy Racers
www.easyracers.com

Fox Racing Shox
(831) 274-6500 (CA)
www.foxracingshox.com

Gary Fisher Bicycles
(800) 879-8735 (WI)
www.fisherbikes.com

Giant
(800) 874-4268 (CA)
www.giant-bicycle.com

Giro Helmets
www.giro.com

Hayes Disc Brakes
(888) 686-3472 (WI)
www.hayesbrake.com

Hope Technology
www.hopetech.com

Hutchinson
tires.hutchinson.fr

Independent Fabrication
www.ifbikes.com

Iron Horse USA
www.ironhorsebikes.com

K2 Bikes
www.k2bikes.com

Kestrel
www.kestrel-usa.com

Klein
(800) 879-8735 (WI)
www.kleinbikes.com

Kona Mountain Bikes
www.konaworld.com

LeMond (Greg) Bicycles
(800) 879-8735 (WI)
www.lemondbikes.com

Lightning Cycle Dynamics
www.ihpva.org

Litespeed Titanium Bicycles
(800) 743-3796 (TN)
www.litespeed.com

Loose Screws
(541) 488-4800 (OR)

Magura
www.magura.com

Marin Mountain Bikes
(800) 222-7557 (CA)
www.marinbikes.com

Marzocchi
www.marzocchi.com

Maverick American
(303) 415-0370 (CO)
www.maverickamerican.com

Mavic
www.mavic.com

Merlin
(888) 563-7546
www.merlinbike.com

Michelin
(800) 847-3435 (SC)
www.cycleus.webmichelin.com

Montague USA
(800) 736-5348 (MA)
www.montagueco.com

NEMA
(714) 841-8384 (CA)
www.nema-usa.com

Nokian
www.nokiantyres.com/bike

Norco Bicycles
www.norco.com

Outland
(888) 222-8981 (WA)

363

Park Tools
www.parktool.com

Pearl Izumi
www.pearlizumi.com

Pedro's
(978) 657-6551 (MA)
www.pedros.com

Phil Wood
(408) 298-1540 (CA)
www.philwood.com

Quintana Roo
(800) 743-3796 (CA)
www.rooworld.com

RaceFace
(604) 527-9996 (BC, Canada)
www.raceface.com

Raleigh USA Bicycle
(800) 222-5527 (WA)
www.raleighusa.com

Rans
(785) 625-6346 (KS)
www.rans.com

Ritchey
(800) 748-2439 (CA)
www.ritcheylogic.com

Rock Shox
(800) 346-2928 (IL)
www.rockshox.com

Rocky Mountain Bicycles
www.bikes.com

Rolf Prima
(541) 868-1715 (OR)
www.rolfprima.com

Salsa
www.salsacycles.com

SantaCruz Bicycles
(831) 459-7560 (CA)
www.santacruzmtb.com

Santana Cycles
www.santanainc.com

Serfas
(800) 424-0047 (CA)
www.serfas.com

Serotta
(518) 584-1221 (NY)
www.serotta.com

Seven Cycles
(617) 923-7774
www.sevencycles.com

Shimano
(800) 353-3817 (CA)
www.bike.shimano.com

Softride
www.softride.com

Specialized
(800) 245-3462 (CA)
www.specialized.com

SRAM
(800) 346-2928 (IL)
www.sram.com

Surly
www.surlybikes.com

Terry Precision Bicycles for Women
(800) 289-8379 (NY)
www.terrybicycles.com

Titec
(925) 484-1200 (CA)
www.titec.com

Trek
(800) 879-8735 (WI)
www.trekbikes.com

Truvativ
(805) 787-0917
www.truvativ.com

United Bicycle Institute
(541) 488-1121 (OR)
www.bikeschool.com

Veltec Sports (Look, Easton, Sidi)
(800) 991-0070 (CA)

Ventana Mountain Bikes, USA
(888) 368-2628 (CA)
www.ventanausa.com

Vision Recumbents
www.visionrecumbents.com

Waterford Precision Cycles
www.waterfordbikes.com

White Brothers Cycling
(970) 241-3518 (CO)
www.whitebrotherscycling.com

White Industries
(707) 769-5600 (CA)
www.whiteind.com

Index

C

S

T